D1104996

GOOD SOUND

FREQUENCY RANGE & HARMONICS

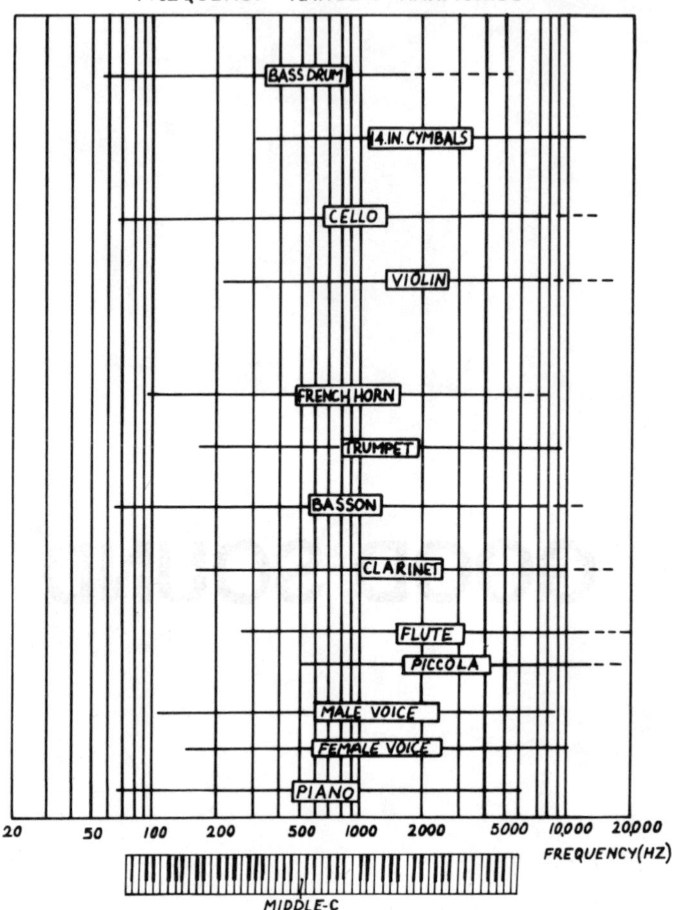
BASS DRUM
14.IN. CYMBALS
CELLO
VIOLIN
FRENCH HORN
TRUMPET
BASSON
CLARINET
FLUTE
PICCOLA
MALE VOICE
FEMALE VOICE
PIANO
20
50
100
200
500
1000
2000
5000
10,000
20,000
FREQUENCY(HZ)
MIDDLE-C

Fig. 1

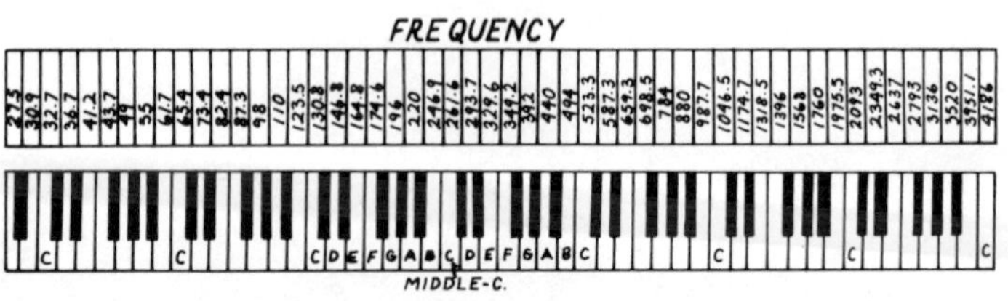
FREQUENCY
27.5
30.9
32.7
36.7
41.2
43.7
49
55
61.7
65.4
73.4
82.4
87.3
98
110
123.5
130.8
146.8
164.8
174.6
196
220
246.9
261.6
293.7
329.6
349.2
392
440
494
523.3
587.3
659.3
698.5
784
880
987.7
1046.5
1174.7
1318.5
1396
1568
1760
1975.5
2093
2349.3
2637
2793
3136
3520
3951.1
4186
C
C
C D E F G A B C D E F G A B C
C
C
C
MIDDLE-C.
PITCH

Fig. 2

GOOD SOUND

AN UNCOMPLICATED GUIDE TO CHOOSING AND USING AUDIO EQUIPMENT

LAURA DEARBORN

QUILL
WILLIAM MORROW
NEW YORK

Copyright © 1987 by Laura Dearborn

All rights reserved. No part of this book may be reproduced or utilized in any form or by any means, electronic or mechanical, including photocopying, recording, or by any information storage or retrieval system, without permission in writing from the Publisher. Inquiries should be addressed to Permissions Department, William Morrow and Company, Inc., 1350 Avenue of the Americas, New York, N.Y. 10019.

It is the policy of William Morrow and Company, Inc., and its imprints and affiliates, recognizing the importance of preserving what has been written, to print the books we publish on acid-free paper, and we exert our best efforts to that end.

Library of Congress Cataloging-in-Publication Data

Dearborn, Laura, 1951–
Good sound.
Bibliography: p.
Includes index.
1. High-fidelity sound systems. I. Title.
TK7881.7.D435 1987 621.389′332 87-22093
ISBN 0-688-06424-8 (pbk.)

Printed in the United States of America

5 6 7 8 9 10

BOOK DESIGN BY MARK STEIN

CONTENTS

ACKNOWLEDGMENTS

Many people have helped bring this book into existence:

Bill Dasheff, who had the idea and who helped shape the contents;

Dave King, who spent many late hours far beyond his role as consultant in thrashing out ideas, fine-tuning systems, offering technical information, suggesting people to talk with and equipment to listen to, and generally giving of his considerable understanding of reproduced music;

Armand Lucchese, for technical information and for opinions that though not always shared, helped to refine some of those offered here;

"Deep Ears,"for his apparently endless trove of records and for the pleasures of the many but always too short hours spent listening to them;

And all those who have cared enough to make good recordings, build good equipment, set up good systems, and spread understanding of music reproduction so that real music, and not just its shadow, can be enjoyed at home.

INTRODUCTION

Music needs intermediaries to bring it to life; otherwise it remains nothing more than a series of black notes on a printed page. Some performers do this well, others poorly—in translating the composer's intentions, intermediaries inevitably add colors and shadows of their own.

Recorded music too must have intermediaries to restore it to life. Like performers, some audio systems do this well, others poorly.

Most people's audio systems are so poor that they hear only a ghost of the music. And most accept this without complaint, not knowing that good sound and a convincing illusion are actually quite accessible with some knowledge and a modicum of effort. There's no need to accept mediocrity.

This is not to suggest that listening to a recording is the same as listening to a live performance. By definition, a recording is a copy and a copy is not an original. But a recording does offer something as valid and important as music experienced live. And of all the sensory illusions that mankind has endeavored to create, the auditory ones may be by far the most potent and convincing.

"Good sound" is important for one essential reason—it makes the music accessible because it reveals more of its subtle *detail*. Rather than sounding "like a recording"—distant, muffled, uninvolving—a recording well played back instead is really able to convey a part of the compelling emotion and intensity of live music.

Anything added or "interpreted" by the system changes the music—you want to hear the music *as it was recorded,* not as your system interprets it. Alter the sound and you've altered the music. So a "good system" is simply one that alters the music minimally—not one that performs a lot of tricks.

Music, at bottom, is sound (more precisely, sound in time). Good (undistorted) sound quality therefore reveals more of the music. The more you can hear the details of the sound, unadulterated and unmuffled by distortion, the more you can hear of the music. Muzak perhaps suffers little from being played on the ubiquitous squawk box of public places—the subtleties have already been intentionally stripped away—but with more complex works good sound is very important, as all the instruments and all the myriad details become easily blurred, like a watercolor that has run.

Bartók, for one, recognized that the quality of the sound can alter the perception and enjoyment of music. His scores are carefully annotated with detailed notes specifying the exact quality of sound he was seeking—for example, that a snare drum should be hit with the flat of a knifeblade. So if your equipment makes a snare drum sound like tin cans falling down stairs, then clearly you will not even come close to hearing the composer's intent.

Try eating a delicious meal with your nose blocked up. Or drink a glass of fresh milk with a little blue food dye added. Both the milk and the meal are themselves unchanged, but how they come to you has been changed and your response to each is therefore quite different—and far less pleasurable. It is hard to "eat past" the blue of the food or absence of olfactory information, but many have become resigned to "listening past" poor sound. We wouldn't accept eating under such poor conditions, but accept listening thus because most of us don't know that anything better is readily available.

"Good" does not mean fancy, expensive, or "state of the art," but simply having fidelity to the recording. All reproduction is a compromise—a copy can never be identical to its original—and with so many steps dividing original from reproduction, there are numerous opportunities for imperfection. But some systems sound "musical," can be listened to with pleasure for hours, and provide a very direct connection with the music, whereas others seem to fight, however subtly, against your access to the music and quickly make you tire of listening.

So the aim of this book is very straightforward—to enable you to get the most music and the most enjoyment out of whatever amount of time, money, and energy you are prepared to put into gaining good sound; to enable you, like Prospero, to summon up your musicians at will.

PART I.

EQUIPMENT

A PERSPECTIVE ON EQUIPMENT

Good sound rests on three equally essential and interdependent pillars—equipment, setup, and the recording. The equipment tends to be mistakenly made the center of attention—people who put thousands of dollars into a stereo system may invest only a few hundred in records and tapes. Yet the point of the equipment is to bring you the *music*.

Ideally, you could listen to a recording just by holding it up to your ear and so dispense with all the complications of equipment. This being impossible, you want equipment that interferes as little as possible with the recording. The equipment is not intended to create the sound (though some equipment adds so much distortion that it does effectively produce a new noise), but solely to release the original musical event frozen in space and time on the recording.

Stereo equipment is commonly viewed as a technological mystery, too complex to understand, let alone control. In truth, you no more need to learn audio electronics to enjoy good sound than you need to study botany to select fresh vegetables. Naturally, you have to know what the vegetable is supposed to be like in order to choose a good one. And you also have to know how to prepare that vegetable to gain the most pleasure from its eating. Similarly, no matter how fine the equipment may be in design, its actual performance is finally in the hands of the user. A system will give back just what you put into it.

People's expectations of what is possible from audio equipment are so low that they will meekly accept the sound quality of a $20 table radio from a system costing many times more. Many not only accept but *expect* "canned sound" from their audio equipment—canned noise is ubiquitous, pursuing one in elevators and supermarkets, on TV and telephone "hold." If cafeteria food is all you have ever tasted, you probably won't know you're missing out on good home cooking. Equally, few are aware of the excellent sound quality available from even modest equipment that has been carefully chosen and set up, and so remain unaware of how much of the music they are missing.

All playback, like recording, is a matter of compromise—the sound of the original performance can never be perfectly captured on a recording, nor perfectly released in playback. A copy cannot be the same as the original. *Some* distortion inevitably is introduced, but how much and what kind are the factors that separate the good from the mediocre. The problem with music played on a poor system is that it loses so much of its "aliveness." It becomes only a referent to the original piece of music, with little if any lingering connection to the emotion, the vitality, and the force of the original. Like a cheap reproduction of a painting, it provides the basic image but loses the significance.

You have to know what it is you want from your system before you will be able to get it. Knowing what you want starts with knowing what you can get—what each component is intended to do, and how to distinguish the few good models from the merely indifferent majority. If you constantly change your equipment because you're struggling to find something but you don't know what it is, then you will have embarked on a very frustrating and expensive search that causes many people to give up and lose the pleasure of music. The fact is that you are always at a crossroads—there is always another step that can be taken, another road to follow. But just because it's there, this doesn't mean you have to take it. Some people live with the same system for a decade and more, just maintaining it and replacing the cartridge yearly. Others change not only the cartridge every year but one or more other components as well.

GETTING TO THE ESSENCE

A component or system that provides good fidelity will always (assuming good maintenance) provide that same quality of fidelity, regardless of whatever technological advances may occur. It may be surpassed by other equipment, but that does not alter its own essential characteristic of fidelity. Old components or old recordings, because they are no longer "the latest," are not therefore inferior. The simple designs of tube amps and preamps can compete with and often exceed the quality of the "more modern" transistor equipment.

High-end audio is a matter of refinement, not of the "latest technology." Refinement means getting to the essence. Remember that playback is not intended to enhance the recording, to wow you with sonics, but simply to reveal the music. The basic technology of audio reproduction has been established, more or less as it is now, for about 100 years. Components from 30 years ago and more continue to be prized for their sound quality today.

In general, the *less* there is between performance and playback, the more faithful the recorded music will be to the original. You want a few elements honed to excellent performance rather than a mass of parts thrown at a problem. Elaborate solutions often indicate a failure to get to the bottom of the problem. This minimalism is a key in both recording and playback—*anything* inserted in the path between the original performance and its playback in your living room will add some distortion, because anything that passes through something else is changed by its passage. Given that the system's goal is to reveal the original performance, change of any kind represents a distortion.

SYSTEM HIERARCHY AND THE IMPORTANCE OF THE FRONT END

All the music you'll ever hear from your system is contained in the recording and it must all be released from the recording—musical detail that is not retrieved cannot be recaptured somewhere down the line. So the quality of the front end is critical.

So a system's *hierarchy,* as first recognized by Ivor Tiefenbrun of Linn, follows the flow of the audio signal. As everything the system has to work with at any point comes from "upstream," then clearly if you have a mediocre front end, even the best speakers won't do you much good—they cannot turn a poor signal into good sound. On the other hand, a system can only be as good as the weakest link in the chain. So even an excellent front end cannot fully compensate for poor speakers. There must be some balance of quality among the components.

Following this hierarchy, the recording itself is really the first component in the system. LPs, CDs, and cassette tapes are not equally good recording mediums. Consider carefully which you want to concentrate on—unless you are prepared to buy all the front ends and put together music collections in all the formats. Read Part III of this book, particularly the sections on analog and digital recording, as well as the front-end chapters in Part I.

THE ROLE OF SPECIFICATIONS

Given that the goal is fidelity to the music, it seems logical to establish a component's quality by how close it comes to reaching that goal, rather than by measuring the playback equipment against some abstract numerical standard. Specs and measurements may tell you how well a component functions *as a piece of equipment,* but not how good or bad the *music* will sound. The issue is not distortion as measured by specs, but *audible* distortion of the music—these two are not synonymous. You would not try to establish how Carnegie Hall sounds without playing music in it. Even with music playing, attempts to spec it out would be of dubious success, because we know very little about how measurements correlate to what we hear. Music playback can be accurately compared only against its original: live music.

THE TURNTABLE SYSTEM

THE GOOD, THE BAD, AND THE COMPACT DISC

The analog LP, while indeed passing into recording history, has yet to be eclipsed sonically by any other medium*—including the digital compact disc. Strip away the hype and keep your mind open and you can hear this for yourself.

Digital recording—on vinyl and CD—owes its meteoric rise to two factors: an enormous publicity campaign and the wretched quality of the turntables generally offered to the public. If turntables of the sort we recommended here were commonly produced in quantity—at the lower prices that this would allow—then the compact disc would undoubtedly be having a much harder time of it.

Actually, the real contest is not so much between digital and analog, or old and new technology, as between mass-fi CD players and even worse mass-fi turntables. A mass-fi CD player may sound better than a mass-fi turntable, but a good turntable sounds better than all but perhaps the few best CD players. The problem lies not with the analog LP record but with the low caliber of the record players, or turntables, found in most homes. While the vinyl disc may be technologically out of style (at least for the time being), proper playback will reveal vinyl's magnificent and as yet unsurpassed sonic virtues.

Like any other audio source, the turntable system has a profound effect on the final quality of the musical experience. The mass market has traditionally underemphasized its importance because conventional audio wisdom long ago concluded that a turntable was a supposedly "passive" device, contributing little to the sonic quality of playback. But this is just plain wrong.

Only very recently, in the last ten years or so, has the significance of the turntable begun to be recognized. (As luck would have it, this has coincided with the untimely decline of the vinyl disc.) Yet despite

*Except reel-to-reel tape.

superb sonic advances in table design, there are still a lot of mainstream reviewers and audio technologists who continue dogmatically to hold to old ideas, refusing to acknowledge the table's true importance.

Traditionally, loudspeakers have been exalted as the preeminent component, the so-called voice of the system. But without an excellent signal from the front end (accurately enlarged by the amplification stage) the speakers wouldn't have a note to give voice to.

The turntable is the *first* component in the system to determine whether what you hear will be a living, breathing resurrection of the original live performance or nothing more than a facsimile. A really good table system can do more to bring alive a lackluster system than any other single investment in the signal chain.

This fundamental misunderstanding helps to make some sense out of how the purveyors of digital have been able to take such a promising recording medium as CD and premiere it to the world in a completely wretched state of development. It has required "obscure" audiophile designers and tweakers, experimenting independently in basements and garages, to reveal finally digital's hidden excellence.

Millions of dollars' worth of publicity and advertising won't change the fact that CD is not inherently better than the vinyl disc, but only an improvement over the vinyl disc played back on a low-quality or poorly set up turntable. A mediocre CD player may not sound as bad as a mediocre turntable, but to get really *good* CD sound you have to use a really *good* CD player. And that genuinely good player may cost you as much as or more than a good table, arm, and cartridge.

Currently the best-sounding CD players are made individually or in small quantities and so cannot be bought off the shelf of any audio store. Nor is it likely that excellent-sounding CD players will be rolling off mass-production assembly lines in the near future. Also, the CDs themselves cost considerably more than LPs, especially now that a lot of vinyl is going for bargain prices.

Not appreciating the profound significance of the turntable exposes a fundamentally inadequate understanding of what a recording is. Records are a lot more than just memorabilia—they are an artistic medium.

The Importance of the Turntable System

Let's not mince words—contrary to conventional thinking and whatever a lot of the old-line hi-fi experts may say, the turntable and arm are freakin' important and don't let anyone ever kid you about that.

The music begins in the turntable system. But it can end there too. Consider that the record contains *all* the music you'll ever be in touch with. Whatever musical information the front end—the turntable—fails to retrieve from the record is lost, *permanently*. It can never be reconstituted, re-created, enhanced, or otherwise rescued by some whizbang component downstream (no, not even by an equalizer!). *The recording is the heart and soul of the system.* What the front end retrieves is the most you will ever hear. Turning this around, the less the front end retrieves, the less your musical experience.

For years, no one, not even the hottest hotshot recording engineers, effectively realized the full extent of holographic imaging and tonal realism caught in the grooves of any decent-quality record. It took tree-worshiping audiophile druids to begin startling people by discovering more musical detail on LPs than was supposed to be there. (Indeed, some "experts" still deny it's there!)

The big revelation came when audiophiles rejected the practice of "enhancing" the recording in order to try to make it sound better. Instead of doctoring the distortions by the use of tone controls and equalizers, they concentrated on eliminating playback distortion in order to *reveal* the recording in all its detail. Remember, whatever is missing from the recording cannot be brought back; and whatever is on the recording cannot be "improved" on—once made, a recording is cast in stone. But even a halfway decent recording has a lot to reveal that most people never get to hear. Yes, you can fiddle around with equalization, but that's only cosmetics at best. On a good, properly set up system, EQ doctoring should never be required. The fact is, on a *good* system, EQ doctoring will only diminish the quality of the recording and therefore your pleasure.

For a good analog system, a good table is absolutely mandatory, so your other fine components won't mercilessly reveal a poor signal source. Even on a lesser system, you need a good front end just as much. Because the other components of a poor system are so veiled (distorted), you've got to deliver a very clear signal to them in order to be left with anything worthwhile after they've whittled away at the music. It's astounding what a good table will do for even a low-fi discount-store system—far more than any "dynamite" speakers or amplifier. Of course, if the table and the rest of the system aren't set up wisely, you might just as well have bad equipment anyway—'cause it's gonna sound like you do even if you don't.

A poor table makes it effectively impossible to assess what's going on with the rest of your system. But establishing a good signal source *first* provides you with a stable foundation from which you can begin to accurately focus in on weaknesses elsewhere in the system. Painstaking experience, along with observing and helping many other people, has repeatedly shown us how much it pays off to start out with a good turntable system, even if it means skimping a bit on the other components.

Also, a poor table system unquestionably helps to harm your records. That's right—this may sound farfetched if you're new to all this, but think about it. If the cartridge stylus isn't being held properly in the record groove by the tonearm and table, then it's inexorably doing some injury to the groove by mistracking. And one thing that mass-fi tables do excellently is mistrack. Cartridge mistracking, along with dirt and a worn stylus, are far and away the greatest ruiners of records.

If you have a large record collection or, for that matter, one of any size that you care about, a top-quality turntable system is an essential investment and should normally be the first major upgrade, along of course with a pro-quality record cleaner like the VPI (see p. 275).

Incidentally, much of the music available currently on LP will never be transferred onto CD and so will be lost. A similar loss occurred with the switchovers from 78s to 33⅓s and from mono to stereo. Each time the format is changed, some of the existing repertoire is purged. However, in earlier switchovers, the library of recordings was smaller and so more of it was able to be transferred. Now, with the repertoire so immense (literally millions of recordings), a substantial chunk of it will just be obliterated. Nor will the winnowing come among the duplications in the repertoire, particularly of classical music, but rather it will come in the material that sells less well and will therefore be chosen not to sell at all. Democracy will in effect be voting on many of the "artistic" decisions made in the upcoming transition period, and we all know that democracy is, by its nature, not the champion of art.

In addition, with real estate at a premium, not even the master tapes of works that aren't being transferred to the new medium are likely to be preserved and stored for future rediscovery of their worth. Like so many of the early films and TV shows, these tapes too will be destroyed, whether they are actually thrown out or merely neglected.

While analog vinyl may not possess the trendy cachet of CDs, the art, emotion, and the sheer humanity stored on millions of LPs is irreplaceable. At some point in the not too distant future, once time has granted enough of us the wisdom of hindsight, the virtue of the analog record will be rediscovered. Then the LPs that people so blithely discard today will become treasures in the analog renaissance. Hold on to and take good care of those prosaic pieces of black plastic. You'll have to pay through the nose to get them back later—if you can at all.

The Turntable System: An Overview

The table system, as its older name declares, is quite literally a *phono-graph*, and the "graph" (writing) it reads is the "phono" (sound) that's engraved in the record. That's why turntables and, by extension, all other music sources are also known as *transcription* sources. The entire *raison d'être* of the table system is to follow exactly and extract this very delicate, complex line of musical information embedded in the record groove.

One of our central themes is that playback is the mirror image of the recording process—it "unrecords" the recording. The turntable system is the playback counterpart of the cutting lathe. It is in effect an "uncutting lathe" and the direct counterpart to the mammoth lathe that inscribed the music into the lacquer at the mastering lab. To retrieve the most music, the playback cartridge (which in our mirror-image analogy is the unrecording counterpart to the cutting head of the lathe) must very accurately retrace the grooves. The more accurately you retrace the groove, the more music you retrieve and the more wonderful the musical illusion. As you deviate from perfect accuracy, you get increasingly distorted sound, less music, and less of a thrill. Now that's a very good test—if your music doesn't keep on thrilling you, there's something drastically wrong with your system. J. Gordon Holt, founder of *Stereophile* magazine, calls it the goosebump test.

Ultimately, the entire focus of any turntable system is on the tiny momentary point in space and time where stylus and groove wall meet, often termed the stylus/groove-wall interface. How accurately this minute contact point is maintained determines how well the stylus reads the groove—and therefore how much music you get.

How successfully the stylus/groove interface is maintained is determined *at least* as much by the table and tonearm as by the cartridge. It's very easy to mistakenly focus on the cartridge as the nucleus of the turntable system—after all, that's where the music is "unwritten" from the record groove and converted into that electrical mystery which travels through the system to come out of the speakers as music (or noise, as the case may be).

But you just cannot take a low-quality table and arm and improve their performance by sticking on a superior-quality cartridge. On the other hand, a truly high-quality, well-set-up table and arm will tolerate all but the crummiest cartridges and still deliver good sound (though obviously the system would be better off with a good cartridge). Besides wasting your money by putting a good cartridge on a mass-fi arm and table, you will actually get *worse* sound because the better cartridge will expose the poverty of table and arm. You might at first be fooled into thinking you're hearing an improvement (there even may be improvement in certain restricted areas). But if you listen attentively, you'll soon recognize that what you're hearing is a *change* rather than an overall musical advance.

What it comes down to is that the table, tonearm, and cartridge must be understood as being inseparable parts of a single system. The performance of any one part directly influences the other parts. To pick up good sound from the tiny intersection of groove and stylus, the table system (and its owner) must strive to accomplish three things successfully: (1) turn the record at precisely the correct speed, (2) rigidly hold the cartridge in correct relation to the groove, and (3) shield the stylus from any extraneous acoustic and mechanical vibrations. All this may sound simple enough, but it remains a very challenging combination of applied physics and aesthetics, something mass-fi table companies try to sidestep neatly—or, worse, aren't even adequately aware of.

Compare the minuscule scale of the music signal (see p. 42) with the scale of the vibrations in your environment coming from airborne and mechanical sources. We're not talking about gross vibrations like footsteps so much as the commonly ignored *microsonic* environmental vibrations that travel up your turntable support and into the platter, or that stem from the motor, the platter bearing, even the microsonic noise of the stylus tracking the groove. These are as loud as or louder than many of the musical "vibrations" pressed into the groove and so fog the music, especially quiet passages and low-level detail. With groove modulations as small as a wavelength of light, spurious movements of even a millionth of an inch can veil, distort, or even blot out musical nuances.

As laughably insignificant as these tiny contaminating vibrations—from an elevator, passing traffic, the fridge, or an air conditioner—may seem from a human perspective, on the scale of the stylus and groove they are serious forces to be reckoned with. The stylus is as undiscriminating as a little seismic sensor.

The whole table system is, in effect, a delicate seismometer that registers every tremor, regardless of its size or source. But while a conventional seismograph is designed to detect all the minute vibrations in its environment, a turntable must *exclude* some and pick up just those pressed into the surface of the record.

Obviously, a stylus cannot "know" the difference between musical vibrations intentionally inscribed in the groove and foreign vibrations from the environment. Once spurious information becomes enmeshed with the music, there is no way to remove it. ALL vibrations, whether intentional or not, are automatically picked up and converted by the cartridge into an electronic signal that will eventually be amplified some thirty thousand times. In this sense, the table, and indeed the entire system, is like a microscope—magnifying mechanical energy from the ultra-minute to the human scale.

The upshot is that, on a less than good table that permits vibrations to interfere with "unrecording" the music, what you hear sounds much less like real music and much more like a car radio—canned sound. Good turntables have what is sometimes described as "pulled-apart" sound, where each individual instrument clearly communicates its own discrete acoustic and spatial identity. The layers of sonic grunge imparted by a mediocre table system obscure the so-important subtle information, resulting in a collapsing and compacting of the sound. What we're talking about here is the difference between a beguiling illusion that draws you in, holds your attention, and *involves* you, and a system that, while it may sound imposing or even impressive, never transports you to the music.

On a really good system, you can identify individual instruments and their specific locations from side to side and front to back—as in the live performance. This becomes particularly striking on good symphonic recordings, where the string sections finally stop being just a smear of violins, a blur of cellos, and so on. Instead of listening to the audio equipment, you are at last listening through to the musical event. This is why Harry Pearson of *The Absolute Sound* magazine consistently stresses "transparency"—you start hearing past the equipment into the music. You want your equipment to be seen but not heard!

Incidentally, extraneous noises on some recordings, such as tape hiss or mild surface noise, which are superimposed over and sonically separate from the music, should be of far less concern than the crucial musical nuances blotted out by distortion. One's musical ear easily learns to ignore tape hiss (like conversation and clinking glasses during a club act—if you don't remember what this is like as a background to the music, listen to *Jazz at the Pawn Shop**). But fine musical detail obscured by distortion is music lost.

This assumes, of course, that you're listening on a good table. On a mass-market table unable to reveal such subtleties, it's hard to get past the surface noise and other obvious grunge—that's why folks get duped into thinking that the CD is *ipso facto* better than the LP.

Any mass-fi table system—even the pricey impress-your-neighbors type—is so unmusical and noisy that the richness of musical subtleties we're talking about is never heard. Getting good sound from a mass-fi table is like trying to learn about French food by sampling the wonders of ''gourmet'' frozen dinners.

TURNTABLES: THE BASICS OF GOOD DESIGN

Just as playback is the mirror image of the recording process, in a similar way *you* are the playback equivalent to the recording engineer. So to have an understanding of what a good table is supposed to do not only helps you choose the right equipment to buy, but helps you operate it intelligently.

The turntable system's job is to play the record groove while minimizing vibrations, which can bombard it from every conceivable mechanical and acoustic source. The degree of protection provided against these vibrations is one of the major differences among a lousy, a good, and an excellent table system.

While the presence of ''sonic garbage'' in the form of microresonances often goes unnoticed because you are probably so used to this muddied sound, its absence is immediately apparent in the overall sound quality. This absence can be achieved through better setup or by upgrading your table. A ''better'' table will have both a better mechanism to keep resonances away and, just as important, precision-machined and -fitted parts to avoid adding resonances of its own.

Turntables, whether belt or direct drive, consist of two basic subassemblies: the *drive system,* which must ensure exact platter speed and

*Proprius LP7778-79.

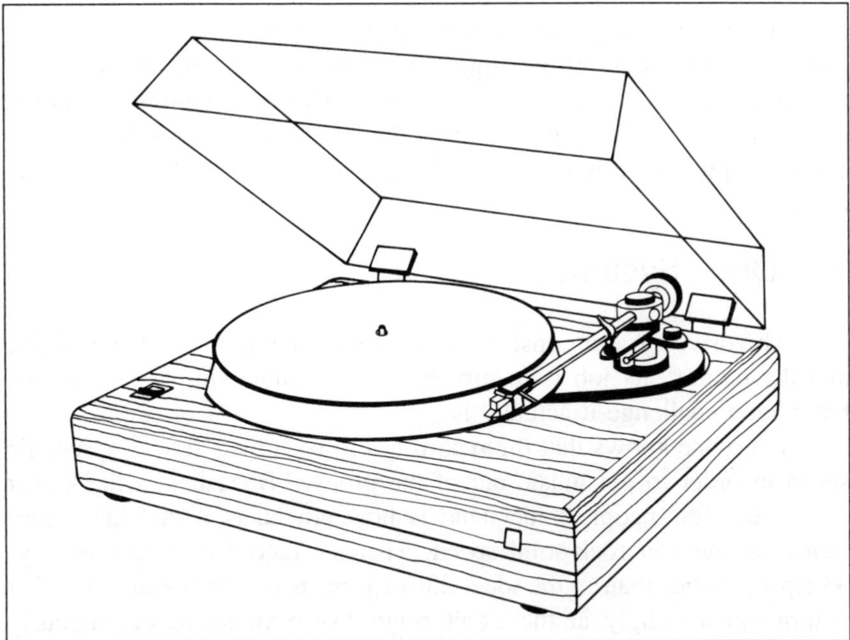

Fig. 3

supersmooth rotation, and the *isolation system,* which shields the stylus from spurious vibrations. The record itself becomes the final unifying element of the entire system. In fact, if there is such a thing as a single paramount ingredient in the vinyl playback system, it is the record. The disc is the software program that directs the stylus—the modulations of the spiraling groove literally drive the stylus, drawing the tonearm across the record.

As far as the plinth (table base) and dustcover go, when *thoughtfully* designed, these can offer some degree of acoustic shielding and of course provide very necessary protection against dust. The plinth, however, is largely a vestigial remnant from the Victorian origins of the gramophone. Stay away from flimsy plinths that sound boxy when you rap them with a knuckle. Boxy plinths resonate like the soundboard of a stringed instrument or piano. A poorly designed plinth and dustcover function like a giant "antenna" conducting mechanical and acoustic energy right up into the record and tonearm—obscuring the music. In fact, in many tables, the dustcover is the primary culprit in acoustic feedback because it acts like a giant diaphragm.

A very few of the finest tables, such as the Oracle and the Mitchell, are plinthless. Elite Rock offers a plinthless table as an option and at a significant saving. Probably the cost could be similarly reduced on most good tables by eliminating the plinth, but people are so conditioned to expect a box topped by a round platter that plinthless tables still remain the exception. As far as the mass-market mentality is concerned, a plinthless table is as unfinished as a Jackson Pollock without a frame.

The Drive System

The drive system consists of the *motor,* the *motor/platter linkage,* and the *platter.* Its job is to turn the record—how simple that seems, but what a challenge it actually is.

Everyone knows that the record has to be turned at a very specific speed in order to get music out of the groove. BUT, here's the kicker . . . what few people understand is how crucial is it that the record turn at a *constant* rock-solid speed. That the record may turn at, say, 33 r.p.m. rather than at the ideal 33⅓ r.p.m. is *less* important than that it turn unwaveringly at the exact *same* 33-r.p.m. speed continuously from one instant to the next. Yes, a speed slightly off from 33⅓ will alter the pitch a shade—turning too slow flattens the pitch, while too fast makes it sharper. But *minor* pitch deviation is not something to fret about greatly, providing it remains rock solid.

On the other hand, speed *inconstancy,* where the speed rapidly fluctuates however so slightly, is far more disturbing to the music than a slightly wrong but consistent, steady speed. Inconstancy alternately causes the sound to speed up and slow down, and the musical part of your mind is incredibly sensitive to this. You may not at first consciously register the changes because they occur so quickly, but keep listening and listen with your ears, not your eyes!

Consider that what makes one C note differ from another an octave higher is the *rate of vibration* of the string or membrane—i.e., time. Alter that time by constantly altering playback speed and you've altered the music. Speed inconstancy is one of the problems of mid-fi systems that leave so many people feeling bored, untouched, and unengrossed by a lot of classical music. Your brain already has a lot of sorting out to do when listening to complex music. If the music is also being frequency-modulated by speed inconstancy, then you'll probably tire of it sometime during the first movement.

The two *conventionally* recognized speed distortions are *wow* and *flutter.* Wow is a long-duration, low-pitch speed instability, the kind of gross distortion that's often heard on a badly warped record. Any table that has wow is really a mess. Wow may also be caused not by the table itself but by a record warp, or a record that's slightly out of round due to its spindle hole having been punched off-center. Check to make sure your arm and cartridge are riding nice and steady and that they're not quivering (that's vertical warp) or weaving slightly from side to side (the result of horizontal warp or an off-center spindle hole).

Flutter, much more common than wow, is a faster, tremulous, and higher-pitched effect, sort of like the sound of ZaSu Pitts's voice or the quivery-quavery soundtrack on some old movies. It refers to speed changes of less than one tenth of a second in duration (i.e., frequencies above 10 Hz). Though harder to detect than wow, its effects may be more fatiguing in the long run. Flutter is especially easy to detect on piano records—the notes warble when they should be steady. By the way, if your table suddenly develops flutter, check to be sure that a problem you're hearing isn't the fault of the particular record you're listening to—an off-speed studio tape recorder is not as rare as it should be. But if you hear flutter consistently with a number of your records, then it's probably your turntable at fault, or else possibly a mass/compliance mismatch between the arm and cartridge. Before racing to the repair shop, check to make sure your belt isn't slipping due to old age or because you've been running greasy fingers all over it. (First try cleaning the belt with alcohol and dusting with talc or cornstarch, next try replacing the belt, and only then investigate the need for repair.)

Even beyond flutter, there is shimmer, what J. Peter Moncrieff of *International Audio Review (IAR)* calls frequency modulation, which grows directly out of what was said about speed inconstancy. Shimmer is an elusive instability or "shakiness" to the sound that's so fundamentally intertwined with the music that often it's most easily noted by its absence. Shimmer is the musical equivalent of gently jiggling the photographic enlarger during printing—it produces a soft-focus, slightly blurred effect, like draping gossamer over a camera lens. Shimmer is usually as much a matter of tiny fluctuations in the evenness of your house current as it is any outright fault of the table motor. Because of this, no matter how excellent the motor, it will always greatly benefit from a top-quality regulated power-line conditioner.

The major effect of flutter and shimmer is to distort the critical time and phase relationships of the music, what's known as *time/phase distortion,* which results in a loss of musical "coherence." This means that the various sound frequencies that make up the music do not arrive at your ears in their correct order. It's not just that speed inconstancy bends the musical notes, but that unless they reach your ear in the same exact sequence and relationships in which they were originally played and recorded, the music will have been changed. This really strains your musical mind and is one of the major causes of listener fatigue. Your ear and mind have a remarkable ability to pick up these unmusical discrepancies and be quietly freaked out by them. Time and phase coherence make up a major difference between live and canned music, and between good sound and bad.

A lot of folks glibly assume that maintaining proper time relations by rotating the platter at an exact speed isn't so hard—after all, the same kinds of motors used on quality tables are used to power clocks that keep accurate time to within seconds a year. BUT, getting the musical information out of a record groove is a physics problem totally different from getting a clock to keep good time. A platter musn't "cog," or jump from one microsecond to the next, the way a clock can ratchet from one moment to the next—the record must turn absolutely smoothly and evenly.

Most people, even old folks, can easily hear sounds of 12,000 cycles per second. That means that the table motor has to be accurate to at least a twelve thousandths of a second, and if it isn't, your ear is going to sense that. What motor for a clock has to be that accurate? A clock can vary in speed from microsecond to microsecond without this ever being noticed, whereas a platter must rotate absolutely steadily with no variation.

If you could watch a clock with the same concentrated moment-to-moment attention with which you naturally listen to a piece of music, then a clock's normal moment-to-moment speed inconstancy would become just as undesirable as it is with a turntable. The clock, while very accurate in its normal time-frame of minutes and hours, would no longer be accurate in the micro-time-frame of recorded music. It cannot be stressed too often how absolutely crucial a constant record speed is. Music is a uniquely temporal art form.

In recognition of this, most of the top table designers have now gone to special power supplies—power line conditioners and regulators, which help enormously to lock in a steady speed and so reduce shimmer. As the minute speed variations of the motor are increasingly reduced, coherence of image and transparency become amazing.

Really, no table can be considered "world class" unless it has its own highly regulated and filtered power supply. In addition to the microfluctuations in voltage that obscure musicality, a lot of "noise" or "hair" normally rides along the 60-cycle wave form coming out of your wall socket and interferes with the music signal, especially in more urban locations. The poor and inconsistent quality of wall current is well recognized among computer hackers, who carefully isolate their equipment against this "line garbage."

The motor of our "world class" table will require, in addition to rock-steady speed, extreme silence. All motors produce vibrations, which, if allowed to reach the stylus, will cause bad sonic problems. All mass-fi tables suffer greatly from this affiliation. Some first-rank table motors, like the Well Tempered and the Merrill, are isolated in a special soundproof housing or pod, packed with an acoustic damping material. The Well Tempered motor is further isolated on a completely separate chassis mounted atop a 12-pound block of lead.

Severe motor vibration (and platter bearing noise) is known as *rumble*. Unfortunately, rumble doesn't limit itself to the bass frequencies, as widely supposed, but infiltrates well into the heart of the music—the midrange—where it causes major sonic dislocation. This is why something as simple as putting black Linn or Merrill oil in your bearing well usually produces a striking sonic improvement. Good tables often use small clock motors because they generate less vibration than larger motors. Their lesser power is compensated for by the heavy flywheel platter.

Some designers like to make a big deal about what particular kind of AC or DC motor they use. It's not so much that one is intrinsically better than the other, but more a matter of *how well* a given motor is incorporated into a *particular* design.

Since the motor's purpose is to turn the platter, there clearly must be a connection between the two. *Direct drive* and *belt drive* are the two basic methods. *Rim drive*, in which the motor is connected to an idler wheel that drives the rim of the platter, is inherently inaccurate, noisy, and obsolete—stay away! You'll never see this on a good table anyway.

Belt Drive

A belt drive (indirect drive) table is by far the preferred choice among discerning listeners, though it is sometimes dismissed by the audio novice or mass-fi technocrat as being an "old-fashioned, low-tech" design. Belt drive is a beautifully uncomplicated method that al-

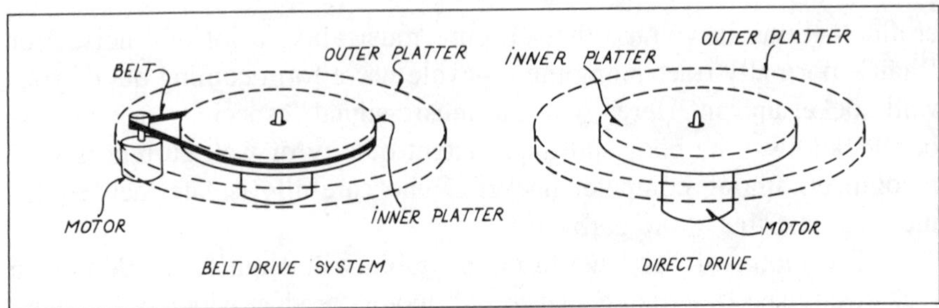

Fig. 4

lows money and effort to go for a high-quality motor and top-notch materials instead of being diverted to juggle a complex design, as in direct drive.

With BD, the motor's drive shaft is linked to the platter by a thin rubber belt (or in the case of the Micro-Seiki, a thin silken thread) stretching between the motor shaft pulley and the platter rim. The belt acoustically "decouples" the motor from the platter by acting as a filter and helping to dissipate motor vibration before it reaches the platter. In even the finest electric motor, the spinning rotor tends to snap back and forth between the magnetic poles, delivering its torque (power) in a series of pulses, known as cogging, rather than as a smooth even flow. When combined with the rotational inertia or flywheel effect of a heavy platter (not the flimsy hollow platters used on mass-fi tables), a belt drive smoothes out microvibrations and unevenness in motor rotation.

Another important asset of the belt-drive system is that, unlike most direct drives, it easily allows for the use of a *sprung subchassis* (also called a suspended or floating subchassis), which helps isolate the record from acoustic and mechanical vibrations. The platter and tonearm are mounted on a separate subchassis that's not only isolated from the motor and the plinth but, theoretically, from the environment as well. Because there's no rigid linkage between the platter and motor, the belt's "give" allows the subchassis to float freely. The subchassis is tuned, usually with springs, to filter out microresonances that would otherwise feed into the cartridge and contaminate the music signal. (More about this under "The Isolation System," below.)

Good tables use a *heavy platter* for two reasons. Weight provides plenty of inertial mass, which acts as a flywheel, greatly helping to smooth out platter rotation and the speed irregularities of the motor. In addition, mass also serves as a mechanical ground or sink for spurious resonances traveling up the spindle shaft and even resulting from the drag of the stylus in the groove. The sound of the stylus tracing the record produces its own nasty little distorting resonances, also called record ring. To listen for this needle talk, turn the volume completely down while playing a record and put your ear up near the table—you'll hear a little chittering sound. Sounds cute, eh?—but it's hell on the music. A good clamp, mat, and platter are the remedy.

The best platters, when tapped, sound "dead." Hold your ear up to the platter as you tap it with a small sharp object. The sound should be only a dull thunk, with no after-ring to it. The best "dead" platters are commonly made of a thick slab of machined plastic weighted with lead, the whole platter weighing as much as 10 pounds or more. Heavy machined-metal platters, which are the next best choice, are usually made in two parts, an inner platter and an outer ring, so that each piece will help to dampen resonances in the other. The metal is generally cast aluminum that has been milled on a lathe, as with the Linn and Acoustic Research tables, though the Source makes a beautiful heavy brass platter. The Rega and Systemdek tables both use a thick glass platter, which while sonically acceptable is far from our first choice of materials. Some of the top designers are now experimenting with the advantages of using machined Benelex, a superdense material made by the Masonite company. Thin plastic or lightweight metal platters are worthless and the sure sign of a mediocre table. All platters, regardless of material, must be precision machined for level surface, roundness, and dynamic balance.

The platter mat and record clamp are integral parts of what makes a good table work—these are not accessories. The designer should have figured out a good clamping method for the particular table design. However, these can sometimes be improved. George Merrill, for example, thinks well of the SOTA reflex clamp for his turntable (see more about this on p. 39).

A precision, highly polished platter *bearing* is essential on a heavy flywheel platter if it is to turn as smoothly and silently as possible. When you consider that an average audio system will magnify the music signal *at least* 30,000 times, then perhaps you can start to credit that it's possible the sound of molecules grinding against molecules can become incorporated into the music.

There are two basic approaches to bearing design. The typical bearing is at the bottom of the platter spindle, so the platter and spindle rotate on the bearing. Very tight tolerances are essential to ensure the spindle cannot wobble in the well. This would cause horrible distortion as the platter tipped from side to side. Some bearings, as on the Linn and Merrill tables, are so exactly milled to such tight tolerances that when you insert the platter spindle in the oil-filled bearing well, the platter can take as long as a day to settle all the way down.

The oil is essential in the design for several reasons. Two very smooth metal surfaces have a tendency to "freeze" together. The oil serves as a third body to keep these metals apart. It also drastically reduces friction and thereby noise and speed variation. It also helps keep the spindle centered in the well. The specific oil you use makes a small but important sonic difference. Yes, that sounds ludicrous, but try it (see p. 252).

A few companies, such as SOTA and the Elite Rock, turn the classic bearing design upside down—the special oilless jewel bearing sits *on top* of the spindle shaft instead of underneath it. This inverted bearing design is based on the premise that the best way to spin a plate (the platter) so it is very stable is to balance it on the stick (shaft) and then spin only the plate. The more conventional arrangement is to attach plate to stick and spin the stick. This upside-down design is called a fitted or zero-clearance bearing because there is no oil as a buffer layer and so contact of spindle and well is very intimate. Zero-clearance fit prevents platter wobble and ensures smooth rotation with no rattle or chatter. The materials used for spindle and well are different, preventing friction or freezing. Usually, the spindle is metal or jewel and the sleeve a polymer like Teflon or Delrin.

Provided the execution is good, both designs—oil and oilless—are probably of equal merit. It's how the table sounds that counts.

Two small disadvantages of belt drives: Speed selection on some models must be changed manually, by removing the outer platter and slipping the belt from one part of the pulley to another. It only takes a moment, but if you change speeds frequently, consider a belt drive that has pushbutton speed selection, like the Merrill or SOTA.

The other minor inconvenience is low torque. Because there's no rigid connection between the motor and platter, it's impossible to apply the large amount of starting torque that's needed to accelerate the platter quickly. Getting up to speed can take a few seconds because only the friction of the belt turns the platter. But why be so impatient? The low torque can be a real inconvenience, though, when using certain record-cleaning brushes that can put enough drag on the platter to stall it. The delicate carbon-fiber brushes will hardly ever do this, however.

Direct Drive

Direct drive (DD), although the most common design in turntables, is used in very few *good* ones. Unless you want to get involved with one of the handful of high-end DD tables, we recommend steering clear of them entirely. The good DD tables start in the $2,000-plus range with the Goldmund Studietto (incidentally, the highly vaunted $14,000-plus Goldmund Reference, the firm's *ne plus ultra*, is a belt-drive), the Mitch Cotter, and the Technics SP-10 DD. Mass-market DD tables should be avoided like the plague, even the fancier, more expensive ones like Denon's, though the boys in the white lab coats won't be happy about this.

In a DD turntable, the platter is directly coupled to the electric motor—in other words, the motor's drive shaft is the platter's spindle and directly drives the platter. On the face of it, this would seem to be an eminently sensible drive system, the rigid coupling allowing no play between motor and platter, thereby providing very stable platter rotation, at least in theory.

BUT, in execution there are some *major* drawbacks to this design. The DD claim for more-stable platter rotation is based on the flawed premise that a motor will turn perfectly smoothly, evenly, and exactly. Even the most expensive motors do not turn perfectly. (Check earlier remarks on speed inconstancy, p. 26).

As mentioned earlier, a motor's spinning rotor tends to snap somewhat in its progression from pole to pole, delivering its torque (power) in a stream of rapid cogging pulses rather than a smooth even flow. Without benefit of a belt to act as a filter and isolate the platter, all DD motor vibrations are transmitted directly into the platter. So in contrast to its seeming simplicity and straightforwardness, direct drive actually requires complicated sensors and servo-control circuitry to compensate for this cogging and its associated vibration.

Good direct-drive motors—those used on $2,000-plus tables—employ complex control electronics, a precision-machined rotor, and elaborately interleaved copper windings. These motors are understandably far more expensive to manufacture than a comparable motor for a belt-drive table, and are far too expensive ever to be used on any mass-market DD.

On top of their other problems, DD tables cannot be conveniently protected from acoustic feedback and mechanical resonances. The motor's direct coupling to the platter not only transmits all motor resonances directly to the stylus/groove interface, but in addition seriously interferes with using a sprung subchassis or other isolating suspension. Directly coupling a vibrating, cogging motor to the platter and finding some way to provide protection against resonances are the two really ugly problems with DD tables.

The main advantages of DD are to the mass-fi manufacturer and not to the *listener*, allowing a turntable to be marketed as an appliance, with "all modern conveniences"; offering almost zero setup time, in contrast to many belt-drive tables; and permitting considerable design freedom with pull-out drawers, gadgets, and twinkling lights that are fun to twiddle and nifty to look at. None of these features, however, add to fidelity of sound—the proof of the table is in the listening and nowhere else.

The Isolation System

An isolation system may provide some protection against such gross vibrations as passing footfalls and the like. But its most important job is to isolate the record and cartridge from the tiny microsonic vibrations emanating from the motor, bearing, stylus/groove interface, and environment.

The suspension acts as a filter that allows very low frequencies (i.e., subsonic frequencies, below the audible range) to get through, but will not pass frequencies higher than its tuned resonance. Any microsonic information that's in the audible band, and so would directly interfere with the music, is therefore filtered out. The lower the frequency that the suspension is tuned to, the less mechanical energy is allowed through and the cleaner your music.

With the cartridge effectively a microsonic detector, it is essential to prevent spurious sonic resonances from being picked up along with the music signal. Just consider the minute scale of the stylus and the record groove—with groove modulations as small as a wavelength of light (a millionth of an inch), the tiniest vibrations imparted to the platter or arm can contaminate and obscure musical information. It's the same kind of thing as preparing tomato sauce in an aluminum pot—you do not expect to single out the taste of the aluminum specifically, but the sauce's flavor will nonetheless definitely be affected by the pot.

And while any one of the many sources of distortion, taken alone, may seem insignificant, their accumulation causes significant muddying of the music, greatly lessening the pleasure of listening and leaving you with nothing more than a canned performance.

A stethoscope can show you just how much microvibration your table must deal with (stethoscopes are expensive, so try to borrow one from a friendly local health-care professional or termite exterminator). With the motor both off and turned on, listen to the table support, the platter, the chassis. Do this at varying hours of the day and night so you can hear the changes in resonances due to traffic and other noises. You'll be amazed to discover the amount of noise that travels up through the floor and walls and through the air to rattle the tiny stylus as it tracks that speeding, twisting, music-packed groove. Then play some music with the volume turned up and listen for airborne vibration.

This airborne or acoustic vibration comes mainly from the system's own speakers (*acoustic feedback*). It masks important low-level information and detail that gives the music much of its "realness." That's why the table should always be kept out of a direct line with the speakers. Lower-frequency drivers are omnidirectional, so placing the table right behind the speakers is not a good solution either.

When severe, acoustic feedback has been quaintly termed howlaround, because it can sound like a storm wind howling around the house. It is now largely a thing of the past, however, unknown today with any table of the quality of an AR ES-1 or better. As a quick check for howlaround, flip on your system, *very gently* place the tonearm down on the record without the platter turning, then *very slowly* turn the volume up all the way (and be ready to turn it down real fast if howlaround does occur). On a good table, you should get none. If you do get any, there's something very wrong with the table.

Any comprehensive suspension that helps block mechanical and airborne resonances is better than none—it may be as basic as special compliant rubber feet, or as elaborate as a sprung subchassis that isolates the table from both external and internally generated sources of resonance.

Tables that have minimal or no built-in suspension of their own are more susceptible to resonances and vibrations, so the surface they sit on must be carefully chosen for absolute stability and protection against footfalls and other gross shocks. Whenever possible, it's always best to use a specially designed support like the Arcici Iron Cloud, secured to a load-bearing (usually external) wall.

When *compliant feet* provide the sole suspension, then only the plinth is being isolated from mechanical and, to a more limited extent, acoustic vibrations. Motor vibrations are filtered from the platter by only a belt at most. This method is commonly used on cheap belt-drive tables and on almost all direct-drive tables. The standard mass-fi compliant feet of coil springs encased in rubber should be avoided, including the handsomely packaged after-market sets. They make lousy acoustic isolators—in fact, if you hit them and listen closely, you can easily hear the springs inside going *pwang, pwang*—BAD! Replace spring feet with Tiptoes or pucks of Sorbothane. *Never* use these spring-loaded feet in combination with a sprung subchassis because the carefully tuned frequency of the subchassis will be confounded.

A *sprung subchassis* is by far the most widely employed means on good tables of isolating the platter from vibrations. (This method is never found on mass-fi DD tables.) On good belt-drive tables, the platter and tonearm are on a floating subchassis mounted on specially tuned springs that isolate platter and stylus not only from vibrations caused by the table's motor but also from the environment.

A way of roughly judging isolation effectiveness is to play a record at your highest NORMAL listening volume. Then, *without changing the volume*, turn off the motor and GENTLY place the stylus on the motionless record. Tap with your fingernail on the plinth and the support surface the table sits on. The quieter the thump you hear from the speakers, the better the table's isolation from vibrations.

One hassle of a sprung subchassis is that it requires the table to be correctly "set up" by tuning the springs for both levelness and correct compliance or tension. The springs, drive belt, and tonearm cable are all that connect the platter and subchassis to the plinth (and environment), and consequently exert a major effect on the table's sound. Nonsprung chassis are far easier to set up but, with very few exceptions (such as the WT and Elite Rock), a sprung subchassis design is the wisest way to go.

There are a number of different sprung-subchassis designs. The first rudimentary versions of this design were disasters because, while the platter was suspended, the arm remained rigidly fixed to the plinth! With the arm going one way, the platter another, severe distortion and even groove jumping resulted. This damaged a lot of records and styli, let alone paining the ear.

Most subchassis designs now derive directly from the milestone three-point system developed by Edgar Villchur for Acoustic Research, circa 1960, and then refined in Britain by Linn and later by George

Merrill in the United States. In this design, the subchassis is suspended from three or sometimes four springs secured to the plinth. Other designs, like the VPI, support the subchassis from underneath on springs. This method of ''support'' rather than ''hanging'' can allow greater lateral or side-to-side movement, which must be corrected for. A spring, when compressed to support a weight, will tend to bend over sideways unless compressed very uniformly. A spring extended by a hanging weight has much better stability and naturally reacts up and down, rather than from side to side.

However, since good sound is always the result of tasteful, workable compromises, there's no single ''best way'' to design a sprung subchassis. The success of any particular suspension seems to have more to do with the quality of construction, and the intelligence with which each ingredient is integrated into the overall table design, than with its ingenuity in the abstract.

For example, rather than springs, the Well Tempered Table uses special neoprene cushions specifically designed and tuned to filter out everything above 15 cycles. Bill Firebaugh of the Well Tempered Lab points out that if you tap the plinth of any sprung subchassis, you can hear the springs ''ringing''—he believes (and he's not alone in this) any spring suspension unavoidably imparts a ''ring'' to the music. Sal Demicco, for one, emphatically concurs—he's a firm believer in unsprung tables like the Technics SP-10. Springs are also inherently unstable, being subject to vertical and lateral movement, and this instability can permeate and distort the music—unless handled just right.

Peter Moncrieff reports that Japanese high-end table designs (which don't see the light of day here) try to minimize the effects of external shock not through springs but through mass. The Japanese too believe springs will color the music by their inevitable movement. Moncrieff reports that the dedicated Japanese audiophile will cut a hole in the floor of the house, sink a huge concrete block into the ground below (without

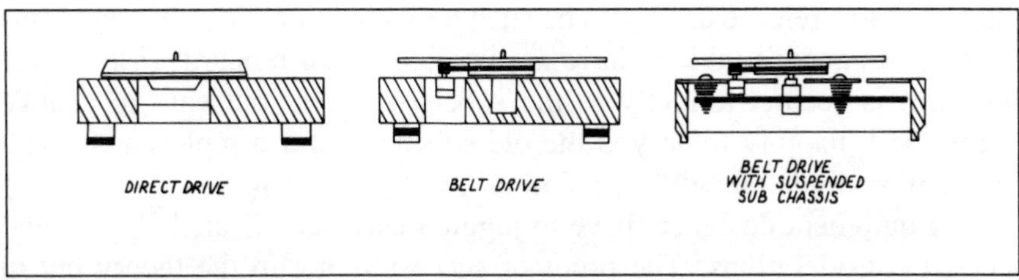

Fig. 5

letting it contact the walls of the hole), and then mount the table on this concrete block.

This *mass-loading* approach to quarantining the record and cartridge from the environment exploits the fact that high mass acts like a sonic sponge to dampen and actually absorb resonances. It is used over here by, among others, Harry Weisfeld of VPI.

The highly respected English table, the Pink Triangle, employs the opposite philosophy. The designers have struggled over the years to come up with an incredibly lightweight but highly rigid design using Aerolam, an aluminum honeycomb-structured material. These proponents of *low-mass* design believe that the *less* mass is used, the less material there is to resonate, and also the less material there is to store resonant energy. Mass loading and low mass are two opposing but equally valid approaches to controlling resonances.

Another important technique for minimizing resonances is the *closed-loop* or *mechanical-grounding-loop* design, employed on all good tables with or without a suspension. In effect, it is also an extension of the mass-loading approach. Visualize a loop extending from the stylus up to the cantilever, into the cartridge, through the headshell and along the tonearm to the arm's bearings, down the arm pillar into the suspension structure, then back up into the platter bearing, up the spindle shaft, into the platter, into the platter mat, and finally to the record, which contacts the stylus and closes the loop.

If all links in this loop are rigidly coupled, then the mass of the entire turntable system is available to each link. Each link of that loop then serves as a sink or ''mechanical ground'' to conduct and dissipate resonances into the total mass of the table before they reach the stylus and groove. Any flaws in this path can result in spurious additions or subtractions to the music from non-music-signal vibrations. It is therefore essential that the connections—between cartridge and headshell; headshell and arm; arm, arm board, and suspension—all be solid and tight.

George Merrill takes the mechanical grounding loop one step further by eliminating some of the linkages altogether. He considers what he terms arm release energy to be such a major source of sonic problems that he designs his table to have no separate tonearm board. Instead, the tonearm is secured directly to the subchassis. (If you want to change arms, he'll happily trade you the old subchassis for a replacement with the new armhole already precision-drilled.)

Equipment designers have to juggle many complicated choices and design considerations. The proof of success is not in the theory but in the excellence or mediocrity of the sound. Good sound is a result of refinements on an already good concept.

Platter Mats and Record Clamps

Both stylus and the vinyl disc vibrate, and they each vibrate differently. These vibrations in turn set up additional resonances in the cantilever, cartridge body, tonearm, and the disc itself. The resonances set up in the disc are interpreted by the stylus as part of the audio signal, intentional elements of the music.

The cure (never total) is to couple the record tightly to another surface that can dissipate the vibrations. This is the function of platter mats and record clamps. They can also help to flatten records, and so mitigate "warp wow" distortions. The perimeter clamp on the George Merrill table is particularly effective here.

Vacuum clamping is an all-out attempt to minimize record vibrations and warps. The record is held by vacuum suction to the platter, thus ensuring both flatness and excellent coupling to transmit resonances away from the record groove. There are claims that vacuum clamping may physically damage the record and increase surface noise. Speculations as to the cause range from the suction pressure embedding dust particles in the vinyl to actual alterations in its chemical balance. Less suction applied continuously is thought to have corrected the problems. However, the results are not all in.

A platter mat plus clamp, while perhaps less effective, serve very well. These accessories—"necessories"—allow you to adjust the sound of your turntable system, sometimes for the worse, hopefully for the better. Be careful not to confuse "different" with better—a change can result in an improvement, an impairment, or simply a step sideways that offers a different combination of tradeoffs.

Some tables come with their own clamping systems, like the Merrill peripheral clamping ring, the VPI spindle-threaded screw-down clamp, the SOTA vacuum-clamping system. Such an integral clamp may be the best choice for that table, or you may want to experiment with other clamps. Some tables also come with special platters, made for example of acrylic, which are intended to eliminate the need for a separate mat. Again, respect the designer's intentions but don't necessarily ignore the possibility of experimenting with mats (as well as clamps) nonetheless. How a clamp sounds may depend on the mat it is used with, so these are best considered in combination.

Mats are placed between platter and record. They come supersoft, soft, medium, and hard. Each represents a different theory about disc/turntable interaction and each represents a slightly different conjunction of tradeoffs and compromises. No two will sound the same.

In addition to damping and isolating the disc, the mat must also provide a good grip for the disc and thus prevent slippage and resulting speed irregularities. It must also not interfere with a tight coupling in the mechanical grounding loop.

As summed up by Peter Moncrieff, the mat should be firm enough to support the stylus in its larger excursions, yet soft enough to terminate the entire surface of the record and table platter so vibrations will die as quickly as possible and minimize smearing of the music. The softness should have a damping rather than springy quality so the mat doesn't store the energy it absorbs from the record only to release it later, thus smearing the music that way.

A hard mat (as a category) will tend to give a more ''lively'' sound to the music, which can be attractive but is actually distortion. Vibrational energy from the record is not being stored and dissipated by the mat but is instead being reflected right back into the vinyl, where it continues to reverberate. There is an idea that a hard mat is most like the LP and therefore, since like materials transmit vibrations between them more easily than do unlike ones, the vibrations will be transmitted through the mat away from the record and then dissipated into the mechanical grounding loop. A soft mat (again, as a category) will tend to reduce transient impact. You really have to listen for yourself on your own system to decide on a mat that matches well with it.

When using a clamp, the stylus tracks better; focus, imaging, and soundstage improve; and the sound is more pellucid overall. The only problem is that some clamps add their own coloration, or rattle and vibrate. Again, audition these in conjunction with your mat.

Record clamps come in three basic forms: a simple weight, a reflex clamp that slips over the spindle and then locks downward onto the record, and a screw-on clamp that requires that the spindle has already been threaded to accept it, like the VPI. Merrill uses a combination of weight and special peripheral clamping ring, which secures the record around its perimeter. Holding the LP both in the center and around the edge, this system is excellent both at locking the record to the platter (or mat) to minimize vibration, and at (temporarily) flattening out warps. This system is almost as effective as a vacuum, while being less expensive and having none of a vacuum system's drawbacks.

The weight style of clamp, which simply slips over the spindle and holds the record by its heavy weight, is probably used safely only on tables whose bearing assemblies have been specifically designed to support this. Such a weight may also slow platter rotation. Though it is better than nothing, it is probably less effective than either a screw-down or a reflex clamp.

Some clamps are friction-fit, like the Souther. A small disc of plastic, this fits snugly over the spindle and couples the record to the platter. The clamp's hole is cut square and on the small side to ensure a tight fit, and the sides expand very slightly to fit a variety of spindle sizes. It's probably the least expensive good clamp around, since the Radio Shack one has been discontinued. With this type of pressure-fit clamp, be careful not to push down too hard, for two reasons: If you become too enthusiastic, you can cause the edges of the record actually to become slightly lifted off the platter, and you can also "bottom out" the suspension. While this probably does no harm, it doesn't feel right and will probably require more frequent adjustment of the suspension springs as a result of their being so often compressed.

Reflex clamps use neither weight nor screw threading nor pressure-fit. This design slips over the spindle, with no pressure applied to the table bearings; then a collet grips the spindle and pulls the clamp slightly downward until it presses against the record, coupling it snugly to the platter. This method, for an aftermarket clamp, is probably the most effective and entails least risk of any possible destructive action. The SOTA reflex clamp works very well and is beautifully made. Audio-quest has a similar design.

The bottom of a reflex or friction-fit clamp should either be slightly dished or use some other method that permits the placement of a spindle washer under the record. Without this washer, when the clamp clamps down on the record's center, its outer edge will be raised away from the mat, negating the benefits of the clamp—and then some.

THE TONEARM

Getting good sound from a record requires that the stylus very accurately trace the groove modulations. Imagine what would happen if you tried to trace a picture while your hand was shaking. If, as the pencil traced the picture, your hand trembled, the tracing (transcription) would be distorted.

The same thing applies when transcribing a record. The tonearm is like your hand, the cartridge stylus like the pencil point. Musical accuracy depends on having an absolutely steady hand (tonearm) and stable surface (turntable). Unless the arm holds the cartridge rock-steady over the groove during the stylus's half-mile encounter with each side of the record, the musical transcription will be distorted. The function of the tonearm is to follow the groove so the stylus can follow the

THE MINUTE SCALE OF RECORDINGS

What makes the table system's job so devilishly demanding is the truly minute scale of the music signal that must be released from the grooves. This signal must be magnified some 30,000 times from the groove to the speakers in order to be heard.

Visualize the fineness of a record groove, and then consider that it combines two distinct channels of information, each with completely different modulations. Some of the signal modulations in the groove are on the same order of size as a wavelength of light, which means the stylus has to "read" a signal as small as a millionth of an inch. Add in all the variation and complexities in the scale of the music itself, from crescendos to pianissimos, from piccolos to contrabassoons, and you can begin to see the stylus has quite a job.

The recorded audio bandwidth is the range of frequencies (i.e., rates of vibration) the human ear can hear, which extends from 20 Hz to 20,000 Hz. Hertz (Hz) is the same as cycles per second. You can hear a piccolo note whose fundamental vibrates as fast as 4,698.6 Hz and whose harmonics extend well up to 18,000 Hz and beyond, and a contrabassoon with a fundamental plunging as deep as 29 Hz. Your ear can also detect ranges in loudness of 60 dB, a ratio of 100,000 to 1. Not only is this tremendous range captured in the record groove, but then the stylus has to release it.

For the half mile or so of record groove per LP side, the stylus must precisely trace abrupt changes in the direction of the undulating groove, sometimes traveling at speeds several times the acceleration of gravity, without ever losing contact with either wall or blurring together the modulations.

Groove friction heats the stylus up to 350 degrees Fahrenheit and the groove vinyl momentarily liquefies each time the stylus passes over it. (This is why one should let a record rest for *at least* 30 minutes before replaying it, and preferably for 24 hours.)

Even though the cartridge tracking weight is commonly set at only about 1.5 grams, the entire weight is supported on the minute side edges of the stylus. As a result, the downforce applied to the groove on a per-square-inch basis is *several TONS*.

Combine these extreme conditions of weight, heat, speed, and need for exquisite maneuverability, then add in the scale of environmental vibrations that interfere with the stylus as it retrieves the music from the groove, and it's extraordinary that ANY music (as opposed to noise) is heard through an audio system. The feat of retrieving all the music from the groove is analogous to an elephant trying to thread a needle.

To help one better grasp the magnitude of the difficulties in retrieving all the music from the record, the Boston Inch Scale (developed by E. B. Meyer and published in the Boston Audio Society's magazine, *The Speaker*) converts signal and table measurements from their real-life micron scale into inches. A micron is a millionth of a meter, or one thousandth of a millimeter, which is equivalent to 0.0039 inch.

Using the inch scale, a stylus is 30 feet high, affixed to a cantilever 50 feet thick and 275 feet long, which extends from a cartridge body 2,000 feet long, sitting 80 feet above the record. The tonearm, 450 feet in diameter, crosses 1,300 feet above the record from its pivot point 4 miles away. On a typical line-contact stylus, the stylus downforce temporarily deforms the vinyl by as much as an inch (20 times the size of a violin harmonic), leaving a stylus footprint on the groove wall measuring 10 inches long and 4 inches wide.

A typical midrange signal demands that the stylus move 16 inches from peak to peak of the wave form. A deep bass note 10 dB louder requires the stylus to move 10 feet 6 inches whereas for a high-frequency harmonic at a very low sound level, the stylus must move only 0.68 inch. Even the simplest piece of music is likely to contain, at any one time, enormous numbers of frequencies at different levels.

(Incidentally, the same microsonic scale applies to compact discs. Though it is technologically feasible to make the pits smaller than they are now, and thus fit more information onto a single disc, the laser fine enough to read those smaller pits has yet to become commercially practical.)

modulations inscribed within the groove, and replicate as closely as possible the motion of the cutting lathe stylus.

Attention has commonly been focused too much on the cartridge, as the component that actually "collects" the music from the groove. But what allows the cartridge to do its job properly is the quality of the arm and table. If these two components do not meet certain standards, the cartridge will not perform up to its own quality. The best pencil in the world is of little benefit in a trembling hand on a shaky surface. You must think in terms of the table *system*—the table, arm, and cartridge form one component. This, and not the cartridge, is the real transducer.

To enable the cartridge to retrieve the most music from the record grooves, the tonearm must accomplish four tasks: (1) provide a rigid platform to support the cartridge over the groove, (2) conduct resonances away from the cartridge while introducing very few (ideally none) of its own, (3) move freely and smoothly across the record, and (4) provide sufficient adjustments so the cartridge can be accurately set up in correct geometry to the groove. (1) and (2) are both accomplished through a balance of mass and rigidity.

High Mass, Low Mass, and Rigidity

Ideally, you would want the tonearm to have *no mass* so it would follow the gradual inward spiral of the record groove, moving without friction and without deflecting the stylus and cantilever out of correct alignment with the cartridge generator.

Yet if the cartridge and arm had no mass, the stylus would have no "anchor" to work against as the groove walls pushed it around. Instead, arm and cartridge body would faithfully match the stylus's every wiggle without resistance, so that the three moved as a frozen unit. No work would be done, no signal would be generated, and there would be no music output. Proper music signals are produced only when the stylus moves *relative to* the fixed cartridge body. If the body wiggles also, then either no signals or wrong signals will be generated.

Therefore, the ideal pickup arm would have *no mass* at superlow frequencies to allow easy handling of LP warps or eccentricities and free movement across the record, but *infinite mass* caused by inertia, at audio frequencies so that the only movement was by the stylus.

Coming back to reality, however, records themselves are not ideal and invariably have flaws. Even seemingly flat LPs actually have tiny surface eccentricities, which the tonearm must be able to follow instantaneously. High mass here becomes a major liability because of its high inertia, which resists changes in movement. A low-mass arm, on the other hand, can respond quickly to record surface irregularities.

Here's an example. An arm with too high mass will travel up the side of a warp, but may then overshoot the top instead of maintaining contact with the surface of the warp and following it down the other side. While a high-mass tonearm can be easily set in motion because its great mass has been counterbalanced on a precision bearing, once moving it's hard to stop. As speed increases, so do inertia and resistance to quick changes of direction.

All records have mini-warps. A warp is like a ramp and, like Evel Knievel, the arm/cartridge comes flying along, shoots up the ramp, and may momentarily take to the air. If, for even a micromoment, the stylus doesn't exactly follow the groove modulation, you get a time distortion, which, as said earlier, is one of the most unmusical distortions to plague playback. Not accurately tracing the groove effectively creates two time domains, one of the cartridge/tonearm and another of the record, whereas the cartridge is supposed to march exactly to the time and tune of the groove.

A very low mass arm can precisely follow record irregularities, but cannot easily dissipate microresonances transmitted by the stylus up into the cartridge, headshell, and tonearm. In fact, with too little mass, the arm is easily driven into resonant behavior by the energy traveling up from the cartridge and record. Rather than serving as an energy drain, the arm will itself start to microvibrate and resonate, feeding vibrations back into the stylus. This, of course, interferes with the stylus's ability to trace the groove accurately and muddies the sound. Another problem with low mass is that the arm, instead of providing a stable support and energy sink for the cartridge, can actually be pushed around by the cartridge, as described in the earlier discussion of the ideal tonearm. As the groove wall pushes the stylus, that motion is passed right along up into the arm. A high-mass (high-inertia) tonearm will most effectively provide an extremely stable, rigid cartridge support as well as being a good energy drain for the microvibrations of cartridge and headshell.

Balancing these two opposing needs of mass versus freedom from inertia is what keeps tonearm designers busily perfecting tonearms. Different designers choose slightly different tradeoffs, but an effective compromise is a medium-mass arm, one that is as light as possible for good tracking of LP irregularities, while still having sufficient mass to resist the stylus movement and to prevent the resonating cartridge body from causing the arm to vibrate. Most arms have a medium 10 to 13 grams of effective mass.

The arm's effective mass is also very strongly influenced by the weight of the cartridge and headshell, since these sit out at the farthest end from the pivot point. The effect of tonearm mass increases with the square of its distance from the pivot point.

The mechanical-grounding-loop principle discussed above (p. 38) also helps to control resonances.

Rigidity and the Tonearm Tube

Rigidity, in both material and design, can help substitute for mass in controlling resonances. Mass and rigidity are balanced and traded off in every aspect of arm design, from the choice of materials through the shape of the arm tube to the choice of headshell material and design, arm bearings, and every other detail.

For example, to minimize mass while maximizing rigidity, the arm tube may be built with a thin wall for low mass but a large diameter for high rigidity. A low-mass arm with a *small* diameter would easily flex when excited by external vibrations, moving the cartridge body all over the place. The small diameter would also make it difficult to provide rigid coupling to the headshell. It's essential that not only the tube be rigid and dead but also the headshell and the coupling between the two. Most arms fail miserably at this.

The more rigid the arm, the higher the resonant frequency and the higher the Q or sharpness of the resonance. Rigid arms must be carefully damped. To check for adequate damping, sharply tap the tube with your fingernail or other small sharp object and listen closely. The sound should be a dull thunk, like a spoon dropped in a jug of whipped cream, with no lingering after-ring.

The Bearings

The tonearm must minimize friction at its pivot point in order to move freely and smoothly across the record. Any resistance interferes with the stylus's accuracy in tracing the groove and also transmits resonances from the pivot point, down the arm tube, and back into the cartridge. Tonearm bearings must be as friction free as humanly possible.

The bearings form a vital link too in the mechanical grounding loop because, if well designed, they will transmit low-frequency energy beyond the arm's damping ability into the much larger mass of the table, where it can be dissipated. To do this, the bearings must be very rigid, permitting no slop or excess play. Such play could also cause audible rattling and chatter.

In fact, bearing rattle is provoked by the stylus vibrations traveling from the cartridge body down the arm tube, and also by acoustic feedback transmitted through either the arm tube or the plinth into the arm base. The vibrations of the rattling bearings then get transmitted back down the arm tube to the cartridge body and wiggle it, thus interfering with accurate music retrieval.

Once again, a tradeoff becomes necessary. Make the bearings tight enough to combat rattling, and the friction increases. Loosen them enough to reduce friction, and they rattle worse. Indeed, all hard bearings have a tendency to rattle more at higher frequencies, regardless of how tight they are. The bearings cannot be tightened sufficiently to move the rattling into the supersonic regions without simultaneously introducing excessive friction.

One solution to this conflict is an air bearing design such as the Eminent Technology arm uses. Correctly designed, it is friction free and nonrattling. Another inspired approach is offered by the Well Tempered Arm's no-bearing design. The arm is suspended on a pair of crossed nylon monofilaments secured to a paddle immersed in silicone damping fluid, an arrangement that allows for high effective rigidity. As a friend explains it, this design produces an effect very similar to trying to swing a Ping-Pong paddle underwater quickly.

In conventional bearing design, this conflict between very tight coupling and friction-free movement is generally best resolved by extreme smoothness and hardness of the bearings, reducing friction while allowing rigidity. Naturally, such a fine-quality bearing ain't cheap.

Tangency Adjustments

The final design goal is to align the cartridge correctly with the record groove, recapitulating the position of the stylus on the cutting lathe.

The first alignment for all pivoting arms is bending the tube at some point(s) along its length to maintain the correct tangency between cartridge and groove. (In geometry, "tangent" means a straight line touching a curve at one point.) A pivoting tonearm will be perfectly aligned with a concentric recording groove only at two points in its journey from rim to center, but with care an overall accuracy of ±2 percent can be achieved. When you're trying to impress friends, give them a choice center cut off your favorite LP, where deviation will be the least.

The equations for calculating the optimum arm length, offset angle for cartridge mounting, and the arm's mounting point on the plinth have been well established for over 40 years. Generally, the optimum compromise for arm tube length is 9 inches, with the cartridge offset by about 25 degrees to the line of the arm.

Arm tubes come in a variety of shapes: straight, S-curve, double S-curve (a Joe Grado special), J-curve, and undoubtedly new ones yet to be dreamed up in the search for ideal tangency. Straight and J-curve arms, which maintain tangency by angling the headshell on an otherwise straight tube, require less material than do S-curves and therefore permit a lighter (lower-mass) arm. Arm tubes that taper, regardless of configuration, stagger any buildup of resonance, because as the tube's diameter changes, so does the resonant frequency of the tube. Resonances can be more readily propagated with untapered arms because the tube's resonant frequency remains constant over its entire length.

Aluminum is often selected for its lightness and strength; alloys of magnesium and titanium have roughly the same strength but will resonate at different frequencies. However, the choice of tube material is generally less important than the mechanical design and execution of the tonearm.

Offsetting the angle of the cartridge on the arm to maintain groove tangency also introduces a bias or skating force. Left uncorrected, the inner (left-channel) groove would have much more force against it than the outer groove, resulting in degradation of imaging and, in severe

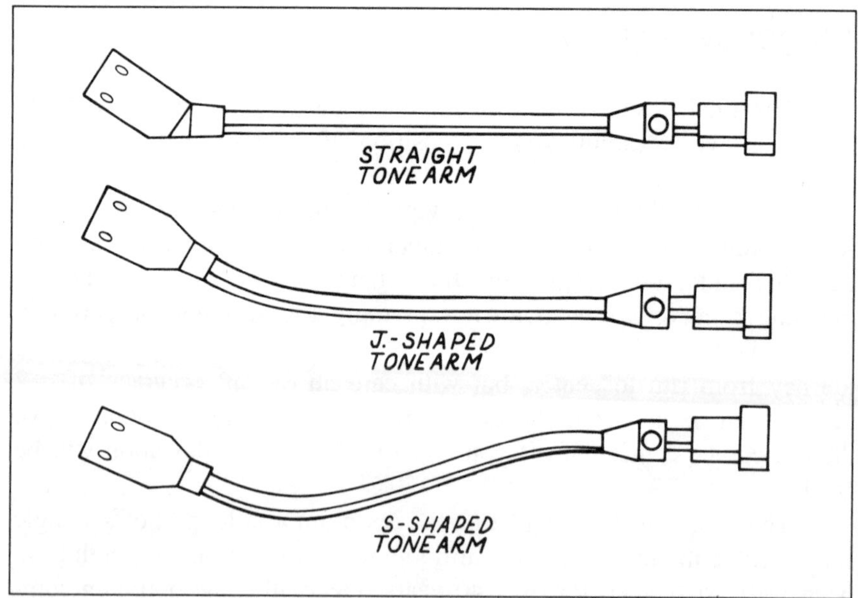

Fig. 6

cases, nasty distortion, as well as uneven record wear. The *antiskate* adjustment can partially counteract the cartridge's "inward pull" on the arm. However, skating force varies with the music's loudness level, since it is a function of the stylus drag and cannot always be perfectly balanced by a constant antiskate force. The most serious problem with this skating force is that it dislocates the alignment of the cantilever respective to the generator *and* the groove. This is one of the advantages of a straight-line tracking arm (see p. 50).

Good tonearms make it possible to swivel the cartridge in all three planes—cartridge *overhang* and null-point alignment sets the lateral tracking angle, *vertical tracking angle* (VTA) adjusts the stylus vertically in the groove form back to front, and *azimuth* establishes the stylus at right angles to both groove walls to ensure proper right and left channel separation. Much more about this in "System Setup" (p. 236).

Precision adjustments for vertical *tracking force* (tracking weight) are also vital. A movable counterweight on the arm tube behind the pivot point adjusts the tracking weight or amount of downforce on the stylus riding in the groove, and counterbalances the weight of your particular cartridge.

The Headshell

The headshell is the platform at the end of the arm tube where the phono cartridge is clamped. A mechanically tight coupling is essential to prevent microrattles and to help conduct resonances away from the stylus. The best mechanical connection is provided by an *integral headshell* as this eliminates any joint between arm and headshell—both are cast or forged together from a single piece of metal. A less expensive and slightly less desirable integral design is to make a permanent joint between the headshell and arm tube, either welded or pressure fit. Permanent glue joints are the least desirable and least rigid due to their compliant adhesive.

When you use a *detachable headshell*, the surface contact between the headshell and arm tube is incomplete. Overtightening the headshell screws in an attempt to improve coupling is likely only to deform the parts and make matters worse. A removable headshell should be made of an inert, very rigid material to fix the cartridge in position as rigidly as possible and transmit resonances effectively without adding any of its own. Metal is best as it permits really torquing down the cartridge screws, thus minimizing "leakage" in the mechanical grounding loop.

Carbon fiber, while a good vibration absorber, is less rigid and is also soft enough that screws cannot be tightened down securely. As a rule, avoid carbon fiber headshells.

Unfortunately, the choice of good removable headshells is quite limited—Sumiko makes one of the very best. One reason there is so little choice is that the good arms almost always have integral headshells and so their designers have thus had no need to develop a replaceable one. Mass-fi manufacturers produce many but without having considered the refinements of what a headshell really has to do.

Pivoting and Straight-Line Tracking (Linear) Arms

The great majority of tonearms pivot from a fixed point on the plinth. The stylus describes an arc across the record that (assuming proper cartridge alignment) kept it nearly, though not perfectly, tangent to the groove at all points.

Achieving *perfect* stylus/groove tangency at all times would seem an obvious advantage in retrieving the most music from the groove. This is exactly what *straight-line tracking* (SLT) arms are supposed to do. In contrast to an arm that pivots across the record and describes an arc with the stylus, instead the entire arm and stylus travel together in a straight line across the radius of the LP. Record-cutting lathes use an SLT arm so, theoretically at least, ''uncutting'' the record the same way it was cut would seem to offer potential major advantages.

The idea of a linear tracking arm always parallel to the groove has intrigued designers for many years. In fact, Edison's early gramophones had all linear tracking designs. But while many SLT designs have been attempted, the vast majority have been unsuccessful. Currently, there are three great leaders—the Souther, the Eminent Technology, and the Goldmund arms.

Stylus/groove tangency may be improved greatly with SLT arms,

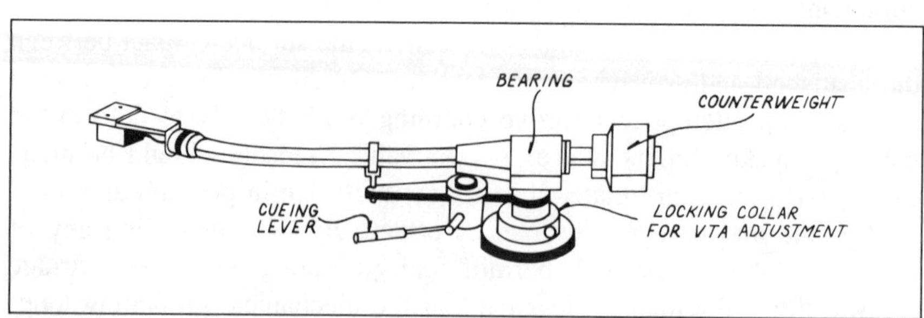

Fig. 7

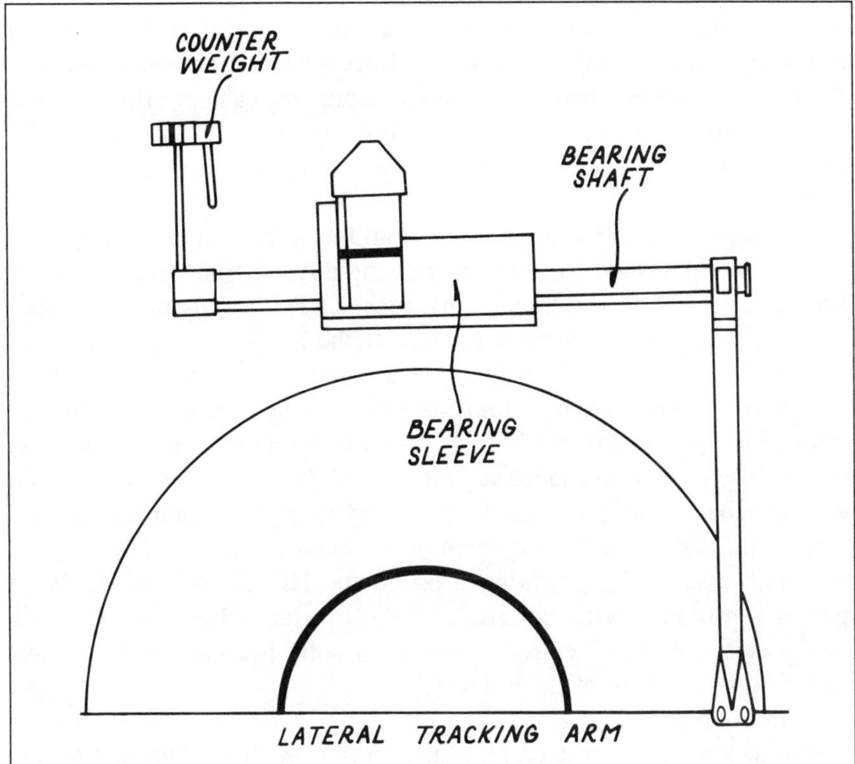

Fig. 8

but in the real world they still remain far from perfect. For one thing, the stylus may not be perfectly aligned when manufactured, or the cartridge perfectly mounted in the arm. Even if all begins well, perfect tangency is impossible to maintain over a period of months since the cartridge changes compliance with use and the stylus changes shape with wear. These changes occur long before they can be seen on even a high-resolution optical microscope, let alone under a magnifying glass. Temperature and humidity will also affect cartridge compliance from one day to the next, and therefore also the sound quality.

SLTs do definitely eliminate some sources of distortion. Perhaps their greatest advantage is the shortness of the arm tube. Shorter arms offer a better combination of low mass and high rigidity, with less arm resonance. Pivoting arms must generally be about 9 inches from stylus to pivot point, whereas an SLT arm need be only about 6 inches, which is the radius of the record.

Another and perhaps stronger advantage is that, unlike pivoting arms, SLTs are not subject to skating force since they move in line with the cartridge across the record. So the cantilever can, in principle, stay neutrally in its correct alignment to both groove and generator. This may account for the SLT's often superior stereo imaging and lesser distortion.

Transmitting resonances away from the stylus, an important factor usually accomplished by good bearing rigidity, can be very difficult to achieve on an SLT. Unlike pivoting arms, SLTs' bearing design is often "noncaptive," meaning not enclosed. If the arm rides on top of rails, only the downward force of gravity is counteracting the upward force of the vibrations traveling from the stylus along the arm tube and up through the plinth and arm base to rattle the bearings. With the bearings not enclosed, the arm can move both up and down vertically on the rails and also back and forth on the rails and therefore along the groove, which will distort the time domain of the music.

However, the air bearing used on the ET, as well as the WTA pivoting-arm no-bearing design, have demonstrated that there are excellent possible alternatives to conventional solid-bearing rigidity. There just need to be more of them developed.

In contrast to the above benefits (fully realizable only in an ideal world) is the real-world complicating factor in SLTs—the entire arm moves and the movements of the front and back ends must be perfectly synchronized. The cartridge end is driven by the record groove and the back end must remain absolutely synchronous. Any error here will throw the stylus out of alignment with the groove walls, negating the primary advantage of SLTs.

There are two basic ways of moving the SLT arm base along with the front: the *self-aligning* and *servo-driven* methods. Self-aligning arms are mounted on a low-friction bearing, as in the Souther, or, in the case of the Eminent Technology, on an air bearing. Whenever the arm moves away from exact right-angle alignment to this bearing, the drag of the stylus in the record groove provides the entire motive force of the arm and pulls the arm base back into correct alignment.

Servo-driven arms employ a more complex and less satisfactory method. Used on all mass-fi linear arms, this is a poor solution. The arm base is actively driven across the radius of the record by a servo-controlled motor that moves it in sync with the cartridge. This would be fine—if records could be cut with a uniform groove spacing; but this could happen only if music had no pitch. If groove size and spacing were always even, then the motor could run at a constant speed and the movement of both the back end and the stylus end would always be matched.

BUT!—music varies substantially in both pitch and amplitude, so groove size and spacing vary enormously—in soft passages the grooves are small and packed closely together, whereas in louder sections the grooves are larger and more spaced out. Just examine a record surface—you can clearly see this. Sensors must detect when the front of the arm, driven by the groove modulations, is not at right angles to the base; the servomotor then reacts to bring the arm base into correct alignment. The base is moved along in quick spurts: One moment it lags behind the stylus, the next it jumps a little ahead of the stylus, then it waits until the stylus catches up, and so on. Stylus and base are never in perfect sync and so stylus/groove tangency is never quite correct.

Some detractors describe servos as in effect ensuring that stylus/base alignment, and therefore groove tangency, is always wrong! And this is the fact—it's only the very error itself that triggers the corrective action. An additional problem is that the motor inevitably introduces vibration. Only Goldmund so far has been able to come up with a servo SLT that manages to sound very good.

So contrary to much of the advertising, whichever SLT drive method you use, it is impossible to maintain zero tracking error—both methods require an error in alignment before the arm base moves. With good design, though, SLTs can be closer to zero tracking error more of the time than are pivoting arms. However, with typical mass-market servo-controlled SLTs, tracking is no better, and is usually worse, than with a pivoting arm, and entails far greater expense and complication.

The fact that SLT arms are inherently more complicated devices than pivoters is a real drawback. In fact, the enthusiasm for SLT arms exists predominantly in America and Japan, and much less in England and Europe. No SLT design has yet survived for an extended period of years, whereas the pivoting arm designs have been around for decades. Any SLT arm is going to require more frequent adjustments and tweaking than a pivoter. Unless you get one of the very few excellent SLT arms, such as the Souther or the Eminent Technology, you're likely much better off with the more straightforward, less complicated pivoting arm, at least to begin with.

THE CARTRIDGE

The cartridge is the electromechanical bridge that carries the music stored in the record to the rest of the system. And as with most bridges, you must pay a toll to get to the other side—even if it's just a wan smile to the bridge troll. The cartridge introduces much of the distortion in the entire playback system.

A tiny electrical generator, the cartridge takes the mechanical energy represented by the record groove and ''collected'' by the stylus, and with it generates a tiny electrical signal (actually, two—one for each channel) that, when amplified, drives the speakers. This energy conversion—from mechanical to electrical—is called *transduction.* There are two transduction points in vinyl playback—when the cartridge uses mechanical energy to make electrical energy, and then when the speakers convert the electrical energy back into mechanical acoustic energy. These two points are most vulnerable to distortion in the entire system.

Even though, strictly speaking, the cartridge is the transducer, really the entire turntable system should be viewed as the transducer since the fidelity of the electrical signal produced depends so intimately on the performance of table and tonearm.

Nearly all cartridges (or pickups, as they were once called) are electromagnetic, working on the principle that when a wire is moved near a magnet, electricity is generated in the wire. *Moving magnet* and *moving coil* cartridges work almost identically. What differs is which element is caused to move in sympathy with the stylus: the magnet (in moving magnets) or the coil (in moving coils). In a moving magnet, the stylus is mounted on one end of a pivoted rod or cantilever and a magnet is mounted on its other end, close to a fixed coil of wire inside the cartridge body. A compliant bushing where the cantilever passes into the cartridge body allows it to pivot freely. As the cantilever moves in response to the record groove, the magnet moves in relation to the coil of wire, so generating electricity.

The only difference between this setup and a moving coil cartridge is that the positions of coil and magnet are reversed—the coil of wire is attached to the cantilever and the magnet is housed, unmoving, in the body.

Fidelity thus depends on how accurately the stylus is able to trace the groove, how precisely that mechanical action is communicated to or

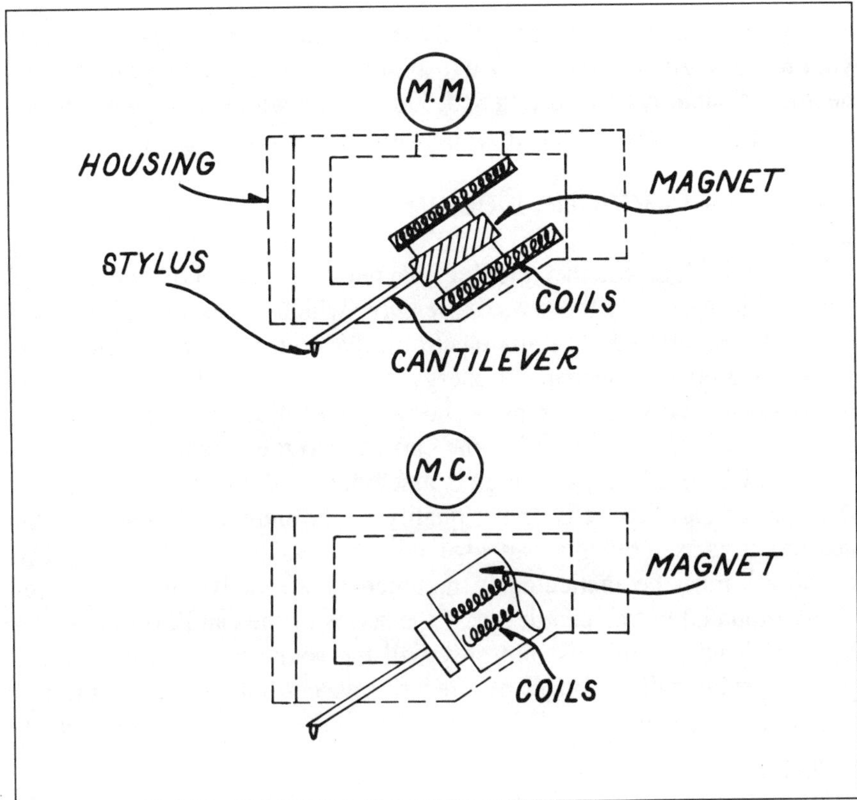

Fig. 9

"seen" by the generator, and how much distortion is introduced by the process of transduction. The cartridge's accuracy in tracing the groove and conveying that tracing to the generator depends largely on the environment provided by tonearm and table.

Fidelity depends on the *relative motion* of stylus to mini-generator. If due to poor tonearm or table stability the cartridge body moves at the same time as the stylus, then the *relative* motion of stylus and generator is altered and so is the music signal.

Unless you have a good arm and table, there is little point in having a fine cartridge, because its quality will be obscured. The cartridge must have the proper environment in order to perform well—its full assets will certainly not be revealed unless the quality of the turntable and the tonearm is *at least as good* as it is.

So until you have a really good table and arm, invest only modestly in your cartridge. Keep your stylus clean and in good condition—

a dirty or worn stylus not only degrades sound but, far worse, damages your records. Also, proper cartridge alignment is essential (see p. 236 for details). A table system costing $15,000 or more won't sound much better than a kid's toy record player if the cartridge is not properly set up.

Basics of Cartridge Design

A cartridge, whether moving magnet or moving coil, consists of three basic parts: (1) the *stylus assembly*, which traces the groove and drives the generator, (2) a tiny electromechanical *generator*, which converts the groove's mechanical energy into an electrical signal, and (3) the *housing*, the plastic or metal body that encloses the generator and provides the means of securing the cartridge to the tonearm.

How carefully the cartridge is assembled and tuned is as critical as the kind of cartridge it is or the quality of the individual elements that go into it. Assembling a cartridge is a process of microsurgery. The cantilever must be meticulously mounted in the body, the stylus precisely mounted on the cantilever. If the stylus or the cantilever is assembled the least bit off-axis, not only will the sound be harsh but, worse yet, the stylus will no longer be a record revealer but a "record eraser," regrooving all your LPs. This is neither a joke nor an exaggeration. It happens.

The Stylus Assembly

This is composed of the *stylus* (nearly always diamond), mounted on a *shank*, fastened to the *cantilever*. When stylus and shank are cut from a single gem, this is called a nude stylus.

Until the 1950s, the stylus was steel—an unparalleled record reamer. Thorn, cactus, and other fiber needles were sometimes used instead, as these caused less damage to records, had a more pleasing, less "steely" sound, and could be resharpened by the user to extend their otherwise very short life somewhat. Steel and fiber needles started being replaced by synthetic gemstone in the early 1950s.

The cantilever is a short metal or gemstone rod that pivots on a bushing in relation to the generator, relaying the stylus's every nuance of vibration. The ideal cantilever material is light, stiff, and dead—and remains all of these from sub- to supersonic frequencies. These requirements tend to be mutually contradictory so, once again, the final choice of materials calls for engineering compromises.

The cantilever is commonly damped (sometimes painted with special gunk, sometimes, if hollow, internally damped) to prevent its resonances from being added to the music signal. "Needle talk" occurs when the cantilever is overly alive and adds its own chattering to the signal. Proper damping is essential in preventing the shock waves and vibrations that travel up the rod from also traveling back down it again and into the stylus to interfere further with the music. This damping in effect serves the same purpose as the surround on a speaker cone.

Hollow cantilevers—either metal leaf rolled into a cylinder or gemstone (often sapphire) bored out with a laser beam—minimize mass. Solid cantilevers of a very hard, jewel rod may ensure that all the frequencies traveling *together* up the cantilever, maintaining time coherence.

Don't fixate on these "exotic" details until your system has achieved the resolving power that will reveal the difference between a metal or gemstone cantilever. Many fine cartridges use a metal cantilever, including the Grado Signatures and the Garrott P-77. These are excellent cartridges that, matched with a good table and arm, will give you a lot of music.

The shorter the cantilever of the cartridge, some feel, the more accurate the transcription. It offers exactly the same advantages as the shorter tonearm tube possible with SLTs—greater rigidity and so less resonance and less flexing. The Dynavector uses a very short cantilever and Decca cartridges have none. Whether or not you'll like the sound of the Deccas is intensely personal, even more so than with most cartridges. Bill Firebaugh, who collects cartridges, says he'll no more recommend a cartridge than he'll give out marriage advice. Deccas (preferably Garrott modified) are the favorites of, among others, Ken Kessler of *Hi-Fi News & Record Review*. The $1,600 Rosewood Signature, also *sans* cantilever, is to some minds the only cartridge able to challenge the Deccas.

Stylus Footprint

The whole illusion of LP recorded sound rests on the tiny point of the stylus. The playback stylus must in essence "uncut" the identical path made by its counterpart, the cutting lathe stylus. Its success in retracing the music's path largely determines playback fidelity.

However, cutting and playback styli have two different shapes. The cutting stylus, which gouges out the grooves in the master lacquer, is deeply beveled for accurate cutting. The same sharp edges on the playback stylus would "recut" the soft vinyl of the groove. Just how closely the stylus can follow all the minute twists and turns of the music groove without ever losing contact with the groove walls is known as its *tracing ability*.

The record groove is roughly V-shaped, with modulations both from side to side and up and down (*see* Fig. 10). Each groove wall, sloped at about 45 degrees, carries a different signal and so has different modulations. (The inner groove wall provides the left channel, the outer groove the right—a handy mnemonic is "Long Island" for left inside.) The groove path is quite complex, swinging from side to side and growing deeper and shallower according to the two signals' interaction.

When the record master is being cut, the sharp edges of the cutter are always on a perfect radius from the center of the record. But during playback, the stylus's two contact points with the groove wall, because the stylus is much more rounded, are seldom on the same perfect radius. *Pinch effect* is one distortion caused by this difference in shape between

Fig. 10

the cutting and playback styli. Because of the chisel shape of the cutter, the record groove narrows as it wiggles. This narrowing, which the blunter playback stylus cannot exactly trace, "pinches" the playback stylus and forces it upward, thus introducing spurious vertical (out-of-phase) movements to the stylus.

As the music's signal level (amplitude) and frequency (pitch) increase, so do the groove modulations. Again, the relatively blunt shape of the playback stylus tip (compared to the cutting stylus) may be at times too crude to follow all these ins and outs. This results in both a loss of high frequencies—sometimes called *scanning loss*—and in *tracing distortion.* Both are unfortunately worst at the end of the record side, which often coincides with the musical climax. These three forms of distortion are ineradicable, but the extent of their severity is a function of stylus shape or *footprint.*

In order to trace the rapid changes in groove modulations, the stylus should be as short as possible so it reads only one modulation at a time (*see* Fig. 11). Yet you also want contact with the groove walls to be as broad as possible, in order to distribute the tremendous downward force of the stylus tip on the record groove. This force measures literally *tons* per square inch. To combine these two requirements, you want the stylus footprint to touch a large area *vertically* on the wall to spread the weight, and only a very narrow sliver *horizontally* to permit rapid movement.

The stylus should ride along the sides of the groove walls, just about in the middle. You don't want it in the bottom of the groove, where it will miss some of the signal and also pick up muck left over from the pressing process along with the dirt that has been accumulating there ever since. It should ride just low enough on the walls to keep well clear of the "horns" or rough edges near the top of the groove, leftovers from manufacturing, as these do cause noise.

Stylus Shape

A *conical* tip is the original gemstone stylus shape, still standard on less expensive cartridges. It traces the groove quite crudely, missing fairly sizable amounts of musical detail. Because it touches the groove wall only at the apex of its roundness, this shape focuses the mass of the cartridge and arm on a small area of the groove wall, resulting in a higher degree of record wear. Fortunately, a record worn by a conical stylus can often be successfully played by a narrow-profile stylus. The

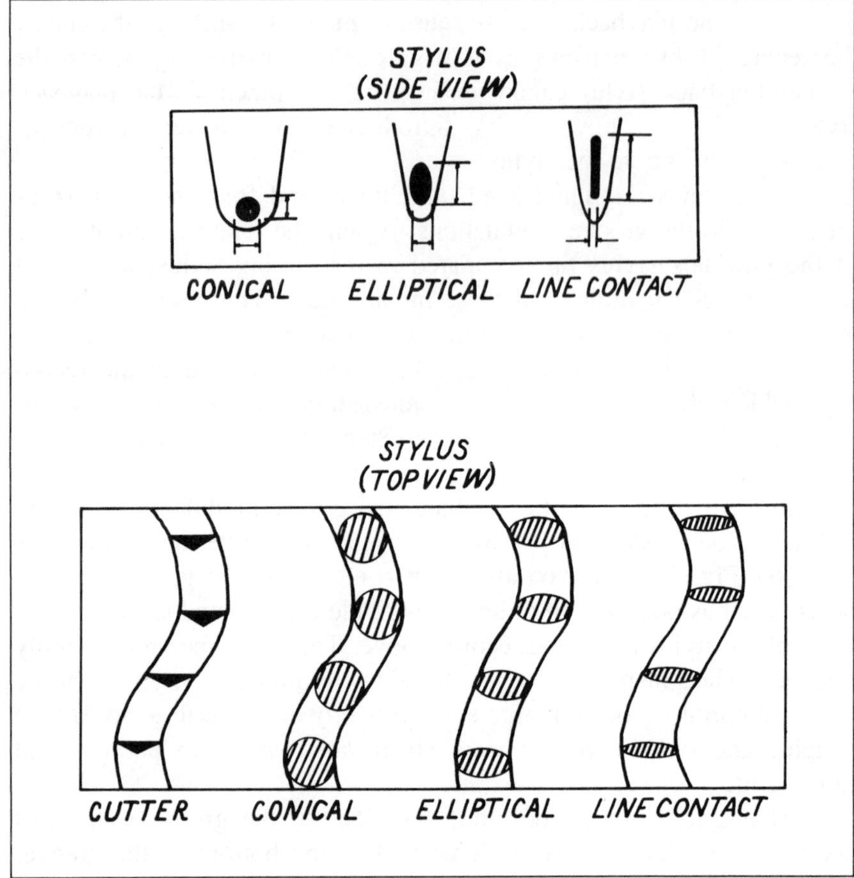

Fig. 11

wear points caused by conical styli are usually high on the groove walls; a sleeker stylus rides below the wear line and so (it's hoped) traces a pristine groove area.

The *elliptical* stylus is a flattened oval version of a conical. Being narrower from front to back, it can more accurately trace fewer groove modulations at a time, without blurring them together. This is particularly important with the denser inner grooves. However, its smaller contact area increases pressure per square centimeter on the record. Sensitivity to setup is also increased.

The most recently developed stylus profile is the *line contact,* a.k.a. Shibata, van den Hul, microlinear, and similar terms. Used on better cartridges, this stretches the elliptical shape both vertically, making it longer, and horizontally, making it narrower. To greatly increase contact up and down with the groove wall, it has two flat faces ground into its surface. Because of this, it imposes less pressure for a given tracking weight, minimizing record wear. In addition, its narrowness means it can track fine high-frequency modulations. These styli are, however, the most demanding of proper setup. Misalignment will significantly increase record and stylus wear and result in bad tracing distortion.

A refinement on this basic design is the *microridge*. A ridge is cut along each face of the stylus where it touches the groove, ''hollow ground'' in the same way a knife is sharpened and for the same reason. This way, even as the stylus wears, its contact area with the groove retains much the same profile—thin from back to front for tracing accuracy, while vertically long to distribute weight and reduce record wear. The degree of tip curvature remains constant throughout stylus life. Microridge styli wear down just as fast as any other, but because their profile remains unchanged much longer, they effectively have a much longer life.

Another advantage is that the very small front-to-back contact area provides a closer approximation to the geometry of the cutting stylus, so the tip is more easily able to follow small-scale, high-frequency modulations. This improved tracking particularly helps reduce inner-groove distortion.

The drawback to microlinear cartridge is that they are *extremely sensitive* to setup and alignment, especially to VTA (see p. 245). Even slight misalignment results in distortion and groove damage. The fine ridge requires meticulous care and handling as it is subject to chipping and easily clogged by dirt.

The *polish* on a stylus tip in many ways is as important as its footprint. A high polish reduces record wear, friction, and the vibrations and the resonances generated by the stylus tracing the groove. Both van den Hul and Garrott are well known for their superpolished styli. Look at a Garrott under high magnification and it's like looking at a blob of mercury—most other cartridges in comparison look bumpy and misshapen.

Here's a (risky) way to hear what your stylus sounds like and what colorations it adds to the music—suggested by Bill Firebaugh. With the table turned off, place the stylus in a blank, unmodulated groove (the run-out or lead-in of a record, or the blank grooves included on some test records). Very gently, by hand, rotate the record a short distance while listening to the sound of the stylus. You must be VERY CAREFUL in doing this—moving the record backward against the very delicate cantilever can bend it or even rip it right off.

The Electromagnetic Generator

Nearly all cartridges produce an electrical signal through electromagnetism. The rare exceptions include ceramics, which are used rarely now except on the cheapest of kids' turntables. These operate on the piezoelectric principle—certain crystalline materials, such as barium titanate ceramic, will when twisted or bent produce a voltage at their surface. To withstand the necessary twisting force, the stylus assembly must be quite strong so these cartridges generally have an undesirably high moving mass. Ceramics produce a much higher voltage than magnetic cartridges.

Moving magnets are the most common type of cartridge. They (and their variations—moving iron, induced magnet, and variable reluctance) move a magnetic field through a coil to generate electricity. A tiny permanent magnet is attached to the end of the moving cantilever and a coil of very fine wire is secured inside the cartridge body. As the groove modulations move the stylus/cantilever, the magnetic field cuts across the coil and induces a voltage. The advantage is a high output level; the disadvantage is the weight of the magnet on the end of the cantilever. It takes force from the record to move this mass, and some transient information is lost by the relatively slow response time of the moving mass. In fact, the magnet must of necessity be kept fairly light and so relatively weak.

Moving coils reverse the positions—an extremely lightweight coil of wire is attached to the cantilever while the heavier magnet structure is housed in the body. The benefit is excellent retrieval of transient and high-frequency information because the movement of the stylus has to drive only light coils of wire, not a heavy magnet. This low mass can respond quickly to rapid changes in the music and so can retrieve music more cleanly and delicately than most MM designs. Also, the magnet housed inside the body can be heavy and so the coil can be low impedance.

The disadvantage of MCs is significantly reduced output level, typically a third less than that of a moving magnet. In an attempt to improve output, sometimes the coil windings are increased, but this also increases the moving mass and so reduces the MC's advantages. These higher-output MCs suffer some loss of fine treble detail and transient attack.

The MC's very low output generally requires an additional stage of amplification: either a head amp (a.k.a. pre-preamp—see p. 127) or alternatively an additional stage in the preamp itself. In addition to adding to the expense of these cartridges, which often already cost more than a comparable-quality MM, the additional amp stage complicates the circuit and can itself degrade sound quality. For there to be any sense in using an MC, the cartridge plus extra circuitry combined must sound definitely better than an MM of comparable price.

Some MCs are designed to have a high output and so do without a head amp. These are also generally considered to sound less good than low-output MCs. As always in audio, compromise and tradeoffs are required. Deciding on the basis of theory is tricky—use your ears as your guide.

While many preamps are now being designed to accept the minuscule output of an MC cartridge directly without a head amp, a lot of these really just amount to a head amp grafted onto a preamp, which neither minimizes the circuitry nor necessarily improves sound quality. GSI's 5TP preamp is a rare exception, carefully designed to have extra gain *without* extra circuitry. Preamps that do add an extra stage of gain should allow you to bypass this stage when using an MM—since you don't need the extra gain, you don't want to be forced to go through the additional circuitry.

MCs have been steadily improving since they were developed back in the 1950s by Joe Grado, who is the father of the MC design and holder of the U.S. patents. They fell out of favor for a number of years and only began to come back again in the mid-1970s, largely picked up by the Japanese designers. Grado himself hadn't made an MC in many years until recently commissioned to design one. Grado's cartridges, including his finest hand-built Signature series, employ his own moving-iron variant of the MM design.

The Sound of Moving Magnets and Moving Coils

There is an ongoing controversy among connoisseurs and designers as to which—MC or MM—is sonically preferable. A number of designers who have ready access to any cartridge choose to listen to MMs. Along with detail and speed, MCs can also have a hard, edgy sound, often characterized as "zingy." They tend to be spitty, as they exacerbate sibilants. They are particularly sensitive to proper setup and are relatively poor trackers. MC styli are also not user-replaceable (because of the superfine coil secured to the cantilever), but this is a minor consideration since good-quality MM cartridges should also be returned to the manufacturer for stylus replacement.

In the end, the sonic differences between a good MC and a good MM are, like much else in audio, a matter of tradeoffs. There can be as much difference from one MC or MM to the next as between the two categories. Neither design is free of characteristic colorations, so it's largely a matter of choosing which colorations you prefer and how these match with the rest of your system. MMs could perhaps be *broadly* characterized as having a "warmer" sound, MCs a cooler, dryer, more analytic sound. However, you can in most cases probably get a better-quality MM than MC for the same price—the Audioquest 404B MC and the Adcom are two possible exceptions.

The Housing

The cartridge body should be strong and nonresonant. In its own miniature way, the body is like a speaker cabinet and any resonances it transmits will color the sound.

Whether plastic, metal, or wood, the housing must be strong enough to permit a good mechanical coupling with the headshell and not distort when cranked down. A solid connection between headshell and cartridge body is essential to prevent microrattling, which, albeit on a microsonic level, is still sufficient to veil and color the music. If the housing is flat on top, it can then be mounted absolutely flush with the headshell and so effectively become a single, solid unit with the tonearm. This helps to damp the vibrations of the cartridge body and maintains the mechanical grounding loop. As a visual aid in setup, a square housing also helps greatly.

ARM/CARTRIDGE MATCHING, TRACKING, AND COMPLIANCE

You cannot stick any cartridge onto any arm and expect the best results. Arm and cartridge must be carefully matched. Specifically what you're matching is cartridge compliance with tonearm mass. *Compliance* (compliant-ness, amount of give, the opposite of stiffness) refers to how much force is required to deflect the cantilever. The cantilever is like a spring topped by the weight of the arm and cartridge body. A low-compliance cartridge is noncompliant and so resists being deflected; it is best matched with a high-mass arm. A high-compliance cartridge is quite elastic and easily deflected and so is best paired with a low-mass arm.

Ideally, the cartridge should be compliant to the audio frequencies so it can accurately trace them, but inert to tracking and warp frequencies, which you don't want the cartridge to pick up along with the music. Again, ideally the tonearm should be the reverse—inert to audio frequencies (so the arm doesn't move along with the cartridge) and compliant to tracking and warp frequencies (so it will promptly follow record irregularities).

If the cantilever "spring" is very stiff (has a low compliance), then it needs the control of a high-mass tonearm; otherwise the spring will throw the arm around. (Obviously you can't see this happening—it occurs on the scale of microresonances.) If the spring is quite soft and floppy (highly compliant), then you need a low-mass arm; otherwise the spring will be crushed. A highly compliant cartridge can more faithfully follow the tiny modulations of the groove than a stiffer one. But on the other hand, the relatively low mass arm it has to be matched up with is less rigid and therefore more resonant—so the potential benefits of improved groove tracing are offset by the problems of arm resonance. Also, a highly compliant cartridge tends to be more vulnerable to groove junk.

The arm/cartridge system's particular *resonant frequency* is also determined by the arm/cartridge mass and cantilever compliance. The arm and cartridge are a weight sitting on the spring of the cantilever. Like any weight on any spring, this system has a resonance—at some particular frequency, even a slight amount of energy can cause the system to vibrate, coloring the sound. Either the higher the mass OR the higher the compliance, the lower the arm/cartridge's resonant frequency. The lower the mass OR compliance, the higher the resonant frequency.

The arm/cartridge match should set that resonance at a frequency where there isn't much to make it vibrate, and certainly below the audible range, ideally somewhere between 8 and 12 Hz. Below that range, resonance can be excited by rumble and motor noise, while anything above 15 Hz enters into the range of what we can hear and so resonances can be excited by the music on the record.

Tracking ability is the ability of the cartridge (in conjunction with tonearm and table) to maintain the stylus in uninterrupted contact with the groove wall. This differs somewhat from tracing ability, which is how accurately the stylus, when held in proper contact with the groove, retraces the groove's exact path. Tracing ability is determined largely by stylus footprint.

All cartridges sometimes mistrack, especially at high modulations when the music gets loud. When you consider the conditions that styli have to perform under, it's remarkable they do so well. The stylus must smoothly hug corner curves as well as track the dips and bumps without bouncing up and out of the groove, all the while traveling at speeds many times the acceleration of gravity. (Superstylus—faster than a speeding bullet . . .)

Listening to mistracking is a little like wearing eyeglasses that aren't quite correctly aligned—your vision is just slightly out of focus. Even if you're not consciously aware of it, the overall effect is disturbing. Poor tracking not only sounds bad, it is also a major cause of record and stylus wear.

Tracking at the lower frequencies is most affected by the cartridge compliance; at higher frequencies, it's most affected by the *stylus tip mass*. This is the combined mass of the stylus and cantilever plus the compliance of the cantilever suspension. This defines just how much weight is knocking against the groove walls. Because tip mass determines the actual pressure exerted against the groove walls, it may be the single most important factor in record wear and damage.

Most higher-compliance cartridges are good trackers—in fact, most competently designed cartridges, providing they're well set up in a good arm on a good table, track well. A commonly offered example of an excellent tracker is the Shure V15 Type V-MR, though some don't like its somewhat clinical, even edgy sound quality.

Mistracking can be minimized by adjusting the vertical tracking force, which is the downward pressure exerted by the tonearm on the cartridge and stylus to keep the stylus in the groove (see p. 245 for correct adjustment). The typical tracking force of 1.5 to 2 grams recommended for many cartridges may seem negligible (and a cartridge manufacturer recommending anything less than this is likely to be a purveyor of "geewhiz" gimmickry). But stop to consider that all of this pressure is focused in one *minute* location—the stylus point usually ranges from about 0.5 to 1 mil (0.001 inch) in radius. So the pressure at the groove/stylus contact point is measured in literally TONS per square inch.

Too much force will cause excessive record wear and reduce the stylus's facility to respond to the groove modulations. But on the other hand, too *light* a tracking weight can be even more damaging than too heavy a force. Underweighted, the stylus can more easily bang around in the groove, hitting against the walls (instead of sliding along them) and actually chipping the vinyl. A mistracking stylus bounces off the walls, regains contact, loses it again, and so on. Even though you may not consciously identify the problem, this distortion is very irritating and fatiguing to listen to as well as extremely damaging to your records. (See p. 294 for a description of how groove wall damage occurs.)

As a general guide in arm/cartridge matching, moving magnets often have high compliance, so they are often best matched with an arm having minimal mass. Moving coils tend to have low compliance (meaning they're stiff) and may require pairing with an arm of medium to high effective mass. We'd recommend selecting a cartridge to match the arm you're using, rather than choosing the cartridge first and then selecting the arm accordingly. As much of a difference as a cartridge can make to the music, the arm surpasses its importance in the system hierarchy.

TAPE DECKS

CASSETTES OR REEL-TO-REEL?

The medium is the message, a man called Marshall used to say, so when you're considering which component—deck, table, tuner, CD player—to choose as your main source for music, your primary consideration should be the fidelity of the medium, i.e., of the music source.

No matter how good any cassette deck might be, the very best it can give you is limited by what the cassette tape itself is capable of delivering. The most the deck can do is live up to the standards of the cassette. And cassettes, as a class, are sonically inferior to LPs. They are also more vulnerable to damage—the tape can stretch, tangle, fade, or bleed through, and the cassette mechanism can jam. Tape and deck alike need regular cleaning and maintenance. However, as long as you're prepared to accept them as a mid-fi medium, cassettes have the solid benefit of being convenient, portable, and inexpensive and they can sound very good, though still not as good as LPs.

As cassettes offer strong advantages and disadvantages, choosing them for your primary, rather than additional, music source will depend on your priorities. For instance, good friends moved to Nepal, taking a Nakamichi Dragon, Marantz 8B, and Proac Tablettes—and *trunkloads* of cassettes recorded during the preparatory year. LPs would have been totally impractical—*two* caravans would have been required for their transport, nor would the discs have survived long in the somewhat rugged realities of Nepal. Incidentally, theirs appears to be the *only* high-fidelity system anywhere in Nepal.

When Philips introduced the cassette tape deck in 1963, it was offered as a simple, convenient office dictating machine—suited for "electronic notetaking" and providing only the fidelity needed to capture the limited frequency range and dynamics of speech. It was never expected nor intended to record anything other than dictation, let alone to be a high-fidelity medium or to supplant reel-to-reel for music. But somehow, given a few refinements, this format came to gain in popularity, and the more this happened, the harder the tape manufacturers worked to improve their tape quality. Each tape generation has been better than the last.

Cassettes are now an excellent medium for many uses—but are still (with rare exceptions) far from being the preferred one for real fidelity. Only the serious decks, of which there are very few and which are generally comparable in price to a really good turntable, can offer good sound quality. Unless you do a lot of recording (or are moving to Nepal), go with the table as your primary source. It offers both better sound and a far larger ready-recorded library of music to choose from. However, a cassette deck wins without contest for ease of use. Certainly as a secondary music source, cassette decks have a great deal to recommend them.

If you plan to do a lot of recording or if you're interested in fidelity, get yourself a *good* deck from the start or hold off until you can. With a mediocre machine, anything you record on that machine will also be mediocre at best and that's a permanent condition—the quality of the recording itself obviously can't be altered by changing the machine you play it back on. When you replace a mediocre turntable, you immediately gain the benefits of hearing all your LPs sound great. When you replace a mediocre deck, nothing will improve the mediocre sound of recordings made on that deck.

Recording LPs

If your main reason for getting a cassette player is to record your records to preserve them against wear, remember that the recording you make can never match the sound quality of the original LP or CD. (This includes recording with digital audio tape [DAT] equipment.) Though home-recorded cassette copies can, with careful soundcraft, sound much better than many prerecorded ones, nonetheless neither can equal the sound quality of a good LP played on a good table.

The cassette duplicate will be sonically degraded in several ways. Anytime you make a copy of a copy, the sound is somewhat degraded, just as a photocopy of a photocopy will not be as clear as the original and every subsequent copy of a copy will be less clear than the previous one. Add to this that cassette tape itself is essentially a mid-fi format (see p. 329 on tape).

Another factor to consider is the quality of your signal source. You will not achieve as good a recording from an expensive tape deck fed by a poor signal as from a mediocre deck driven by an excellent signal. The copy can sound no better than the signal it receives. And the signal's quality, in turn, depends on the twin factors of its own origins and the equipment processing it.

Keep in mind that cassette copying, like photocopying and software copying, is against copyright law. Copying your own recordings for your own archival purposes seems legitimate enough, but copying recordings you don't own is an infringement. You may be indifferent that this takes profits away from the record companies, but consider that it also takes royalties from the artists, whom you may well want to be supporting (considering you like their music well enough to copy it) and most of whom need all the legitimate financial support they are due.

The Advantages of Reel-to-reel Decks

While recorded sound has existed for over 100 years, tape recording has a much shorter history—Dr. Goebbels hastened its development during World War II to broadcast the Führer's voice from moving trucks. This was a wonderful means of spreading propaganda. (Note that neither Edison's machine, the German tape deck, nor Philips's cassette deck was developed for music but simply for voice reproduction.) After the war, its advantages were quickly recognized for music. Recording studios tossed out their direct-to-disc equipment and replaced it with this new technique (which didn't sound as good but was much more convenient to work with). From then on, all recordings, with the exception of the rare direct to disc, were first put on tape and then transferred to LP, cassette, or CD. These reel-to-reel decks, also called open reel, used by the recording studios are sonically a quite different story from cassette decks, and offer the best *combination* of sound quality, reliability, durability, and editing flexibility of *any* format.

Reel-to-reel at home is a connoisseur's listening medium. The equipment and tape are expensive, working with the tape is awkward, and availability of prerecorded tapes is extremely limited. In fact, Barclay Crocker, the last commercial producer of prerecorded open reels, closed down in 1986. So access to music is restricted and you really have to make your own tapes. If you make your own recordings of live music on open reel or have access to master or early-generation tapes, then an open-reel deck is the king. Reel-to-reel offers amazing performance, but at a price and inconvenience that make it appeal only to the superdedicated.

However, there are a good number of those superdedicated out there, and for them Teac introduced—long after the CD's success was a certainty and reel-to-reel therefore seemed all the more anachronistic—an open-reel "budget" model comparable in price to a serious cassette deck (i.e., much less expensive than any previous good open-reel deck). Perhaps there'll be enough interest for tape manufacturers to improve the quality of open-reel tape, which, unlike the cassette tape, has seen no refinement for many years. (On the other hand, cassette tape is still trying to catch up with open reel's superior sound quality.) Even with the deck's price comparable to that of a serious cassette machine, it is still more expensive to operate because of the tape costs—open reel's higher speed and wider tape about doubles the operating expense.

The Disadvantages of Cassette Decks

In theory cassette decks operate on the same principle as reel-to-reel decks. But in actual practice, reel-to-reel and cassette are only distant cousins and as similar as a Thoroughbred to a burro.

A goodly amount of the cassette system's sonic problems are caused by its very miniaturization. The small capstan (the device that pulls the tape across the tape head) reduces the possibility of attaining real speed accuracy, so important to fidelity. A speck of dust on that small capstan causes proportionately worse speed irregularity than the same speck on an open-reel capstan. Similarly, the inevitable wear on parts will cause proportionately greater error on the small scale of cassettes than on the larger scale of open reels.

So in exchange for convenience, the cassette format trades away fidelity. (Sound familiar?—the fast-food heaven of audio, or is it really more of a Faustian pact, substance being sold for form?) The wider tape and faster recording speed of open reel ensures far better fidelity because more oxide particles pass the head in a given period of time. The combination of wider tape and higher speed passes more tape per second under the recording head for the same amount of music signal—so there's plenty of room for the information to be "laid down" without being compressed. This is similar in principle to LPs, where the less music per side, the more room the grooves have to spread out in, and so the less compressed the music signal. Higher speed also reduces flutter, wow, and the audibility of tape splices and dropouts.

Cassette tape, on the other hand, is recorded at much slower speeds—it creeps along at about 1⅞ inches per second (i.p.s.) compared to open reel's 15 i.p.s., 7½ i.p.s., or, at the very worst, 3¾ i.p.s. The less tape passes across the recording head for a given amount of music, the less room there is for the music signal to fit onto, and so the less the fidelity because the music is compressed. Compounding this problem is cassette tape's narrowness—⅛ inch compared to even the narrowest open reel's ¼ inch, with additional open-reel choices of ½-inch and 1-inch tape. Then the already limited amount of tape room for the music signal is still further reduced by cassette's quarter-track format—*four* tiny tracks across that ⅛ inch—instead of the half-track (two-track) format preferred by serious open-reel users. With this kind of miniaturization going on, it's not surprising that wow, flutter, and splice/dropout distortion are audibly worse with cassettes.

Given the popularity of cassettes, tape manufacturers have been steadily working over the past 15 years or so to overcome the format's limitations of dynamic range, signal-to-noise ratio, frequency response, and headroom. Each tape generation has been better than the last.

To compensate for the slower speed and narrower tracks, cassette tape manufacturers have been steadily increasing the quantity of magnetic particles they cram onto the tape. Since the effect of high speed and wide tracks is that more particles pass the head in a given space of time, increasing the count per square inch does compensate for slowing and narrowing the tape.

To fit into the cassette shell, the tape must be very thin, which allows *print-through* more easily (as well as stretching, rippling, twisting, and scraping). The music recorded on one section of tape over time slightly magnetizes (imprints) the section of tape lying up against it. You'll hear a "ghost" of the print-through music playing right along with the music that was intentionally recorded on that section of tape. This is also called pre-echo and occurs sometimes on LPs for two reasons: Old master tapes can suffer from the problem and when reproduced on LP reveal their age; cutting the grooves too close together will cause one to sonically "bleed" into the other.

The longer the cassette's playing time, the thinner the tape has to be in order to fit into that same-sized cassette shell. Therefore, the more easily damaged it is. Buy the shortest time per side that you can use—longer playing time per side may save you money and you won't have to change tapes as often, but the tradeoff is in both fidelity and durability. This might not matter for recording an interview or conversation or dictation, but for music you want to keep, it can be critical. Sony, in fact, recently discontinued its C-120 tapes. C-90, or 45 minutes per side, is the *maximum* safely recommended recording time for good musical fidelity (as opposed to speech). Check whether you can hear better fidelity with a C-60 tape (30 minutes per side). (Open-reel, on the other hand, allows 2 or 3 hours' total recording time, depending on whether you use a 7-inch or 10-inch reel.)

HOW A CASSETTE TAPE DECK WORKS

The Tape Heads

The recording and playback heads are transducers, meaning they convert one form of energy into another, and they do this by means of electromagnetism. An electromagnet consists of a coil made of many turns of very fine wire—similar in its effects to a permanent magnet but requiring an electric current passing through it to create a magnetic field—and then in turn the coil is wrapped around a permanent magnet. This permanent magnet is constructed to leave a small gap at one end and so the magnetic "circuit" isn't complete. As a result, a fairly intense magnetic field is generated at the gap. This field fluctuates either in accordance with the strength of the electric impulses applied to the head by the mike, in the case of the recording head, or, in the case of the playback head, in accordance with the strength of the magnetic impulses from the tape.

In both recording and playback, the audio signal is constantly changing. If these changes are to be accurately recorded (or played back), then the magnetic field must be concentrated on a very small portion of the tape, which necessitates a very thin-line air gap. The *recording head* is analogous in function to the cutting lathe head used in making the LP master. It uses the mike's electrical input (an analog of the musical sound waves) to imprint the magnetic particles electromagnetically on the tape in a physical analog of the music signal.

The billions of tiny magnets uniformly coating the tape are, before recording, randomly oriented in all directions. When exposed to the magnetic field of the recording head, their alignment becomes organized in a specific pattern of magnetization, which should form a true analog of the audio signal. This pattern remains imprinted on the tape until either it is erased or it fades over a period of years.

The *playback head* works in reverse. As the recorded tape passes across the playback head, the magnetic impulses imprinted on the tape cause very small voltage changes in the windings of the coil. This electrical signal is then passed on to the amplifier. The playback head is the equivalent of a phono cartridge—it "reads" the signal on the tape and translates the electromagnetic energy into electrical energy to be fed to the amplifier.

The *erase head,* fulfilling its name, simply erases signals previously put on the tape when so instructed. It does, unfortunately, leave behind noise, so the erased tape is not as clean as a virgin tape. A bulk eraser may do a better job.

Two- and Three-Head Decks

All cassette decks have a separate erase head, but the recording and playback functions are often combined in a single head. Better decks—both less common and more expensive—have individual heads for recording, playback, and erasure.

For the highest fidelity, recording and playback each demand a slightly different head gap (see Fig. 12). Trying to combine both functions in a single head necessitates a compromise in the spacing of the gap, with the result that each function will be performed less than exactly.

In the case of playback, the narrower the magnetic gap, the more extended the frequency range that can be reproduced, which especially affects the higher frequencies. The higher the frequency, the more the

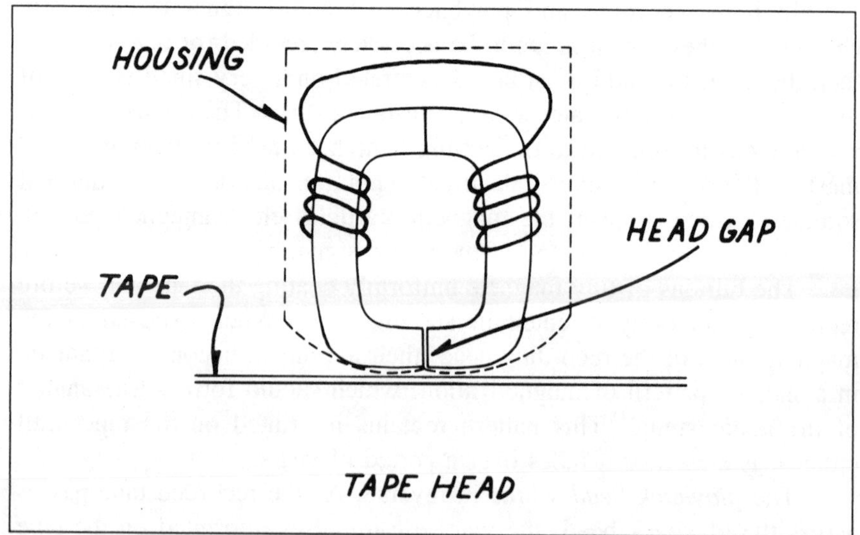

Fig. 12

magnetic particles packed on the tape, and the narrower the gap needed to receive each note *accurately*. The magnetic gap should be no wider than about 1 micron (roughly the size of the period at the end of this sentence).

Recording, on the other hand, benefits greatly from a large gap, as much as 3 to 5 microns, as this makes it possible to put a strong enough signal on the tape to provide a good signal-to-noise (S/N) ratio (see below). Clearly, the conflict between the least gap for playback and the most for recording is pretty stark and any attempted compromise to enable a single head to perform both functions will be crude at best.

The additional advantage of having three tape heads is that this allows monitoring a tape during recording. Using the preamp's "tape monitor" switch, you can switch back and forth between the tape you're in the process of recording and its music source, in order to compare relative sound quality and make adjustments to the bias or volume to ensure the tape isn't "oversaturating." By monitoring, you can also be certain that a recording is indeed being made and that you're not just listening to the original playing. For anyone seriously recording music, this is a very valuable feature.

Azimuth

Correct vertical alignment of the recording and playback heads—known as *azimuth alignment*—is fundamental to good sound. It's as important to tape playback as is cartridge setup to LP playback. Azimuth error prevents flat frequency response and also causes loss of signal. This loss becomes greater as the frequency rises—the higher frequencies, having the shorter wavelengths, are the most easily lost. The importance of high-frequency information is that it provides much of the sonic detail that permits imaging and makes recorded music sound convincingly alive.

The head gap must be absolutely perpendicular to the direction the tape moves in. As critical as this is, azimuth alignment can never be continuously right because the tape is not a rigid ribbon moving past the head gap but has a tendency to skew or scrape or otherwise fail to maintain its correct vertical orientation. Manufacturers have worked very hard to try to make the tape behave like a rigid object, with some, but not complete, success. Another problem is that the head may be mismounted, so its gap is slanted in relation to the tape path.

Because recorded wavelengths on tape are as short as 3 microns, a fraction of a degree of deviation has an audible effect—even as little as a few minutes (1 degree contains 60 minutes) can be heard.

Relative azimuth error is what we're really concerned with, meaning the relative degrees of azimuth error between the head that was used in making the recording and the head used for playback. This is one advantage of using the same head for both recording and playback—azimuth error is identical and any errors incurred during both the recording and playback are likely to cancel each other out, providing the tape is played back *on that same deck*. With a three-head system, the recording and playback heads must be kept meticulously aligned to eliminate azimuth loss. One excellent solution is to have the three heads located within the same head block. With this setup, it's impossible to get the record and playback heads out of azimuth with respect to each other, yet the head gap for each can be optimized.

Most cassette decks have small adjusting screws that permit realignment; a test tape and test meter can be used to check and then adjust for proper alignment.

The Tape Transport

Tape recorders are primarily mechanical devices, as are turntables. Regardless of how good the electronics may be, if the mechanical standards of the tape heads and transport mechanism are not up to a high level of precision, then, just as with a table, playback (and recording) will be mediocre at best.

The tape must be guided past the tape heads at a constant speed and with absolutely steady movement for faithful recording or playback. This is critical. It's essential that all moving parts be balanced and centered so the mechanism rotates with a minimum of vibration to prevent frequency modulations and variations in pitch. Constantly altering the musical frequencies, however minutely, throws off the tonal and timbral relationships of the music—your musical mind will be able to hear the wrongness even if you aren't consciously alert to it. The slightest speed variations result in the dreaded time and phase incoherence, and in the worst cases, in clearly noticeable flutter or the more severe wow (see pp. 26 and 165 for more discussion on the distortions of frequency modulation.)

The tape is pulled past the tape head by means of a *capstan*, a rotating metal shaft that revolves at a constant speed and holds the tape against a *pinch roller* or rubber idler. When the pinch roller is disen-

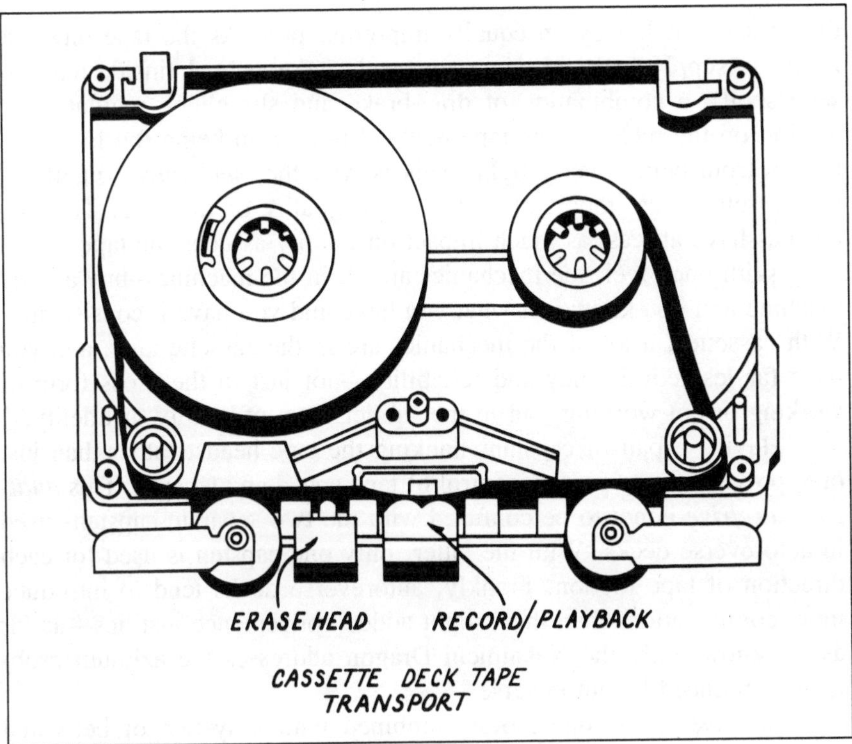

Fig. 13

gaged from the capstan, the tape doesn't move. Both capstan and pinch roller must be exactly contoured and centered to keep the tape movement at the necessary, precisely constant speed.

Speed accuracy within 0.1 percent is considered good for consumer equipment. Professional recording studio equipment is not always as accurate as it should be—you can often hear the slight warble of speed inaccuracy, especially on a piano recording, so don't confuse inaccuracies recorded on the tape with any inaccuracies being caused by your deck. If the problem you're hearing turns up consistently on all your tapes (assuming these weren't all taped on the same deck) then the problem is with your tape deck. If the inaccuracy is only on certain tapes, then the problem is with those tapes.

The job of the tape transport is not just a simple matter of maintaining a constant speed on the capstan. The tape itself is constantly stretching, squashing, rippling, and scraping, all of which counteract the speed steadiness of the capstan and wreak havoc on your music. So while the capstan and pinch roller control tape speed, the reels inside the cassette shell play an equally important part. As the tape unwinds from the supply reel and winds up on the take-up reel (inside the cassette shell), a combination of drag-brake and slip-clutch regulates the tension on the reels, so the tape neither spills from being too loose nor breaks from being overly tight. This is why the *mechanical* quality of the cassette is as important as the *sonic* quality of the tape. The mechanics have at least as much impact on fidelity as does the tape.

With open reel, the mechanics are all in the machine—buy a good machine and you know just what you have and you have it consistently. With cassettes, a lot of the mechanics are in the cassette tape, and you have far less consistency and reliability—not just in the gross form of working or not working, but in the subtler form of quality of fidelity.

Having a pair of capstans flanking the tape heads, rather than just one, provides more precise control of tape speed and tension. This *dual-capstan drive* is not to be confused with the two separate capstans used in autoreverse decks. With the latter, only one capstan is used for each direction of tape motion. Frankly, autoreverse decks tend to introduce more complications than their slight added convenience justifies—as far as we know, only the Nakamichi Dragon addresses the azimuth problems introduced by autoreverse.

In most cases, one motor combined with a system of belts and pulleys drives the capstan, plus the supply reel and take-up reel. Better machines use one motor to drive the capstan and another for the reels. The best machines use three dedicated motors, one each for the capstan, the supply reel, and the take-up reel. This system is the most mechanically reliable and produces the least speed error. Also, the fast forward and rewind functions are quick and easy to use.

Bias, Equalization, and Noise Reduction Circuitry

Tape is nonlinear in its frequency response—only a small section right in the middle of its response curve is a relatively straight line. If the audio signal could be limited to just this linear part of the curve, then one would gain an undistorted recording (relatively speaking). This is exactly the function of the *bias current*. This is a constant AC signal of ultrasonic (and therefore inaudible) frequency—about 70 to 200 *kil*-*o*hertz—that is fed to the recording head along with the audio signal. Correct bias is critical: Even 1 or 2 dB of difference is easily audible in a good system.

Tape *equalization* is comparable in principle to the LP's RIAA curve

—it's a system of frequency alteration that allows more signal to be squeezed onto the tape with the least distortion. In recording, it consists largely of treble boost; in playback, of bass boost. The combination, including the frequency alterations of the tape itself, provides the playback result of a flat frequency response. Playback EQ is standardized, with one 120-microsecond curve for Type I tape, and 70 microseconds for all the others. In recording, each type requires a different EQ.

Usually a tremendous amount of preemphasis is applied during recording to overcome the high-frequency losses inherent both in the tape and in the playback process. A property of the magnetic characteristics of the tape formulation is that the tape saturates beyond a certain point. This is called MOL for maximum output level and results in the high-frequency roll-off so common in tape recordings. However, by adding preemphasis to try to secure the highs, the tape can overload and distort when high-frequency energy comes along from cymbals, vocal sibilants, trumpets, percussion transients, and so on. Either increasing the speed and tape width (i.e., using an open-reel tape) or else increasing the density of the coating (as done with cassette tapes) can help alleviate the problem.

Different tape formulations require different bias settings. Most decks now provide switchable bias for tape Types I, II, and IV, which require increasing amounts of bias. (Type III requires a little more than II but is rarely used in the United States). If bias is set too low for the tape being used, low frequencies can become distorted. Use too high a bias and the tape becomes saturated, causing compression at high frequencies. "Saturated" simply means the tape has absorbed all the signal it is able to. Once the tape is saturated, trying to add more signal is like trying to add more liquid to a glass already filled to the brim—it just spills out all over the floor. You can pack more lower-midrange energy onto the tape but only at the expense of high frequencies.

In theory, a given tape type, regardless of brand, should conform to an industry standard and therefore take the same bias. But in practice there are differences from brand to brand. The bias setting for each tape deck is factory aligned to match one specific brand and this brand is often recommended to be used on that deck. If you use a different brand, even if it's the same tape *type,* the bias will probably not be optimized. So unless you stick to the tape brand recommended by the manufacturer, getting a flat frequency response off the tape is somewhat hit-or-miss. Anyway, the manufacturers often poorly calibrate the machines. It's best to have the settings checked by a specialist and calibrated to one particular tape brand, or else you can do fairly extensive experimentation to find the tape that works best (keep good notes as you go along).

Some decks have "user-adjustable" fine tuning for bias setting, which allows you to optimize bias for different brands—at least once you've established through experimentation just what the optimum bias should be. Remember—lowering the bias level boosts the high frequencies. If you increase the bias, the bass becomes less distorted but the treble tends to become more muffled.

Most decks have an equalization switch for each particular tape type. This applies an EQ treble cut during playback to complement the treble boost or preemphasis applied during recording. Setting the switch in the wrong position for the tape being played will result in the music's sounding either too dull or too bright.

Noise Reduction Systems

The development of noise reduction techniques was really the turning point in the widespread acceptance of cassettes. Tape hiss stems basically from the grain structure of the magnetic particles coating the tape. Even the best recording tape retains traces of this high-frequency hiss, just as the smoothest photographic film retains traces of grain in the image. Amplifying the signal in playback amplifies tape hiss right along with the music.

Cassette tapes are inherently noisier than open-reel tapes because of their relatively slow speed and narrow track width—only a limited amount of music information can be put on the tape before the tape saturates, and so the noise floor appears more prominent in relation to the music. Noise reduction systems in principle are like the LP's RIAA curve. They boost parts of the signal during recording and this boost is reversed during playback. Playback noise reduction on your tape deck is only a decoder—it is the second half of the encoder used during playback. It can have no noise-reducing effect on any recording made without noise-reducing encoding, and so cannot reduce noise from old tapes or records or from radio programs.

Because tape hiss is high-frequency noise, noise reduction systems boost the relatively weak treble signals in recording and then cut them back by an equal amount in playback. Tape hiss and noise are thereby reduced while maintaining flat frequency response. A noise reduction system is a *compander,* which stands for compressor/expander. During recording, it expands or increases the recording level for low-level high-frequency signals, leaving the stronger portions of the music alone. This improves the *signal-to-noise ratio*. S/N ratio is the range or distance between the noise floor and the highest amount of signal that can be put onto the tape. The S/N ratio is enhanced by emphasizing the upper portion of the audible frequency response curve during recording, thus exaggerating the separation between the music and the noise. The noise is still there but the separation has been exaggerated.

Then during playback, these same expanded signals are now compressed by (ideally) the same amount as they were boosted during recording. Assuming the compression and expansion operations exactly match (which cannot be guaranteed), the correct frequency balance is restored while tape noise remains reduced. Improper matching of recording and playback levels (mistracking) harms frequency response, usually causing a loss of the high frequencies and therefore an overall flattening-out of the sound.

One has to be careful with noise reduction. Tape hiss is high-frequency noise; reducing the hiss can result in shaving off the music's high-frequency information right along with the noise. Tape already has a problem with recording high frequencies and you don't want to run the risk of losing any more of them. When this happens, there is an antiseptic cleanliness to the sound because the ambience and imaging information, which are largely contained in the high frequencies, have been knocked off.

It has become a point of fashion to be worried about surface noise. Under good recording conditions, tape hiss is really not something to make a big deal of. We all of us have a whistling in our ears—when you're in a very quiet place, this whistling can become more noticeable. Yet we all listen past our "ear noise" with no problem. Tape hiss and other surface noise, on a good system, is about as disturbing as ear whistle. However, some people appear to be more bothered by it than others. If people only spent as much time worrying about sound quality! A good system, contrary to popular belief, tends to make noise less objectionable (whereas mid-fi tends to make it worse).

Another drawback to this equalization is the extra circuitry through which the music signal has to go, both during recording and playback, sacrificing some of its quality. However, overall cassette quality is poor enough that this reduction in fidelity is seldom noticeable.

Three different noise-reduction systems are available on cassette decks: *Dolby B, Dolby C,* and *dbx*. (Dolby A is a professional NR system.) Dolby B, found on virtually all music cassette decks, reduces high-frequency noise by about 10 dB, supplying a 60 dB signal-to-noise ratio, about the minimum acceptable. This is also the standard system used by manufacturers for prerecorded cassettes. Dolby C is like combining two Dolby B systems operating at different signal levels and in slightly different frequency ranges. It provides up to 20 dB of noise reduction and covers nearly the entire audible range.

Careful pairing of recording and playback response levels is essential. Dolby C tapes can be played back on Dolby B decks; Dolby B can be played back with no Dolby decoding, though this will result in a very bright sound. Similarly, Dolby C tapes played back on a Dolby B deck will sound bright. Dolby C tapes played back with no Dolby decoding will sound extremely bright and will in addition "pump" and "surge," becoming unlistenable.

Be aware that dbx-encoded tapes can be played back *only* on systems with dbx-decoding circuitry. They cannot be played back on Dolby systems and, if played back with no decoding, are unlistenable. The dbx system operates over the full frequency range and reduces noise by as much as 30 dB.

TUNERS

For us, the main value of a tuner lies not in its fidelity—which, even in FM, is not high—but in its tremendous variety as a musical resource. A tuner is like a lending library—you can roam at will through all the stations, stopping to listen to whatever you want, then either passing it by or going out to purchase a copy of your own. Some of the music you could never hear anywhere else.

It's worthwhile to get a good tuner because otherwise you probably won't listen to it much. With FM fidelity less than great to start with, you don't want to add more distortion from the equipment or be unable to pick up the stations clearly. Instead of adding a tuner as an alternative front end to your main system, you may want to set it up as a separate system in another room where you spend a fair amount of time. You can enjoy some semibackground music and also keep semi-alert for "discoveries." In this case, a receiver (tuner and preamp/amp combined in one chassis) may be the most economical approach, though you'll never match the quality of, for example, a Magnum/dynalab FT-101 by taking this route.

WHAT IS A RADIO-FREQUENCY WAVE?

Tuners are unique as a signal source in that they do not retrieve signals that have been physically notated on a piece of plastic, as do LP, CD, or tape, but literally pluck music signals out of the air.

These signals are traveling at the speed of light, bouncing against walls, buildings, trees, the curvature of the earth, and even combining with competing signals from the 8,000 or so commercial radio stations that broadcast in the United States alone. They also suffer interference by electrical signals from passing jet planes, vehicles, air conditioners, toasters, and so on. Whew, what a mess! It's amazing broadcasting even works, let alone maintains some semblance of fidelity.

Radio-frequency waves are of course different from sound waves. They travel at the speed of light (about 186,000 *miles* per second) and do not need a medium such as air to move in. In contrast, sound waves travel through the air at about 1,130 *feet* per second. Radio waves and sound waves are alike in that they both vibrate at a given frequency, measured in cycles per second (renamed hertz in honor of the discoverer of RF).

In any radio transmission. the information being transmitted, whether music, speech, or any other kind of sound, is carried on a signal called—would you have ever guessed—a *carrier signal.* This carrier signal is then modulated to correspond with the audio signal.

AM (amplitude modulation) broadcasting, even at its best, has sound of only mid-fi quality, regardless of the receiving equipment and setup, because of how the signal is transmitted. The information is transmitted as variations (modulations) in the strength (amplitude) of the carrier signal. The tuner then ''skims'' this information off the carrier and translates it into an audible signal for amplification.

The problem is that AM transmissions are very much subject to atmospheric and man-made electrical interference. Most sources of *radio-frequency interference* (RFI)—car engines, electric motors, electrical storms, and the like—are AM in nature, because noise deviates with amplitude, not with frequency. So noise, like the AM signal, is easily carried right along with the intentional signal, creating distortion.

The prime advantage of AM over FM is that it can travel much greater distances than FM's limited 60- to 80-mile average range. AM's longer-wavelength transmissions will bend to follow the earth's curve and will also diffract around obstructions. With this asset, however, comes a disadvantage—in traveling farther, AM is more likely to pick up distortion and interference from distant stations on the same frequency.

Another limitation, though not inherent, is the cutoff of the frequency response at about 5,000 Hz. Even modest audio systems can reproduce from 80 to 15,000 Hz. Restricting AM to a 5,000-Hz maximum was a decision by international broadcasting regulators to reduce interference between AM stations by limiting the transmitter bandwidth.

Inexpensive portable, table, and clock radios offer AM reception alone because reproduction of its limited frequencies is cheaper than including a capability for FM's much wider range.

In *FM (frequency modulation) broadcasting,* the amplitude of the signal (and thus the power) remains constant while the frequency of the broadcast signal varies according to the audio signal.

FM has two outstanding advantages over AM: It is far less sensitive to noise and interference than AM, and it can transmit a wider

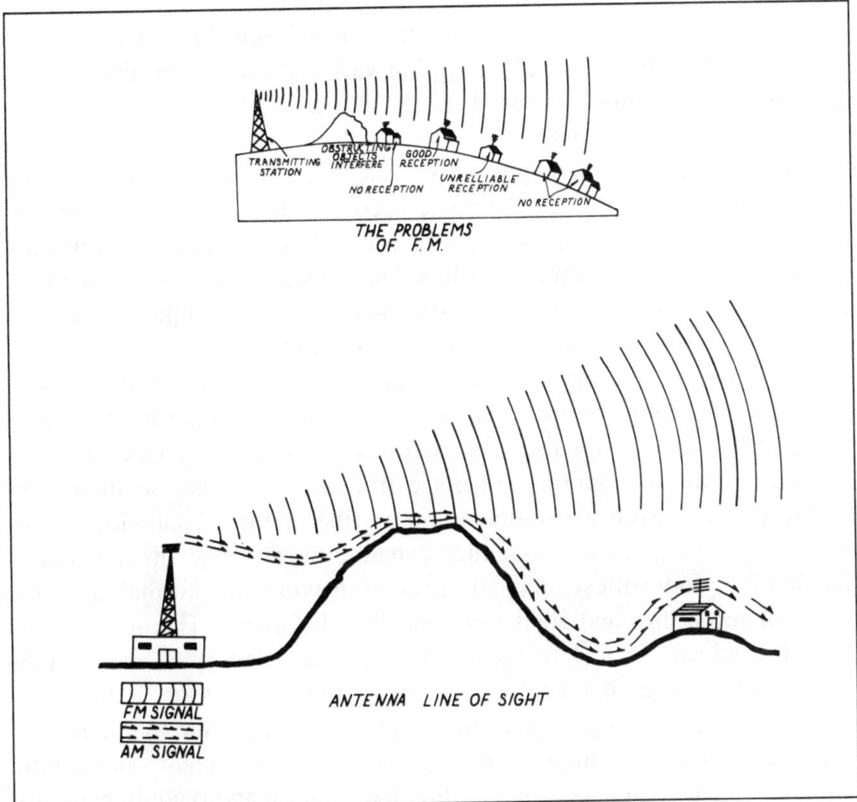

Fig. 14

range of frequencies. It is true, the Federal Communications Commission restricts these to a 50- to 15,000-Hz bandwidth, thus cutting off the extreme highs and lows of the music. But contrast this to AM's upper limit of 5,000 Hz. FM, relatively speaking, is a high-fidelity transmission.

The FM requirement for a wide bandwidth (about 300 kHz for a stereo channel) potentially poses serious interstation interference problems. But using VHF (very high frequency) transmissions, which do not bend around the earth's surface as do lower frequencies, minimizes these problems and ensures that each FM transmitter has a well-defined service area. As the airwaves become increasingly crowded, however, FCC regulations are changing and broadcasting areas are becoming less distinct.

The use of VHF, however, is responsible for FM's outstanding *dis*advantage—its distance limitations. Unlike AM, FM reception is essentially limited to locations that are in "line of sight" of the transmitter (see Fig. 14). "Fringe area" reception varies according to time of day. A basic rule of thumb is that if *both* the transmitting antenna and the receiving antenna are 100 feet above sea level, then FM can broadcast about 30 miles; if the height above sea level of both transmitter and receiver is 1,000 feet, then the range becomes about 80 miles. In mountain areas, antenna elevations may be high enough to permit a 150-mile range. The average range is a broadcast distance of about 60 to 80 miles. Where hills and buildings obstruct the line of sight, the quality and range of reception will obviously be degraded.

Ultimately, the most important factor in FM fidelity is the attitude of the radio stations themselves, many of which are quite indifferent to the quality of their signals. Most stations use a low-frequency filter to eliminate turntable rumble and noise from their signals, so their low-end response is even worse than the prescribed limited bandwidth. Most also use a "compressor" to reduce dynamic range (the contrast between the loudest and softest sounds), thus destroying the normal dynamic range of recordings and adding considerable distortion. (This may change with the advent of CD or it may remain the same if no one can be bothered to change it.) The point of using the compressors is to ensure broadcast over the largest possible geographic area, while maintaining a volume level always high enough for an adequate signal-to-noise ratio and to "catch" listeners scanning the dial. Station audio equipment also is generally not built from the standpoint of fidelity, but rather of durability and reliability (as with most recording studios).

FACTORS AFFECTING A TUNER'S SOUND

So, the two main factors affecting a tuner's sound quality are (1) the quality of the transmitted signal, in terms of noise level, dynamic range, and so on, and (2) the sensitivity, selectivity, and fidelity of that particular tuner (and antenna). Obviously, you have little control over the signal transmitted to the tuner, just as you have limited control of the quality of a recording—if you want to hear what that particular recording or station has to offer, you have to take it as is.

However, you can select the particular tuner attributes in addition to fidelity that are most important to you, given where you live. If, for example, you live deep in the heart of the country and far from radio stations, you may need a tuner with particularly good sensitivity. If you live deep in the heart of a city, and so can receive a proliferation of signals, you'll need a tuner that can cope with the fuzz of multipath distortion. No one tuner will excel at everything, so it is a matter, as usual, of determining and then accepting the tradeoffs.

How a tuner sounds in the end really depends on the reception problems in your area. So before buying, find out what kind of reception you can expect to get for the stations you want to listen to. If you are in a poor receiving area, it may be that the best tuner will not be able to sound good, so it probably doesn't make sense to spend a lot of money on it. Consider a less expensive one and invest the savings in buying records or upgrading other components.

If you are some distance from FM stations, you may find that in stereo a tuner provides only noisy reception, whereas in mono it brings the station in fine. Stereo reception requires twice or more the incoming signal strength that mono does, so while in mono the FM signal may extend 100 miles, in stereo it will broadcast less than 50 miles. If your tuner doesn't automatically switch to mono to compensate for weak signals, switch it over manually. FMX may turn out to be a solution: Recently developed by CBS, it is a method of stereo broadcasting that is designed to extend the range of stereo reception to be almost equal to that of mono.

Regrettably, *sensitivity,* the ability to pick up weak signals, and excellent sound quality are seldom combined successfully. If you want to listen to local stations or even to distant ones with strong signals, you needn't worry too much about sensitivity and can instead concentrate on good sound. If reception is poor, however, the best sound quality is obviously irrelevant if you can't hear the broadcast. Sensitivity specifically refers to how strong the station's signal must be before the tuner can pick it up. The more sensitive the tuner, the weaker the signal you can get away with and still gain clear FM-stereo reception. The *lower* the sensitivity figure, as expressed in microvolts, the better. This is also expressed in terms of decibels, in which case the 50-dB quieting figure is the one that ensures the signal will be quiet enough to provide audio worth listening to.

Selectivity identifies the tuner's ability to deal with interference from other station signals; in other words, it refers to how well the tuner can bring in one station while rejecting others nearby. This is also called alternate channel separation. It is expressed in decibels, the higher the better, and indicates the difference in loudness by which a tuner screens out nearby channels. In urban areas especially, where many stations crowd the airwaves, this is important to consider. A rating above 50 dB is acceptable; above 80 dB is considered excellent.

Multipath distortion is the prime enemy for urban and suburban listeners. In such areas, in fact, regardless of how good your tuner is, multipath causes serious sound degradation on the majority of stations.

Multipath distortion occurs when the broadcast signal arrives at your tuner not by one direct path from the transmitting antenna but instead via multiple paths. (This is sometimes loosely compared to the ghosts on TV screens.) These paths are the result of the signal bouncing off mountains, walls, buildings and other large steel structures, and the like. Each of the reflected signals will have traveled a somewhat different distance and so some will arrive at your tuner's antenna later than others and become echoes, delayed both in time and in phase.

These time and phase delays are a serious source of distortion and listener fatigue. As discussed elsewhere through the book, music is a uniquely temporal art—to alter its time relationships is like putting a turpentined rag to a still-wet oil painting and smearing it. Once these problems are a part of the input RF signal, there is very little your tuner can do to remove them. Tuners with good AM rejection and capture ratio can ameliorate certain aspects of the problem, but the problem still remains. A good antenna is critical (see below).

Capture ratio is the tuner's ability to cut down on multipath distortion by suppressing the weaker of the two signals coming in on the same frequency so the stronger can be clearly received without interference. This helps protect not only against "ghosts" but also against receiving two stations' broadcasts simultaneously. As new stations proliferate, the likelihood increases that some will interfere with others in RF-congested parts of the country, particularly California and New England. Capture ratio is expressed in decibels; the lower the figure, the better. Two dB or less is considered good; slightly less than 1 dB is the best that can be achieved.

AM rejection (or suppression): "AM" in this case doesn't refer to an AM radio station signal but to "amplitude-modulated" noise distortion. Many man-made devices, including appliances, elevators, and spark plugs, produce amplitude-modulation components that interfere with FM reception (and interfere even more with AM reception). Lightning and multipath signals also cause the same problems. Tuners must be able to ignore these forms of interference and, obviously, this is particularly important in urban areas. Rejection is measured in decibels, as the ratio between the AM and FM signal components at the tuner's antenna input and its audio output. Probably the minimum you should accept is −45 dB (meaning the noise being rejected is 45 dB *less in amplitude* than the wanted signal); −60 to −80 dB is preferable if you're in a problem area.

S/N ratio: This is the ratio between the received signal's maximum strength and its background hiss. It relates directly to sensitivity. The ratio is expressed in decibels, the higher the better; but keep in mind that few FM stations broadcast better than a 60-dB signal, though many tuners have measures ratios of 80 to 90 dB.

Stereo Separation: This is the separation between right- and left-channel music signals. It is expressed in dB—the higher the figure, the better the separation. Listen for stereo separation also with the noise reduction switched in, as this can reduce separation. If the left and right channels are not perfectly in phase, or synchronized, this will also reduce the perceived sense of separation. Average is about 50 dB.

SCA Rejection: "SCA" stands for subsidiary carrier authorization, which allows FM stations to piggyback specialized programs, such as store background music, onto their regular broadcasts. If a tuner doesn't adequately filter this out, the piggybacked signal tends to cause increased background hiss, high-pitched twittering or chirping (known as "birdies"), and high-frequency distortions. Again, as with AM rejection, the numbers will be negatives, for example −75, indicating that the piggybacked signal is 75 dB less in amplitude than the signal you want to receive.

DIGITAL TUNERS

With all the excitement over "digital" these days, the term is thrown around pretty loosely. Here's what they're *really* talking about.

A *digital station readout* is nothing other than a bunch of light-emitting diodes (LEDs). Instead of reading a needle on a dial, you read an "alphanumeric display." This is not part of the RF or audio signal path and has NO effect on the tuner's sonic performance. Its advantage is the unambiguous identification of which frequency you're tuned to, which with analog dials can be somewhat unclear. The disadvantage is having to learn the numbers of the stations, instead of just their locations, though digital readout users claim one adapts very quickly. Some prefer the appearance of a dial to that of LEDs.

Digital station tuning, on the other hand, actually is digital and is in the signal path. It has its advantages and disadvantages. The main advantage of this digital tuning is that you are always at the exact center of the station selected, which assures minimal distortion. You needn't even pay any attention to fine tuning—just select the station and the tuning is automatically taken care of. But exact-center tuning is a practical advantage only if the rest of the tuner's circuitry is of comparably low distortion.

The very serious disadvantage, which overshadows this modest benefit, is that you cannot "detune" a station slightly to achieve better real-world reception; the digital tuner is set only for "perfect" reception and will permit nothing else. For example, when you want to listen to a weak station that is neighbored by a stronger one, you get a lot of distortion and modulation from the stronger one. But by slightly "detuning" the weaker station to the side opposite the strong one, you can often get an acceptable signal. The station you want is weak enough that you don't notice the slight distortion added from detuning, and you lose much of the interference from the competing station. Digital tuning doesn't let you do that. That's bad. Some cable stations intentionally shift the frequency of the channel they broadcast over by 20 or so kHz. You don't want your tuner to lock in only to where the signal "ought to be" instead of where it is.

The reason you can't do it is because digital tuning is performed by a *frequency synthesizer*—a preprogrammed microprocessor that "knows" where the station "should be" and will permit adjustments only in gross increments of 5 kHz or so. When detuning a station to minimize neighboring interference, you want a subtle alteration of only about 1 or 2 kHz, not a crude leap of 5 kHz. Analog tuning has almost infinite fine-tuning capability.

Now, here's another twist added to confuse. Analog tuning *controls* may be applied to either analog or digital station-selection *circuits*. Analog controls are very nice because you can travel in either direction on the dial, and can go exactly as fast and as far as you want. Digital tuning controls are much more limited—you can only do what they've been programmed to do. They'll require "less labor" of you than analog, but also give you less choice.

Manufacturers will continue to prefer digital station tuning, not only because their marketing departments tell them they should, but also because it is far less labor intensive. Analog tuning has a large manual labor budget in its cost, whereas a digital tuner can be pretty much completely machine assembled and tested. Magnum/dynalab, widely acclaimed for its sonic excellence and good looks, combines analog tuning controls and analog station selection with digital station readout.

THE PURPOSE AND IMPORTANCE OF THE ANTENNA

An antenna has to do two basic things. First, it has to *tune in* the signal frequency you're trying to pick up. Second, it has to *tune out* multipath and other distortions. This is how Peter Moncrieff describes it.* In fact, he enjoins one to think "negatively"—you've tuned IN the station and now you want to tune OUT multipath. By selecting only one out of the multiple reflected signals that hit your antenna, you can largely eliminate the multipath problems of general fuzz along with time and phase incoherence. Selecting only one from among the many is possible because each echo or reflection of the main signal tends to come from a slightly different direction—by carefully rotating your antenna, you can pick up the best one.

What should you be listening for? You're NOT seeking the *strongest* signal, because this strength comes from a conglomerate of reflections. Nor do you necessarily want the signal on a direct path from the transmitter. It's unlikely there is such a path, especially in built-up areas, and certainly not to an indoor antenna—the signal by then has bounced all around your building. Even if you do manage to tune in to a direct path, it's likely to be accompanied by a strong ghost reflection coming from almost the same angle. That's why in New York City, every TV program is hosted by a twin ghost of the World Trade Center.

What you ARE seeking is the *cleanest* of all the paths, and this will be the one that has no close followers. It's fairly easy to hear the difference between good and poor antenna orientation, but trickier to pick up the subtler benefits of the "right" compared to just "good" antenna tuning. A signal that contains more distortion will usually sound louder

---

**IAR Hotline*, nos. 6 and 7.

and brighter than a less distorted signal. Listen for a quiet, dull signal because this will be cleaner and less distorted, and will bring you more of the music with less listener fatigue over time. As you attune your ears to recognizing a good signal, the subtleties will no longer be regarded by you as mere subtleties but recognized as important distinctions.

Keep in mind the basic human/audio truth that as you eliminate grosser problems, the smaller ones thus revealed will move into the foreground and become annoying in their own right.

Changing the orientation of your antenna in two dimensions will gain you the best signal. You should not only rotate it on its axis but also tilt it so its bars are no longer horizontal to the earth—the reflected RF waves will not be horizontal. Tilting the antenna will orient it so it's parallel to the signal.

Obviously, tilting and rotating an outdoor antenna each time you tune in to a different station is very awkward—even if you employ expensive servomotors. Moncrieff recommends building a one-fourth-scale indoor antenna and mounting it on an inexpensive ball-socket tripod head, which you can then tilt, rotate, and swivel to your heart's content. And, more important, because you can, you will. Yes, a smaller antenna will provide a lower signal strength, but for local stations at least you will have more than enough. To bring in weaker, more distant stations, you could switch to a full-size roof antenna. Probably only serious DXers (radio enthusiasts who like to pull in as many distant stations as possible) will feel the need to do this. A well-regarded commercially available indoor antenna that permits easy swiveling and rotating is the GC Electronics.

The primary benefit of an outdoor antenna is its height above ground level. Each foot above ground level adds 1 mile to the receiving distance, just as, if you are 6 feet tall, you can see a distance of about 6 miles to the horizon; 5 miles if you are 5 feet tall.

Dipoles, Rabbit Ears, and Outdoor Antennas

There are three basic types of antennas, which run in simplicity from dipoles through rabbit ears to outdoor types. The only reason outdoor antennas are best is their higher location. The farther you are from a station, the greater the benefit of *any* good antenna.

A *folded dipole* is the standard antenna supplied with a tuner—a long, plastic-coated pair of wires (called a twin lead) forming a T. The two arms of the T constitute the antenna, which receives only in a direction at right angles to its length. The upright of the T terminates in two bare leads, which screw or clip into the antenna terminals on the back of the tuner or receiver. Dipoles have a fixed length approximating the center of the FM band (which may not be where you do most of your listening) and they are hard to orient in a particular direction to optimize reception. If you're in an area of high signal strength, then a dipole can provide adequate, though certainly not great, reception.

Dipoles do not cope very well with multipath distortion, the perennial problem especially of urban areas. Dipoles, being "dipolar," meaning two-sided, accept signals as easily from the front side as from the back side (though who's to say which is front and which is back?). So they pick up twice the amount of multipath.

Rabbit ear antennas are a small step ahead. Their advantages are twofold: They can be "aimed" in the best direction to enhance reception, and their length can be adjusted to the wavelength of a particular broadcast. Some advise using the standard indoor TV-antenna rabbit ears rather than ones specifically designed for radio. These latter cost quite a bit more and not only may gain you no improvement but even sometimes sound worse.

These are really your only two useful options for an indoor antenna. Add a 10- or 15-foot length of cable onto your dipole or rabbit ears to improve reception, and play around with the antenna's positioning.

Mounting the antenna on a photographic stand makes it very easy to move around to the best receiving position. Lowell makes an excellent one. This company also offers rolling wheels to add to its stand, which can be locked and unlocked with foot action. The wheels make it even more convenient to use as an antenna stand or as a light stand to provide closeup lighting on your turntable or cleaning area.

Another type of antenna can be used indoors, which can help considerably in picking up weak signals, in reducing multipath problems, and in coping with adjacent station interference. This is an antenna that effectively incorporates a "pretuner" stage, like a preamp, which manipulates the signal before it reaches the tuner proper. The Magnum/dynalab Signal Sleuth is a well-regarded example.

Outdoor and rooftop antennas, if practical for you, can make a big difference. Rooftop TV antennas don't help FM reception much, and while there are combination TV/FM antennas available, the best results are obtained with dedicated FM antennas. These consist of a dipole with additional elements known as directors and reflectors. They are designed to increase gain and improve directionality to help limit multipath distortions. The more of these directors and reflectors, the greater the gain and directionality.

Omnidirectional outdoor antennas need no aiming, but on the other hand this means they can't be aimed *away* from undesired signals. *Directional* outdoor antennas generally provide good protection against multipath distortions and so give the best reception. They are commonly sold for ''fringe'' areas as they have the strongest pickup, but are beneficial in protecting against multipath fuzz in built-up areas as well. The only problem is that you'll need to tune in the antenna for each station by using a remote-control antenna rotator. Remember, you're not necessarily looking for the strongest signal, but for the clearest, cleanest one.

An outdoor antenna should be located in the highest place possible and, ideally, well away from obstructions like walls that the signal could bounce off, increasing multipath. Keep the antenna well away from anything metal, including furniture, railings, roof eaves, TV antennas, and so forth, as these will increase AM interference.

Incidentally, running the round 75-ohm transmission line from any antenna is a better choice than that 300-ohm line because, though bulkier, it is shielded against interference. The 300-ohm line, being unshielded, picks up noise; though, being flat, it slides easily behind furniture and hides neatly under carpets. Choose your priorities.

COMPACT DISC PLAYERS

Ten years after the first digital recordings were released on LP, the compact disc was launched in 1982–1983 and digital audio was firmly established with its own unique playback format and equipment. It promised perfect sound quality, no defective discs, and no wear. None of these claims were true.

However, the launching of the CD was successful. In an unprecedented agreement between the hardware and disc manufacturers, there were no battles over which format of digital disc to adopt. A single type—the optical compact disc using a semiconductor laser to read pits pressed into the disc—was settled on for *all* discs. Philips teamed up with Sony to develop the medium and gained a strong base in Europe and in Japan, origin of most disc players. Enormous promotional efforts successfully established the CD in the mass marketplace, though market penetration remains little more than 5 percent. The Compact Disc Group formed and bankrolled by manufacturers to promote the CD finally disbanded in 1985, stating its job was done and there was no need for it to maintain its PR efforts—this at least was *one* truthful statement it made.

Meanwhile, in the high-end audio community, the widespread reaction was that CD did not sound good, regardless of the claims to "perfect sound forever." Prospects of a digital future seemed grim. Mike Moffat of Theta pretty much summed it up—if you want to age ten years, listen to a bad CD player. Until in 1986 there was a breakthrough—a handful of audiophiles had each independently come up with ways of significantly improving digital sound. While not yet comparable to analog, it was clear that it held promise.

As Harry Pearson cogently put it, the CD is currently the audio novelty of the computer age, but if, as the novelty wears off, the pleasure of listening to music disappears along with it, then where will we be? Small audiophile companies like PS Audio, Mod Squad, Theta, and Perfectionist Audio, fusing a passion for music with a penetrating exploration of audio technology, have started to answer this question by designing customized players. These early generations of high-end compact disc players demonstrate that digital really does have both potential and promise. California Audio Labs has made a tube CD player incorporating some of Theta's digital section upgrades.

Despite claims of "perfection," CD players have gone through a number of generations, each one usually sounding a bit better than the last. The differences between generations have not been merely cosmetic, or a matter of features, but clearly audible. Curiously enough, the specifications have changed very little from one generation to the next, not reflecting the very definite sonic changes that have occurred. CD players, in fact, including even the cheapest, have "better" specs than the best turntables, despite sounding far less good.

One problem for which there is no excuse is the poor quality of the analog section of the player, which even in many expensive mass-market models would embarrass a boom box. Improving this section helps the overall sound. But the analog section is only part of the problem. Integrated chip design is an area few analog designers are familiar with, and regrettably the people who are the experts on the chips tend to know little about listening to music. With any luck, these two groups will be able to get together and combine their expertise.

For all its problems, a CD player can be an upgrade from the standard mass-fi turntable having a misaligned and probably worn cartridge. There's no worry about proper turntable setup, or table, arm, and cartridge matching, or any of the other irritants more or less cheerfully put up with by enthusiastic listeners to gain good music. What we may be seeing here is a compromise *downward* in quality in order to bring overall better sound to a wider audience—good sound that is better than what the majority is used to but less good than what can already be readily attained with a little knowledge, a little effort, and the exercise of taste.

As was pointed out above in "The Turntable System," in order to gain good sound from a CD player, it is necessary to spend as much as you would on a really good turntable. It is also essential to take into consideration the much higher cost of compact discs compared to LPs and the more limited repertoire. Nonblockbuster music and performances are unlikely to show up on CD while costs are high and production remains tight. One good point is that old releases are being brought out of storage and reissued on CD.

The primary consideration is which you think sounds better—analog or digital. Read Part III, on recordings, do plenty of listening, and above all, listen for yourself. Don't simply be swayed by the enthusiasms of others—a new technology is always exciting.

And digital technology is in a state of flux. Some believe the new

DAT (digital audio tape) format will supersede the compact disc altogether, as it offers the advantage of recording as well as playback. The major controversy delaying DAT at this point is copy protection for commercial recordings. Record companies do not want to lose any of their revenue by having their expensive CDs copied by DAT home recorders, the way that LP revenues have been lost by cassette copying. A DAT recorder that can dub CDs will even be easier to use than a regular cassette deck—there will be no recording level, Dolby, bias, or EQ to set.

So copy protection is still being worked out to prevent digital-to-digital copying, but it will almost certainly also degrade the sound. Here is a new digital recording/playback system being developed with an intentionally added sound defect.

Unless there are releases that you feel you must have that are coming out on CD only, we would recommend holding off until the dust has settled a little more.

HOW A COMPACT DISC PLAYER WORKS

Instead of a stylus tracing a groove whose shape is the analog representation of the original sound wave, a laser beam pickup scans the pits on the underside of a single-sided CD disc as it spins first at 500 r.p.m., gradually decreasing to 200 r.p.m. as the laser reaches the disc's center. Each change in reflected light is sent to a photodiode, where it is converted into the electrical signals that form the bit stream. This bit stream information is first sent through an error correction and concealment circuit, and then on to the digital-to-analog converter, where it is changed into analog signals so it can be heard as music.

Certain physical obstacles will always be in the way of reading with absolute accuracy the billions of bits embossed on the disc. The *error correction* process reconstructs the original numbers or at least "guesses" at a reconstruction, based on the signal just before and after the error. If the error is too great to be reconstructed, then it must be covered up by *error concealment;* and, when the errors are too severe even to conceal, the system goes into "mute." A moment of silence is preferable to a very nasty popping noise that could damage components and hurt your ears. But all these corrective measures operate only on the *digits*—they cannot identify what the original sound of the live music was.

And because the sampling rate in digital is limited, errors must occur in converting analog wave forms into numbers, and then again in re-creating analog audio signals from numbers. Even if many more levels were used than is the case today, the sampling points of the original sound wave probably lie somewhere between any two levels. A digitizer rounds off the sound to the nearest whole number. When converting these numbers back again to sound, the level generated will be that of the recorded number, not of the exact original sound, so error is almost certain. To increase accuracy, some players use *oversampling*. Here again, many things can go wrong.

This gives an immensely simplified impression of what is actually a very complex process. Digital recording and playback are in fact so complex that it is difficult to come up with a simple explanation that is useful to the consumer. As many problems as analog reproduction is subject to, the greater complexity of digital offers far more opportunities for something to go wrong. Aside from recording and playback circuitry, the disc itself may also contain manufacturing defects, ranging from pin holes to dust contamination to an off-center hole, all of which affect the player's ability to retrieve the music. You may not hear the ticks and pops of LPs, but instead you will get the increased distortions of error correction, covering up for the CD equivalent of LP surface noise.

Every player approaches the problems somewhat differently. Even if you are able to understand how the digital technology works, this probably does you little good because there is no consistent evidence that one particular approach is better than another. As experience and understanding develop, it will probably become possible to correlate techniques with sound quality. Until then, concern yourself less with the manufacturer's claims and more with the sound of the music.

THE AMPLIFICATION STAGE

The role of the preamp and power amp, whether they are separate or combined as an integrated amp, is to do exactly what their names indicate: to amplify the music signal. The difficulty is that the signal must in no other way be altered. The signal coming out should be identical to the signal that went in in every particular except size.

The tiny signal from the cartridge (or other front end) is not itself directly enlarged. Rather, it is used to control an enormously larger current—the wall current—which thereby takes on the pattern of the smaller. Think of a photograph—the original photo or negative cannot be made any bigger; only a copy modeled on the original can be created in a larger size. Just as a copied photo can never be quite as good as its original, so the enlarged audio signal is never identical to the signal it is modeled on. Some distortion is inevitably introduced.

The basics of amplification circuitry have been effectively established for decades and most circuit designs today remain essentially the same as those of years past. Some amps made 20 to 30 years ago are still among the best-sounding components available. Nonetheless, though the basics may be well established, the different combinations, compromises, tradeoffs, and permutations are innumerable, even in a minimalist circuit.

Building a good musical instrument—for example, a violin—to a design that may have been essentially laid down a century or more ago does not thereby reduce it to the merely routine; there is no formula that can be followed by rote by an apprentice. On the contrary: The exact piece of wood selected; the glue used; the methods of steaming and joining; the length of the throat and the shape, size, and placement of the opening; the precise millimeter choice of where to affix the bridge; and all the myriad other tiny details, right down to the mood of the builder and that day's air temperature and humidity, are just some of the elements that create the unique voice of each violin.

Component building is much the same—that a component is commonly viewed as a mass-produced machine does not reduce the artistry required. The right selections must be made from among the hundreds of possible resistor and capacitor values, materials, brands, and designs; the capacitance and resistance of the circuit board and hookup wire must be balanced in with the overall design; even the way the circuit is laid out on the board can alter the sound. Every element affects all the others, so each decision must be balanced within the overall larger design. It is not enough to be logical and technical; one must also be intuitive—the final test comes in the listening, regardless of what the measurements may say.

In effect, instrument builders have now found new materials to work with. Instead of using wood and gut and felt to build machines for music, they now have oxygen-free copper and glass epoxy and titanium to manipulate. But just the fact that these materials are associated with technology doesn't make these new instruments "merely technological." Pianos are built of levers and hammers, using technology that was advanced for its day. Just because a piano doesn't use capacitors and resistors, it is not therefore technologically inferior to a preamp; because the piano is more complicated—more technological and mechanistic—than a simpler harp or set of panpipes, it is not therefore less capable of producing real music.

DESIGN FUNDAMENTALS

High-end designing, as with listening, is an exercise in *refinement*. Much more than the latest circuit layout or technology, good sound is a matter of good engineering, irrespective of the particular choice of technology used. As often as not, "new" takes over from "old" not because of innate superiority but because "new" excites the mind. The refinements of the old are often overlooked, at least initially. Progress generally includes throwing out at least some part of the baby along with the bath water (and then, often as not, trying to retrieve it later). This happened with tubes when transistors arrived.

The transistor revolutionized audio by making it available to large numbers of people, and the vacuum tube was almost instantly relegated to the ashcan of history. The new "wonder technology" superseded everything learned before.

Unfortunately, the sound that transistors made so widely available was less good than that of tube equipment. Fortunately, some people refused to believe the ads if it meant disbelieving their ears and so continued listening with tubes. Certain designers went right on designing with tubes. William Zane Johnson of Audio Research experimented with both tubes and transistors and returned to tubes. David Hafler of Dynaco, having since the mid-1950s offered amp equipment that for a low price would also bring you close to the best sound available at any price, made the switchover to transistors permanently. To many ears, his transistor equipment, while very good, has never quite matched the sonic quality of his tube equipment, though his recent XL 280 power amp may indicate a return to his early days of remarkable excellence.

Solid state was so warmly embraced for a number of reasons. For the manufacturer, transistor amps could be made less expensively and assembled more easily—large sections of circuitry that before had to be hand-assembled were now neatly contained in a single chip that took but a moment to secure to the circuit board. Transistors also made possible a new, sleek component profile—they weren't bulky, they gave off very little heat, and they were light. Consumers liked the novelty, liked being "in fashion," and liked the convenience of not having to bother with biasing and replacing tubes. This was the period when even the minor control of equipment care and maintenance was taken away from the consumer and replaced by "pretend control" in the form of multiplying switches and lights on a front panel that rapidly developed—or deteriorated—into a knob-twister's delight. Equipment was becoming feature oriented rather than benefit oriented.

Since the late 1970s, the best solid-state and the best tube devices have been gradually converging in sound quality. Tube and transistor designs, when carried through well, offer alternative compromises and tradeoffs. Let your ears make the choice for you, rather than being led astray by the grossly mistaken notion that tubes went out with the dodo. (Ken Kessler calls this fear of tubes "reverse technofear.")

Choice of Technology: Tubes, Bipolar Transistors, and FETs

A good amplifier is a good amplifier, regardless of the amplifying device used. Nonetheless, all amp devices are nonlinear (meaning that what comes out is not identical to what went in), and tubes and transistors have their own characteristic "sonic thumbprints," which you should become familiar with before buying. Probably you will prefer the general sound of one type over the other. The better the amp, the more alike tubes and transistors sound, as they both come closer to live music.

In sheer numbers, transistor amps rule the market until you get into the high end. However, moderately priced tube equipment has been

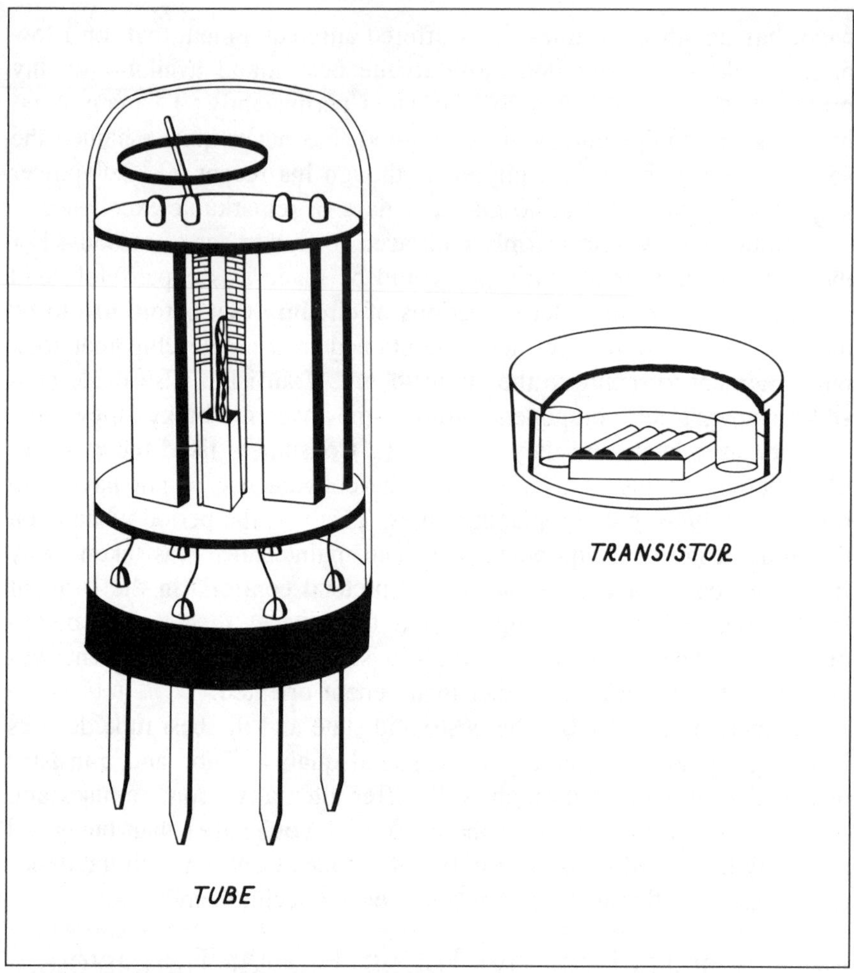

Fig. 15

coming out recently and the excellent used tube equipment from the past 25 years or so is available at budget prices. So you really are not limited to transistors just because of budgetary constraints.

Tubes, in general, excel through the all-important midrange and into the treble—they tend to have a transparent midrange; delicate, sweet, unshrill, nonpiercing highs; a less punchy, even somewhat flubby, bass; and very good soundstaging. Power is relatively low, but usually ample for most speakers in most rooms. Tubes are inherently more linear, simpler amplifying devices than transistors, and allow a much simpler circuit. Top rock musicians choose tubes for their music amps, like the Mesa Boogie.

Transistors, on the other hand, as a class are generally high-powered and have a strong, tight bass; highs that are often more extended but also tend to be hard, at times even shrill and piercing; a less good midrange; and a smaller, more "collapsed" soundstage. Transistors can have great precision, detail, and control—they can also be a little hard to take from the midrange on up.

You must be prepared to pay some attention to tubes—check the bias, replace them every year or so, hunt for better tubes. Solid state you can set up and forget—it either works or it doesn't. On the other hand, if something goes wrong, simple repair and even maintenance are far harder than with a tube amp. Transistors are more delicate and so more easily damaged than tubes. Transistors have a lifespan of as much as 20 years, compared to an output tube's life of about 1,000 hours, but you can replace an old tube yourself. An integrated circuit, once gone, may mean the end of the amp. Transistor amps also cannot easily be upgraded, as can tubes.

FETs (field effect transistors) appear to combine the sonic benefits of tubes and *bipolar transistors,* as well as operating more like tubes. Bipolars are current devices; FETs, like tubes, are voltage devices. (And music is a voltage phenomenon.) FETs have less distortion than bipolars but also less power. FETs are faster than bipolars and slower than tubes in terms of time delay.

One way to try to have the best of both worlds is to bi-amp (see below) or to combine tubes and transistors in different components. For example, a good choice is to use tubes in the preamp where the signal is very sensitive, and transistors in the power amp for good oomph. No tube amp can match the low-end range and control that a solid-state amp can have over a dynamic woofer; no solid-state preamp can match the sweetness and musicality of good tube preamps. A tube is a voltage device, which is what you need in the preamp and up until the amp's output stage; a transistor is basically a current device, which is what you need in the output stage.

Just remember that each system's sound depends on the matching of components, the setup, room acoustics, and your own preference for one sonic thumbprint over another. All components err; you want to keep all of yours from erring in the same direction.

Amplifying Circuit Designs

Probably the most basic amplifying circuit is *tubes with transformers*. It is also one of the most consistently sonically successful designs—it is much harder to design a poor tube circuit than a poor transistor circuit. Classic examples are the Dynaco Stereo 70 and the Marantz 8B, which have served as models for many successive designs, including the mono Quicksilvers. These particular designs are somewhat power-limited. The Stereo 70, for example, is 35 watts per channel, but note that tube watts are more powerful than their numerical equivalent in transistor watts. For example, 35 tube watts is comparable to about 50 transistor watts. Large tube designs, such as the Acoustic Research D-250 or Conrad-Johnson Premier 1, are heavy and expensive. It is harder to find a very modestly priced tube than a modestly priced transistor component. However, more and more inexpensive tube amps are being produced.

By far the most common amplifying circuit design is the *transistor Class A/B* (see below for more on "class"), which is both the most efficient and the most reliable—the NAD 3120 is a classic example of a good Class A/B. Transistors require much larger amounts of negative feedback (see p. 117), which can be a sonic disadvantage.

A *tube circuit without an output transformer* is rare—only a few are designed this way. It is an expensive and difficult design, which is pursued because transformers are a source of distortion. The best known output-transformer-less (OTL) design is the Futterman, now produced by Harvey Rosenthal. In conventional transformer/tube amps, the output tubes have a very high impedance and high voltage output. To match this to the speakers, a transformer is needed to step down the impedance and voltage while stepping up the current. OTL amps instead use several special low-impedance output tubes in parallel, which are capable of putting out a reasonable amount of current. These can then match directly with the speakers, eliminating the need for a transformer.

A more recent development has been *tube/FET hybrid* amplifiers, which can combine the advantages of "tube sound" with no output transformer and the efficiency of transistor A/B design. A tube circuit is used for all stages up until the output, where FETs take over, eliminating the problems of a transformer (and adding the power benefits of transistors). In theory, hybrids should combine the sweetness and transparency of tubes through the midrange and treble, with the solidity and control of transistors in the bass. Hybrids can also be made less expensively than all-tube designs.

The term "Class A/B" refers to the operation of the output stage of the amp (see p. 115). Preamps are in Class A operation throughout; amps operate in Class A until the output stage.

Excellent preamps and amps exist in each of these categories; so do poor ones. The final issue is not the particular approach used but the results when listening.

Passive Components

Fidelity of both the preamp and the amp depends most on the quality of the parts *(passive components)*; the quality of the *power supply,* both within the amp and from the wall; and the intelligence of the *circuit design,* more than on the choice of specific amplifying device or approach. Passive parts include the assemblage itself—sloppy work and "blob construction" methods (where solder is incorrectly used as a mechanical, structural part) are strikes against good sound.

The quality of the passive components the audio signal has to travel through is as important as the quality of the wall current it uses to build the amplified signal. The resistors, capacitors, and wire in the signal path behave like filters and gates, filtering the signal or actually halting it before letting it go through again. "Everything has a voice" is how Ed Dell of *Audio Amateur* and *Speaker Builder* magazines describes it, and the voice of those gates and filters will be imparted to a greater or lesser degree to the music signal passing through them.

You may not *want* to believe this can make a difference, but it does. How can bits of wire alter sound? you may ask—but they do. Who would *dis*believe that the particular characteristics of the reed used in the bassoon's mouthpiece can subtly alter its "voice"; that the horsehair used for a violin bow is chosen over catgut or nylon not because it is cheaper or stronger or more available, but because it sounds a certain way; that the felt used to pad the hammers of a piano has a direct and strong influence on the piano's tone; or that a performer's breath and finger/hand/arm movement alter in subtle detail the quality of the notes? Yet, that this also holds true with electricity is regarded with disbelief. If bits of wire and foil can transmit energy and sound, then it stands to reason that they can also alter that energy and sound.

The behavior of water is often used as an analogy for electricity. Think of a stream flowing over various streambeds and consider the effects the rocks and pebbles and fallen branches and variations of the streambed all have on the water's flow.

Similarly, the music signal may meet with greater or lesser resistance from the capacitors, resistors, and wire that it must flow through. All the frequencies of the signal may flow through simultaneously—some may be held back slightly while others flow through faster. Even though the speed differences may represent only a microsecond or less, even this is sufficient to alter the signal, affect sonic fidelity, and actually change the music.

The difference between the still highly prized, classic tube amps of 25 years ago and the best amps being produced today is often largely a matter of the passive components—these *have* improved in quality over the intervening years. Replace the old passive parts with the new and you are likely to have something that competes directly with the best amps of today. And at a very great saving—you can pick up a Dynaco Stereo 70 tube amp in good condition for probably about the price of a cheap and nasty transistor amp. *Any* component with a good power supply and basic circuit layout can be significantly upgraded by changing the passive components.

Even with recent amps, you may find that upgrading to better-quality passive components is worthwhile. This is a fairly inexpensive way to substantially improve the sound quality of a component. Not using the *best*-quality parts in a component is not, by the way, necessarily any indication of ignorance or shoddiness on the part of the designer, unless the design is sold as being "cost no object." The standard industry formula for the "parts cost multiplier" is four or five times—if a better-quality capacitor costs $1 wholesale, it adds $5 to the price of the component at the retail level. Multiply this by the number of caps, resistors, and other little parts in an amp or preamp and the increase in price in substantial—so much so that it could make the component unsalable to the particular market for which it was designed. The parts cost multiplier has to cover the costs of factory labor, overhead, manufacturer profit, dealer costs, and dealer profit.

Nothing prevents you from upgrading these components yourself. Be sure to match exactly the values of anything you replace. It may also be advisable to call the designer first to make sure there are no hidden design elements you should be aware of. We recommend solder, hookup wire, and caps are recommended in "Fine Tuning" (p. 255).

Power Supply

The power supply is at least as important as the amp circuit because it provides the material from which the enlarged music signal is constructed. If you use mediocre ingredients in a dish, then results will be mediocre (unless you spice it up with a lot of extra ingredients to distract attention from the basically poor materials you used). While a poor amp circuit can undo the benefits of a good power supply, conversely a poor power supply will hinder the best amp circuit. Mediocrity in either circuit or power supply can be spiced up with mid-fi-style boom and sizzle, but the discerning ear will not remain fooled for long.

The function of a power supply is deceptively simple. It must rectify the wall current, meaning convert it from AC to DC, and then it must filter and regulate the power to provide a steady, exact, and always available supply to the audio signal. It is essential that the power supply's voltage, the "building material," be absolutely rock-steady so that only the electrical signal from the cartridge is varying. Really, what the amp does is to modulate the power supply. This is the same in principle—electrically—as the need for the cartridge body (power supply) to be absolutely stable so that only the stylus (AC music signal) moves, or for the record groove, turntable, and speakers all to be steady and nonresonant in order to reproduce an undistorted signal.

The material the power supply works with is the AC wall current. Any computer user knows, probably from painful experience, that the juice from the wall is dirty, spiky, variable in power. Altogether, it does not live up to its image as a clean, predictable, and dependable source. It works reliably for relatively crude applications like running your lights, refrigerator, and toaster, but for delicate precision applications like audio it leaves much to be desired.

One person living right down the block from a power station was constantly blowing fuses and burning out tubes. A test of the wall current measured it at 133 volts!! While line current always fluctuates slightly around the ideal of a steady 120 volts, this aberration was extreme. The solution—at least a temporary one—was to add a 50-foot extension cord, coiled up behind the sofa. This sufficiently increased resistance to bring the voltage down to a normal 120. No more problems. (A varistor would probably cause less sonic degradation than an extension cord.)

If you are using a dirty, spiky, variable material to build up your ever larger signal models, then chances are you will end up with some

CAPACITORS

A capacitor stores and releases an electrical charge—it has "capacity" or a reservoir of energy available for use on demand. It must release its charge instantly and linearly (without alteration).

Its construction, in essence, is very simple—two electrically conductive plates are separated by a dielectric, or nonconducting, insulator. Each plate is connected to the outside world by a lead-out wire or terminal. Because these terminals are electrically insulated from each other, a capacitor cannot pass a direct current but does pass alternating current, such as the music signal. In fact, it presents an impedance that decreases with rising frequency; thus it can also be used as a filter, for example in a loudspeaker crossover.

No capacitor can perform to its ideal—all capacitors, like all audio designs, are approximations and crude ones at best. Each is imperfect in a different way, which is why each capacitor model sounds different.

There are hundreds of capacitor manufacturers, offering thousands of different capacitor choices. Options are not simply a matter of capacitor values, though that is clearly one element, but also choices of dielectric, type of construction, and quality of manufacture. This last is as important a sonic factor as the dielectric—some would say more important. Basic design and construction considerations such as height in relation to diameter, rolling (winding) versus stacking of the dielectric, tightness of the winding, microphonic characteristics (with the system on, tap a cap with a pencil and listen to the *thunk* coming out of your speakers), and placement of the tab connectors all take their sonic toll.

Unquestionably, capacitors can make a major sonic difference in your equipment, as important as a change in circuit design. This is true not only of the caps in the signal path but also of the caps *outside* the signal path, for example in the power supply. Granted, the signal has already been through innumerable and probably lousy caps in the course of recording, but this is no reason to add to the injury—changing even one cap in your playback system can change the sound. The preamp is especially sensitive to the choice of cap. While the amp can generally tolerate polypropylenes, the preamp will generally benefit from a better cap. However, as with much of audio, this is not an absolute.

If you replace your capacitors (or have them replaced), be sure to use good solder and to allow a few days' "burn-in time" for the caps to settle into their true sound. One of the worst feelings is to change caps only to be horrified by the results—bright, hard, edgy, unlistenable—until they've had a chance to break in (see p. 257). A tweak: Stan Warren of Superphon recommends wrapping caps tightly in tape to help reduce blur.

Below, capacitor dielectrics are listed in *descending* order of sonic quality (and of price). The importance of the dielectric is that it affects how quickly that reservoir of energy is released and how much of the charge the dielectric holds on to, releasing it moments later, smearing the sound.

Wondercaps, Sidereals, and Rels are widely considered to be among the best of the generally available caps. However, as the sonic role of cap quality is further explored, chances are that the accuracy of this brand-name information may change or be expanded.

1. *Vacuum:* Actually used in caps by a few companies, but they are very expensive and, being very inefficient, must be very large in size to store a useful charge. This sets up sonic problems, in addition to the practical ones of size and expense.
2. *Air:* Also not very efficient, breaks down easily, and contains water, which provides leakage paths.
3. *Teflon:* Stable and predictable, but very expensive. Makes for less mushy sound because charge from the music signal is not greatly absorbed and so does not get held and then released later to interfere with music. However, some say it can add glassiness to the sound.
4. *Metallized film* (in descending order of price and sound quality):
   Polystyrene: Yields good sound; soldering runs the risk of changing the capacitance value.
   Polypropylene: Most cost-effective for good sound, but styrene is better.
   Polycarbonate: Very reliable, durable, but not a very good dielectric. Same as the CD base material.
5. *Mylar:* Some of these caps in particular are microphonic; OK for noncritical use.
6. *Ceramics, etc.* This category includes naturally occurring materials and their derivatives, such as glass, mica, and ceramics. These are better than electrolytics for dielectric absorption but tend to add a grainy, sandy sound to the music, like the material they are made from.
7. *Aluminum electrolytics:* Allow an enormous amount of capacitance in a small package. Used in the power supply to smooth out current ripples—a combination of high capacitance, reasonable size, and modest price assures their use here. *Not* used as signal path elements except in cheap solid-state equipment and speaker crossovers. Widely recognized as making the poorest-sounding caps of all. Even when used outside the signal path, electrolytics nonetheless affect sound quality.

pretty poor results. To help protect against this, the component must have a good power supply; it should be plugged into its own electrical circuit; and it may benefit from a line conditioner (see below). If the amp must share an electrical circuit, be sure anything else on the line will not be in use at the same time that you are listening. A refrigerator, appliance, or anything else that draws a lot of juice, and/or cycles on and off, is to be shunned. Some people even bring in a dedicated power line—this may seem extreme but has its rewards, if your system is sufficiently revealing so as not to camouflage the improvement with its own grunge.

The power supply consists of three elements: a *transformer,* which steps down the wall current for transistors or steps it up for tubes; a *bridge rectifier,* which converts the transformer's AC output to the DC used by both transistors and tubes; and a *reservoir* of capacitance, which holds a pool of power always at the ready and smooths out all ripples in the power. How constant the power supply is depends on the current drawn by the amp and the size of the reservoir. Sometimes a regulator, which is a feedback circuit, is added to reduce ripple further.

The power supply is often the most expensive part of the circuit to build and so tends to be skimped on. It is particularly important in the preamp, where the fragility of the signal allows it to be easily distorted.

Though you cannot really upgrade the power supply yourself, you can make its job a little easier by cleaning up the wall current. You should investigate special power cords, such as the Discrete Technology Power Bridge, and line conditioners. The latter have been seriously investigated for some years now. The problem with most of them is that they can do almost as much harm as they can do good. None have yet been specifically developed from scratch for audio; all have been borrowed from other applications. Like any other hand-me-down, they really do not quite fulfill the goals of audio, however excellent they may be at line filtering.

Minimal Circuitry

The simpler the circuit, the fewer parts the audio signal has to go through, and the fewer opportunities for distortion to be introduced. (Better still would be if one could just slap a recording up to the side of one's face and listen to it directly, eliminating nearly *all* the distortions introduced by playback equipment.) This is audio's Holy Grail of "straight wire with gain"—the mythical nondistorting pathway for the music, consisting of no more than a straight wire that would somehow amplify the signal (the Immaculate Magnification).

Simplicity, or minimalism, is a recognized and increasingly observed design philosophy. (And one that applies equally to many recordings, as discussed in Part III.) However, here as everywhere, there are tradeoffs to be chosen and careful balances to be maintained. If a circuit is made overly simple, then each part has to do more than it is best suited for and so, pushed to the edge of its limits, it will become extra-sensitive to changes in wall current or other aberrations. It is also likely, pushed to its limits, to have a shortened lifespan.

A ''short-trace'' circuit uses the least amount of wire possible without degrading the circuit. All the wire that the signal has to go through acts as a lens—the thicker the lens, the greater the diminution and distortion of light passing through it. Einstein advised: Simplify as much as possible and then no more.

A complex circuit, on the other hand, as well as increasing sonic colorations, tends also to be less reliable. Excess circuitry, or as GSI's Andy Fuchs terms it ''audio verbiage,'' offers many more opportunities for something to go wrong. Complex designs can sound as if the music is coming to you through a London fog. Good circuits, like most good design solutions of any kind, are inherently elegant.

Incidentally, just because a transistor amp may *look* simple when you open it up doesn't mean it *is* simple—just that it's harder to tell what's going on. One of those innocent-looking IC chips is built up of anywhere from 50 to 100 layers of screen, each screen about one molecule thick and intentionally containing impurities. The carefully established impurities in each silicon screen determine the chip's resistance and conductivity.

Complexity may enable the unit to perform better *on the test bench,* to test more linearly (with less distortion) in terms of measurements, but a sonic price is exacted in exchange for the good advertising copy. Each additional component in the design contributes its own aberrations. These will either remain audible as a distortion or else have to be corrected for by other components, and then in turn these additional components will either be heard or have to be corrected for, and so on and so forth, like those wooden dolls that nest one inside the other. Unfortunately, designers may have an incentive to complexify a circuit to ''justify'' what consumers may otherwise perceive to be a high price.

Keeping the amp circuits as simple, short, and minimal as possible reduces the potential for distortion. Conversely stated, the more complex the circuit path, the greater the opportunity for distortion to enter the signal and be amplified many thousands of times along with the music. Elaborating on a minimal circuit is like accessorizing a musical instrument. The whole purpose of audio is the attempt to capture the music *as it was performed by the artist* and then to transport that communication from the room where it was performed to the room where you are listening. Some designers sometimes seem more eager to demonstrate their own technical brilliance than to reveal the performer's work.

BASICS OF PREAMPLIFIERS

The preamp and power amp, though they are both amplification stages, perform quite different roles. The preamp can be viewed as a continuation of the front end—it enlarges and controls the signal to prepare it for the amplifier. The power amp (often called simply the amp) is somewhat like a motor for the speakers. Its function is to add power to the signal to enable it to do the work of driving the speakers.

Preamps sound more different from each other than do comparably good amps (assuming the amp has been correctly matched to the speaker)—the preamp signal is so small and delicate that the circuit has a substantial effect on it. A stronger signal is less easily distorted. Vintage preamps tend to compare less well with present-day preamps than do vintage amps with their modern siblings. While amps age well, preamps have unmistakenly improved over recent years. Perhaps only the Marantz 7C and the Dynaco PAS 3, in unmodified form, are still in the same league as today's high-end offerings.

The preamp involves three main sections or stages: the *phono stage,* the *line-level input,* and the *line section.*

The Phono Stage

The phono stage is used only for the phono cartridge signal—all other music sources bypass this initial stage. For phono cartridges, the phono stage supplies the first and main preamp boost to the signal, increasing usually from between 0.25 (low-output moving coil) and 1.5 (moving magnet) *milli*volts up to anywhere from about 0.5 to 1.5 volts.

The phono stage must also EXACTLY reverse the RIAA equalization curve used in cutting the LP. RIAA equalization has nothing to do with improving sound quality (in fact, the opposite); it simply makes it possible to fit more music onto each record side by cutting back the bass and boosting the treble. Left untreated, the bass notes would take up a great deal of space on each side, so they are cut back a sharp 20 dB to conserve space; at the same time the treble is boosted 20 dB in order that the bass needn't be cut back still further. Boosting the treble also improves the signal-to-noise ratio, because when the treble is cut back during playback to restore it to its natural level, noise (which was not boosted along with the signal) is also being cut back. The more accurate the preamp's equalization correction, the flatter the frequency response.

Before the RIAA curve was finally agreed upon as an industry standard, each major record company developed and used its own EQ curve; sometimes this varied even from one record to another within the same company. Amps were sold with multiple "compensators" to de-equalize each major record label's EQ curve.

The Line-Level Input

All music sources other than the cartridge are connected into the preamp at the line-level input stage, thus bypassing both the LP's RIAA correction and the initial gain stage. Tape decks, tuners, and CD players are called line-level sources because their output is sufficient to go directly into the line stage.

This stage also contains all the controls, including the input selector switch and volume control. You want as few controls as possible, for two reasons. First, anything in the signal path—where obviously the controls must be, in order to control the signal—degrades the sound to some degree, however small. The less in the signal path, the less the opportunity for degradation. Second, many controls claimed to "improve" the sound are in fact performing as camouflage, attempting to cover up problems that originate elsewhere in your system or setup and that should be corrected at their source, rather than compensated for later. You have to pay a steep price to cover up what shouldn't be there—you pay once just by having the problem and then you pay again in the further degradation of additional controls. Scratch and rumble filters have blushed themselves right off most faceplates, but there are still plenty of other embarrassments.

A basic selection of controls on a good preamp includes: an *input selector,* which switches between the music sources of turntable, tuner, tape deck, and CD player, and also ensures that the music source signal is inserted into the correct stage of the preamp circuit; *volume and balance controls,* which may be combined; perhaps a *mono switch,* and perhaps a *mute button.* This last is definitely useful—the phone rings or someone's at the door; you can pause briefly and return to listening without having to reset the volume level. Any other controls are really unnecessary and you should think and think again whether you really want them. Their presence may also indicate other areas of compromise that you would prefer not to have to live with.

The volume control is basically a variable resistor that either allows the signal to pass at full volume or throttles it back to the desired level. Turning up the volume does not amplify the signal: The maximum volume is always available, but as you turn the volume down, resistance is increased so that less signal passes through. By turning the dial up again, resistance is reduced and so more volume is released. Treble and bass *balance controls* also are variable resistors.

The Line Section

The output of the control section is fed into this final ''line stage,'' which provides an additional fixed amount of gain, on average about 20 to 30 dB. The preamp's output impedance must be low enough to drive a length of interconnect and be less susceptible to radio-frequency interference (RFI) and cable characteristics. A cathode follower is sometimes added in a tube preamp to reduce output impedance so the signal can drive a longer interconnect. The tradeoff is a more complex circuit and therefore slightly degraded sound. However, if the signal can't drive the cable and is obscured, the preamp's better sound will do you little good. The boosted and equalized preamp signal then travels to the power amplifier through interconnect cables or, in the case of a receiver or integrated amp, directly through the circuit board.

THE POWER AMP

All electrical systems either manipulate information, do work, or both. So far, the signal has only manipulated information and performed no work. Electricity always combines current, voltage, and resistance, but in differing proportions. The particular relative proportions determine how the electricity behaves. In the preamp, the voltage signal kept it traveling through switching devices and cables to reach the amp. Now in the amp, that voltage has to be converted to watts or current in the output stage so it can perform the work of driving the speakers.

The power amp consists of three basic selections: the *driver stage,* the *power supply,* and the *output section.* The driver stage is a voltage-gain stage, much the same as the phono stage of the preamp, and usually has about 25 to 30 dB of gain.

The output section is current gain and supplies a good deal of power either directly to the speakers or, in the case of tubes, to the output transformer, which in turn drives the speakers. In addition to providing power, the output stage must also isolate the amp from the very low impedance of the speaker.

Again, as with the preamp, the power supply (see above) plays a critical role because it supplies the material used to make a larger copy of the musical signal.

The Output Stage: Class A, B, and A/B Operation

Most amplification stages are push-pull operations—two devices or groups of devices working together in such a way that when one device is conducting current, the other is not (or when one is conducting more current, the other is conducting less). The music signal is split in half when it enters the amplifier, each half is separately amplified, and then the amplified halves are recombined in the output stage to emerge as one again. Obviously, there is tremendous opportunity for mishap in how the music signal is split and how it is recombined. This push-pull operation also gives rise to the classes of operation.

No mode of operation is in itself any assurance of excellence, even though a Class A rating is sometimes touted as if it were the equivalent of USDA Prime for meat. Until the output stage of the power amp is reached, all amplifying stages operate in Class A, as this is the most linear mode. Because it is also very inefficient, most amps switch over in the output stage, where the "work" is performed, to a combined Class A/B operation.

In *Class A* operation, the amplifying device, whether bipolar transistor, FET (field effect transistor), or tube, puts out full power at all times, even when no signal is being conveyed. This altogether eliminates the switching distortion, which occurs as a device switches on and off. Most devices increase in distortion the closer they approach to their turn-off region, so if the device is never switched off, then it is always operating in its most linear region.

Class A therefore offers low distortion and also a desirably low output impedance. The tradeoff (you've been waiting for this) is in its great inefficiency, since it maintains full power even when no work needs to be done. In order to ensure that both parts of the push-pull configuration are never off, the idle current, or standing current—i.e., that level of current which exists when a signal is not passing through—must be set high enough to ensure that both devices are conducting throughout the entire wave form, rather than one conducting more, the other less. The power supply of all Class A amps must be capable of delivering *continuously* more than double the amp's maximum output power.

A great deal of the power generated is therefore wasted as heat. Efficiency (power output relative to power drawn from the power supply) is as low as 25 percent. In the earlier amplification stages, this is really not a consideration because no work is being performed. But in the output stage, where currents are high and heating effects significant, it becomes a prime consideration. Class A output certainly keeps the power company happy and your listening room warm—perhaps nice in the winter, not so good in the summer.

In fact, these amps are as expensive to buy as to operate. Class A transistor amps require sizable heat sinks to dissipate the heat so that heat-sensitive circuitry isn't damaged. Class A design for high-powered transistor amps has really been feasible only since the late 1970s, when transistor power devices were developed to have sufficient high temperature reliability and current ability. In some cases, fan cooling, which can be noisy, must be resorted to. Class A tube amps (which all tube amps used to be) don't need heat sinks because the glass envelopes of the tubes radiate the heat directly; generally more output tubes are required and the output transformer has to cope with a high idling current. Class A amps are physically larger and heavier for a given output than Class A/B, which sets a rather practical limit to their power.

In *Class B* operation, when no signal is passing, no current is conducted and the output devices switch off. Since no work is expended when there's no signal to convey, efficiency is very high, about 70 percent (i.e., only 30 percent of the energy put in is wasted as heat). Class B amps can also be smaller and lighter and can provide a much higher power output. Requiring no heat sinks or fans, no heavy-duty power supply, and no high electricity bills, they are generally less expensive to buy and to operate.

However, they also don't sound very good. Their serious disadvantage is severe switching (crossover) distortion. Each time the amplifying device switches on or off, it must travel through its nonlinear region, with some unpleasant-sounding results. Crossover or switching distortion also cause problems with time-delay distortions (see p. 27 re music and time) since there must be a lapse of time, however seemingly minuscule, between a device's receiving instructions to switch on and its actually doing so. Class B operation is considered to have been a major cause of the harsh sound of early transistor amps.

A compromise blends the benefits of both Class A and Class B—this *Class A/B* has become the norm. A standing current is maintained so the output devices never completely switch off, though they do not, as in Class A, maintain full power at all times. The greater distortion of A/B is theoretically put to rights by negative feedback (see below). Class A/B is not one single standard—there are a number of gradations and combinations of A-ness and B-ness possible. The closer to A, the better the sound (all things being equal).

Negative Feedback

Negative feedback was developed in the 1920s by Bell Labs for the purpose of reducing distortion in long-distance phone lines. Phone lines are still not exactly high fidelity—spend an hour on a call and you can get off with a headache (quite apart from the bill).

This is the classic method used in nearly all audio-amplifying devices to reduce distortion, increase bandwidth, and lower output resistance. The more feedback is applied, the lower the distortion. During the late 1960s and into the 1970s, ever-increasing amounts were used in the pursuit of vanishingly low distortion figures. Even today, it continues to be misused to give poor equipment the *appearance* of being good—measured distortion can be brought down to less than 0.01 percent. While this appears impressive on paper, unfortunately, as with so many other specs, the measured distortion is not confirmed by what the ear hears—the ear hears further than the eye can see. For one thing, if the amp is constantly clipping, which is high distortion, then it doesn't really matter a great deal if its measured distortion is low during the small amount of time it is not clipping.

William Zane Johnson of Audio Research describes feedback as "electronic whitewash"—a cover-up rather than a solution. Those who recognize that "less is more" are prepared to accept specs that *appear* to be less good in the knowledge that the overall sound reaching your ears—as opposed to the sine waves reaching the test scope—achieves truer fidelity.

Feedback is an error correction technique. Described very simply, the negative feedback circuit compares the distorted output signal with the undistorted input and applies a corrective signal corresponding to the difference between the two. The result should be that output and input more closely mirror each other and the amp is therefore more "linear." The problem is that you are trying to correct the error on a signal that is already gone. There are also time delay problems, with a blurring especially on the transients, as the feedback circuit takes a moment to latch onto the signal and make its correction. Transistors generally need more negative feedback than do tubes, and generally are given a lot more than is necessary.

In the late 1970s, high-end designers started to turn away from the ever-escalating quantities of feedback. Amps began to be designed to perform as well as possible *before* the application of feedback. Feedback has been found to work best when applied not in massive doses to the entire circuit but instead locally, within each stage.

Exactly how much should be applied remains an issue. While negative feedback reduces *measured* distortion, it trades higher amounts of low-level second- and third-order harmonics for low levels of higher-order harmonics (see Fig. 1). Higher-order distortion is subjectively more unpleasant. If the amp is well designed, and feedback is applied locally, very small amounts will suffice. A few amps have been successfully designed using *no* feedback.

Fusing the Output

Transistor amps are commonly provided with some form of output protection against electrical back pressure from the speakers, which could damage the chips. If a chip receives a signal it is not suited to receive, even if only momentarily, that chip will be damaged and the transistor will fail. Tubes are far less delicate and more tolerant of overload.

The commonest and simplest form of protection is a fuse but, as always, there are tradeoffs. A fuse acts as a resistor so the amp's output capability is somewhat compromised. In addition, the fuse's resistance varies as it heats and cools in response to the current passing through it and this signal-dependent fluctuation can produce clearly audible distortion.

Some designers prefer to do without fuse protection. If nothing ever goes wrong, then this is quite safe. The risk is that a short circuit across the amp's output terminal when a signal is passing through will in all likelihood blow the output transistors. For instance, if you carelessly disconnect the speaker cable from the speakers while the amp is on, and the ends of the cables touch, you will short out the amp. Be very careful. If you suddenly get no output from the speakers, especially if in one channel only, immediately turn off the volume and check the speaker wiring for a short.

Power Output

There is a basic tradeoff between power and sound quality. One can have a clean, lucid-sounding amp of relatively low power or a powerful amp that tends to be prone to more distortions, especially in terms of high-end roughness. More power requires a more complex circuit, with the accompanying increase in distortion. The classic method of compensating is negative feedback, but this solution introduces problems of its own.

There is also a simple inverse relationship between speed and power. If the parts of the output stage are made rugged enough to handle high power, then they cannot also be made fast enough (at least at a reasonable price) to respond very accurately to the music signal. This is another source of distortion.

Power output is really not the big issue it is cracked up to be. It is only one element out of a number that should be considered. If you need to fill a large room, listen at very high levels, or have extremely inefficient speakers, then it may become a primary consideration. Generally, the far more important factors are how the amp sounds when playing the average levels of the music and how harshly it clips when it runs out of headroom at some of the music peaks.

In addition, amps with nominally equivalent power output can display marked differences in the loudness levels to which they are in real life able to drive speakers. There are rated 25-watt amps that can outpower some 100-watt designs.

Drive a pair of Spica TC-50s with a 25-watt-per-channel Dynaco Stereo 70 tube amp (modified by GSI)—the match is beautiful. Several factors contribute—the Spicas are reasonably efficient and don't go much lower than a clean 55 cycles; a 25-watt tube amp is the equivalent in solid state to 50 or 60 watts; and the Stereo 70, like most tube amps, clips very gracefully.

The Spicas are also 4-ohm impedance speakers, unimportant in the case of tube amps, but very significant with transistors. As the speaker impedance halves—from an 8-ohm speaker load to a 4-ohm load—transistor power delivery doubles. So an amp that can deliver 100 watts into the standard 8 ohms will deliver 200 watts into 4 ohms.

The differences in volume resulting from an amp's power output are negligible—a 50-watt amp and a 100-watt amp are almost identically loud. Doubling the power has almost no effect on volume; to double volume, you need to increase the power tenfold. As there are no 500-watt amps, the difference in loudness between 50 watts and the most powerful amp made is insignificant.

Greater power output is less an issue of volume than one of bass extension. Most of an amp's power is used up by the lower frequencies; therefore, a more powerful amp will be able to take you down further, or at least take you down with less distortion. A 100-watt amp with 3 dB of headroom is generally enough to produce a full range down to 30 cycles. However, if your speakers do not go down this far or your room is too small to support 30 cycles of bass, there is little point in having an amp that will produce it (see p. 139). In fact, it is likely to be a disadvantage as, all other things being equal, a larger amp tends to sound less good than a smaller one. A lower-wattage amp will give you just as much bass—since your speakers and room, not the amp, are the limiting factors here—along with probably better sound.

Music does not consist mainly of transient peaks but of a ''mean'' or average; there can be as much as a 20-dB difference between these peaks and averages, requiring as much as a 100-to-1 difference in power. Because the amp must be designed to handle the peaks, it has more power than it needs for the mean and so most of the time, even at fairly high listening levels, an amp delivers only a small fraction of its power output. However, with an average music level of 10 watts you would need 1 kilowatt of power to meet the peaks, and no amp, not even a very powerful one, can provide this. Every amp runs out of *headroom* and will *clip* during the course of the music. *How* the amp clips and then recovers is a very significant difference between amps and is an area where tubes excel. Headroom is the ability of the amp to go beyond its rated power for short durations, in order to meet musical peaks without clipping.

What happens when the amp clips at a transient peak is that the top and bottom of the wave form are chopped off—"clipped"—with the result that large amounts of high-frequency distortion are generated. (On an oscilloscope, you can see when the normally rounded tops and bottoms of the wave form are clipped off square and flat.) An amp clipping is like a singer going beyond the voice's normal range—the voice can go shrill and screechy, which is what tends to happen with solid-state amps, or may go a little soft, as happens with tubes. Though both are distortions, the tube's softness is easier on the ears.

Persistent clipping is damaging to the speaker's tweeter. Clipping transposes low frequencies into higher frequencies, which are then directed to the tweeter. The tweeter, which must be light for quick response, therefore has a very small voice coil, which provides little heat dissipation. If it keeps getting hit by clipping frequencies, the coil will overheat. It won't usually burn out the first time but gets progressively mauled.

With a more powerful amp, clipping occurs less frequently so that tweeter is less likely to suffer damage. Instead, the woofer is at risk of bottoming out with more bass than it was intended to handle. Nonetheless, as a general rule, more speakers are damaged by low-powered amps than by high-powered ones.

Dual Mono and Mono Block

Dual mono is a somewhat loosely applied term and may be confused with *mono block*. Mono block is literally what the name suggests—a complete mono amp, self-contained on its own chassis, used for either the right or left channel, with another amp used for the other channel. Each has its own power supply, its own on/off switch, and its own transformer. The advantages of mono block are the individual power supply for each channel and the lack of interaction between the channels. With good channel separation, and so no cross-talk and smearing between channels, the imaging and soundstage are wide, exciting, and deep. Each mono amp can also be located very close to its speaker, offering the benefit of very short cable runs.

Another approach, which also uses two chassis, is to place the amplifying stages on one chassis and the power supply on another. With more space to spread out in and the heavy power supply off on its own, the designer can use the best components, which usually weigh more, and space them farther apart to minimize any undesired interactions.

Another benefit is better signal-to-noise ratio, because the hum-inducing power supply transformer is removed some distance away from the audio signal path.

Most dual mono amps share the same chassis but the implication is they do not share the same power supply—that each channel has its own. More commonly, there is something like one and a half power supplies, with some parts, but not all, doubled up.

Bi-amping and Bi-wiring

In a *bi-amped* system, two amps are used to drive the loudspeakers, one amp for the bass, the other for the midrange and up. (*Tri-amping* uses separate amps for bass, midrange, and a tweeter.) This requires the insertion of an active crossover between the preamp and amp (see p. 176 on active crossovers).

Bi-amping has two advantages over mono-amping. Low frequencies are kept out of the treble amplifier, thus eliminating a major source of intermodulation distortion and reducing the power requirements of the treble amp. In addition, the bass amp can exercise better control over the woofer cone because the woofer-circuit resistance introduced by the speaker's passive crossover is eliminated.

A drawback to bi-amping (even greater with triamping) is that one can sometimes hear the "seaming" between the two amps—each sonic signature will be heard as being different, lending a slightly different coloration to the bass on the one hand and to the midrange and treble on the other. This can be quite disturbing. So amps must be carefully matched to prevent this from happening.

Using identical amps for top and bottom will eliminate the problem. But there are definite benefits to using a tube amp for the top and a solid state for the bottom. At the low frequencies, a current device like a transistor will give you the control and oomph you need for bass; a voltage device like a tube will give you the best midrange and high end. This is one advantage of a servo subwoofer designed with its own integral amp, like the Spicas, Janis, or Vandersteens.

Bi-wiring represents a less expensive means of achieving similar ends, as only one amp is involved. In its simplest form, it consists of separating the bass and treble sections of a two-way speaker system, then running separate speaker cable to each section. This can reduce blurring of the signal because each cable carries a narrower bandwidth and can be more closely matched to its signal. You can use a cable excelling in bass to carry the amp signal to the woofer, one that excels in midrange and treble to carry signal to the midrange and up. However, your speakers must be set up to be bi-wired.

Bi-wiring presents none of the problems of getting the sounds of two amps to blend really well. *Tri-wiring* can be done with a three-way system.

AMP/SPEAKER MATCHING

This is really a matter of matching efficiency (see below). You wouldn't use a team of Clydesdale horses to pull a pony cart or expect a pony to pull an oxcart. Any speaker that is difficult to drive—inefficient and low impedance—needs solid state and brute-force solid state. An easier load can be driven by either tubes or transistors—electrostatics can sound their best with tubes. OTL (output-transformer-less) tube amps may be best matched with high-impedance speakers—as they give their most power into 16 ohms, half that into 8 ohms, and half again into 4. This is the reverse of bipolar transistors, which double their power with each decrease in impedance—100 watts into 8 ohms will give you 200 into 4 ohms.

Speaker Loudness

There are two methods of measuring how loudly a speaker will play. The "loudness" being measured is more accurately called *sound pressure level* (SPL). When a sound wave is propagated in the air, the pressure of the air at any point will vary above and below the normal ambient pressure; this difference from the norm is the SPL, perceived as "loudness."

Efficiency, one method of gauging SPL, is a measure of acoustic power out for electrical power in. It is tested by feeding in 1 watt of electrical energy and measuring the speaker's acoustic output with a mike placed 1 meter away. This is expressed as dB per watt per meter—for example, 83 dB/1 watt/1 meter. A rating of 98 dB is very efficient, 87 dB is average, and 79 dB is poor. The problem with this measurement is how to establish the 1 watt input—with a sine wave there is no problem, but with music, input varies with the musical frequency.

Sensitivity provides a more accurate reading of SPL made possible by the advent of transistor amplifiers. Transistors behave as a voltage

AMPS THAT MEASURE THE SAME DO NOT SOUND THE SAME

It is a persistent misconception, put forth by the audio establishment, that if two amps measure the same, they will therefore sound the same. This is not true. Amps that measure alike do NOT all sound alike, and amps that measure alike do not even all sound equally good but different. Specs are not an adequate measure of an amp.

Aside from the fact that by the evidence of multiple pairs of ears amps don't sound alike, there are other problems with the notion as well. It presupposes that we have the ability to measure *all* parameters relating to sound. If that were the case, the science of psychoacoustics would be an open book and acousticians would be able to identify exactly how to build a good music hall (sadly far from being the case). Stradivarius's unique violins would no longer be unique: Their measurements having been taken, they could be replicated. But the years of research on Stradivariuses have been unable to match measurements to sound and we remain unable to identify what makes them so different from any other violin, yet so distinctly themselves.

There are too many subtle and as yet unidentified factors that go into signal processing to permit one the certainty that a few relatively crude tests have sufficed to identify all the sonic aspects. Just because the sonic differences do not show up in the measurements—as we presently know how to measure—doesn't mean our ears deceive us. Our own senses are extremely sensitive measuring devices; we give them too little regard and test instruments too much.

It seems logical enough to expect that amps all *ought to* sound much the same—electricity is not considered to have any sonic character, the amp is not a transducer, and there are no mechanical problems to contend with. However, the fact remains that, despite everything, amps do sound very much different one from another. Those who deny this are in the position of the philosopher who concluded that if the facts do not fit the theory, then so much the worse for the facts.

A curious example of the dissociation between measurements and sound occurs with CD players, which have "excellent" specs. Yet the specs of the latest players, four and more generations after the first, are virtually identical to those of the earliest players, which sounded far different. The substantial improvements in sound in the best CD players have not been reflected in the standard measurements.

On the whole, it's a good idea to mistrust what is presented as an absolute. As much as we do know, there is probably as much or more that we don't know about the faithful transmission of sound. So if reality flies in the face of theory, don't deny reality—throw out the theory and think again.

source, maintaining the same output voltage regardless of speaker impedance or music frequency. Sensitivity is measured with a standard input of 2.83 volts (the voltage needed to produce 1 watt dissipated into an 8-ohm resistor) with the mike placed at a 1-meter distance. Sensitivity is restrained by the least efficient part of the speaker system, which is usually the bass. High-sensitivity speakers therefore tend to be a little light on bass.

A typical speaker is only about 1 percent efficient—for example, for every 50 watts per channel of input from an amp, only 2 or 3 acoustic watts of sound will be produced. Even a highly efficient speaker (10 to 12 percent) will put out only 5 watts or so for every 50 watts in.

A 200-watt-per-channel rating for an amp may impress one as being very powerful, but the fact is that it will deliver to the speakers an *average* of less than a couple of watts, with only an occasional peak of 10 to 20 watts. The ability to provide these power peaks is absolutely essential—to gain the necessary doubling in sound pressure level when you go from a quiet passage to a loud orchestral one, the power output must increase tenfold.

Matching amp power to speaker efficiency/sensitivity may require a quality-versus-quantity tradeoff. Often, the better-sounding amps are low-powered, while the better-sounding speakers are inefficient. So while a high-powered amp would seem the best match for an inefficient speaker, this will cost you in the sound quality of the amp (as well as the dollar cost of the amp). On the other hand, using a lower-powered, better-sounding amp with these inefficient speakers will also cost you sonically because the speakers will be less well driven. A good all-around compromise is to use an amp that offers the best sound quality/power tradeoff in its price range, or else to settle for slightly less volume.

Some speakers, regardless of the power put into them, just cannot put out a lot of volume without distorting the sound and/or damaging themselves—this is true of most electrostatics. While low output may be a matter of poor design, it is often a deliberate design compromise, trading off quantity of sound for quality of sound.

Reproduced music is rarely as loud as live music. Different music needs to be played at different volumes—large-scale orchestral needs the largeness of high volume, whereas folk should be played more softly. Music is composed to be played by specific instruments at those instruments' characteristic volumes—the playback level should reflect the original live intention.

On the whole, with modern good-quality speakers (at least with dynamics) and amps, you'll be able to safely produce about 95 dB in a modest-sized room. To put this in context, a (live) orchestra, at the climax of a major orchestral work, and measured from the front rows, will produce about 105 dB (and a 1-watt output). Discos play as loud as 120 dB (hang out at enough of these and you soon won't be able to tell the difference between a department-store rack system and the best system in existence). The average sound level of a voice talking in a quiet room is about 74 dB. Background music is usually about 10 dB lower than this.

A good rule of thumb is to to double the speaker manufacturer's recommended amp power rating, since these recommendations tend to represent the minimum. Small speakers are less efficient and need a larger power amp to drive them. Dipoles also tend to have low efficiency.

Perceived loudness is also a function of distortion—the more distorted a system, the louder it will be perceived to sound. Many people actually turn up their systems just enough that distortion becomes perceptible.

An amp's power rating is not the full story—two amps rated the same can sound quite different in loudness when going into the same speaker. This is because the "test measurement world" of resistors and sine waves is very much simpler than the "real world" of speakers and music. If the sensation of loudness is very important to you, then you would be wise to try to hear amp and speaker together before buying (which is always a good idea anyway).

Speaker Power Rating

A speaker's *power rating* tells you only how much electrical input the speaker can *absorb* without damage to the voice coil, cone, or suspension. It does not tell you anything about how much the speaker can put out. Speakers with a higher power rating are usually less efficient, which is why they need a more powerful amp to drive them.

Too much power can burn out the drivers' voice coils. The tweeter is particularly susceptible since it uses a tiny voice coil and the very fine wire often contains too little metal to carry off the heat generated by the coil. Tweeters can absorb large amounts of power *providing* that it's delivered for only a few *milliseconds* at a time, and that the tweeter has a chance to cool off between signals. Classical and acoustic music, even played loud, is seldom a problem because it consists of peaks and valleys, allowing plenty of cooling-off time between peaks. But rock and pop present a continuous power delivery into the speakers, with very little letup. This is what blows drivers.

More likely to happen with a high-powered amp played at high volumes is damage to the woofer. If you hear some loud clicks, immediately turn down the volume—this is the sound of the woofer cone extending itself to its full excursion and beyond, known as bottoming out. Get the volume down fast enough and the woofer will have sustained no damage. With a low-powered amp, you'll more likely damage the tweeter. More speakers are damaged by low-powered amps than high powered ones because the amp's clipping will burn out the tweeters (see Amp/Speaker Matching, above).

Impedance Matching

A speaker's *impedance* must also be considered in power rating when being matched with a transistor amp. Impedance indicates the degree to which the speakers impede or resist the flow of electricity from the amp. Measured in ohms, speakers are generally characterized as being 4 ohm or 8 ohm, more rarely 2 ohm or 16 ohm. An 8-ohm speaker resists twice as much as does a 4-ohm speaker. This means a transistor amp can put twice as much power into a 4-ohm speaker as into an 8-ohm, which has double the impedance.

PRE-PREAMPS

A *pre-preamp,* also known as a step-up amp or head amp, is a very low noise gain circuit for the purpose of bringing up the level of low-outout moving coil cartridges—as little as 0.25 millivolts—to that of moving magnets—about 1 volt—so the preamp's phono stage can "see" it. Hum and noise are severe problems because of the tiny signal size and its subsequent high amplification.

There are two basic kinds of pre-preamps—*active* designs and *transformers*. Active designs can either be battery operated or use AC wall current. The battery-operated designs, all things being equal, have a reputation for sounding the least good.

Step-up transformers are essentially impedance-matching devices, matching the low impedance of the MC cartridge to that of the preamp's input. There is debate about these—some say they present all the same problems as the transformer in a tube amp; others believe step-up transformers are the best approach because MCs deliver high current, and a transformer is a preferred current-amplifying device. Transformers will, to varying degrees, reduce the speed and transparency of the signal and slightly "mellow" it, like a soft-focus photograph. On the other hand, they tend to sound better than *many* active designs. It is easier and cheaper to build active devices, such as battery and AC-powered head amps, but passive devices are often considered sonically superior.

Active designs are tricky because the signal is so small and needs to be amplified so much, and yet remain otherwise unaltered. A really carefully designed active circuit can sound excellent. AC-operated pre-preamps may be tube or transistor. Tubes tend to sound better, transistors to be quieter. Transistors are increasingly being built into preamps as an extra gain stage. Providing this stage can be taken right out of the signal path when using an MM cartridge, this is a fine approach. It tends to be quieter than either battery or transformer designs.

Keep a pre-preamp well away from the hum-inducing magnetic fields of transformers in your other equipment. Transformer step-up devices are especially sensitive to this. RFI interference must be well shielded against, both by the chassis casing and by careful shielding of interconnects.

EQUALIZERS

Home equalizing of the recording, by adding or reducing bass or treble or otherwise "enhancing" the signal, is a step we generally recommend staying away from. Any additional circuitry the music signal must travel will sonically degrade that signal. If you feel you need to doctor the sound, consider whether what you really need to doctor is your system, not the recording. Get your system working really well first, and then equalize a poor recording if necessary. EQ should not be used like Accent, as a flavor enhancer to mask poor sound quality caused by your equipment, setup, or room acoustics.

Equalizers will *not* give you higher highs or deeper bass. If your system plays down to 50 Hz, then even with an equalizer it will go no lower—at most, the bass will just be exaggerated by playing *louder*, but not any deeper or with less distortion.

Remember also that equalizers are frequency-selective, not instrument-selective. The instruments that need a boost (or a toning down) will get it, but so will the other instruments that don't need it but that play within the same frequency band.

On the other hand, the fact is that an equalizer can render listenable what would otherwise be unlistenable. Just do not rely on it as a Band-Aid to cover up the problems in your system. It is basically no more than a glorified set of tone controls.

THE LOUDSPEAKER SYSTEM

It's ironic that speakers have for so long been exalted by the audio orthodoxy as the "voice of the system" and the primary investment component. Though many of the orthodox would like to deny it, the speaker is in truth the most *undeveloped* component of the audio chain.

Nonetheless, since the earliest days of "hi-fi," loudspeakers have been regarded with an almost mystic reverence. It could even be said that they've become the totem images of the audio world.

In fact, given the way a lot of speakers are sold—and the way a lot of people buy them—one might get the notion that the loudspeakers *make* the music. But obviously they don't: Their performance depends on the quality of the music signal supplied to them. Speakers cannot "improve" on the recording or the previous components, but only reveal what is given to them, and will, like any other component, inevitably add their own degree of further distortion. If *any* audio component has to lag in quality behind the others, it should be the speakers, at the very end of the signal chain.

In all fairness, what a good speaker has to do—mechanically, acoustically, and electronically—is an enormous job that, despite all the technological wizardry of our age, has yet to be effectively addressed. Speakers are unique in the number of factors that affect their performance.

Some are completely beyond the control of the designer—the acoustics of your listening room, the speakers' setup in that room, and the speakers' setup in relation to you.

Others require choosing among tradeoffs—the design must compromise among loudness capability, speed, low distortion, and neutral tonal balance. For example, a large woofer in a speaker will give more bass with less distortion, but it will have less good transient response and so may sound sluggish. A small woofer will respond faster, but will distort its higher frequencies and give less powerful, more distorted bass. Decisions like these are required over and over, each one affecting every other aspect of the design. Different groups of compromises are chosen by different designers; you have to choose which genre of balancing act you prefer and then, within that genre, choose from among the more successful attempts.

So you can see that to build a speaker that functions convincingly is hard enough. To get one to operate on the scale and within the degree of accuracy necessary to realistically portray the illusion of a live performance taxes the talents of the most gifted designers.

This partly explains why there is such an extraordinary quantity of speakers available to choose from—the varieties of distortions and colorations that speakers can inflict are seemingly infinite. Most speakers, unfortunately, do nothing especially well except placate the naïve listener, much the same way that canned soup companies depend on salt and sugar to fascinate naïve tastebuds.

American mass-market companies typically design their speakers for "more"—more detail, more impact, more liveliness. But the only "more" the discerning listener wants is more accuracy and fidelity to the recording. This is not a goal that seems to be recognized by most speaker designers. Whereas the sound of good moving-magnet and moving-coil cartridges and the sound of good tube and transistor amps have been slowly converging over the years toward the mutual goal of accurate reproduction of live music, such convergence among speakers is far behind.

Ten years ago, audio salesmen would ask speaker customers whether they were looking for California sound or New England sound (also called Boston Bland by its nonproponents). The West Coast sound was typified by JBL speakers, with sharp highs, a very "pushy" midband, and overblown bass. The New England sound, typified by (Boston-based) Acoustic Research speakers, was rosier and warmer. Then there's the rather similar "polite" English sound, from a country where speakers are commonly designed to be mellow and easy to listen to. Both New England and English sound are characterized by a somewhat distant or recessed upper midrange and treble, the regions primarily responsible for a component's sounding too hard or too bright. The Japanese tend toward brightness with something of a emphasis on bass. Now the Laplanders . . .

Audio taste buds vary from one region to another, from cultural group to cultural group. Clearly, all these different sounds are designed to be ingratiating rather than to be faithful to the music. Nonetheless, the goal remains a speaker that adds minimal coloration of its own to allow you to hear the music as it was recorded.

Let's pause for a moment to remind ourselves of what we want from speakers. The entire playback system is there to serve the recording, to "unrecord" it as accurately as possible. Playback is not an issue of ''state-of-the-art'' technology but ultimately a matter of the art—music—prevailing *in spite of* the technology. Don't get hung up on razzle-dazzle speakers that promise to perform audio stunts for you—go for the music. You want speakers that perform *with excellence within the limitations of speaker design,* rather than ones that try to deny these limitations and end up achieving only mediocrity.

The most creative and perceptive designers in the high-end audio community achieve their greatest successes when they achieve *nothing*—that is, when they concentrate on designing their components to come as close as possible to having no effect on the audio signal in the way of adding to, subtracting from, or otherwise altering or coloring the recording. In other words, fidelity comes about through striving for transparency. Rather than a voice, then, the speakers would be better described as the *windows* of the system, the final transparent opening onto the recorded performance.

It is extremely difficult to build a speaker that can, with minimal distortion, reproduce the entire audible frequency range (20 Hz to 20 kHz). In truth, it's not only extremely difficult—it has yet to be done. To reproduce the entire audio band is a real challenge; add to this the inherent physical difficulties in reproducing bass notes, which demand that a great deal of air be moved in the room, and treble frequencies, which demand the utmost precision and delicacy to be reproduced accurately. Then consider that these must commonly be reproduced simultaneously, and in multiples at a time. It may be easy enough to pass simple sine waves accurately but quite a different ball game when dealing with the complexities of even simple music.

Take the energy of a kick drum, which at live levels can reach over 25 acoustic watts (the equivalent of a box speaker being driven by a 300-watt amp!) and contrast this with a piccolo, which, along with the piano, produces the highest fundamental of any instrument, at over 4,698 Hz, with harmonics extending out beyond the audible range. Just the fourth-order harmonics are over 18 kHz. These markedly different instruments—drum and piccolo—must be reproduced accurately (at times simultaneously) by the same loudspeaker.

For speakers to reproduce simultaneously the complexities of music, the performance's acoustic space, the ''presence'' of the players, all accurately and without time or frequency distortion, is a truly extraordinary, generally underappreciated, and seldom achieved feat.

CHOOSING WHICH SPEAKER IS FOR YOU

All audio is about compromises and tradeoffs, the striking of a balance among multiple colorations and distortions. *Good sound is the consequence of the tasteful combining of complementary nonlinearities.* Because the speaker is sonically the most backward component, each speaker design will have its own distinctly different sonic signature. Different designers have different listening styles (not to mention business priorities) and so choose different sonic and design compromises.

While no speaker does everything well, there are a small number of speakers across the audio price range that do a few important things very well. The real key to locating which speaker variant (within any given price range) is the right one for *you* is to get to understand *your* listening style.

For example, the major division among speakers is between the ubiquitous dynamic or box speakers and the "high-tech" dipole speakers, like the Quad electrostatics or the Apogee ribbons. In bass impact, power handling, and dynamic range, conventional box speakers can better their high-tech counterparts. Dipoles, on the other hand, tend to reveal more of the musical nuances and remove an additional veil of fuzz and haze. (They are also far more room sensitive, amp sensitive, and limited in selection and price range.) Which of these groups of characteristics is more important to you is a matter of personal priorities.

The perceptive way to begin choosing a pair of speakers is NOT to study specs and reviews but to consider how and where you expect to be *listening to music*. If the answer is that you don't know, not to worry—just keep reading to find out. If you're anything close to a sentient being, you at least have some hidden preferences; these can (with a little patience) guide you to the right speakers for you.

Striking the Balance

The argument is sometimes put forth that because speakers are so problematic, you must invest in an excellent pair, normally taken to mean an expensive pair. Some even advise that, when budgeting for a new system, you should spend half this budget on the speakers. However, read on.

You can't *necessarily* upgrade your system by just adding a better pair of speakers. Yes, changing the speakers in a system often considerably changes the system's sound. But remember, as we continually stress: A *change* in sound, even if at first impressive, doesn't necessarily mean an *improvement* in sound.

So striking the proper balance between the resolving power and tonal qualities of your speakers and the rest of your equipment is fundamental to putting together a good system. Adding excellent speakers to what is otherwise a mediocre system—or superb speakers to what is otherwise a good system—will only cruelly reveal all the system's defects. As a result, you'll be listening to the equipment instead of to the recording—the very thing you want to avoid.

Harry Pearson has long pointed out that the wider you open the window, the greater the *potential* for more muck to fly through. You've got to be careful not to throw the sonic balance of the system out of proportion. Many listeners have frustrated themselves into a state of terminal disappointment by making an excessive upgrade of their speakers.

Nonetheless, mass-fi audio shamans continue to emphasize the transcendent importance of the speakers. Good sound, however, is about balance among components, poise—concern for good sound has to start with the recording and travel downstream from the recording, to the turntable or other front end, to preamp and amp, and then finally to the speakers. If you let yourself be seduced into working from the opposite end by starting with the speakers, you may never progress past boorish sound.

What all this boils down to is that IF the quality of your speakers has to be out of balance with the rest of your system (and that's likely to be the case), then it is generally preferable that the speakers be a little *less* good than the rest of the system rather than clearly superior. Yes, ideally you would want your speakers to be of equal quality to the rest of your system. But unfortunately that kind of neat match is not always so easy to pull off.

Therefore, contrary to classic audio advance, the speakers are NOT where you initially want to sock the better part of your money. In fact, doing that is a major self-defeating investment. As stressed before, the place to make your first sizable outlay is with the transcription source, i.e., the front end—*this* is where getting the music begins. Whatever musical information the front end fails to retrieve is gone and stays gone; no speaker on this green earth can ever bring it back.

Your Listening Style: Audible Wallpaper Versus Concert Style

You won't (it's hoped) know of many people who would attend a concert and read a book at the same time (or crochet a potholder, string popcorn, carve a napkin ring . . .). Similarly, there are a lot of enthusiastic music listeners out there who "attend" a recorded performance the same way they would a live one—when they're listening, they do nothing else except sit in front of the speakers and groove on the music.

To reap the full benefits of this "concert-style" listening, precise speaker setup is essential for a good soundstage and accurate tonal reproduction. And even if you listen more casually, correct speaker setup will still bring you audibly better sound.

Good recordings are good precisely because, among other things, they have been carefully produced to be played back in a specific manner. This means that, if you want to hear the recording in its true and finest incarnation, you have to set up the speakers in a particular way for accurate playback, just as the engineers had to set up the mikes in a particular way for accurate recording. More than likely, this will require some rearranging of your room (see more about this below). Of course, with a group like the Stones, whose music and performances are fantastic but whose recording quality is so embarrassingly muddled (especially considering the kind of money they've had at their disposal), there isn't all that much quality to reveal, even using the best equipment and setup. But still, even with this kind of recordings, what *is* there greatly benefits from the resolving power of a good system.

On the other hand, if you play recordings primarily as background music—what's often called audible wallpaper—then your listening circumstances are less demanding and the advantages of really critical speaker setup are reduced—but still worthwhile. Less precise setup gives you less good sound. At most, you will get only a partial (through probably still engaging) experience of what is happening in the recording. The image is diffuse and crucial aspects of tonal and spatial detail are sacrificed. These effects of poor setup apply even with the world's finest equipment.

The advantage of the concert-style speaker setup is that, with a little extra effort, you not only have excellent background music but you can also, whenever you want, take to your select concert seats and be transported through space and time back to the original recording venue for a private performance. If may be hard to understand what we're talking about until you've heard it for yourself, but it's what J. Gordon Holt is referring to when he talks about his "goosebump test." All we can say is that once you've had the experience, you'll be hooked. And the most important prerequisite to achieving it is *the quality of the setup*. The better the speakers, the more *intense* the experience can be, but the system must be well set up to reveal it in the first place.

Directionality

How you listen should also be a strong consideration in your choice of a "beaming" versus "nonbeaming" speaker. Some speakers are very *directional,* meaning that they beam, or disperse, the sound out in front of them at a fairly narrow angle. When a speaker diaphragm is smaller than the wavelengths it's radiating, sound will be dispersed very broadly, which is the advantage of the point source (see p. 149). As the radiator becomes as large as or larger than the sound waves, then it becomes increasingly directional.

That's why most dynamics tend to offer good dispersion—the drivers decrease in size relative to the wavelengths they reproduce. Most dipoles, on the other hand, tend to beam quite a bit, because of their very large diaphragms. Something of an exception are the Quad electrostatics, which Peter Walker carefully designed to act as a point source.

Speakers with a beamy, narrow, highly directional radiation pattern tend to sound sharper and clearer, offering better imagery but at the expense of a very restricted listening position—sometimes so restricted it can turn into a "listening prison"! Certainly the "sweet spot" is often confined to just one person, which is OK if you "attend" your music sessions and are a solo listener, but if you prefer listening with company or want to hear good sound over a broader area of the room, then it's a problem. Other drawbacks include a limited sense of scale or image size.

Less directional, wider-dispersion speakers energize the whole listening room, providing a good sense of scale and dynamics. However, they can also smear detail and provide poor imaging. Because the whole room is energized, the reflections of your listening room are mixed in with the music signal and may be insufficiently delayed for the ear to be able to distinguish them as separate, secondary sounds. This is known as the Haas effect. The right balance between the arrival of direct sound and reflected sound is essential in making the music come to life.

Musical Preferences

Another important consideration in speaker choice is what kind of music you mainly listen to. Ideally, all good speakers would be able to reproduce the entire audio range linearly, from 20 Hz to 20 kHz, ensuring extended highs and authoritative bass. But this is something that no speaker has yet fully achieved and that few listeners even approach enjoying. Not only is it very difficult and very expensive to design a speaker both full-range and linear, but in addition your room imposes severe limitations of its own. In the meantime, until there is a loudspeaker breakthrough, here are some guidelines in making the inevitable compromises.

Large-scale orchestral pieces, in order to be fully and musically reproduced, demand the more extended bass and highs of wider-range dynamic speakers matched with a good, authoritative amp. The more sound pressure level (volume) and extension you want, the more efficient the speakers you'll need and/or the more powerful the amp.

But the biggest speakers and most powerful amp may still give you wimpy sound if the size of your room limits the bass you'll hear and its cleanness. A small room cannot really support clear, extended bass, even with the fullest-range speaker. Such a speaker may even make matters *worse* by interacting with your room in such a way as to actually increase distortion. In this case, you may be better off with the relative ''bass-shyness'' of a dipole or smaller box speaker.

If you listen mainly to smaller-scale groups, like jazz, folk, vocal, and smaller classical pieces, then the comparative bass-shyness and inefficiency of dipoles and smaller box speakers may not be a significant drawback. Small dynamic speakers often have a sound surprisingly more lucid than larger ones, which will benefit smaller musical groups whose original performance has a corresponding shortage of bass response. A well-designed smaller enclosure has fewer resonance problems and costs less to build, allowing the quality to go into parts of the design other than the cabinetry. Dipoles tend to provide a sense of openness and transparency of sound. But one of the factors to keep in mind with them is their large size and need for placement well away from walls. You must be certain your room (and its other uses) will allow for their proper setup or once again you'll just be wasting your money.

Your Room as the Final Component

How you listen and *what* you listen to both affect speaker choice, but—as you've probably figured out by now—so does *where* you listen. The speaker is not the last component in your system—your room is. How the speakers acoustically couple with your room will determine *their sound in your room,* as much as their design does. In certain ways, the importance accorded the speakers really belongs to the room—many people will mistake what is actually the sound of the room for that of the speakers.

Of course, some would argue that your ears are the final component, but we maintain it's the room because the ears normally offer little hope for adjustment—although who knows what the future may hold in store. Possibly Ed Dell, in addition to his two highly respected periodicals, *Audio Amateur* and *Speaker Builder,* may someday publish a third magazine entitled *Ear Tweeker* (perhaps in conjunction with the *New England Journal of Medicine*).

Just as a speaker cabinet, enclosing the drivers, should add no resonances or colorations of its own, so your room, which is enclosing the speakers, should add minimal resonances—or at least *euphonic* ones. So their positioning, and yours, along with the room's size, shape, and furnishings, can be almost as important to the final sound as your choice of speakers. A normally vibrant pair can be nearly extinguished simply by poor placement.

To have good sound, you really MUST set up the speakers properly—to say this one more time. You must devote as much attention to their placement with respect to the room's acoustics (not its decor) when unrecording as does a good audio engineer when recording. (For details of speaker setup, see p. 203). One thing this means is that NOTHING should be placed in front of the speakers except your ears. Anything in the sound path between speakers and your ears will distort the sound waves before they reach you. This will especially interfere with the small-wavelength higher frequencies. If, for example, you've had one speaker tucked beside the sofa and the other diagonally across the room behind a potted plant, things are gong to have to be rearranged if you want good sound. Equally, just shoving each speaker off into a corner is going to sound little better, even if the sound path to your ears is unobstructed. (Try correctly setting up the pair you're using now—even if they're not very good, you should hear a distinct improvement.)

For the best sound, your listening chair(s) and the speakers should be positioned at the three angles of an isosceles triangle. Some speakers sound best placed closer to the wall, some several feet away. Dynamic speakers vary in their preferred positions with the particular design used—check with the manufacturer and other users.

Dipoles, because they emit sound from the rear as well as the front, must be placed well away from walls, which will guarantee they become a focus of attention. Their placement is far more sensitive to room positioning than that of dynamic speakers. So it makes no sense to buy expensive dipoles that will require a well-tuned room to sound good, unless you (and the rest of your household) are quite prepared to rearrange the room to meet the standards of the speakers.

Where *you* sit in relation to walls also has an effect on the sound. If you're very close to them, you may get excessive reflections. Unless you're fortunate enough to have a separate music room—specifically dedicated to listening—then realistically your speaker system has to fit in with the room's other uses. This means you should first consider speaker size and setup very carefully *before* you go out and fall in love with something quite impractical.

Bass Extension and Your Room

A too seldom acknowledged fact is that room *size* limits the quantity and quality of bass that you hear. Even if you have the most authoritative, deepest-bass speakers in the world, unless your room is big enough to accommodate those bass waves, they'll never be able to develop—it's against the laws of physics. All that you'll hear is a muddy, boomy, muffled sound as the waves bounce off the opposite wall and tumble back on themselves—like ocean waves breaking against a jetty. You need a distance of *at least* 20 feet between speaker and opposite wall in order to support extended bass below a real 40 Hz or so.

Good bass is the most difficult and expensive part of music for the speakers to reproduce really well, if only because of the sheer length of the sound waves—as much as 36 feet between the top of one wave to the next. For a diaphragm to move such a volume of air with minimal distortion is a major challenge. For a room to propagate that large a bass wave—cleanly and accurately—is also no mean feat.

So if you have only a small room, *don't* throw away your money on expensive bass extension—there's no point in paying for it if it only ends up sounding muddy. You also need a powerful amplifier to generate that length of wave. Altogether, producing articulate bass, the only kind worth having, is not easy. Accept from your system, as most experienced listeners do, a bass that is less deep but undistorted.

Most LP recordings don't extend much below 40 Hz in any case. In the case of live music, the very lowest frequency produced by any musical instrument is 16 Hz, put out by the lowest note of an organ. The next deepest instrument, the contrabassoon, goes down to only 27 Hz, and the piano to 30 Hz. Significantly, the fundamental frequencies of these low tones are considerably weaker than their second- and third-order harmonics. For the lowest note on the piano, this means 60 and 90 Hz respectively. Unless you're listening in a very quiet room (normal background noise of even a quiet room is 30 to 35 dB), you won't be able to hear the fundamentals except at high volume levels. It's not the fundamentals but the harmonics that gives us the pitch of these low notes.

As a general rule of thumb, then, you'll probably be doing yourself a favor to concentrate on the midrange and accept having reasonably undistorted bass extension down to about 40 Hz or so, which is actually quite deep. (Most boom-and-sizzle speakers don't go down much lower than around 55 Hz—they just distort the bass in the crossover to "sound" lower.) The Spica TC-50s go down to a *clean* 55 Hz, which is generally quite satisfying.

In fact in most cases, "bass" is achieved at the expense of midrange resolution. A boosted bass nearly always adversely affects the resolution and sensitivity of the midrange—where the heart of the music lies. Poorly designed speaker systems (which are in the majority) deliver bass as a repetitive, thudding, one-note noise—what Sal Demicco calls thud-and-whack sound—not the actual bass notes of real music.

Bass and Listening Levels

Our sensitivity to sound depends on its frequency and the volume at which it is played. When music is played at low volumes, we hear lower frequencies more weakly than the higher ones and much more weakly than the midrange. This means that a lowering of the volume causes an even steeper drop in our perception of the bass. As the volume rises, the low tones and the midrange perceived as more equal in loudness and the ear becomes increasingly sensitive to the higher frequencies. This psychoacoustic phenomenon is known as the Fletcher-Munson curve.

Listening to music at a volume comparable to the one at which it would be performed live is essential to hearing it as it was originally performed. Playing music at too low a volume will cut back on the perceived volume of the bass and make it seem bass-shy. This is not the fault of your speakers or the rest of your system but a function of how we hear.

This Fletcher-Munson curve is why mid-fi equipment commonly has a bass-boost or loudness compensation control to reequalize and artificially increase the bass when listening at the low levels suited to background music. When comparing two components—say, two speakers—it's essential to play them at the *identical* volume to make a legitimate comparison.

SPECTRAL BALANCE AND THE IMPORTANCE OF THE MIDRANGE

Now, having worked out *your* attributes—listening style, musical preferences, room realities—let's consider some speaker attributes. Given that one cannot have a speaker that is at once full-range and truly linear, at least at this stage in speaker design, then it's best to focus your attention on the midrange, where the heart of the music resides. Clear, tight, extended bass is certainly enjoyable and, even more important, it provides a foundation, an underpinning, for the upper registers. Its presence means that the music is more completely represented. But bass at the expense of an accurate midrange is a very poor tradeoff.

In fact, without a good midrange, you cannot have accurate bass. Strike a bass drum and the beginnings of all that sound are midrange and higher-frequency transients, only afterward followed by bass waves, which have a much slower rise time. Without a good midrange, a drum will not sound convincingly like itself, no matter how much bass you have. You may accept it as a drum but only in the same way that you accept Wonder bread's distant connection with the second part of its name.

In addition, *most* LPs don't go down much below 40 Hz and many CDs, which have potentially much lower reach, are nonetheless compressed to leave little below 40 Hz anyhow. So why pay the cost of extended bass when you're not going to hear it anyway?

One of the most critical characteristics of a loudspeaker design is that of balance. A speaker with good *spectral balance*—meaning balance across the entire spectrum of the audio range—will not emphasize or minimize any frequency in the audible range. It's far easier to design and build a speaker that does emphasize a particular part of the audio spectrum, most often either bass and/or treble. While this may sound superficially attractive when first listened to, the ear soon tires of this distortion.

The difference between a successful speaker design and a less satisfactory one is often a matter of how tastefully the designer has managed to roll off bass and treble extensions in order to gain the most linear midrange. It's better to have a system that's balanced, clear, and articulate but a little rolled off on the ends than to have just extension, which in and of itself does not equate with good sound.

The ear prefers a balance between the upper and lower reaches. A system whose highs are extended, for example, sounds unnatural without also having a proportionately extended bass. So to whatever extent a speaker reaches beyond the midrange, it should strike a careful balance in both directions. Consider the BBC's LS3/5A design, which spawned numerous offspring and is now into its second decade as a classic. It has a lot of problems—compressed dynamics, scant extension at either end, not the greatest of soundstages—and yet it has been widely and legitimately acclaimed for its truly musical sound overall. The same is the case with the Spica TC-50, which excels in the midrange and extends bass and treble in a balanced way.

Most speakers are marketed to inexperienced listeners who buy them on the basis of scintillating highs, thumping bass, and sheer loudness, while the midrange is largely ignored. (Loudness is partially a function of distortion—a more distorting speaker tends to sound louder.) Prominent bass and treble are impressive in the store. To the unaware, these can even make a system seem lively, exciting, and powerful, at least for a short listening time, but such emphasis on drama isn't musical. After a few hours (meaning once you've already got them home and you own them), this kind of sound becomes fatiguing, even irritating, something your musical mind rejects even if you remain consciously unaware of or unable to verbalize the problems. "Boom and sizzle," as it's known, may seem enjoyable for background audible-wallpaper sound or singing along in the shower, but it offers little of lasting musical substance. Poor speakers are one reason that many systems, bought with enthusiasm, end up sitting there mute and in the way.

The midrange isn't just a gap between the important stuff in the bass and treble, *the midrange is where the* HEART OF THE MUSIC *dwelleth.* Without a good midrange, all you're left with is the sis boom bah of metallic highs and thudding lows. So concentrate on this "musical majority" and fret about the fringes later. If the system can't reproduce the midrange well, so that the instruments sound like themselves, then neither great bass nor brilliant highs nor anything else is going to compensate for the absent heart.

It is these reaches beyond the midrange that are the most costly to reproduce—either to the music or to your wallet. The economics of speaker design are quite straightforward. The reach of typical mass-fi speakers is achieved at the cost of their midrange response, with exaggerated or distorted heavy bass and hot highs. The reach of an excellent speaker is achieved only at a cost to your wallet—a stiff one. *Or*—providing you choose wisely and set up carefully, you can get the midrange plus a goodly amount of reasonably undistorted bass and treble with simply a good, modest system. This is known as the knee of the curve—you can get right up to the knee with reasonable value for your dollar, but beyond the knee, each small increment of better sound will cost you handsomely. Refinements always cost the most because they are hardest to get just right.

GENERAL THOUGHTS ON LOUDSPEAKER DESIGNS

Now that you're more or less oriented and ready to think about speaker selection, it helps to have some basic understanding of just how loudspeakers work—both in order to choose the right ones for you and also to use them most effectively. *All* speakers work on the same principles, which should be understood first before moving on to the finer distinctions between the two major speaker categories, dynamics and dipoles.

Speaker design is uniquely challenging in that it is at once *mechanical* (the enclosure and the mechanical behavior of drivers), *acoustic* (the air being pushed by the drivers to reproduce sound and room interaction), and *electrical* (the signal from the amp to the voice coil, which acts as a motor to drive the diaphragm/cone and also the crossover network). Each of these elements must be worked out for both accuracy of reproduction and the minimal addition of resonant colorations.

Following the recording playback mirror analogy, the speakers are the mirror image, or inverse, of the recording microphone. Both are *transducers*. Any transducer—from the recording mikes, to the tape head, to (in the case of analog vinyl) the cutting head and playback cartridge, and then to the speakers—is a primary introducer of distortion.

The recording mikes at the original performance receive the live sound waves and convert them into electrical signals. In playback, the speakers must reverse this, receiving the electrical signal from the amp and converting it back into audible sound waves.

But speakers have a much harder job to do than mikes, and do not do it as well. Speaker playback quality has lagged behind mike recording quality for quite some time. Evidence of this is the excellence of the late 1950s and early 1960s RCA and Living Presence recordings, which rival today's state-of-the-art recordings. (That is, when heard on today's playback systems. In their own time, though appreciated, the full extent of their quality went unrecognized by most, because the playback equipment was still relatively crude and could not reveal it.) Mikes, in comparison to speakers, are less backward—they have yielded themselves to intensive research more readily than speakers because the scale of complications with mikes is much smaller. Complications become more extreme as the scale gets larger.

In addition, mikes are essentially *passive* devices, which *respond* to the live sound waves. Speakers are *active* devices—they must act on the air surrounding them to replicate those original sound waves. An active device must add more distortion by its action than does a passive device.

Mass Versus No Mass

Mikes and speakers share a weakness common to all electromechanical transducers: Once set in motion, they cannot immediately stop again in sync with the audio signal. But the problem is more severe with speakers. Because mikes have only to *respond* to sound waves, they have small, light, diaphragms able to react quickly and accurately to the music with low inertia. But speakers have to *reproduce* those same sound waves at their original live volume. To push that much air, the speaker diaphragm must be comparatively large and heavy.

This might not be such a problem if the speakers had to reproduce only a single continuous tone. But music consists of short-lived, or transient, events. And each time the audio signal changes, the diaphragm must respond exactly synchronously—*any* deviation distorts the music. But to respond to a given signal requires changing direction, so the diaphragm first has to slow down to change direction, and then speed up again. Meanwhile, the audio signal has already moved on and is by now requiring something quite different of the diaphragm. So inevitably, the motion of the diaphragm lags momentarily behind the music signal. This diaphragm lag is called *overhang* and results in a muddying and blurring of the sound. It occurs to varying degrees with all driver types and all speaker designs.

Ideally, the diaphragm would have *no mass* so as to be able to start and stop in absolute synchronism with the electrical signal. But this would pose another problem: Without mass, the diaphragm could move no air and no notes would be reproduced.

So—while accuracy of sound requires no mass, reproduction of sound demands mass. Loudspeakers must fulfill both of these two conflicting goals. The usual compromise is to use the minimum amount of mass that still permits music reproduction.

Dynamics and Dipoles

Two quite different, but successful, compromises have developed to address this contradictory ideal of massless mass: *dynamic* speakers and *dipoles* (see Figs. 16 and 19).

Dynamic speakers (also called box, cone, or moving coil type) make up nearly the entire speaker market. They consist of a cabinet; two or more drivers, each best suited to handling a specific limited frequency range; and an electronic crossover to divide up and direct the audio frequencies to the appropriate driver. Higher frequencies are routed to a small, lightweight, low-mass driver, which can respond very rapidly to high-frequency signal modulations. Midrange and bass are directed to one or two larger drivers able to push sufficient volumes of air to reproduce these longer sound waves.

Dipole or panel speakers were actually the first type explored by C. W. Rice and E. W. Kellogg (originators of the modern-day speaker) at Bell Labs back in 1923, but were soon dropped in favor of dynamics—the technology necessary to make them work had not yet been developed. Now, after a long hiatus, they are back in favor again. Dipole speakers, so called because they emit sound from both the front and the back, include electrostatics, ribbons, and magnetic planars. Often, a single diaphragm is used (usually able to cover most but not all of the audio spectrum), which eliminates the need for distortion-producing electronic crossovers or multiple drivers. The diaphragm is a very thin, light tympanic membrane held by its edges to a frame. Its great lightness and flexibility provide excellent high-frequency handling and transient response, while the overall large size makes it possible to move sufficient air to reproduce lower notes.

Two of the major issues in speaker design—handled differently by dipoles and dynamics—are driving the air accurately, and dealing with the back wave that inevitably accompanies the front wave reproducing the music. Each time the driver pushes forward in response to the audio signal, there is an equal rarefaction or back wave. If left uncontrolled, this can muddy up the music severely because the front wave can be sucked in by the semivacuum created by the back wave.

To date, three possible solutions have been developed. One is the open-baffle method of mounting the drivers in a wall so the back wave can never come around to muddy up the front wave. This method has now (understandably) largely fallen out of use. Dipoles let the back wave go its way but delay its arrival at the listening position—this allows the mind to distinguish between direct and reflected sound. Dynamic speakers use the third method, which is to try to control and isolate the back wave by trapping it inside a box.

A Condensed Comparison of Dynamics and Dipoles

We've already touched on the inherent advantages and disadvantages of dynamics and dipoles (see p. 133), but we want to go over the subject quickly here. We assume, of course, that the speakers are well set up and all the components preceding them are good. No dynamic speaker can provide good bass if the front end and amplification stages don't pass on the bass signals well, or if the room is too small to support it. No dipole can be articulate if the front end and amplifiers aren't at least as articulate.

Bear in mind that the following comparative points about dynamics and dipoles are only *guidelines.* Designers work to maximize the good points and minimize the negatives of any given design. Keep in mind also that the success of any speaker depends *equally* on the artistry of the designer and the diligence and precision of the execution. A great design, if sloppily executed, can result in a poor speaker. Jim Cox of New York Acoustics likens speaker building to gourmet cooking—successful design is a matter of fine ingredients meticulously assembled in a balanced, symetrical way, so that no single element in the concoction overpowers any other element.

In the areas of bass impact, power handling, and dynamic range, conventional speakers will almost always be better than dipole designs. They are also more forgiving of room vagaries and, because they're available in small sizes (though these *must* be used with speaker stands), your room's other uses may also be more forgiving of their presence. Selection and price range are also much greater.

But where dipoles generally excel is in their accuracy and clarity. This is for two reasons: The very light diaphragm is able to respond very quickly to musical transients, reducing driver overhang, which muddies the sound; and, probably even more important, dipoles are free of "boxy resonance colorations" inevitably caused by the cabinet of a dynamic speaker. So dipoles are *capable* of being more transparent, open, airy, and articulate than dynamics. (Dynamics always have at least the potential to be better at bass—there's no way to get around the need for mass to move those 36-foot bass waves.)

Whenever two or more drivers are used—whether in a dynamic or to extend the range of a dipole—some *seaming* will inevitably occur where they sonically meet and overlap each other. Visualize dropping a pebble into a pond and watch the ripples spread out in a circle all around. Now drop a second pebble close to the first. The two sets of ripples overlap and distort each other. The same thing happens with sound waves. Even if you don't consciously identify this seaming as a distortion of the music, your musical mind will be disturbed by it. So this is another advantage of dipoles or any other single-driver design—they can be sonically "seamless" because a single dipole diaphragm can be made to function across a broader audio band than can a single dynamic driver.

If a dipole design uses two drivers in order to extend the audio range it can cover, at this point you've reintroduced two of the problems of dynamics: a distorting crossover and multiple drivers. You're still free of the boxy resonances and you've still got the clarity from the quick transient response of a very light driver.

Dynamics as a rule are more efficient than dipoles and will play louder. This counts for a lot if you like to listen to rock, large-scale orchestral music, and other big pieces that really need strong sound-pressure levels to sound convincing. But remember, you have to have a room large enough to propagate the bass waves in order for dynamics to demonstrate this advantage.

Dipoles, in general, are best suited to smaller-scale music. For bass, they can be paired with a subwoofer, though this introduces the problems of seaming and matching the different sonic colorations of two drivers (more about this under Subwoofers, p. 183). They can, however, be easily blown by loud volume (subwoofers somewhat ease this problem while adding other problems of their own).

Dynamics can be blown too, but dynamics are a lot easier to repair—your audio dealer can generally handle it, or a screwdriver and soldering pencil may even enable you to make the repair yourself. Dipoles are not as easily repaired and in most cases really have to be sent back to the manufacturer. And there you are without music in the meanwhile (which can be a long while).

Dynamic speakers are more practical than dipoles as a rule: more efficient; sturdier and easier to repair; less room sensitive and more widely responsive. They also come in a much wider range of designs and prices. Owning dipoles may involve a strong element of audio status seeking. A lot of people who buy them can't even enjoy their advantages because of poor setup, room problems, or wrong amplifier choice.

If you're starting out, dynamic speakers are recommended, unless you have fallen in love with the sound of dipoles and are really prepared to go the distance to get the most from them. Dipoles also tend to beam more, which means the best listening spot, the sweet spot, may be quite restricted and best suited to those who are anti- or asocial in their listening preferences.

Incidentally, of all audio components, speakers *least* lend themselves to evaluation by technical measurements. If you want good speakers, you're going to have to rely on your ears to find them. There's a famous phrase: "I may not know great (*fill in the blank*), but I know what I like." This is one case to which the statement may actually apply. You want to start to learn about great speakers but still hang on to your own ability to determine what you like—and to be able to really distinguish between merely "impressive" sound and an accurate representation of the music. It's how speakers sound to *you,* in *your* system, in *your* room, with *your* music, that ultimately counts—and is really *all* that counts.

Exotic Speakers

Plasma drivers like the Ionovac or Plasmatronic use ions—instead of a diaphragm—in order to modulate the sound waves directly. Their drawbacks, however, are substantial—they are very inefficient and their

LINE SOURCE, POINT SOURCE, AND PLANE SOURCE

The ideal speaker in terms of imaging would be either a line, a point, or a plane source of sound. A *plane source* has never really even been approximated—it would radiate the full range of sound with no boundaries, as if an entire wall were radiating sound. This means there would be no limitation of a sweet spot; instead, the image would remain unchanged regardless of where one listened, and there would be no seaming effects.

A *point source* would be an infinitely small radiator that would provide excellent dispersion of sound all around. Any radiator that is physically smaller than the wavelengths it is radiating will disperse sound omnidirectionally. As it approaches or even exceeds the size of the wavelength, it becomes increasingly directional. (Dipoles tend to beam for this very reason—the size of the diaphragm is larger than many of the wavelengths reproduced). The disadvantage of a point source is that you can get a high degree of reflected sound, and thus confusion and diffusion of the image. For example, a single cone driver radiates in a spherical pattern, so the sound bounces off not only the walls but also the ceiling and floor.

A *line source* is an infinitely tall and infinitely narrow source of sound, thus combing the benefits of a point source in the horizontal plane and a plane source in the vertical plane. Dynamic speakers with multiple drivers, for example, are designed along the principles of a line source—the vertical array of drivers provides height; the decreasing size of the drivers in relation to wavelength reproduced provides good sound radiation. A line source radiates in a cylindrical pattern, meaning that the sound, while it still reflects off the walls, does not also bounce off floor and ceiling.

In terms of efficiency, the plane source is the most efficient because it offers (theoretically) the best acoustic coupling with the room. The huge surface area is more efficient at moving air. A point source is least efficient, having no surface area to move air. A line source, which combines plane and point, also combines their efficiency.

loudness capability is minimal. The other primary disadvantage is that they ionize the air, producing a great deal of ozone, which in the relatively large doses needed for these designs is deadly. A demonstration of the Threshold speaker at a CES (the Consumer Electronics Show held twice yearly—winter in Las Vegas and summer in Chicago) sent designer Nelson Pass straight to the hospital. In a *Wall Street Journal* news piece, Pass humorously reported that his plasma speakers had the three qualities desired by all audiophiles—it was ridiculously expensive, poisonous, and unavailable!! These days Pass uses more conventional speaker designs, which are well thought of. This ozone problem can be eliminated by ionizing an inert gas such as helium, as used by the Plasmatronic.

John Iverson (of Eagle amp fame) worked on a design in the mid-1970s that was to be probably the world's first full-range diaphragmless speaker system. It requires its own very high voltage, monster power amp and operates by phase modulation of alpha particles. Apparently, this speaker works in such a way that even if you plug your ears, the sound doesn't change—the speaker modulates right through to your cochlea. (The military has been *intensely* curious about Iverson's discoveries.)

Surround Sound

The benefit of two speakers and two-channel stereo is not exaggerated right- and left-channel separation but enhanced realism—the possibility of an almost holographic, three-dimensional image, creating a "you-are-there" illusion. But the illusion is only in front of you—stereo really cannot re-create the sensation of being in the hall where the performance is occurring and being surrounded by that hall's acoustic. All the hall's space and depth is around and behind the speakers, while behind *you* is the quite different acoustic of your own room.

Surround sound, in theory, offers a further extension and solidifying of the stereo illusion by placing the hall's ambience all around you. The point of ambience reproduction or surround sound is not just to provide some reverb behind and to the sides of you, but to provide the illusion of the *entire* acoustic field.

Early reflections have proved to be of immense significance in determining the sound of concert halls. The directions from which these reflections arrive (walls, floor, ceiling), their relative strengths, and their frequencies are all critical factors in a room's acoustic colorations. But in two-channel stereo recording, these important details must be "folded into" the front signals, with an accompanying loss of ambience and realism. Surround sound methods of recording and playback, by providing more than a left and a right channel, make it possible to capture more of a hall's ambience.

The first attempt at ambience retrieval was with quadraphonic, or four-channel, sound in the late 1960s and early 1970s. It was a sonic and commercial disaster. Competing quad systems confused and finally drove away the consumer. Recordings encoded on one system could not be played back very well, if at all, using another system's decoder and seldom sounded good if played back with no decoding.

While each present-day system—whether Ambisonics, Dolby surround sound, or any other—is somewhat different, all use the same basic technique. All surround information in two-channel (nonquad) stereo recordings is encoded as antiphase—left minus right channel—which contains all of the stereo image's spatial and depth cues. Even stereo recordings that are not specially encoded for surround sound can be used because about half of a hall's ambience is random and therefore antiphase. The antiphase signal can be extracted from the main stereo signal and fed to the rear speaker(s). In fact, it can be isolated without even the need for any electronics—simply connect an extra pair of speakers in series between the left and right hot outputs of your amp. (This also reduces the load impedance on the amp, so be careful not to push the amp too hard or it may clip—this both sounds nasty and may destroy your tweeters.) While cheap and easy, this is not the best solution—it reduces channel separation of your main speakers.

Surround decoders increase separation between the front and back images by using a rear-channel delay. Some also employ *logic steering,* which enhances separation in all directions. This latter is considerably more complex and more expensive and will not necessarily offer an improvement for your situation.

Unlike signal processors or equalizers, decoders do not "create" ambient information. A false sensation of ambience can be produced with tricks of artificial reverb or echo, relaying the signal through delay lines, or playing with phase, but these tricks won't fool the ear for long. Instead, decoders extract what is already on the recording and help to separate the ambient sounds from the direct sound. Each recording will therefore sound different, according to where it was recorded. Signal processors tend to impose a uniform ambience on all recordings.

Surround sound has come a long way since the fiasco of quadraphonic. We feel it still has a long way to go, at least for reproducing music that is just for listening, however good it may be for video sound tracks. Any signal processing inevitably degrades the sonic quality of the signal. A surround sound system has far more processing than a stereo system—it involves three to six speakers, three to six channels of amplification, a great deal of wiring, and a lot of additional chips. But to a number of musically trained ears, any such degradation is fully compensated for by the benefits of greater ambience.

Surround sound also introduces a new set of questions about music playback. What musical effects are you seeking in your living room—do you want "music in the round" as heard in many movie theaters, or a more realistic concert-hall situation with the music in front and the sound of the hall behind you? What should happen in the case of rock, which is seldom performed live, so that "the music in front and the sound of the hall behind" makes little sense? Is this system good for acoustic music or best suited to "created" and sound track music?

With surround sound being approached musically now, rather than just commercially, it holds promise. However, it is not going to cure any problems with your stereo system. First get the stereo working really well, and only then start worrying about surround sound.

DYNAMIC SPEAKERS

If an international symbol were ever developed for audio speakers, the image used would be that of the dynamic speaker—a box with drivers.

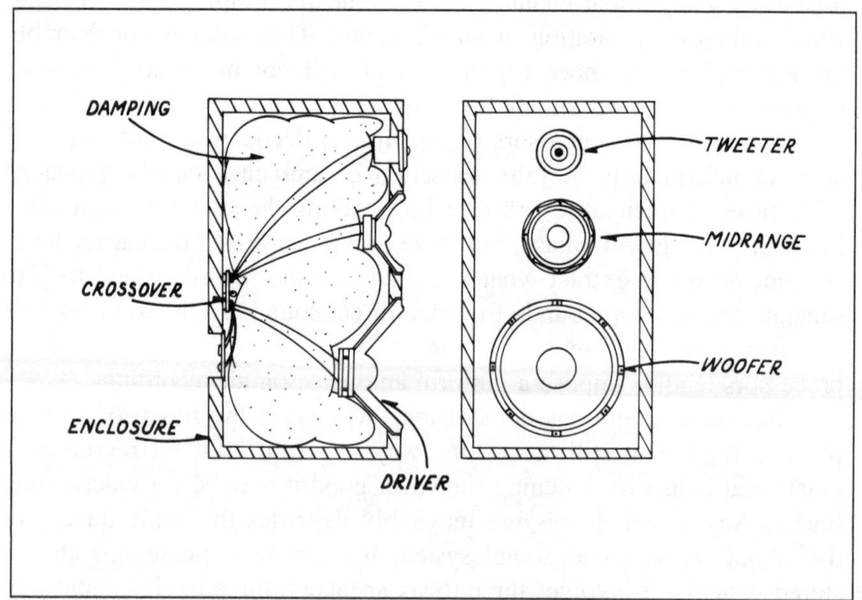

Fig. 16

Found everywhere from TV sets to telephone receivers, elevators, airplanes, bus stations, you name it, these may seem rather routine, old-fashioned, outmoded. Don't be fooled by their unassuming appearance—not only are there some really superlative designs on the market, but dynamics also offer some very significant advantages.

What gives dynamics their ho-hum reputation is that most of the hundreds of dynamic speakers on the market are "cookbook designs," whose manufacturers should more accurately be called box stuffers. They follow a standardized "recipe," using run-of-the-mill cone drivers, routine crossover theory, and marginal-quality cabinet construction. However, what is probably the most expensive speaker system in the world, Dave Wilson's $45,000 WAMM system, is predominantly a dynamic design.

Dynamics, also called moving coil speakers, box speakers, or two- or three-way systems (according to the number of drivers), all combine two or more cone *drivers,* an electronic *crossover* network, and a cabinet *enclosure,* which is normally filled with a damping material such as polyester fiberfill.

Simply put, a loudspeaker converts the electrical energy it receives from the amp into acoustic energy, i.e., sound. The signal from the amp drives the speaker "motor," which drives the attached cone, which drives the air and causes it to vibrate, creating sound. The pressure waves produced in your room should (ideally) replicate the pressure waves produced at the original performance.

A diaphragm has to vibrate thousands of times a second over a very short distance in order to reproduce high-frequency sounds; to reproduce sounds of low frequency, it vibrates far fewer times a second, perhaps tens of times, but must move farther and push a lot more air. The design requirements to respond quickly to high frequencies contradict the design requirements of mass to drive sufficient air to reproduce the long, low-frequency sound waves. So though using one driver to cover the full frequency range would offer many advantages (including no crossover, no problems with seaming, point-source imaging), in reality one needs several drive units of differing size and mass to handle the different frequencies.

In dissecting the workings of a dynamic speaker, it would seem logical to start with the drivers as they actually reproduce the audio signal. But instead let's start with the enclosure and the configuration of the drivers—all the advantages of superior drivers and the best crossover network can be instantly destroyed by a poor cabinet or poor driver layout. These are also the easiest areas for you to spot quickly as problems. If they are not well executed, there's little point in investigating driver and crossover details—unless you have very good reason to think there is still something special about the speakers *despite* their evident flaws.

Bear in mind that speaker design is above all the art of compromise and accommodation, trading off weaknesses and matching elements to achieve maximum symbiosis. What may seem like a strange or poor decision from the outside may have been necessary within the overall context of design, manufacture, and market. While it very much helps to learn the specifics outlined below, the final test—always—is in the listening.

The Cabinet Enclosure

The speaker cabinet is not just there to hide some ugly stuff inside. It's a fundamental part of the design because it helps control the sound waves. A speaker cone moves in and out in response to the audio signal. Each time the cone moves forward, pushing the air in front if it and increasing its pressure (compression), there results an equal and opposite decrease in air pressure (rarefaction) behind the driver. And each time the cone moves backward, the reverse occurs.

The problem is that the compression of air in front of the cone tends to get partially canceled by the accompanying back wave (rarefaction) behind the cone—in other words, the sound at the front is sucked in by the partial vacuum at the back. The result is distortion of the music signal and less sound emitted. So to prevent distortion and even, in severe cases, cancellation, the compression and rarefaction waves must be kept separate.

The most effective method of separating the back wave from the front wave is one still used by a few dedicated audiophiles (which, by the way, means literally lovers of sound, not lovers of equipment, though the meaning is often bastardized by labeler and labeled alike)—mounting the drivers in a wall. This is called an *open baffle* and ensures complete separation of compression and rarefaction waves. (It also very effectively eliminates any problems of boxy reasonances.) Unfortunately, an open baffle has to be BIG—to isolate a 50-Hz wave form (a level of bass that most audio systems can reproduce) the baffle would have to be 11 feet across. It's also kind of hard to set up your living room walls at the proper angles to provide a good stereo image! This solution was more popular among hobbyists back in the days of mono systems.

The more usual method of preventing the front wave from being sucked in by the back wave is to sequester the back wave in a box—i.e., mount the drivers in a cabinet. An enclosure is essential for the woofer and valuable for the midrange, though the tweeter can be left exposed, as the treble waves are so short that the drive unit itself acts effectively as a baffle. You can't see a tweeter move and in fact can barely even feel it tickling you if you touch it. (By the way, it's generally not a good idea to finger the drivers—you can inadvertently dent one or leave greasy fingermarks, which can actually alter driver response.) However, mounting the tweeter in a box may be a good idea to help protect it against acoustic vibrations.

Midrange and tweeter drive units are often self-enclosed in the back even before being mounted in a cabinet. Nonetheless, they should be mounted in subenclosures separate from the woofer; otherwise the woofer's back wave will interfere with the action of the smaller midrange and tweeter.

Boxing in the drivers neatly takes care of cancellation and antiphase (back wave) distortion but introduces two drawbacks of its own. The cabinet, excited by the back wave and the motions of the drive unit, contributes its own music-distorting resonances (''boxy'' colorations), and also greatly reduces efficiency.

Efficiency is reduced for two reasons. An obvious cause is that half the sonic energy produced by the speaker (the back wave) is trapped inside the enclosure and so doesn't contribute to the acoustic output. The other reason is that the entrapped air acts as a spring cushioning the driver, making it harder to move. The cone in effect is made stiffer and so harder to drive. That's why a driver in a sealed enclosure needs more electrical (amp) power to produce the same amount of acoustic power (volume) than that same driver in its ''free air'' unenclosed state. The crossover network further loses efficiency because the signal traveling through capacitors, resistors, chokes, wire, meets resistance and so some of its energy gets lost as heat.

Dynamic-loudspeaker efficiency is very low, ranging from 0.1 percent up to about 1 percent for a high-efficiency speaker. And it's usually in inverse proportion to the smoothness of the response—in other words, the unfortunate rule of thumb is that the smoother the frequency response, the less efficient the speaker. All loudspeakers inherently have a lot of distortion—from the enclosure, the drivers, the crossover network. Good speaker designs absorb these distortions either electrically (in the crossover network) or acoustically (by cone and enclosure damping), but this also absorbs sound. The more distortions are absorbed, meaning the better the loudspeaker, the more sound is also absorbed, reducing its efficiency.

On the other hand, enclosing the drivers in a box is also the best way to make a loudspeaker give a large volume of sound in a small area. One reason is that if the back wave isn't isolated you won't be left with much of a front wave either, and clearly half a loaf is better than none. The other reason is that once the driver is sealed in a box, its back wave or rarefaction has to move only a very limited amount of air, instead of a whole roomful of air.

The enclosed air also acts to damp excessive cone resonance. Peter Moncrieff offers the analogy of the damping pads on a piano. Press the damper pedal (which lifts the dampers from the strings) and run your finger up and down the keys. The strings keep vibrating long after the hammers hit them and together soon create MUD. The damper pads prevent excessive vibration. Similarly, the air pressure in the enclosure actually helps to dampen and reduce distortion, especially in the low frequencies.

Unlike musical instruments, speakers are *re*-producers of sound, NOT originators—they should introduce no sound of their own. A box that does is a bad enclosure. But ALL cabinet enclosures vibrate in response to the drivers—you can feel this with your fingertips when the speakers are playing.

Even though the vibrations are small, much smaller than the motions of the driver diaphragms, the cabinet's surface area is greater than that of the diaphragms. In a poor enclosure, the total cabinet output can even exceed that of the drivers at certain frequencies. The cabinet resonances continue, in effect, "talking" after the drivers have stopped. This results in blurring, overhang, compromised detail. Cabinet resonances also introduce new frequencies that weren't in the original music. Our ears receive all sounds through vibrations in the air—both the intentional vibrations caused by the audio signal and the unintentional by-products from the enclosure. The ear and brain cannot receive the one and refuse the other.

Historically, in the early days of recorded sound, speaker enclosures were *supposed* to play an active part in the sound of a speaker system. A great deal of effort was put into building the enclosures. Then Edgar Villchur came along with the small sealed box enclosure, at which point it seemed that the enclosure was nothing more than a simple box with its air volume being the only important variable. Cabinets came to be viewed as passive and solely decorative devices.

However, it had been demonstrated that identical drivers and crossover network in different enclosures sound quite different. Celestion took the seemingly outrageous step of selling an existing speaker system simply repacked in a different enclosure and priced much higher when it introduced the SL-6. But this "more expensive box," made of Aerolam, clearly demonstrated the vital impact of the cabinet on the sound of a speaker. The enclosure is not passive; it does play an active role in coloring the sound of the speaker, and *this is undesirable.* A lot of work is being done to eliminate the sound of the box while retaining its active role in segregating front and back waves and generating bass.

Most cabinets are veritable rattletraps of vibration. Rap the cabinet with your knuckles—the less resonant it sounds, the less distortion it will introduce to the music. You'll inevitably hear some resonances, but listen for a tighter, higher note that will interfere less with the music. Most cabinets, where they should produce a solid *nick-nick* sound, make instead a hollow *boink-boink.*

Cabinet distortions can be reduced by cabinet *rigidity,* which is determined by a combination of choice materials, shape, and solid construction, and by *damping* the back wave inside the box.

Rigidity: Materials, Shape, and Construction

Just about all cabinets are made of plain old particleboard, usually covered with a wood veneer. Particleboard's resonance is quite well damped because it's made up of lots of little chips, which all resonate differently. Also, unlike plywood, it has no voids or poorly glued layers that can rattle. If the cabinet is well put together and securely braced inside, this kind of material can make a perfectly good and economical enclosure.

Exotic cabinet materials are being experimented with, to reduce resonances further by maximizing rigidity. As rigidity increases, it raises the resonant frequency and reduces its amplitude (sound volume). When you knock, it has a higher tighter ring that dies away more quickly. The higher the resonance, the smaller the resonating wavelengths, and so the more easily they can be damped away with fiberfill.

In cabinet materials, just as in turntable design (see p. 38) and equipment setup bases (see p. 219), there is the same duality of approach about how best to deal with vibrations and resulting resonances. The proponents of mass damping exploit the fact that high mass acts like a sonic sponge to dampen and actually absorb resonances. Also, mass can drive the resonance way down to below the speaker's ability to reproduce those frequencies. This can work on a two-way system that doesn't go down very far. The opposite philosophy recommends a light and very rigid, well-braced cabinet on the premise that the less mass involved, the less material there is to store the resonant energy, while rigidity raises the resonance.

When properly executed, both contrary approaches are equally valid for controlling resonance. The minimal-mass approach offers in addition practical advantages in shipping costs and maneuvering during setup.

Rauna and a few other speaker companies, mainly in Denmark, use a heavy, extremely rigid, poured-cement compound. Several companies have been exploring Benelex, a dense, rigid, and quite heavy material that when rapped sounds almost like china—a nice high note. It was developed by the Masonite company during World War II as a steel substitute.

Honeycomb materials offer the desired combination of light weight and great rigidity. B&W has developed a honeycomb enclosure material called Matrix, which is an interlocked grid of very stiff cross-members within the cabinet, braced at closely spaced intervals, and filled with acoustic foam. Celestion employs the special Aerolam, a lightweight and superrigid honeycomb structure of aluminum borrowed from aircraft construction by Celestion's designer Graham Bank.

When he temporarily moved over to Wharfedale, Bank experimented with laminates as a less expensive alternative to Aerolam. The advantages of sandwiches, or laminates of several different materials, is that each layer has its own acoustic characteristics. Because different materials transmit different sonic frequencies, laminates are more likely to be acoustically opaque at all frequencies. They can have a very high stiffness-to-mass ratio, offering a combination of light weight and rigidity.

But—unless a cabinet is well constructed, even the best material will be of little worth. And while one would suppose that any manufacturer aware enough to use a special material would use it correctly, this isn't always true. Double check for yourself. The box must be rattleproof and airtight. Even the smallest air leak can cause noise and, if sufficiently severe, can reduce bass. All joints should be glued and screwed. The cable entry should be well sealed and drivers mounted with a flexible rubber gasket between driver and cabinet and then well tightened down. It's a good idea to retighten these screws periodically as the constant vibration tends to loosen them up over time.

Shape can also greatly improve rigidity and reduce sonic colorations. The conventional rectangle is the easiest to manufacture, ship, and inventory. The problem of boxy colorations could most effectively be dealt with by *not* using a rectangular cabinet. Cylinders and spheres don't have the resonance problems of boxes. All else being equal, a tubular or half-tubular cabinet will be sonically superior to the rectangle—curved walls are inherently more rigid and therefore less resonant. Also, what musical instrument have you ever seen built in the shape of a box? The resonances set up by boxes are particularly disharmonious and unmusical.

Some cabinets are tapered, either with all four walls narrowing toward the top (a style Ken Kessler christened the Truncated Pyramid), or else with just the front baffle sloped. Tapering the box constantly alters the dimensions and has much the same effect as tapering a tonearm—stray resonances, if distributed over many frequencies, can't build up. In a triangular cabinet, because the front and back walls aren't parallel, the back wave is broken up rather than being reflected back to the driver and interfering with its action. (This is why a cube is an especially poor shape—all dimensions are the same and each back wave ricochets over and over again.) Sloping the front baffle also physically time-aligns the voice coils of the cones.

Damping

Now that the back wave is securely entrapped inside a minimal-resonance enclosure, what do you do with it? Left untamed, the back wave would swoosh around inside the box, setting up all kinds of spurious resonances. It would also reflect back into the speaker cone and interfere with the music signal.

Stuffing the box with damping material will absorb some of the resonances and prevent others from developing. The back wave's energy, by pushing the stuffing fibers against each other, is converted into friction and lost as heat, which does no sonic harm.

Two of the best damping materials are considered to be long-staple (long-fiber) wood and long-staple polyester fiberfill—they're very springy and have millions of tiny fibers, which interlock and cause friction. Long-staple wool is particularly prized because it absorbs sounds at low frequencies better than any other known damping material. It's also very expensive. Fiberglass and foam are usually less effective than either wood or polyester, and impart a "drier" tone. John Bau, Spica's designer and all-round mensch, likes 100 percent cotton batting best.

Sometimes you can add stuffing yourself or change the kind of stuffing used. But you must be careful—you can lose the bass by over-damping the resonances between the diaphragm and air compliance, and end up just absorbing too much sound.

Enclosure Design and Bass Loading

Enclosure design doesn't end with entrapping the back wave in a rigid box and then damping it to minimize resonances. Enclosing the drivers in a box is also the best way to make a loudspeaker give a large volume of sound in a small area because it ensures that the sound wave created by the driver has a chance to propagate, rather than being sucked in by the vacuum at the back of the driver.

While the open baffle or hole-in-the-wall approach mentioned earlier is the most effective, a more conventional and useful variation is to mount the drivers in a totally enclosed box (TEB). This is often called an *infinite baffle* because it separates and isolates the driver's back wave from the front wave as if it were an infinitely large baffle.

The disadvantage of this design is that the enclosure must be quite large, otherwise the enclosed air trapped inside the cabinet tends to behave like a spring pushing against the driver. The "stiffness" of this spring raises the resonance of the drive unit, meaning that the frequency at which it will naturally resonate is pushed higher. (Remember—as in building the cabinet, increasing rigidity raises resonant frequency. This is great when you want to get rid of the cabinet's distortions but not so good when you want to produce sound with drivers, as you'll see when you read on.)

All drivers lose the ability to produce sound below their resonant frequency point, so the higher that resonance point is pushed, the less bass will be reproduced. (Again, this same principle applied to cabinet building is great because there you *want* the maximum rigidity/stiffness to push the box's resonant frequency as high as possible so it cannot reproduce sound below that point.) For small boxes, the stiffness of the enclosed air raises the driver's "free-air" (unenclosed) resonance by a factor of *two to three times*. That's why speakers for a long time were very large boxes with minimal air stiffness.

This was the situation until Edgar Villchur figured out a way to take advantage of the spring of the confined air in a smaller box, and designed the *acoustic suspension* enclosure in the mid-1950s. (Somewhat reminiscent of Henry Ford also making use of what he could get for free—he bought his engines from the one company that would agree to crate them to his precise specifications. When the crates were carefully disassembled, they were ready-cut to perfect size to be transformed into the floorboards for his cars. By a little foresight, he'd secured for himself both free lumber and free labor.)

Getting back to Villchur—founder of the Acoustic Research speaker company, and later creator of the venerable AR turntable, he experimented with reversing the compliance ratios of the box-confined air and driver. Instead of partnering a stiff driver with easy-going, compliant air (i.e., a large box), he matched a floppily suspended, compliant driver with a small box in which the confined air acted as a stiff spring.

With a very loose compliance, a smaller driver is able to move more air because of its longer throw. "Floppy" compliance is set by the *surround,* meaning the flexible rubbery lip around the cone's edge that seals diaphragm to basket. This surround largely determines how far the cone can move in its excursion or *throw*—the distance it can travel in response to the audio signal—and also how compliantly and easily the diaphragm moves. A smaller driver is thus able to produce as much volume and bass as a standard-sized driver in a larger cabinet.

What restores the cone to its resting or "neutral" position in between excursions, without a stiff surround to do it, is the stiffness of the air in the box. Some claim the air's "spring" provides a more linear restoring force than can any mechanical cone suspension.

In addition to the practical benefits of costing less to produce and taking up less space, a smaller speaker also has inherently fewer resonances because the smaller panels for the cabinet walls are more rigid. The original drawback to this design was its poor efficiency, so acoustic suspension speakers required a more powerful amp to drive them. This is really no longer true.

Villchur's timing was excellent. When stereo was introduced shortly thereafter, necessitating two speakers instead of just one, the demand for a small speaker cabinet that would take up less room (at less cost) was high and AR was ready.

One thing a small box has a great deal of difficulty reproducing, however, is bass. There is an analogy likening a bass driver to a canoe paddle. As the frequency to be reproduced gets lower, the paddle gradually changes into an ever smaller teaspoon, whereas the ideal would be a paddle that grew larger and larger. The remedy is either to use a bigger paddle, or else more paddles, or to sweep further with each sweep of the paddle. This last is the idea behind the design of a *bass reflex speaker*.

The ported (turned port) or bass reflex speaker, often used for small two-way designs, makes use of the back wave to actually *reinforce* the front wave, thus strengthening bass but also decreasing speaker efficiency. In its earlier incarnations—and even now when poorly designed—reflex speakers tended to have a boomy rather than better bass, and inferior transient response.

A vent or port in the front (or sometimes back) of the cabinet releases the sound waves (back waves) generated from the rear of the drivers. Routed back up to the cabinet port, the back wave arrives *phase inverted* just in time to add to the compression wave. Because it is phase inverted, it doesn't cancel out but instead reinforces the front wave and improves flat frequency response. Because the driver is moving more air, it can reproduce deeper bass—but at the expense of efficiency, precisely because it does have to move more air. In fact, any small speaker can retain halfway decent bass only at the expense of efficiency/sensitivity.

The port is positioned in the back rather than the front of the cabinet for two reasons. The phase-inverted sound wave inevitably causes some distortion, which is somewhat masked by the port being pointed backward. Adding a port to the front baffle would further weaken it and increase resonance. The baffle is already weakened by the driver holes and is subjected to a great deal of driver vibration. Two ports may be used to double the benefits of sound reinforcement.

What must be very carefully tailored with this design is the resonance of the enclosure. Any vented enclosure has its own particular resonance. The bass reflect design is in effect a variation on a Helmholtz resonator with a driver installed. When you blow across the mouth of a glass bottle, that tone is its Helmholtz resonance. Similarly, the box's resonant frequency is determined by the internal air volume and the size of the port hole. The vent is designed to tune the cabinet to the driver's resonance so the air resonating in the enclosure will augment the driver's low-frequency acoustic output. In some designs, the vent is covered with a *passive radiator*—sometimes called a drone cone. Though this looks like a driver, it has neither voice coil nor any electrical connection to the amp. It's part of the venting system and helps to tune the port in very small enclosures.

Ported cabinets have a tendency to be less resonant and therefore have less distortion than completely sealed cabinets because less pressure builds up inside the cabinet. A curious detail—some designers believe that the wood of fully sealed, infinite baffle cabinets actually deteriorates more rapidly because the shock waves and pressure buildups gradually pulverize the molecular structure of the wall material. One can only speculate on how long this might take to have any sonic effect.

Transmission line cabinets are the third—and least common—basic dynamic design. Also called folded port or labyrinth, this is essentially a tunnel folded back and forth on itself a number of times and comes the closest in its effect to an open baffle. Any pressure buildup inside the box is dissipated in the well-padded labyrinth, and the cabinet is extremely well braced against resonances because of the tunneling—both these factors minimize colorations. Some say this is the most accurate way to propagate bass, but transmission lines tend to be complex, large, and expensive speakers. Irving ''Bud'' Fried is one of their major proponents and has done much to promote them.

Driver Geometry

Believe it or not, how the drivers are mounted on the front baffle of the enclosure is sonically just as critical as the quality of the cones, the crossover, or the enclosure. Misplacement will distort the sound and damage imaging, regardless of how great the other elements of the design are. Each detail is interdependent with all others, from the scale of wire, to components, to system assembly, to the setup and the room.

Baffle Diffraction

This is a problem that has long been recognized, is easy to solve, but remains too often ignored. What happens is that a sound wave generated by the drive units spreads out across the front of the surface until it comes up against the cabinet's edge. At this point, instead of smoothly traveling across the edge and continuing on, it breaks up and scatters. The sudden ''step'' off the edge causes a reradiation of the sound, at a lower level and delayed in time. This is a particularly severe problem with the critical mid- and high frequencies. The diffracted sound radiations are out of phase with the original sound and can cause phase cancellations, alter the frequency response, and the obscure low-level detail that conveys acoustic information and solidifies the image. It's easy enough to eliminate the problem by carefully contouring the baffle edges. Another approach is to put a very narrow front on the cabinet so only the highest frequencies are supported by the baffle. Slightly rounding off the edges is then sufficient. All edges in the sound path should be strongly rounded, sharply beveled, and/or foam or felt padded. (Be sure also that *nothing* in your setup protrudes over or even comes flush with the front baffle of the speakers, such as a shelf, as this too will cause diffraction.)

Driver Array

How the drivers are positioned can also have a strong effect on sound. As discussed on page 149, two of the ideal and strictly theoretical speaker designs are the infinitely small point source and the infinitely long and narrow line source. Sound radiating from a single point source is less subject to phase shift and interference effects than multidriver systems. Physically a point source more closely resembles the physical action of the mike that captured the sound.

A line source combines the theoretical ideal of a plane source (which radiates to the full range of sound with no boundaries) and a point source. It is a plane source in the vertical, as the array of drivers covers (ideally) the full audible frequency range, and it is a point source in the horizontal, thereby offering the advantages of excellent dispersion. So drivers in multidriver systems are best positioned vertically, rather than side by side. A midrange and tweeter set one above the other in line source configuration will sound far better than these two side by side. This latter might seem to approximate point source benefits, but in fact produces "venetian blind" aberrations in the stereo image. The listener MUST be equidistant from ALL drivers in order to hear the music correctly phase aligned and to receive a good stereo image. Vertical alignment provides a phase-aligned window that is reasonably broad horizontally to allow a realistic listening spot.

Some speakers use a "multiple-array" configuration, replacing one large driver with several smaller ones (all of the same size) wired together. They move the same volume of air but have the quicker transient response typical of smaller drivers. In addition, multiples provide a larger wave front than a single big driver, and so greater volume and the ability to handle greater power. Any driver has a lower distortion and flatter response when working at a power below its rating. With power divided up among a quantity of drivers, in theory small-driver arrays should have a lower distortion and smoother frequency response.

On top of this, when drivers are mounted close together, each cone helps to "load" the other. With this mutual loading, two identical speakers close together can theoretically radiate four times the power at low frequencies that a single driver can. This allows the use of smaller drivers with light cones, which will have better transient response.

How the drivers are positioned in relation to the baffle front of the speakers also has a sonic effect. In theory, symmetrical positioning is more like a true line source. However, symmetry may double all resonances caused by baffle diffraction because these occur identically on both sides of the drivers. If, however, the drivers are staggered, there will be more different kinds of resonances but, not being doubled, each will be of lower amplitude and therefore less likely to be noticeable.

Time and Phase Coherence

The importance of time and phase coherence (phase response) has been increasingly recognized during the past decade. The notes coming out of the speaker must emerge with their original time character intact. If the treble and bass notes go into the speaker in a certain time relationship, they should come out to your ears the same way. A difference of microseconds between arrivals of the high and low components of the signal smears it in time and alters the music. Just as you want an orchestra to play together, you want all the drivers in a multidriver system to begin to speak at the same time. Time and phase distortion is a *major* cause of listener fatigue.

Dahlquist, B&O, and KEF did a lot of the early research in this area. The Dahlquist DQ-10 brochure waxed quite eloquent on the subject. "If time warps, reality warps. Our impression of the world—and of the music—is distorted. Uncomfortable." Time is the cue that allows us to judge distance, space, and size. When frequencies reach our ears in the wrong order, even if the "wrongness" is a delay of microseconds, our musical minds are disturbed. We know, through our daily experience with live sounds, what are the proper relationships of phase, frequency, amplitude, and decay in recorded sound. When any of these relationships are off, then the sound is not real, not right.

Speaker phase coherence is attained in the crossover network,

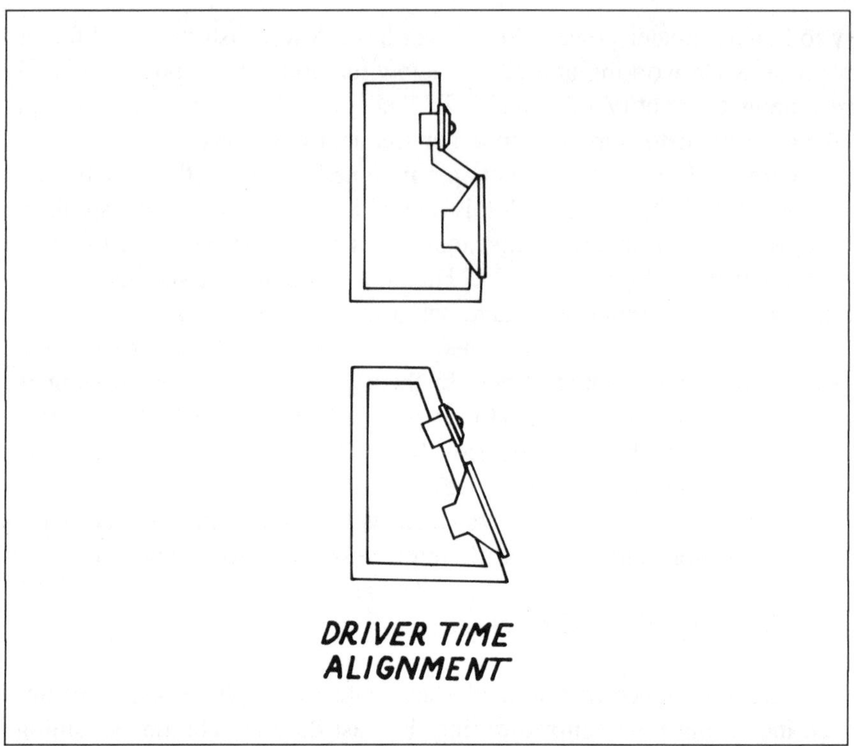

Fig. 17

through which all the audio frequencies must travel in the same time. Time alignment is best achieved by driver placement. If this final physical time alignment is wrong, then any trouble taken to ensure phase coherence was a waste—wrong time alignment negates proper phase.

Most dynamic speakers don't provide time alignment. The drivers are mounted by the front edges of their cone on a common vertical baffle, ensuring time *mis*alignment. Because the woofer's generating system—magnet and voice coil—is quite a few inches farther away from you than the tweeter's, its acoustic output has a longer distance to travel to reach you. The woofer is already further behind in time because of its greater weight and more sluggish response to the audio signal.

Proper time alignment is attained by physically aligning the *acoustic centers* of the drivers so they are all equidistant from your ear. This can be done by sloping the front baffle of the speaker. The voice coil is the source of the signal; the cone is only the volume booster. When correctly aligned, the voice coil of the tweeter will be located behind the woofer's.

While poor time alignment may be compensated for in the crossover, this is much less satisfactory than just physically time-aligning the voice coils. There's really no reason to complicate the crossover, which inevitably adds sonic degradation.

Cone Drivers

Ah, finally, you say, we're getting down to the heart of the matter—the drivers. But take note (especially those of you who've skipped over the preceding and jumped here directly): The best drivers in the world won't sound much different from the worst if they're put in a poor box or arranged incorrectly. Since the quality of the cabinet design and that of the driver geometry are a lot more apparent than the quality of the drivers, focus on these considerations first.

Cones are used in everything from the cheapest portable transistor radios to multithousand-dollar speakers. The most efficient driver yet designed, the cone is in effect a motor connected to a pistonlike device that generates enough "push" to drive the air.

Working on the electromagnetic principle, a cone consists of a simple motor assembly made of a permanent *magnet* that produces a strong magnetic field around the *voice coil,* simply a coil of wire fixed to the neck of the cone-shaped diaphragm made of a special paper pulp or plastic. When an AC signal from the amp passes through the voice coil, this produces a magnetic field around the coil that builds up and collapses in response to the frequency of the current. This field interacts with the permanent field of the magnet to apply force to the coil. The coil moves in response to the AC frequency and the attached cone is moved backward and forward in sympathy. The magnetic force varies in strength according to the current going through the coil, the length of the wire in the coil, and the intensity of the magnetic field of the permanent magnet. Ideally, the sound waves should exactly correspond to those captured by the recording mikes at the original performance.

The cone shape is chosen for its rigidity, enabling the driver to serve as a piston pushing relatively large volumes of air in response to the audio signal. It is made usually of paper pulp (preferably "doped" or painted with liquid plastic) or thin plastic (metal is rarely used). The cone profile is usually curved because, like a sail, this allows it to push more air and also helps to control resonances. The exact shape of the curve is a complex design issue. Cones that are slightly dished (concave) tend to behave better than straight-sided ones. Shallow cones also

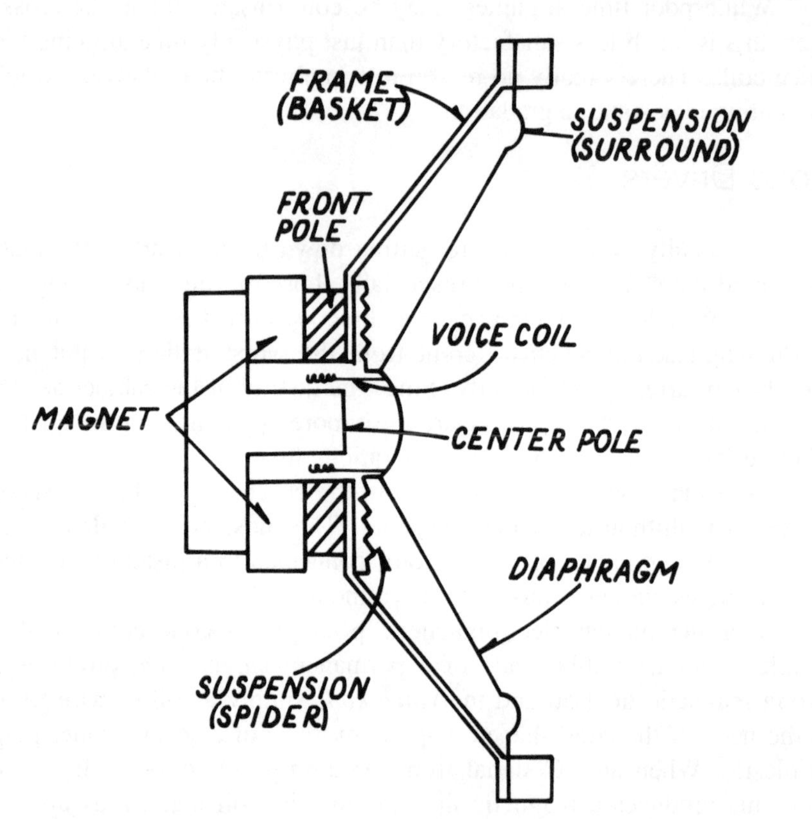

The diaphragm, mounted on a strong metal frame, or *basket,* it is supported at its wide end by a flexible gasket or *surround* and at its apex by a device called the *spider,* which keeps the voice coil centered in the magnetic field. The surround provides a flexible airtight seal between diaphragm and frame, and also terminates or dissipates bending waves set up in the cone. In any driver's upper-frequency range, the cone starts to flex instead of acting like a rigid piston. The waves of flexing travel outward to the outer edge. Unless they are effectively damped here by the surround, they will bounce off and be reflected back onto the cone. Not only will they continue to radiate their own sound but they'll also interfere with the new musical information traveling out along the cone. So the surround is not just a neat way of joining basket and diaphragm but also plays an important role in preserving a driver's transparency and subtle detail.

Fig. 18

tend to be more efficient radiators than deep ones, allowing better dispersion of the sound over a wider area.

Polypropylene cones are considered by some to offer the benefits of greater resistance to flexing and buckling than paper cones, combined with greater sensitivity in responding to the music signal because plastic is a relatively lighter-weight material.

Sometimes the output of the cone is directed into a megaphone, called a *horn,* to further increase volume. These efficient "horn-loaded" drivers are currently popular among Japanese audiophiles. The first horn-loaded speaker was designed back in the mid-1940s by Paul W. Klipsch; called the Klipschorn, amazingly enough it's still in use. The great Klipsch advantage is efficiency—you can run these speakers on about 10 watts.

That the diaphragm is driven only from its relatively small apex (where the voice coil is located) is one drawback of the cone design. The cone, intended to be a rigid air-pushing piston, in reality flexes. Flexing and buckling, which occurs to some degree with all cones and a lot with poorly designed ones, causes uneven frequency response and harsh muddled reproduction. The sound is smudged and muddied because, once the cone starts buckling, it is no longer controlled by the voice coil and instead moves on its own, independent of the signal. Buckling also absorbs energy so the cones are less efficient and dynamic.

Reinforcing the diaphragm with a stiffening coat of plastic or "doping compound" to try to control flexing must be done very carefully. While it may somewhat limit buckling, it also increases mass, which can slow the quick transient response essential for accurate music reproduction.

This is one of the conundrums of speaker design we've discussed. Ideally, in order to start and stop in absolute synchronicity with the music signal, the diaphragm should have *no mass*—except that, having no mass, the diaphragm could then not move any air and so no notes would be reproduced. Therefore, dynamic speaker design divides up the audio frequencies into different bands and then tailors a driver to a given frequency band. Each driver can then be built with just the right amount of mass needed to reproduce the notes in that range but no more mass than is necessary, so as not to slow transient response.

The audio range is commonly divided up among a *tweeter* for high frequencies, a *midrange* driver, and a *woofer* for bass, with sometimes a *subwoofer* for deep bass, usually in a separate cabinet. To review again the basic reason for a woofer and a tweeter: The woofer needs to move a lot of air comparatively slowly but quite a distance, while the tweeter has to move a little air very fast but only a short distance. Two-way speakers consist of a tweeter and a combined midrange and bass, sometimes called a *midwoofer*. Further subdivisions can add a high-frequency tweeter, and split the midrange into upper and lower. More drivers are not necessarily better.

The Tweeter

The Tweeter—so christened for the birdlike high frequencies it reproduces—is small (typically 1 inch) and has low mass in order to respond quickly and accurately to the very short, high-frequency audio waves. It is limited to reproducing *only* the upper frequencies, as it has too little mass and size to move enough air to reproduce the larger, lower notes. Often, the tweeter driver itself comes with its own sealed back and so needs no additional enclosure other than for aesthetics and proper time alignment. However, sealed backs can set up their own distortions and a separate tweeter enclosure may be preferable.

Tweeters are almost always *dome drivers*—rigidity of the dome shape replaces the normal rigidity of mass, allowing the driver to be smaller and lighter and therefore have faster transient response. The dome is sometimes mistakenly considered to provide better dispersion but it's the driver's small size that offers good dispersion, and rigidity of shape that allows the small size.

Soft domes typically use fabric impregnated with a "lossy" damping compound; these tend to have a sonic character that is soft. At their worst, they can be somewhat vague and underdifferentiated in presenting instrumental timbres because, while the periphery is secured to the voice coil and so well controlled by it, the center of the dome is not. The conventional materials used aren't stiff enough to ensure that the entire dome moves in concert.

Hard Domes—not surprisingly—use a highly rigid material like stiff plastic, or metals such as copper, beryllium, titanium, or aluminum. These behave very well until a certain critical frequency (characteristic of the particular driver) is reached, at which point they tend to display a pronounced "ringiness." They can also be quite hard to drive. They developed a poor reputation because their early designs were characterized by a sharp high Q, or resonance, only just out of the audio band, as well as low efficiency and some manufacturing problems.

Wharfedale and Celestion in particular have corrected the problems while maintaining all the good points of smoothness and detail.

The Woofer

Woofers must have a large cone diameter to drive sufficient air—8 inches is usually the bare minimum, for it takes a powerful piston to push enough air to reproduce bass notes. This means woofers must also have a large voice coil to dissipate the considerable heat built up, and therefore a strong magnet to move the heavy cone and voice coil, and therefore a powerful amp to drive it. The bigger the cone, the more its large area is subject to flexing, and so the heavier and stiffer it must be made to counteract flexing. In addition, construction must be strong because the diaphragm takes a pretty heavy beating from low-frequency vibrations, and compliance should be high so that less force is required to move the cone any given distance. Because greater mass requires more energy to be moved, these larger drivers are less efficient.

Compliance is often achieved by having the cone only loosely connected to the frame by the gasket or rubber lip or surround. This surround, in conjunction with the suspension and the *spider* (voice coil support) determine the length of the throw. A longer throw means the driver can push more air with more acoustic efficiency, volume, and bass extension. There is a tradeoff—this can also increase intermodulation distortion (see Subwoofers, p. 183).

Although woofers with smaller, lighter cones are more easily controlled, large cones usually have a smoother frequency response because the cone controls the wave for a slightly longer time. (Of course, this also depends on the cone material. If the larger cone is flexing and breaking up, then it's not going to provide smoother anything.) The increased mass of a larger cone also lowers resonant frequency, so it can reproduce lower notes.

The Midrange

A midrange driver could easily be mistaken for "whatever fills in the gap between treble and bass." Its colloquial name, the "squawker," is all too revealing of its orphan status. But since, as we have said, the midrange is truly the heart and soul of the music, this status is a really mistaken one.

A *coaxial* driver is two drivers mounted as one. It may have a tweeter mounted in the center of a midrange or midbass driver, or else a midrange mounted on a bass driver—"coaxial" means two on the same axis, one in front of the other. In theory, this gives the "ideal" single-point-source setup and offers advantages of economy. It's typical of recording-studio monitors, such as the Altec. However, it commonly results in intermodulation distortion because, even if the two coaxial drivers don't physically vibrate one another, the lower frequencies will nevertheless acoustically modulate (alter) the upper ones. This design had fallen largely into disuse except in studio monitors, until recently introduced in one speaker by Technics.

Two- and Three-Way Systems

Realistically, cones perform best within *at most* a four-octave range, whereas the full audible spectrum covers ten octaves—from 20 Hz to 20 kHz. (Most people, however, hear over a range of only eight octaves. But there is serious belief that even sounds beyond our audible range "reflect back" into the audible spectrum and can thus be heard indirectly. The indirectness makes them no less important.) So accurate reproduction of the full frequency range requires at least two cones, often three.

While more driver units can be added, "more" by no means necessarily signifies "better." The best-sounding designs are usually the simpler ones.

Some of the advantages of simpler two-way systems include less sonic seaming because of fewer drivers, a simpler (and therefore less distorting) crossover, a smaller and therefore inherently more rigid enclosure, and a more economical design, requiring fewer parts and less cabinet material.

The advantages of three-way systems include a considerably broader frequency range without increased distortion. Each driver is able to operate well within the confines of its greatest linearity and need not be stretched to handle more of the audio band than it should.

The archetypal low-cost speaker system, since the mid-1970s, has been a *two-way system* consisting of a box with an 8-inch midbass unit (midwoofer) and a 1-inch dome tweeter. The 8-inch driver has to cover a more extended audio spectrum than it's suited for. It must be able to reproduce the midrange, some lower frequencies, and even stretch up into the higher frequencies in order to match seamlessly with the tweeter.

To respond fast enough in the midrange and upper-midrange frequencies, the midwoofer must be reduced in mass. In a larger cone like this, the lighter weight generally involves some sacrifice in rigidity, therefore also in the ability to push large volumes of air, reproduce bass, and perform without the breakup and buckling that smears the music. To reduce mass further, the voice coil is kept small, driving the cone from only a small circle at its apex, increasing the likelihood of flexing and spurious resonances (accurate reproduction depends on the entire surface area of the driver moving *in unison* like a piston).

This compromise results in reduced bass and generally less accurate frequency response. Because the same driver has to reproduce both low and higher frequencies simultaneously, the two will inevitably interfere with each other, the bass notes altering the higher frequencies. The result is increased distortion and blurriness. However, these criticisms are in reference to a standard of excellence. A good two-way system can be a very good choice and the best compromise of budget, size, and musical quality. Everything—especially in speakers—is a matter of tradeoffs.

The *three-way design* adds a third driver, so that the speaker incorporates a tweeter, midrange, and woofer, improving accuracy and especially bass extension. Each driver can be optimized for a more limited frequency range, where it can operate with the least distortion.

But this does require other compromises in exchange. Increasing the number of drivers adds complexity to the design and the crossover network. Time and phase coherence must be more carefully designed for with three drivers than with two. Each driver type has a different coloration/distortion signature—combining colorations can further confuse and complicate the sound. Dispersions will likely vary, so there may be very obvious seaming problems where the sound of the tweeter, midrange, and woofer don't blend quite successfully. Three-way systems also usually require larger enclosures to house them. Larger enclosures, made up of larger panels of material, generally resonate more, adding still further colorations. This particular problem can be treated with special highly rigid cabinet materials, like Benelex or Aerolam, or with substantial internal bracing.

These are all expensive problems to solve and usually only the better systems solve them even somewhat successfully. Inexpensive multispeakers will often sound far worse than a two-way system selling for about the same price. The simple woofer/tweeter combination often represents the optimal compromise among cost, complexity, and performance. In fact, a three-way needs to be exceptional to justify its price.

Speakers that are four-way or more will generally have more drawbacks of complex crossover and driver seaming than can justify any possible advantages of each driver's working well inside its narrow band of linearity. However, one of the world's finest speakers uses 105 drivers!! But looks deceive. These drivers go to a three-way crossover network no more complicated than that for a three-driver system. The quantity of drivers offers two benefits—good efficiency and a (nearly) true line radiator. This is the Infinity IRS (for those in the upper tax brackets).

Omnidirectional speakers, such as the Bose 901 and the Linn Isobarik and, more recently, the AR MGC-1, add a spatial element to the sound that's missing with forward-radiating speakers. This is not necessarily a particularly accurate sound, though. By reflecting off all four room walls, thus increasing the amount of indirect sound, omnidirectional speakers attempt to create a live, concert-hall flavor. One problem is that, in a typical listening room, the reflected sound arrives with too short a delay time after the direct sound, so the ear has a great deal of difficulty in distinguishing one from the other. That's why many of these speakers often provide imprecise, undetailed reproduction.

The Crossover Network

When more than just a single driver is used, a crossover network is needed to divide the music signal into different frequency bands and route each to the appropriate driver. While the crossover adds its own distortions, it also enables each driver to operate within its best frequency range and reproduce the music with better linearity.

The more drivers used, the more complex the network must be. But the simpler the crossover, the less distortion it will introduce—the shortest, simplest circuit path is always the best. A simple crossover also represents an easier load for the amp to drive and less power waste through electrical resistance and the resulting heat.

The crossover network filters frequencies. The crossover for a two-way system uses a *high-pass filter* to pass highs to the tweeter while holding back the lows, and a *low-pass filter* to pass lows to the woofer while holding back the highs. A three-way system's crossover adds a *band-pass filter* to pass the middle frequencies to the midrange driver while holding back both highs and lows.

To focus in on this a bit more, what happens is that the particular frequency band best suited to a given driver is allowed to pass through the network unimpeded while the unsuited frequencies are *rolled off,* i.e., impeded by the use of either capacitors for the higher frequencies or chokes (coils) for the lower.

There are two kinds of roll-off—acoustic and electrical. *Acoustic roll-off* is determined by driver size. Each driver couples most efficiently with the air within the specific frequency band—above and below that band, its efficiency rolls off and it reproduces frequencies less well. *Electrical roll-off-off* is accomplished through the crossover. The accepted design practice is to roll off a driver electrically about one octave before its natural roll-off point. This way, the driver is operating well within its best linearity and efficiency. This is not a "brick wall" filter that cuts off sharply, but a gradual roll-off. If the driver's natural roll-off, for example, is 1,000 cycles, then the electrical roll-off will be one octave before that, i.e., at 2,000 cycles or higher. (An octave higher is double the hertz or cycles; an octave lower would be half the hertz, 500 in this example.)

To maintain a seamless, continuous response through the audio range, the individual frequency characteristics of each driver must overlap each other slightly. The point at which the drivers overlap or cross over is the *crossover point;* the frequency at which this occurs is the *crossover frequency.*

How steeply the frequencies are rolled off, and at just what point between drivers, are sonically critical, quite complicated, and subject to no hard-and-fast rules. It's essential to understand *all* the parts of the equation before you can judge whether the sum total is correct—either that or use the guidance of your ears. Having a little technical knowledge is just as likely to throw you off course as it is to give you true insight. For example, how the crossover rolls off the frequencies in and of itself tells you little—you would also have to be familiar with the behavior of the particular drivers being used. It's the *combined effect* of the roll-off of both crossover and drive units that is the important consideration, not just how the filter rolls off on its own. There is a mind-numbing combination of variables to juggle in designing a crossover.

Crossovers are generally mounted inside the speaker cabinet and never seen. The practical benefits for manufacturers are cosmetics and no extra expense of another box for the crossover. Sonically, however, there are definite advantages to mounting it quite separate from the cabinet. Crossover parts are sensitive to vibration, found at high levels within the speaker cabinet. Also, Martin Colloms, world-acknowledged speaker authority, explains that the current-induced magnetic fields in the crossover wiring and inductors can interact with the varying magnetic fields produced by the dynamic drivers, adding to distortion. An externally mounted crossover eliminates these problems and can also facilitate bi-wiring (see p. 122).

Active Crossovers

The crossover network described above is the standard *passive* one, which divides up the audio signal *after* it has passed through the amplifier, and one amp is used to drive everything. An *active* crossover divides up the signal after the preamp but *before* the amp, and a separate amp is used for each speaker driver. A two-way system would use two amps, a three-way system three amps, and so on. This is called bi-amping, tri-amping, etc.

The advantages of active crossovers are that the signal division comes earlier, at the more manageable line level of the preamp where you're dealing with mere volts and milliamps, as opposed to tens of volts and many amps in a passive crossover. Active crossovers can more closely tailor the signal. In addition, each driver has its own dedicated power amp. A transistor amp can be used to provide good power to the base, while a tube amp provides linearity on the midrange and highs. (See also p. 101 on amplifiers.)

The drawback to active crossovers is that there are not a lot of good ones on the market. The GSI is very well regarded. Dahlquist used to make a good one, and you may be able to find one of these on the used equipment market.

Speaker Size

A larger enclosure inherently permits lower bass, tighter bass, more efficiency, and more loudness capability. A smaller enclosure compromises these but offers other benefits in trade. In balancing ideal speaker size for the music with realistic speaker size for the room, household, and neighbors, smaller dynamic speakers, called *monitors,* mini-monitors, or bookshelf speakers, may provide the best compromise. More than half the speaker manufacturers now offer at least one small two-way system for those with limited space, a limited budget, or a limited desire to let the audio system become a focal point in the living room.

When properly designed, small speakers can sound very good. The

FILTERS AND ROLL-OFFS

Electrical filters always roll off at rates that are multiples of 6 dB per octave. A first-order filter rolls off at 6 dB per octave, a second-order filter at 12 dB per octave, a third-order filter at 18 dB per octave, and so on.

The first-order crossover (6 dB per octave) is the simplest crossover and also the only one that introduces no phase distortion, so the original wave form of the input signal is maintained. This crossover also maximizes transient response. However, drivers used with a first-order crossover must have extended response characteristics beyond the crossover point.

A second-order crossover (12 dB per octave) is the simplest with which true acoustic roll-offs can normally be achieved, because a drive unit's inherent roll-off is usually second order. However, this crossover has problems with both frequency response and phase shift. Phase shift causes an alteration of the signal wave form. The accepted solution is to connect the drivers 180 degrees out of phase, and designers who do this insist you cannot hear that the drivers are now out of phase. Others believe that in-phase speakers provide greater dynamic range, ''attack,'' and listening ease. If the drivers are out of phase, time compensation becomes virtually impossible.

Third-order slopes (18 dB per octave) produce a phase shift in the crossover region but do produce flat amplitude. Nor do they require extended frequency response or greater power-handling characteristics of the drivers, since each driver operates within a limited frequency range and is rapidly crossed over.

As a rule of thumb, phase distortion worsens the higher the order of the crossover, though some designers consider that the phase distortion introduced by third- and fourth-order crossovers is still insignificant. Fourth order, however, is usually the highest encountered. The 24-dB-per-octave roll-offs are usually steep enough and the crossover is already quite complicated.

For this reason, some designers stay with the lower-order crossovers, which are simpler—capacitors and inductors have a deleterious effect on sound quality, so the fewer the better. In any case, its considered good engineering practice to achieve a design goal as simply as possible.

two drivers' being so close together allows a near-point-source radiation pattern, which provides for very good imagining. The Spica TC-50s are particularly notable for this. So too are the ProAc Tablettes and the Celestion SL-600s. Having such a small enclosure (often made still more rigid by the use of such special materials as cement and Aerolam), monitors suffer relatively little cabinet diffraction and resonance. As a result, they can sound very articulate and detailed, with little coloration, and have a focused soundstage with excellent coherence throughout the audio range. The relatively small front panel also minimizes vibration, which mitigates intermodulation distortion, increasing clarity and definition. Monitors are less efficient than full-size speakers, but a powerful amp can compensate for this.

Where you lose out the most is in the fact that they usually roll off at about 70 Hz, whereas most larger speakers go down to about 40 Hz. The high frequencies are also rolled off to maintain a proper spectral balance. Small speakers are therefore best suited to smaller-scale music like jazz, folk, and chamber, where you can get away with a less extended frequency range and lower listening volumes. More complex, larger pieces will definitely suffer from the shortage of bass and power. Some people are more sensitive than others to this drawback—you may be perfectly happy to accept this particular compromise.

While small speakers offer compactness, quality, and economy, they absolutely must be placed on speaker stands (see below). Stands add expense and also make the speakers more obtrusive in the room.

Full-range speakers, usually three way, offer a sense of ease and effortlessness, a reserve of headroom unmatched by any small speaker. And for extended bass and treble, a two-way can't even come close. On the other hand, large speakers are more difficult to design because of their more complex three-way crossover, harder to build, and quite a bit more expensive. The larger enclosure will probably suffer more cabinet colorations unless meticulously and rigorously constructed and braced. The very rigid cabinet materials being introduced in small speakers remain, so far at least, too difficult to work and too expensive to be suitable for use on a full-size speaker.

DIPOLE SPEAKERS

Dipoles radiate sound equally from the back and the front, with the sound from the rear reaching you by reflection from the walls, ceiling, and floor. Since the reflected sounds arrive a microsecond after the direct sound from the front of the panel, this can add a sense of depth and realism, or else it can muddy the sound, depending on room acoustics and speaker placement. You want to delay the back wave sufficiently so the ear can clearly distinguish between the direct and delayed sound. This can be done by absorbing the back wave within the speaker (as Quads do), by absorbing it on the wall with acoustic treatment, or by keeping the speaker well out from the wall so the reflections are well delayed. Any of these can help with the mid- to upper frequencies, but not with the long lower frequencies.

Dipoles are therefore quite particular about positioning and must be placed well out from any wall. Combined with their larger physical size, this can cause room placement problems.

A single large, flat diaphragm, rather than a cone, covers all or most of the audio range. Unlike a dynamic speaker, where the driving force is applied at a single point of the cone driver, a dipole's driving force is applied uniformly over the entire diaphragm. The diaphragm can therefore be lightweight for low mass, enabling it to respond very quickly and accurately to the stop or start of the audio signal. At the same time, it can be be nonrigid (having no need to act as a piston) and so freer from resonances and breakup.

Dipoles tend to reproduce low-level detail particularly well; this gives a sense of realism to recorded music. Dipoles offer more uniform frequency response, excellent transient response, and low distortion. Not being enclosed in a cabinet, they suffer from no boxy colorations. Time alignment is good, even when more than one diaphragm is used, as both lie in the same plane and the woofer section is very light and so can speak almost as quickly as the tweeter.

On the other hand, dipoles are also less durable, produce less volume, and have a more limited frequency range, especially in terms of bass, than do dynamic speakers. To provide sufficient bass power, the diaphragm must be very large to compensate for the much smaller amount of movement possible than with the cone of a moving coil speaker. Because the back wave is not separated from the front wave by being enclosed in a cabinet, but only by the width of the diaphragm, longer waves can come around and cancel the front waves. This will happen with all frequencies low enough that the sound wave is longer than the radiator (diaphragm) and so no longer blocked by the radiator.

Because the higher frequencies are also reproduced by a large diaphragm, they tend to beam rather narrowly—to provide good dispersion, a tweeter must be smaller than the sound waves it produces.

Dipoles remain expensive because they can use no off-the-shelf stock parts—everything must be designed and built from scratch. They still have problems with reliability, though this has improved over the years. (The excellent Quads have a notoriously slow repair time—not speeded up any by the company's being in England. On the other hand, Quad continues to service its equipment even long after it has been discontinued.)

Yet despite their important drawbacks, many consider they give the best sound reproduction possible from a speaker at this time. Those who take their listening seriously may be very happy to accept these tradeoffs in return for the often greater clarity and detail of dipoles. Just be aware that dipoles tend to be much fussier about the other components they are matched with.

Types of Dipoles

When Kellogg and Rice, the originators of the modern-day speaker, were still trying to figure out just how to design one, they first explored using *electrostatic* principles. But the need for very high voltages posed too many practical problems at that time. Instead, they moved on to designing the first dynamic speakers in 1925.

It wasn't until the late 1950s that insulating materials and signal-transformer core materials were able to handle the high-voltage needs of electrostatics and make them reliable enough (more or less) for commercial production.

At that time, Peter Walker in the United Kingdom developed the original ESL Quads, still highly prized today and represented now by the ESL 63 model. Arthur Janszen in the United States put out the Janszen speaker, which later became the KLH line. Janszen's company now produces the electrostatic panels used for the midrange of Dave Wilson's remarkable $45,000 WAMM speaker system.

Electrostatics use static electricity to generate sound—this is a principle completely different from the electromagnetic one used in dynamic designs. The driving force is applied uniformly over the entire large, flat diaphragm, rather than from a small apex as in a cone driver, so the diaphragm need not be stiff. This offers two great advantages—the diaphragm can be extremely lightweight for low mass, therefore

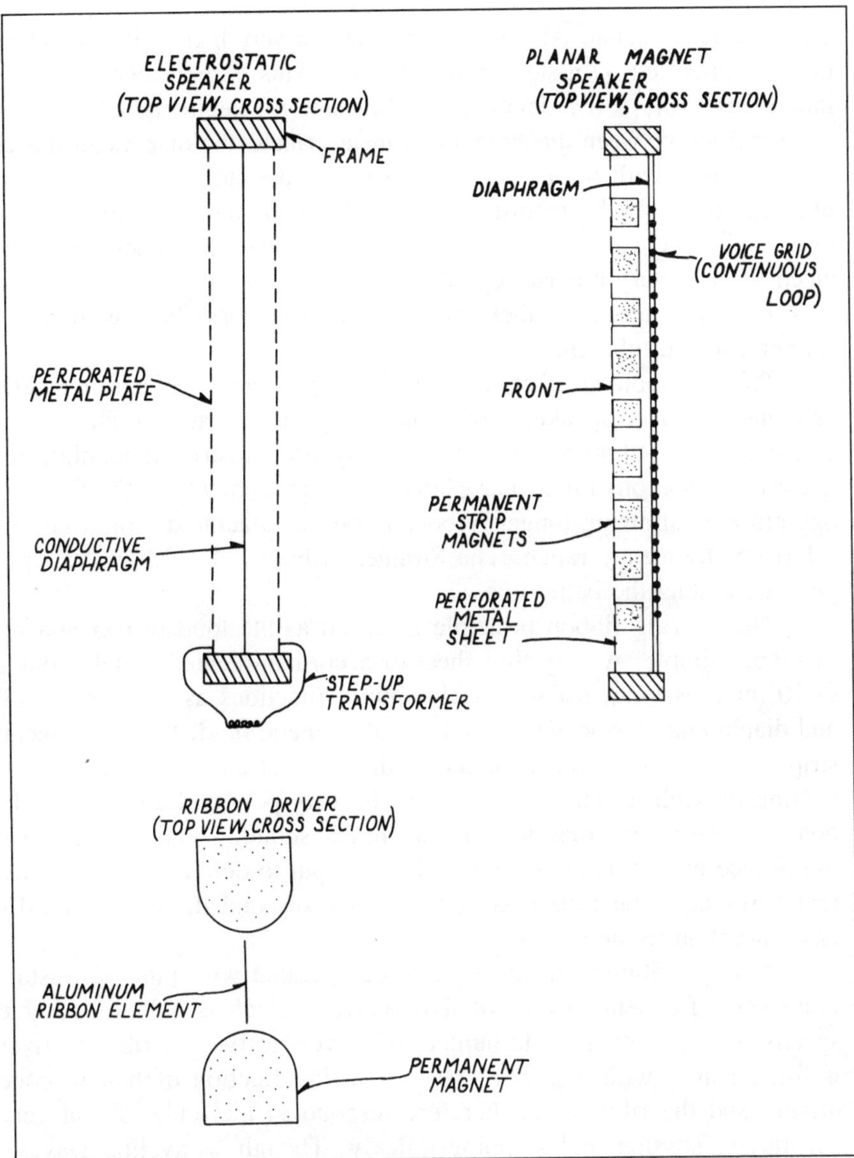

Fig. 19

having very good transient response, and it can be limp, offering freedom from resonance.

The diaphragm is a light, microns-thin plastic sheet coated with a fine metallic layer. This is electrostatically charged and suspended between two perforated metal panels, which are connected to the amp and carry the audio signal. All electrostatics require very high voltages, which must be provided by a step-up transformer. This transformer inevitably introduces some sonic degradation. Because of electrostatic attraction and repulsion between diaphragm and metal panels, the diaphragm moves in accordance with the audio signal, causing the surrounding air to vibrate in analog to the recorded music. The diaphragm's extremely low mass and the close control exerted over it by the electrodes make the electrostatic a very precise reproducer.

Electrostatics are widely considered to perform best with transformer-coupled tube amps.

Ribbon dipole speakers are a very simple form of electromagnetic or dynamic driver speaker, but avoid many of the usual limitations of the dynamics. Ribbons had until recently been restricted to high-frequency applications (and microphones), but refinements in the technology are now allowing longer ribbons to be manufactured, able to cover a broader frequency range. The Strathern ribbons and full-range Apogees are among the better known.

The moving ribbon principle is as old as the loudspeaker and remarkably simple. A very thin sheet of accordian-pleated metal about 2 to 10 microns long, usually of aluminum, functions as both voice coil and diaphragm. Suspended loosely in a magnetic field, the entire metal strip responds to the music signal in the form of an alternating current passing through it. The magnets must be very powerful and/or the ribbon very large in order to generate much sound. Very low intrinsic impedance means many amps will be hard put to deliver sufficient current. Providing the ribbon is very floppily suspended, there is hardly any coloration to the sound.

A single ribbon driver can now be operated with minimal distortion over a frequency range of five octaves, which is half the audible spectrum, thus reducing the number of drivers to two. A ribbon driver is often paired with a planar. Mass is a tiny fraction of that in cone drivers and the ribbon can therefore respond to the audio signal very accurately, starting and stopping quickly. Though "traveling waves" (like ripples on a pond) move up and down the length of the ribbon, these can be effectively damped by a spongy material placed at each end, or else by depositing the ribbon on a thin plastic backing.

Heat dissipation is a problem. Aluminum, the sonically preferred material, has a low melting point and deforms permanently at temperatures well beneath its melting point. Therefore, to effectively dissipate heat to the surrounding air, the ribbon must have a very large surface area; otherwise it cannot handle continuous high wattage.

Planar or *isodynamic* dipoles are also electromagnetic speakers, often confused with ribbons. Essentially, a planar is a moving coil speaker that has been "flattened out" so the voice coil is dispersed as a lightweight winding on a large, stretched film diaphragm. It is either etched from a thin copper layer deposited on the diaphragm or formed by wire bonded to the surface. Bar magnets positioned in rows on one or both sides of the diaphragm provide the magnetic field. The diaphragm is driven over its entire surface.

Planars are sturdier than ribbons, but their acoustic efficiency is low and bandwidth is generally limited to the bass and midrange, due to the relatively high mass of the diaphragm and magnets. They are often used in combination with ribbon tweeters.

The first planar was developed by Peter Winey, an industrial engineer and home audiophile, who loved the sonic advantages of electrostatics but wanted to use the more efficient, and less expensive, driving method of electromagnetics. His speaker was eventually marketed as the Magneplanar and has achieved great success in the high-end market.

SUBWOOFERS

The purpose of subwoofers would seem self-evident—to provide more extended, more powerful, and less distorted bass. However, their chief benefit is in improving the *midrange*! Specifically, a subwoofer can provide a substantially improved lower midrange, which is where most music and most musical instruments play their fundamentals and first overtones and where the ear is far more sensitive to distortions than in the bass region.

The improved midrange is due to the relief a subwoofer provides to a two-way system's midbass driver or a three-way system's bass driver. It no longer has to handle as broad a frequency band and therefore is able to operate over only its most linear range. (Naturally, an additional crossover is required when the subwoofer is added to the system.) The result is the effective elimination of *intermodulation distortion* (Doppler distortion). This occurs when the cone, driven by a lower frequency, moves back and forth with a long excursion and alters the character of another, higher frequency being simultaneously reproduced by the same cone. That character alteration is distortion. The only way to reduce this distortion is to severely restrict the cone's excursion, which can only be done by sending the lower frequency signals to a different driver—the subwoofer.

Unfortunately, many devoted listeners feel that the majority of subwoofers on the market leave a great deal to be desired. Most consist of a simple acoustic-suspension box enclosure with a heavy coned (for low resonant frequency) woofer subjected to large excursions in order to pump out a lot of woolly bass. A typical problem is that if you turn up the woofer loud enough to hear any benefits, it won't integrate with the music and can even smother some information in the midrange. Many listeners would prefer just to do without. The fact is that the whole question of low-end sound has yet to be properly dealt with technologically—the world still awaits a really convincing subwoofer.

However, in the meantime . . . it's best if subwoofers are driven by their own separate amp. This can be done by bi-amping the system, using one amp for the mid- and upper ranges and another for the bass. Often the choice is to use a tube amp for the top and a transistor amp for the bass. Subwoofers may also be designed as *active speakers* having their own integral amps designed into them, such as the Janis or Spica subwoofers. The problem with a speaker having a dedicated amp is that its sonic character is quite dependent on the amp's colorations. Either buy a matching system like the Spica TC-50 with subwoofers, or else carefully investigate the crossover information *before* you buy. The wrong crossover network can ruin the entire speaker system's sound.

Traditional wisdom holds that bass is omnidirectional, therefore only one subwoofer is needed. This traditional wisdom has recently been questioned. Some people say directionality can be heard well into the bass. On the other hand, a large number of recordings are cut with a mono blend in the bass, meaning that the bass is combined into a single channel. While one subwoofer can be better than none, two are better still, and for a number of reasons in addition to directionality. Two subwoofers can produce more powerful bass with less distortion. Two allow greater flexibility in avoiding bad room interactions when setting up the speakers.

A third reason is stressed by Peter Moncrieff. On most recordings except coincident mike ones, there are severe phase and time differences between bass notes arriving at one mike versus another. If these are electrically or acoustically combined by a mono woofer, than you'll get random interference patterns—in the form of either cancellations or additions. This gives a very distorted picture of the original event. Using stereo subwoofers prevents these phase and time aberrations.

SPEAKER STANDS

Speaker stands play a vital and integral role in the sound of small and medium-sized speakers and must be regarded, for many speakers, as an essential part of the purchase price. In order to release the signal accurately, the speakers must be kept absolutely still, or every microscopic shift of the cabinet will distort the movement of the cone and therefore the music. The principle is very similar to that of the stylus—subject either to any resonance and the signal will be distorted. Stands "lock" the speaker solidly to the floor through mass coupling and so help dissipate cabinet resonances. Just as important, the stands also bring them up to the correct listening height. If the tweeter is level with your knees, the high-frequency notes may never get even as high as your ears.

You may not be able to see this rocking motion, but you can feel it. Place your fingertips on various objects around your room when the music is playing and you can judge for yourself how much resonance they have. You can easily feel the speakers vibrating as well. Adding a heavy weight on top, such as a cinder block or some heavy books, will mass-load the cabinet and prevent it from rocking so easily. More effective (and more attractive, though also more expensive) is to use stands.

Substituting a shelf for stands is not a good idea. Shelves don't lock the speakers to the floor and so can't act as an energy drain. Shelf placement is more likely to actually *add* resonance of its own and muddy the sound. And two speakers on one shelf will only excite each other and vibrate even more. If the shelf protrudes by the slightest amount over the front of the cabinet, it will cause diffraction (see p. 163). Also, most speakers sound best some distance away from the wall, so a shelf won't work for this reason as well.

By putting a speaker on a stand, you are trying to fix it immutably in space. The stand itself must have mass because you don't want the speaker cabinet to be able to shake the stand. The mass gives the combined speaker and stand, an inherently unstable tower, a lower center of gravity so it doesn't rock back and forth. If you can move either the speaker on the stand, or the stand itself, then you will lose information, dynamics, and therefore music. You also want to be sure that any ringing is well damped.

The accepted solution for ensuring that the stand is physically and acoustically inert is to fill the hollow tubes of the stand with sand or lead shot (which is amazingly expensive), or a mix of lead and sand. This last is both less expensive than pure shot and, according to the theory, superior in that the smaller sand granules fill the interstices between the shot pellets and so create a better energy dump.

Stands can be quite deceiving as to the amount of filling they will require, so if you do use shot, be prepared to pay handsomely. If you choose sand, be sure it is clean, not beach sand. The salt in beach sand will in time corrode the metal tubing. The sand used in the public ashtrays in hotels and large office buildings works excellently, because it both is clean and has a fine grain that packs down well. Tap it down with a rubber mallet and then seal the opening with a removable, nonhardening claylike substance like Mortite.

The stands must be meticulously adjusted so there is no perceptible movement of either stand or speaker when rigorous attempts are made to rock them. Spikes should be provided on which to rest the speaker, or alternatively some other secure clamping method, and spikes should couple the stand to the wood floor or through the carpet. Spikes improve rigidity because they mass couple the entire weight of the cabinet onto a tiny point, so you get more mass per square inch than if the speakers rested on a solid platform. This helps transmit the resonances more effectively into the ground.

Arcici uses three spikes on the bottom of its stand to facilitate level coupling to the floor and minimize any risk of rocking, but uses four spikes directly under the speaker. The reason is very interesting—speakers actually rotate as they play, because the diaphragms are never perfectly balanced and so the lopsided mass will push one side more than the other, setting up a rotating motion in the cabinet. Four spikes help to prevent this rotation and so provide much more effective support. Arcici also makes a highly regarded stand specifically for the Quad ESL-63.

The alternative no-mass approach used in some table design and table-support design can be experimented with here by substituting vermiculite or foam beads for the sand and shot. These will dampen resonances without adding mass. Mass coupling of resonances will depend on the spikes. This approach is recommended by Linn and may be worth trying, although it is not the accepted high-end wisdom at this time.

If the stand is steel (metal stands provide much better rigidity than do wooden ones), there should be some provision to keep the speaker cables away from the stand to avoid magnetic interactions.

Adjustable stands offer the great advantage of easy height alteration but usually at a cost—try finding one as rigid as nonadjustable stands. A rare exception is Arcici's adjustable stand. Rigidity is vital and height adjustments can be achieved by other means with a little ingenuity. Sal Demicco likes acrylic plaster blocks under his equipment and this can certainly be used to raise height. Cinder blocks, painted or felt or fabric wrapped if you prefer, are another alternative.

CABLES AND INTERCONNECTS

Good interconnects and speaker cables (combined, these are referred to simply as wire) are as important a component in your system as any other audio equipment. The right wire can significantly improve overall sonic performance. Good wire will not make a bad component or system better, but bad wire will certainly hide a good system's qualities.

The first inkling that wire was anything more than just wire was in an article published in 1977 by French audiophile/designer Jean Hiraga. It took nearly another decade before designers and listeners really took the subject seriously, and then a flood of new wire designs started coming out. The better cables today are a major improvement over what was available even a few years ago.

The difficulty with selecting the right interconnects and speaker cables for your particular system is that wire is highly equipment and system specific—what sounds excellent on one system can sound mediocre on another. In addition, the range of choice is bewildering. No one formulation has yet been found to be *the* right one that works best with all types of components—good wires are widely divergent in their materials and construction types. Wires vary in impedance, inductance, capacitance, dielectric properties, resistance, delay characteristics, and more, and each of these characteristics appears to affect the sound. Speaker cables are the most system specific of wires—the interaction between cable and amp is almost impossible to predict. Your choice can affect the apparent amount, tightness, and extension of the bass.

Days of listening may be needed to figure out whether a cable is an improvement, merely a change, or even somewhat worse overall. Just because one wire reveals something that another does not, don't get carried away. It is very easy to chase after one detail or another, only to find after longer listening that you've lost the music.

As even good wires can sound very different from each other while none of them is clearly right or wrong, subjective preferences—unfortunately too often accompanied by a lot of voodoo and of the competition—may be the final factor. Don't believe wild claims you may hear about wire. Some wires are very expensive, but expense does not always equate with quality—$25-per-foot wire can sound worse than some costing $3 per foot. This doesn't necessarily mean the $25 stuff is a ripoff, just that it does not work as well in your system.

Good wire may reveal some of the deficiencies of your system that less good wire covers up—along with the music. Some wires sound euphonic on certain systems, but you have to consider whether the euphony is music being revealed or coloration added by the wire. The coloration may be pleasant, and then you have to choose whether what you want from your system is pleasant sounds or fidelity to the music.

Fortunately, there are a *few* very general rules of thumb. High-impedance sources, such as MM cartridges and some tube preamps, are notoriously poor at driving capacitive loads and suffer noticeable high-frequency roll-off under some conditions. You may be best off with a cable that has a high output impedance designed to compensate for these high-frequency roll-off tendencies—one that may even tend to sound bright or "tizzy" when used with low-impedance sources, such as MC cartridges and the better solid-state preamps. The difficulty is that the manufacturer's quoted output impedances may not help you much in choosing, because the outputs of many components, particularly preamps, rises sharply as the frequency rises. But almost any tube preamp will work fine with runs of 6 feet or less of any interconnect. The final decision should be made by your ears, rather than "by the rules."

If you hear no differences between cables, then we'd recommend using the inexpensive Straightwire Flexconnect—this is like the Grado MTE + 1 of wires. It gives you most of the performance of Straightwire's LSI (generally regarded as one of the cables that is consistently most neutral on a wide range of systems) at a third the price—a best buy and an absolute minimum for any system.

Some Basic Wire Background

The music signal travels down the wire at the speed of light. It is an electromagnetic signal, made up of electric and magnetic fields. Both fields interact with the wire—the electric field with the wire's capacitance and dielectric, the magnetic field with the cable inductance. The signal's amplitude is reduced by resistance.

There are two primary factors that affect the sound of wire: resistance and self-inductance. Secondary, though very important, factors include the dielectric material, the cable-weaving design, and the purity and construction of the conductors.

When an electrical current moves through wire, it encounters an energy-sapping phenomenon called *resistance*. The conductor's atoms impede the flow, causing power to dissipate as heat. Resistance is the other side of the coin of conductivity; both are inherent properties of a material. At normal temperatures, silver is the best conductor available, copper a close second. After that, there is a sharp drop-off to gold, followed closely by aluminum. Resistance is also directly related to length—the greater the cable's length, the higher its resistance. However, increasing the diameter of the cable offsets increased length.

The chief sonic result of resistance is in frequency response. Less resistant (whether shorter, fatter, or of a more conductive material) cables produce a different change in frequency response than do more resistant cables and therefore sound different, though not necessarily better (or worse).

Any impurities in the material degrade conductivity, hence increase resistance. Oxygen-free copper (used extensively by Hitachi) and silver (Siltech) are 99.9 percent pure or better. Linear crystal copper and silver are being used for some cables. LC manufacture encourages the formation of a homogeneous structure with large crystals to minimize voids and the number of boundaries between crystals. However, the sonic difference between the poorest copper in 16-gauge zip cord and the best oxygen-free copper is much less significant than making a small change in the design of the cable.

Self-inductance is the result of a change in the current flow; any change sets up an opposing current. The faster the change, the greater the opposing current. So the faster-moving, higher-frequency music signals create more of an opposing current than the lower frequencies, and so will reduce themselves more. Thus the high frequencies are rolled off. The shorter the cable, the lower the inductance; the wider the cable, again the lower the inductance.

There is an additional phenomenon known as *skin effect*. The core of the wire conducts the best. But as current increases, so does resistance. So while the lower frequencies (with lower current) travel through the core, the higher frequencies (higher current) travel along the surface of the wire, where they encounter less resistance. While some designers address themselves to skin effect, others consider that it is insignificant at audio frequencies, at least compared to the properties of inductance and resistance.

Another sonic factor is a wire's *capacitance*. Wire can be thought of as a long capacitor, with the conductors serving as plates and the insulation being the dielectric. The electric field of the music signal interacts with the dielectric, which absorbs a tiny fraction of it. This absorbed energy is then slowly released, long after that part of the signal has gone by. Transients are smeared. Dick Olsher of *Stereophile* compares this to loudspeaker cabinet resonances: The cabinet soaks up energy from the cone's back wave and then releases it as a time-delayed and frequency-smeared version of the input signal. Following a vacuum and air, Teflon is one of the best dielectrics. Unfortunately, it is also expensive and stiff.

Capacitance seems to be an issue only for very long cable runs and for high-impedance sources such as MM cartridges, MC transformers, and some preamps.

Wire Geometry

The geometry of the overall cable is important. Some feel that twinax cable (with symmetrical hot and ground returns within a shield) seems to sound better than coax (a single hot with a shield). This may be because the electric fields are balanced and symmetrical in twinax.

The geometry of the conductors themselves is also important—there are sonic differences between solid conductors versus stranded, tinned or plated versus pure, finely stranded versus coarse, interconducting strands versus Litz versus separately insulated parallel strands (the object of this last being to lower self-inductance). Litz construction—multiple insulated strands in parallel for each conductor leg—is intended to minimize high-frequency attenuation by increasing the available surface area.

RF Shielding

The signal level at the front end and preamp is so small that it comes very close to the ambient electrical noise fields. So the wire used for the front end/preamp/amp interconnects must be shielded against the ubiquitous radio-frequency signals floating around in the air. Otherwise, without *RF shielding,* the wire would be likely to pick up hum and other noises. Even with shielding, the wire may still pick up fields radiated by sizable currents flowing in speaker cables, so keep your speaker cables and interconnects well separated.

RF shielding must be designed properly or it can itself degrade the sound. If the shield is too close to the conductor, it will reflect electromagnetic energy into the nearest strand as well as change the self-inductance of that strand.

Dave Salz of Straightwire recommends for better RF rejection that the shield be connected at the preamp end between signal source and preamp, and at the amp end between preamp and amp.

Terminations

Finally, the quality of the *connectors* and the soldering at the ends also affect sound. The connectors matter in terms of the conductivity and sonic quality of the material used, but also, and at least as importantly, in terms of the quality of the mechanical/electrical connection they make. For good electrical contact, you want a solid, airtight contact over as much surface area as possible.

RCA jacks are used on nearly all interconnects. The drawback to this design is that the hot connection is made and broken before the ground. The long center plug, which is the hot, makes contact before the outer ring, which is the ground. This is what causes that awful *bzzzzzz* if you connect or disconnect while the system is on (which, of course, you shouldn't really do in any case). Only a very few jack designs connect the ground first. Aside from this, the main sonic difference in quality among RCAs is not whether they are plated with gold or anything else, but whether they give you a positive connection that stays connected. Expensive connectors tend to do this better than inexpensive ones. Tiffany and Monster Cable connectors are good at this.

Speaker connections aren't terrific either. On the backs of most speakers are the much-scorned five-way binding posts. While these accept spade lugs, a looped wire, a straight wire, a banana plug, or even the long-departed pin plug, the electrical connection possible is not a very good one and these posts are widely considered to degrade the sound. Banana plugs can lose their tension and leave you with a poor or intermittent connection.

Spade lugs, simply crimped very tightly onto bare or Tweek-treated wire, are our preferred. Solder is audible, however slightly, so should be avoided where that's an option. Be careful, by the way, whom you get to terminate your wires—a poor job could leave you worse off than using zip cord! Monster Cable's X-Terminators pair up well with spade lugs—they are quick and easy to connect and disconnect from the back of the speaker, and yet ensure a positive and intimate connection because the center pin expands as you lock it in place.

PART II.

SETUP, OPERATION, AND CARE

SYSTEM SETUP

THE IMPORTANCE OF SETUP

Having a good violin does not mean you will play good music. Having good equipment does not ensure you will get good sound. You have to learn how to "play" your system in order for it to release the music.

Two essential aspects affect the sound of a playback system—aside from the recording: (1) the equipment itself, including component matching (both discussed earlier), and (2) how that equipment is affected by its environment—the mechanical environment of resonance, vibration, and acoustic feedback; the electrical environment of your house current; and the acoustic environment of the room, particularly how the speakers couple with it.

This impact of the environment on the system is what setup is all about. Setup is not just a matter of making sure sound comes out of your system, it is a matter of ensuring you get the *best* sound from your system. You must be meticulous about setup to enjoy the full extent of good sound and imaging available from your system—it really is extraordinary how unaware most people are of its vital importance.

Good setup is like good cooking—the better the ingredients, the better the results. But even undistinguished ingredients can, through good cooking (like good setup), be made satisfying. The very best ingredients, however, like the very best equipment, cannot compensate or cover up for poor cooking or setup.

You can walk into listening rooms that enshrine systems costing a good year's income, yet the music sounds like Muzak! Taken individually, the components are perfectly good. The ingredients of good setup may even appear to be there—the table properly placed on a Lead Balloon or other "isolation platform," the tube amp's transformers suitably capped with VPI bricks, the preamp neatly isolated on Tiptoes, the speakers reposing on stands. But good components and the "right" accessories are no substitute for proper setup—accessories can enhance an *already good* situation but they can do little to transform a poor one.

Careful setup can bring a component or system right up to the limits of its best. It cannot alter the fundamental way a system works but it can allow the system to do well what it has been doing only crudely before.

Setup involves two phases: the foundation of correct installation and operation; then the fine tuning, an ongoing process of refinement that relies on listening and improvisation. Fine tuning is a matter of optimizing your own particular circumstances of equipment and acoustic space. What works in one situation may not work in another.

The goal is to come as close as possible to "transparency." A system that is transparent enables you to listen right *through* the equipment, the recording, the recording studio, and the distances of time and space, to reach the original performance with as much directness and immediacy as possible.

A system should be seen but not heard. The system should (ideally) *add nothing* to the recording—neither expression nor interpretation nor distortion. The recording, not the system, is intended to be the focus of attention. The system should convey the music as neutrally and exactly as possible. As playback is brought up to increasingly transparent and undistorted standards, the recording becomes progressively unveiled. Transparency is inversely governed by distortion.

The issue is not whether or not the equipment works—merely operating mechanically or electronically does not fulfill its function of fidelity. Any operating hi-fi or mid-fi system can cause the notes on the recording to be restored to sound, but not any system can allow the *music* to be restored to life. Both the quality of the component and the quality of its setup in a system in a particular room will determine its success at conveying art. Otherwise, it remains nothing more than an appliance suited perhaps for auditory lavage but not for any greater purpose.

If you treat audio equipment like an appliance, it will do the minimum of what it is intended to do—it will make the recording audible. There is an essential difference in the roles of an appliance and a high-fidelity component—the one relieves you of a task, the other reveals art.

The notion that you can simply go out and buy a system, then bring it home, pop open the boxes, and start listening is a promo man's fantasy. If you haven't the patience or time to do it yourself, pay an expert to come out to your house and make a proper installation. Beware, though, that not every self-professed expert is necessarily an expert in the claimed area. A pro is someone whose own system sounds musical, enticing, enjoyable for hours on end—that's the only credential needed. Accept no mere proclamations of pro-dom as a substitute.

Even after benefiting from the services of a system setter-upper, don't be afraid to move things around. *You* are the one spending extensive time listening and can perhaps focus in on the system even better over time. Just be sure, before you move anything, that you clearly mark its *exact* position so you can restore it if you want. China marker pencils are great for temporary markings on wood floors—the waxy color is easily wiped off when you are done.

Equipment designers cannot know the specifics of room acoustics and other variables that influence a system's performance, so audio components can be designed only for "general use." Just as a recording is incomplete until it has been played back, so in a sense is a component "unfinished" until it has been set up as part of a particular system within a particular room. The identical component in two different systems or two different rooms will sound different. For that matter, the same component in the same system and same room can sound very different depending on setup. Consider how much live music can change according to the environment in which it's played, or how the "sonic signature" of the same orchestra may change with its conductor. Just as performers adjust their playing to accommodate their environment and their co-performers, so must you "adjust" components to the system and room.

Remember that high-fidelity sound (HFS) occurs on a literally microscopic and submicroscopic scale. From the minute signal generated by the cartridge, tape head, or laser beam to the fully amplified signal fed to the speakers, amplification may be easily 30,000-fold. High-pitched violin notes occupy spaces smaller than a millionth of an inch in the record grooves or on tape; small excursions of the speaker diaphragms replicate the captured sound waves, conveying all the drama and largeness of a brass marching band. On this infinitesimal scale, seemingly insignificant factors can, indeed do, exert disproportionately large effects on sound quality.

When system setup is poor, the finest, most advanced components will deliver no better than a middling performance. Even the digital compact disc, widely heralded as the greatest convenience since the seedless grape, has been found to be surprisingly finicky and setup dependent. So no matter what anyone may tell you, equipment that is simply pulled from its boxes, connected, and played cannot be expected to deliver good sound.

Minimize Distortion

Distortion all along the reproduction and playback chain is the sole force preventing perfect playback. Minimizing distortion is therefore the master key to good sound. Distortion can never be eliminated, but it can be *reduced.* It is a ''nonlinearity'' (what comes out is different from what went in) that emphasizes certain aspects of the signal, resulting in a particular coloration such as brightness, or upper-midrange glare, or muddiness.

More often than not, people unwittingly arrange their systems in ways that greatly *exacerbate* distortion. A reasonable system well installed will always outperform an excellent system poorly installed. Proper attention to detail can turn a mediocre system into an enjoyable one, a good system into a commanding one. Neglecting these details will result in unmusical sound, no matter how expensive and potentially excellent your equipment may be.

HFS is like a telescope—if you're trying to see something millions of miles away, then the slightest tremble will make the object look as if it's jumping around the sky, or it's even possible the telescope may miss the object altogether. Recorded music must travel across great expanses of time and distance. The slightest tremor in the physical, mechanical, or acoustic environment will distort and even altogether lose musical notes.

But distortion is more than a matter of colorations; it's a matter of *intelligibility,* the ability of the system to convey the music clearly and therefore the listener's ability to comprehend it clearly.

For example, a complex classical work, when unfamiliar, can be a bit of a struggle to understand. But, if heard on a poor system, it can be rendered incomprehensible, meaningless. So many of the notes and the silences between the notes are blurred together that the structure, and so much of the feeling and meaning, are obscured.

As your system becomes more transparent—through better setup and perhaps upgraded components—you'll notice that you hear more of the music, hear notes you've never known were there before, and suddenly complex musical passages become clear—the musicians' message is getting through. A frequent response to a genuine upgrade in your system's sound is not only to rediscover all your favorite records but also to discover new favorites in performances that before left you indifferent.

As you reduce distortion, it may take a while to adjust to the better sound quality. Many listeners get so used to hearing severe distortion in recorded music that it becomes a part of their expectation of how recordings ought to sound. One response is to keep turning up the volume until the system just begins to distort, in order to get back that old familiar (distorted) sound. As Robert Blake points out, if you keep a dog chained to a stove for years and then one day let him loose, at first he'll turn and run right back to the stove. Don't just hit the volume control—consider the live listening level for that particular kind of music. A symphony played at quiet background levels isn't going to sound particularly realistic—it will sound distant and small. A chamber ensemble blaring forth at an orchestra's 100-dB level will also sound unnatural.

The Importance of Fine Tuning

Having eliminated the grosser distortions and imperfections, all the subtler imperfections will now be revealed. Basic setup has brought the system into rough focus; now you want to sharpen that focus. This is like a microscope that has both a coarse- and a fine-tuning knob.

In fact, you really need to put yourself on the level of the stylus to gain good sound. The audio signal exists on a microscopic scale until it reaches the speaker diaphragm, and so one needs to view the signal's environment from a microscopic perspective.

Fine-tuning changes generally cannot be measured. Some (even many) respond, "If it can't be measured, it doesn't exist." We say, "If it can't be measured but can be heard, we just haven't figured out how to take the right measurements yet." How else explain a clearly audible improvement that occurs even though the equipment specs remain unchanged? Obviously, there are things we can hear but cannot yet measure. Our ears are remarkably sensitive and critical—we can perceive distortions we have no way of measuring and don't even have names for yet. But this does not mean they don't exist. Our ears and brain still retain their edge over man-made instruments. So just because we don't have scientific verification yet doesn't mean a given change didn't occur.

If measurement were everything, Newton and Einstein would have dismissed their ideas on account of their being "unmeasurable"—only years of intensive exploration established scientific verification of their flashes of imagination. Scientists are still trying to figure out what makes the Stradivarius violins sound unlike any other. But, even though scientists have not yet found an answer, no one has had the temerity to proclaim that these violins don't sound the way they do.

Only in audio, this strange meld of art and science, do we seem to lack faith in what our own senses tell us and instead feel more secure depending on "objective" measuring instruments to tell us what we're hearing.

You cannot really lose out in your efforts to fine-tune a system—improvements can be made at the price of *time* rather than money. There are simple things you can try at minimal expense and no risk to the system. Go ahead and experiment—if you hear no difference after a fair trial, then don't continue. But try several things before you give up, as the effect is cumulative. Also, listen for a while before dismissing their worth—you cannot get instant sound any more than you can get a good cup of instant coffee. However, a cup of fresh-brewed coffee requires that you take the trouble to note the distinction between fresh and just fast. If these distinctions do not interest you, then HFS may not be for you. By all means take the convenience route and don't bother yourself.

You probably have a job to do, a home to run, if you're lucky a garden to tend. You wish your system—with a little care—to be a source of relaxation and enjoyment, not an instrument to be constantly worked over in hopes of wringing out the last percent of a degree of improvement. It is possible to maintain a reasonable balance between convenience foods and gourmet cooking. Fine tuning, best carried out over a period of weeks, even months, of listening, need not be an all-absorbing nor endless process. Assuming you don't change components or rooms, you can bring the system to a point that satisfies you and then leave it at that. Thereafter, just regularly maintain the system to protect against the ravages of entropy. On the other hand, some people get so enthralled with tweaking that it turns into a hobby itself—they spend more time fine-tuning the sound than listening to the music. But tweaking is only rarely addictive—experiencing a little doesn't mean you'll turn hardcore.

Keep in mind that what you are trying to accomplish is not really to fine-tune the *system,* but more accurately to fine-tune your access to the music. Keep your awareness music-focused rather than equipment-fixated.

If you listen seriously to more than one program source, you must play them *all* as you fine-tune. Otherwise, you run the risk of compensating for the colorations of one signal source only, to the possible detriment of the others. If you listen to one as the primary and the others only as secondary sources, then optimize for the one you listen to most.

Make One Change at a Time; Keep a Record Log

As you start really tuning the system in, go slowly and if you have the patience, *keep notes* (Larry Smith of Perfectionist Audio stresses this). Listen carefully to each change. It's very easy to imagine or assume an improvement when all you may have actually achieved is a change. It's also possible to gain a real improvement but overlook in your excitement that you have lost something valuable in the tradeoff—it's quite possible to improve one element of the sound while sacrificing more than you've gained. It will probably require extended listening over several days to decide which way gives greater overall fidelity. This is where keeping notes is so helpful—by the time you've made up your mind to restore the system to its earlier way, you may have forgotten just what that way was! Notes are particularly important for speakers, whose sound is so greatly affected by how they interact with the room's acoustics.

Some people find it almost impossible to resist making six different changes all at once. The problem with this approach is that when you finally sit down to listen and find yourself not altogether satisfied (a common enough state of affairs), there's no way to identify where you may have gone wrong. In order to do so, you would have to *undo* all the changes you have just made and then redo them one by one, listening carefully in between each change. It is easier if you just go ahead and do it this way in the first place. *Make only one change at a time*. Be patient—tune the system, listen to what you've done (and listen over a period of time, not just briefly), then proceed with tuning again until you've either reached satisfaction or else had your fill, for the moment, of playing with the system rather than listening to music.

Some tweaks can actually make your system sound *worse,* not because the tweak itself is bad but because it unmasks problems elsewhere in the system. Keep track of the tweaks that don't work and try the same change again later on—you may be pleasantly surprised. It is also possible that a particular change may establish a *non*complementary nonlinearity in your system.

Perhaps for these reasons, tweaking has received a poor reputation. Just to hint at the possibility that some tweaks make an important sonic difference is enough to produce those significant glances that warn of the presence of a loony. There are many doubters who refuse to see the hand before their nose. The fact is also that tweakers have a vested interest in hearing an improvement, not simply a difference, from their adjustments so claims are made that are not legitimate or are legitimate in only a few systems.

Still others, trying out a recommended tweak on their own systems, cannot hear the promised change and therefore deride the tweakers as crazies or voodooists. They disregard the possibility that their systems may be at fault, operating at too crude a level for that tweak to make an audible difference. Or it may be the tweak won't work with your particular combination of components and room acoustics. Just because aspirin doesn't clear up every headache doesn't mean it's ineffective.

There is without doubt a great deal of voodoo going around in audio—whether from plain ignorance, ignorance combined with a reluctance to reveal it, or a desire to keep others ignorant and so hold on to one's own (imagined) power. But, despite a healthy distaste for audio voodoo, it's essential to remember that seemingly insignificant factors really can exert disproportionately large effects on sound quality. Any single refinement alone may not make much of an audible difference, but combine several and the cumulative musical effect can be the difference between a good system and a great one. Small adjustments can slowly produce very substantial results.

Always keep your goal of live acoustic music right in the forefront of your mind. Though you will never match it, it's the direction you want to move steadily toward. A system that sounds good consistently will make you feel good; you can listen hour after hour without fatigue or irritation, with involvement, satisfaction, and stimulation. Your music system is not a substitute TV—listening to music is generally an active, involved, engaging activity.

Truly, though many may not believe this, while setup tends to be time consuming, tedious, sometimes frustrating, it is not difficult and does not require brains or great coordination (except in the case of cartridge setup) or even "mechanical aptitude." It's perfectly straightforward, and once you start to miniaturize your thinking down to the scale of the musical notes, it all becomes reasonably clear.

Sequence of Setup

The transducers—speakers and turntable/cartridge system—will benefit the most from really meticulous setup. Any point where energy is converted from one form into another is always a primary source of distortion, which can either be mitigated through proper setup or else aggravated by its absence. Once the transducers are correctly set up, only then should you turn your attention to the rest of the system, because only then will such refinements really be noticeable.

Cartridge and speakers have in common that they can accurately convert the music signal only if the proper element (whether speaker diaphragm or stylus cantilever) moves *in relation to* its motor. If this *relative* movement is interfered with by resonance or vibration, then the signal will consist of distortion in addition to music. So it is fundamental to good fidelity that the *relative* motion be precisely preserved. In addition, both stylus and speaker diaphragm must be set up exactly "in orientation to" a specific object—the stylus to the groove, the speaker to the room and listener. If either of these essential setups is wrong (and commonly both are), then you have mediocrity, regardless of the excellence of the components.

Speaker placement, because it has such a profound effect on the system's sound, should be established first and then the other components arranged in relation to the speakers. So whereas in most aspects of a music system, the hierarchy of priority follows in the direction of the signal—the signal source being of first importance and the speakers of last—this sequence is reversed for basic setup.

The first step, therefore, is to set up your speakers and then position the other components in relation to the speakers and in relation to the mechanical and electrical environment. For example, the turntable must be out of the path of acoustic feedback, while interconnect and cable runs should be kept as short as possible. Component supports are very important for minimizing vibrational distortions.

SPEAKER SETUP

The speaker is not the last component in your system, your room is the final component. How the speakers acoustically couple with your room is as crucial to *their sound in your room* as is their design. They must be "locked into" your room just as the stylus has to be "locked into" the LP grooves.

The speakers are the playback mirror image of the recording mikes. You, as "playback engineer," have to devote as much attention to speaker placement as a good recording engineer has to devote to mike placement. Your job differs from miking, though, in that you do not want your room's sound added to the sound of the room the music was recorded in. The acoustic of the hall in which the recording was made (at least in the case of classical music) is an integral part of the performance and should be preserved and revealed intact.

So just as the speaker cabinet that encloses the drivers should ideally add no resonances or colorations of its own, your room, which serves as the enclosure to your speakers, should add minimal resonances. How and where you position the speakers (and your listening position) in your room (along with room size, shape, and furnishings) is certainly as critical as which speakers you buy—an otherwise vibrant pair can be extinguished simply by poor placement.

Some, wanting the sensation of sound filling the entire room, hang the speakers from the ceiling or other strange locations. You'll get sound throughout the room this way but its quality will be less than good. The intent of "high fidelity" is to try to regain as much of the original experience as possible, which means the speakers should be at "seated-ear" height and placed so as to allow the re-creation of a stereo image. in fact, there is no point in spending good money and effort to get equipment that has the ability to convey music transparently if you then set it up so that it cannot do so. The intent of "stereo" is to provide the illusion of three-dimensional sound. Placing speakers so the two channels cannot "rejoin" in such a way as to re-create a stereo image will actually alter the music, because its elements will be reaching you in time relationships different from the original performance.

If you want sound throughout the room, explore surround sound or speakers that intentionally aim the sound sideways as well as forward (see pp. 150 and 173). Consider very carefully before making such a choice. Though this may be, as many claim, the way of the hi-fi future, its successful realization, to our ears at least, still remains somewhere in the future.

Carefully set-up stereo speakers will always sound best when listened to from one particular location. This doesn't mean you can't listen from anywhere else—just that the speakers are optimized for a certain listening position, the sweet spot. Speakers correctly placed in the room, that have, so to speak, found the "voice" of the room, will even when you're not sitting in that sweet spot still sound better from *every* point in the room.

Speaker setup involves a lot of variables that must all be considered simultaneously and usually compromised among. Remember, as you try out the results of the compromises, that though speaker placement most greatly affects the bass, the most important part of the music is the midrange. Midrange clarity is always to be preferred over a position that provides slightly stronger bass but muddies the midrange.

Certain aspects of speaker setup remain absolutely nonnegotiable: The speakers and the listener must form approximately an isoceles triangle, there must be no line-of-sight obstructions between speakers and listener, and both the speaker placement and the speakers'/listener's environment must be sonically symmetrical and balanced.

Anything in the sound path between the speakers and your ears will distort the sound waves before they reach you. NOTHING should be placed in front of the speakers except your ears. Sound waves are like light waves, in being easily reflected, deflected, diffracted, and absorbed by objects in their path. The smaller-wavelength higher frequencies are especially vulnerable as they are most easily absorbed, by even just their passage through the air. If, for example, you've had one speaker tucked beside the sofa and the other diagonally across the room behind a potted plant, something will have to be rearranged if you want good sound. Even if the sound path to your ears remains unobstructed, just shoving each speaker off into a corner is not going to make a great improvement because you and they should also be set up to form a triangle. (Try correctly setting up the pair you're using now—even if they're not very good, you should hear very definite benefits.)

Speaker placement may be dictated by the architecture of your room in terms of doors, fireplaces, windows, and the like. Try not to let existing room decoration dictate placement. Don't assume you should leave the chair or couch where it's always been—it was put there for a completely different purpose: for aesthetics or socializing or the sake of the view out the window, but not for music listening. Experiment to find the best sonic location, then rearrange the furniture around this. At least try it before rejecting the idea out of hand. You can move all the furniture back if you decide the improved sound is not really worth the dislocation of your room.

If there are other members of your household who feel strongly about where the furniture should be, for heaven's sake try to figure out a workable compromise before you all stake out your positions so rigidly that any mutually satisfying arrangement is that much more difficult to arrive at. Not everyone finds good sound more rewarding than good decor, and not everyone is in a position to blend the two successfully.

Speakers, Room Boundaries, and Bass

If speakers could be put nowhere, they wouldn't suffer from room effects, just as dipoles benefit from not having to contend with speaker cabinet effects. One wouldn't be plagued by problems of standing waves (see below) and the like. Free-standing speakers, designed to be placed well away from any walls, as a general rule will give the best imaging and least time smearing without the need for special room treatment. *IAR* recommends placing speakers at least 5 feet away from any reflective (untreated) wall. Good advice but, in order to follow it without having the speakers sitting in your lap, you probably have to be living in a loft or an old house with dimensions more generous than the norm these days.

Walls most influence sound in the bass and lower midrange. The closer to the walls or floor you place the speakers—this is called *boundary reinforcement*—the more they will set off room resonances in addition to giving the *impression* of more bass. The room's standing waves can be excited, adding a vague heavy ringing boom to the bass. Speakers positioned some distance away from walls, floors, and corners receive the least bass reinforcement but also as a result benefit from the lowest bass coloration.

Placing speakers close to one surface increases bass, placing them close to two surfaces, a wall and the floor, further increases bass, and placing each in a corner, with three surfaces, increases bass most of all. Each increase in bass is accompanied by an increase in coloration. Therefore, "more," once again, is not necessarily "better," and indeed usually means "more distorted." However, speakers that sound too thin and lean, like some mini-monitors, can be placed closer to walls to boost their warmth and upper bass. The tradeoff is that this may also degrade imaging and increase time smearing from wall reflections. Worse yet, midrange performance could suffer by becoming honky and boxy sounding. Pick your poison.

In a rectangular room, placing your speakers against the longer wall will generally result in a softer, more resonant sound. Bass waves will not have a sufficient distance to propagate. Place the speakers against the short wall so they are firing down the length of the room and you will get more bass; other room problems can then be treated.

Peter Walker of Quad developed a working formula some years ago for speaker placement that many have found provides the least colored results. The Walker dictum is: "The best position for any loudspeaker is one third of the distance along the diagonal." Once you understand what that means, it's an easy and handy formula to remember (makes for impressive cocktail chatter too). Visualize a line crossing your room from one corner to its diagonal opposite. Mark off one third of the length and place one of your pair of speakers at this point. Repeat for the other speaker, starting from the other corner of the room.

If this lands you with one speaker beside a solid wall, the other next to a doorway that mustn't be blocked, then compromise the dimensions a bit (some say the formula ranges from one third to one fifth of the diagonal distance).

Walker's dictum is a very useful guide but not a law, because each room and speaker will interact differently. It offers a solid starting point, a sort of "X marks the spot" from which you can start exploring. Speaker location is critical to within an inch, even, without exaggeration, to a quarter inch. By critical, we mean that one can hear the sound suddenly lock in due to a minute repositioning. It is like hearing the image lock in when you have your stylus finally set up just right.

The one important problem with the Walker formula is that it leaves out the critical third dimension of height. There are two heights that are important and therefore two adjustments that need to be made. The bass height off the floor needs to be optimized—the closer the driver is to a surface, the more bass reinforcement but also the more bass coloration. The tweeter height must then also be optimized in relation to your (seated) ears. High-frequency energy is easily absorbed, even by just the obstruction of the air it passes through before reaching you. If the tweeter is either significantly above or below ear level, you may miss out on this part of the audio signal altogether. Once your bass driver height is established, tune in the tweeter/ear level by adjusting the height of your listening chair.

There is no rule of thumb for how high off the floor the bass driver should be. Some speakers are designed to be *floor loaded,* meaning they use the floor to provide beneficial reinforcement for the bass. Other speakers will sound bottom-heavy if too close to the ground. Placing the bass driver at the wrong height can produce low-frequency cancellation when the bass frequencies are reflected out of phase to the original wave form by floor and wall. Get the advice of the manufacturer and other users, then experiment with the particular vagaries of your own room and system.

The Importance of Symmetry

For the best sound, your listening chair(s) and the speakers should be positioned approximately at the three angles of an isosceles triangle. Certain speakers sound best a little closer to each other than they are to the listener, like the Spicas. Quads often sound best spread a little farther from each other than they are from you. Follow the manufacturer's advice but also talk with other users and experiment for yourself.

If you spread the speakers too far apart, you will get a "hole-in-the-middle" effect, a space between the speakers that is empty of sound. Bring them too close together, and the sound field from each speaker will overlap and cause a sense of blurring of the soundstage.

If you distance yourself too greatly from the speakers, imaging will fall apart. Sit too close and it's like listening with a pair of giant headphones.

The speakers should be exactly equidistant from wall, floor, ceiling, and listener. Don't just eyeball these distances, measure them—an inch can make a difference. This symmetrical placement will ensure that the room's effect is the same on both speakers. However, this also presumes a room symmetry that is not always available.

Room symmetry, in terms of both the room's architecture and its furnishings, is as important to setup as speaker symmetry. Room and speakers invariably interact, the room becoming in effect a form of enclosure for the speakers. This "enclosure" (which will be set into resonance by the speakers) should be the same on both sides of the speaker position. For example, don't, if you can help it, place one speaker beside an open doorway and the other speaker beside a wall, because then the two speakers will sound different. If that location is your only choice, then try to fake a wall by hanging a heavy rug over the open doorway to prevent the sound from leaking out into the next room.

If an asymmetrical environment cannot be avoided, then try moving the speakers around a bit—you may be able to compensate for the imbalance by a slight imbalance in the speaker placement. By the way, correcting such imbalances is NOT what your tone controls (if you have any) are for. These should be used, if at all, only as a last resort for correcting *recording* imbalances.

Start to look at your room's architecture from its "sonic" perspective and try to identify what kind of an environment it provides for sound waves. For example, the front baffles of well-designed speaker cabinets have all edges well rounded to prevent diffraction of the sound waves. The same holds true in your room as well—avoid having the speakers fire across any sharp edges.

Another vital aspect of the sonic environment is your furnishings. Sound is like light in that it can be reflected by hard surfaces, diffused by irregular surfaces, and absorbed by soft ones. These surfaces too should be somewhat symmetrical—if the left-channel side of your room is all metal and glass, but the right side is full of overstuffed furniture, then the sonic environment will be unequal. You will probably get a relatively hard, bright sound from the left channel and a dull, absorbed sound from the right. You'll also run into time and phase anomalies and other nasty distortions as those right- and left-channel sound waves, which should be reaching you simultaneously, in fact arrive milliseconds apart (the ear can readily distinguish delays of a few milliseconds) because the sonic environments the sound waves have to traverse are so different. The left-channel signals may richochet off the hard surfaces and arrive at your ear diffracted and muddied, while the right channel arrives with rolled-off highs, having lost a good deal of upper-frequency information in all that upholstery stuffing. Regardless of whether you can consciously dissect all these distortions, their effect on the music is to take away its "realness" and leave it sounding "recorded."

What you want in your room is a balanced ratio of absorptive to nonabsorptive materials. If that overstuffed furniture were distributed evenly around the room, then probably the acoustic problems would be largely eliminated. (See more on p. 259.)

There are some places, however, where you do *not* want symmetry. Sound waves, like light, reflect off the room's walls and other surfaces. Where there are parallel walls, the sound will bounce back and forth between them. Carpets, curtains, upholstered furniture will pretty much take care of this problem in the upper frequencies by easily absorbing the short wavelengths. It's the lower frequencies that are harder to deal with, having longer wavelengths.

Often, standing waves are set up in the room. These occur at frequencies having wavelengths that are twice a given room dimension. The result is that in some parts of the room the bass is unnaturally emphasized, in other parts unnaturally deemphasized. In addition, only certain frequencies of the bass are either emphasized or minimized, so you get a very inconsistent sound, with some notes pounding out and others nearly inaudible. If you can stroll around the room and the sound remains consistent wherever you stand, that is a very strong sign of a good room environment. If you do hear changes, just be sure neither your speakers nor listening chair is placed in a standing wave peak or null area.

To minimize this problem, avoid making any setup dimension either the same as or a multiple of any other. It is best if your room dimensions are all unlike also. While each speaker should be the same distance as its paired mate from any room boundary (wall, floor, or ceiling), the distance from the speakers to the wall should *not* be the same as or a multiple of the distance from the speakers to the floor, and so forth. For example, if the speakers are raised 2 feet off the floor, you don't want them to be exactly 2 feet or 4 feet out from the wall—make the latter 3 or 5 of some other nonmultiple, or else change the height off the floor.

A Few Particulars on Dipoles

Because the dipole's back wave is not absorbed in a cabinet, the speaker's setup must be very careful to minimize the amount of the back wave that bounces off the rear wall and is reflected forward to the listener. As it bounces forward, it radiates into the room and mixes with the original forward wave form. This causes both reinforcement and cancellation interferences at different frequencies, plus time smearing. In addition, the diaphragm is so light that it may be driven by this acoustic back wave bouncing forward off the rear wall, and so the diaphragm will no longer represent the original music signal.

It's essential that dipoles be placed well away from any reflective surface. It is especially important that they not be placed *parallel* to any wall when dipoles are properly set up, the radiating back wave has a sufficiently long delay time before reaching the listener so that it can be clearly distinguished by ear and brain from the front wave, and just adds a nice rich sense of ambience.

Subwoofer Setup

Asking around about subwoofer setup will get you a lot of conflicting information. Some say subwoofers must be carefully time-aligned with the rest of the system, which certainly seems to make sense. On the other hand, Paul Klipsch, among others, believes that if the subwoofers are placed too close to the rest of the speaker system (which would be necessary in order to time-align them), then you will get intermodulation distortion. You will have to experiment, keeping in mind what was said earlier in this chapter about bass reinforcement and also what was said in the chapter on speakers about the purpose of subwoofers. If you have subwoofers, these should be set up first for clean strong bass, then the speakers should be set up in respect to the subwoofers.

Your Listening Position

Where you sit in relation to the room is as important as where the speakers are placed. Remember the advice of Roy Allison (designer of Allison speakers) that, through symmetry, the room's effect is the same even when listener and speaker positions are reversed.

What applies to the speaker position therefore also applies to the listening position, with one exception. Whereas you want the room surfaces around your speakers to be *non*reflective because you don't want reflections mixing with and distorting the original music signal, this is not true of your listening position. Here, the reflections that come at you from the sides and back enhance the sense of the original ambience in the stereo recording. They also help to defeat your knowledge that you are in a relatively small space rather than in a concert hall. However, it is best that you, like the speakers, be at least 5 feet away from any reflective wall to avoid time-smearing reflections that blur sound and stereo imagining (see p. 259).

The better your speakers are at re-creating a stereo image and the more carefully they are set up, the more critical it is that you sit at the exact spot where imaging is sharpest, which is a point precisely equidistant from both speakers. Compare a good-quality camera lens to a very high quality one—the higher the resolution that the lens is capable of, the more critical the focus, because the *disparity* between being in and out of focus increases with the resolution. In the same way, an ordinary mass-fi speaker is less fussy about how it's set up and where you sit than is a high-resolution speaker, because the ordinary speaker is limited in its capability. It will reveal no more with a more precise treatment, just as the merely good lens will, after a certain point, be unable to focus any more sharply however exactingly it is adjusted.

Like speaker placement, the listening position must be set up in all three dimensions: *distance between* speakers, *distance from* speakers, and *height* off the floor. Naturally, since the listening dimensions are predicated on the speakers' position, the speaker setup must have been established first.

To determine your listening distance between and from the speakers, the easiest method is first to establish a center line. Measure and mark the center point between the speakers, then extend this point out into a line to your chair. Extending a point into a line without a second reference point to guide you is very tricky—it's easy to drift off course if you just eyeball this line, even using a straightedge. Say you start with drift of perhaps an eighth of an inch, barely visible; by the time you extend the line 6 feet, which is probably the closest you will be sitting, that eighth of an inch has expanded into a couple of inches.

The surest method is to take a length of *nonstretching* twine, center one end of the back of your listening chair (either pin it in place or have someone hold it), and pivot it in an arc from one speaker to the other. Be sure to measure from the same (mirror image) location on each speaker. Align your chair into the center. *Mark this spot*—use masking tape as on a stage or a thumbtack or nail polish or anything else, so long as it is semipermanent. Chairs are easily moved and you don't want to have to be constantly remeasuring.

Only one center line is exactly equidistant from both speakers. Sitting off that line unfocuses the image. A mono recording is a useful test. The music should come from a narrow line between the speakers. If it is diffuse, covering a wider area, then somehow the channels are blurring, probably because either the speakers or your listening position is set up imperfectly. You must use a genuine mono recording for this, not just a stereo one with your preamp controls switched to mono. On a stereo recording, the music from a center-stage soloist is fed to both channels. The same music signal comes out of both speakers but, if you are sitting off-line, will reach your ears at slightly different arrival times for the left and right channels. Therefore, the coherence of that soloist's image will be shot.

To set your distance from the speakers, always move back and forth along that central line. You want to maintain approximately an isoceles triangle, but again, quarter-inch subtleties can make a difference. High frequencies fall off in amplitude over distance, so the farther away you move your chair, the weaker the high frequencies will be by the time they reach you, and so the duller the sound. The closer you sit to the speakers, the more high frequencies you will hear. This measurement may vary with refinements in setup and even sometimes with the recording. You may move your chair back and forth periodically, whereas you never move it off-center or adjust the listening height (unless you also change the speakers).

The third and final dimension is your listening height, which should match tweeter height. Otherwise, you will lose much of the high-frequency information essential for conveying the sense of air, ambience, and other very fine detail of a recording. Listening height also affects image height. For example, if you are sitting higher than the tweeter, this can compress image height perspective, resulting in the illusion of looking down on the performers. A quick way to judge the difference in sound is to sit on a pile of phone books to raise yourself if you are too low and then listen to the music. If you are too high, get a lower chair or at least scrunch down a bit. Just be sure you do not scrunch below the level of the chair back or you will lose the important reflections off the rear and side walls.

To finalize your setup, measure the tweeter's distance off the floor. Then have a friend measure the distance from the floor to your ear when you are seated *naturally* (whether slumping or erect) in your listening chair. Adjust the height of your chair accordingly. You may have to change chairs or add cushions.

Using a Spectrum Analyzer

A spectrum analyzer can help you more quickly determine speaker placement so that it neither (a) is totally arbitrary, nor (b) requires weeks of painstaking experimentation. If you're blessed with a friend (or can hurriedly cultivate one) who has an Ivie, or the almost as good and a whole lot more economical Heathkit 1308 real-time half-octave spectrum analyzer,* well, then, your problems are largely over. You can determine the best (NOT meaning biggest, but smoothest and least distorted) bass response. Incidentally, take Roy Allison's advice—stick the speaker where you think *you'd* like to sit and then move yourself around the room holding the analyzer (be sure the speakers are connected up and playing). Through symmetry, the room's effect on bass response is the same even when speaker and listener positions are reversed. It's an awful lot easier than lugging speakers all over the room and reduces the risk of damaging them.

---

*Reviewed in *Stereophile,* vol. 9, no. 3, and in *Audio Amateur,* March 1985.

The Heathkit is sold only as a kit, requiring a generous 40 hours to build all three pieces—spectrum analyzer, pink/white noise generator, and power supply/rack mount accessory. It's time consuming, but consider that you are getting more features at a lower cost than in competing assembled units such as the Ivie. Though this job is probably not recommended for the novice kit builder, the instructions are reasonably clear to follow—something Heath has always been known for—and it's not outrageously hard to do, providing you have a good soldering hand. You must also be methodical—there is a very large quantity of parts.

Fine-Tuning the Speaker Setup

With the speakers correctly positioned in the room, and rigidly locked into place, now you can fine-tune their setup by angling them in relation to your listening chair. There is debate as to whether they should face straight forward or angle in slightly to aim directly toward the sweet spot. Toeing in tends to increase high-frequency response and so sharpens and focuses the image. Pointing straight ahead, some feel, gives a greater sense of depth to the image and slightly better resolution. It also offers a three-person wide listening position. Toeing the speakers out may give a greater sense of ambience. Results will be influenced by room acoustics. Experiment all ways.

If you do toe them in, you then have to decide whether you want the imaginary lines of the speakers' firing to cross slightly in front of you or just beyond. This too is debated and probably the final answer simply depends on your system in your room combined with your own taste. Aiming speakers at your ears or just beyond theoretically reduces cross-talk between the channels and so increases channel-specific information, giving better imaging, soundstage resolution, and other benefits of stereo. Crossing them in front, if you toe them in too much, can result in a mono image, as the two channels will merge together before reaching your ears.

Place the speakers so their axes cross just in front of your ears. If you sit exactly in the middle, the signals from both speakers are equal, giving a central image. If you move over a little to the right, then actually you are moving into the region where the left speaker is stronger and the right weaker. This will compensate for the fact that you are nearer the right-hand speaker and so will tend to push the image back into the center. If the axes crossed behind you, then as you moved

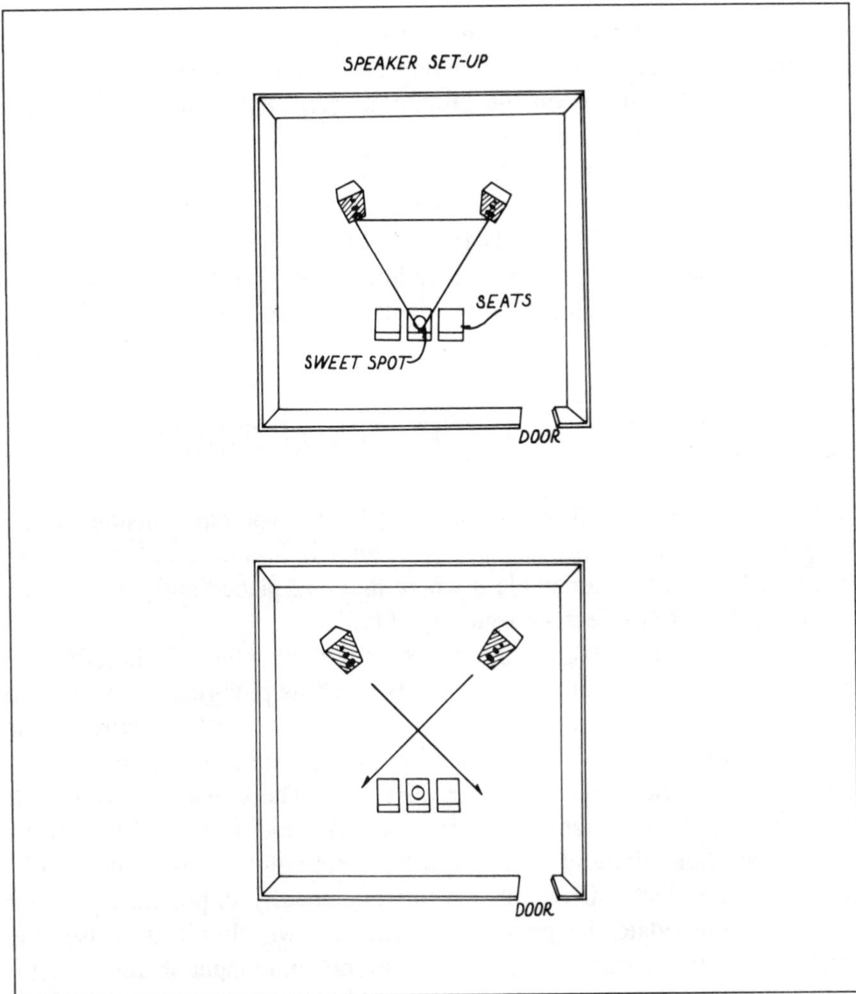

Fig. 20

closer to one speaker or the other, the image would tend to slide into the speaker you were closer to.

Whichever arrangement you decide on, the angle of the speakers must be exactly the same. There are a couple of ways to check this. One is simply, as you sit in the sweet spot, to compare how much of the side of each speaker you can see—if it's an equal amount of both sides, then the angles are the same or very close. A more accurate technique is to place a plastic protractor on the floor at right angles to the center line you marked, take the same nonstretching string you used to set up the basic speaker position, and secure it to the center back of the listening chair. Align the string along one side of one speaker and note the angle of the string on the protractor. Repeat for the other speaker and adjust so both angles match.

Sometimes a non-time-aligned, two-way speaker will sound better if you tilt the face up a little so the acoustic centers of the drivers are vertically aligned. The signals from woofer and tweeter may therefore reach the listener more nearly simultaneously, improving time alignment. However, unless the crossover is phase-coherent, this will be of little benefit.

PLACEMENT OF COMPONENTS

Once you have decided where the speakers go, you can consider where to place the other components. Their setup is less critical than that of the transducers, but nonetheless where they are placed and on what can have a substantial effect on sound quality.

Wherever possible, components should be plugged directly into wall outlets, not into other components (such as plugging the table into the preamp) or extension cords. Any unnecessary lengths of wire, in the form of extension cords or connection through other components, further increases the opportunity for distortion. The extension cord itself acts in effect as an antenna and increases RFI (radio-frequency interference) distortion. Preferably, every component would be plugged into its own separate electrical circuit. As this is generally impractical, at least try to accommodate the power amp with its own circuit as it uses the wall current to enlarge the signal. Be sure no component shares a circuit with a refrigerator, air conditioner, furnace, or other power-hungry object.

Yes, this may sound farfetched. And unless the equipment itself has the resolving power to reveal the difference between direct plugging and using an extension cord, such considerations are unnecessary. Some audio equipment—and not only the kind you have to mortgage your house to buy—can reveal the difference very clearly. An essential point to keep in mind is that good setup, like good equipment, is a matter of attention to detail. If you let all the details go by, you won't hear good sound; take care of all the details and the cumulative effect can be startling.

Because it operates at the lowest energy state in the entire system, the table (and any other front-end component) must be carefully protected from its environment. The electrical signal that passes from the cartridge to the preamp stage is minuscule and very fragile. The slightest spurious resonance is enough to add distortion, which will be amplified right along with the music until it comes out of the speakers.

The turntable must be protected from both acoustic (airborne) and mechanical energy. Do NOT put your turntable in front of the speakers, behind the speakers, on the same shelf, or anywhere near them—acoustic feedback will cause distortion and, even if you are not consciously aware of this, will wreak havoc on your music. The table base and to a lesser extent the dustcover may offer some, but at best limited, protection against acoustic feedback and so cannot be depended on.

The preamp must, because of the short tonearm cable (you can't drive a long cable with the minute cartridge signal), be placed within a few feet of the table. Even if you have a separate cartridge/tonearm-to-preamp cable, as with a Well Tempered Arm, the maximum length should be 1 meter or about 3 feet.

Place the preamp (or integrated amp or receiver, both of which contain a preamp section) to the RIGHT of the turntable, the side farthest away from the table motor and its stray magnetic field. The preamp's phono circuitry (on its left side) should be kept away from this magnetic field as it can interfere with the music signal, causing intermodulation distortion.

Equally, any hum fields, such as that from the preamp's transformer, should be kept well away from the cartridge as well. The music signal generated by the cartridge, being so minute, is easily damaged by the slightest distortion.

The power amplifier, tape deck, and AC power cords should be kept well away from the phono circuitry (left side) of the preamp. Also keep the amp well away from the cartridge and phono cables because of its transformers.

As a matter of choice, components should not be stacked, tempting as this may be. For one thing, they need ventilation so the heat given off by each component can easily dissipate. Also, there is an electromagnetic interaction that can cause intermodulation distortion and other problems. Furthermore, the transformer in each component puts out strong enough vibration that you can feel it with your hand. This vibration is transmitted between components and blurs the sound. However, many people do stack their components and suffer little or no noticeable degradation. Listen and judge for yourself. But if there is a way to avoid stacking, do so regardless of sonic degradation because heat shortens equipment longevity.

If you must stack, the preamp should go on *top* of the tuner (which you should turn off when playing records), the amp should be on its own. Preamps and amps, whether tube or solid state, give off a goodly amount of heat and need plenty of air circulation.

Components pushed up against a wall, if stacked or on shallow shelves, will not get enough circulating air even if their vent holes are not actually obstructed. Lifespan will be greatly shortened; sound quality will degrade over a period of time. Just one detail of what can go wrong: If the buildup of excessive heat from the resistors cannot readily dissipate, then resistance values can change, causing the sound to change. At worst, resistors can actually self-destruct.

Do not ever, under any circumstances, place the turntable (or any other signal source) on top of the speakers. Not only will you get terrible acoustic feedback, but the speakers vibration will interfere with the stylus's ability to trace the the grove accurately.

Interconnects and Cables

Speaker cable and interconnect runs should be kept as short as practical. Longer runs degrade sound quality and also get into a tangled mess. The ideal would be to eliminate the need for signal leads by *hard-wiring*—soldiering one component to the next with only a minimum length of wire, 1 inch or so, between them. Remember the audio verity that *everything* has a voice—the less you introduce into the circuit, the less distortion is introduced into the signal.

With this in mind, keep all signal leads as short as possible and only just long enough to reach between the two components being connected, plus another foot or so for maneuverability. *Keep both channels the identical same length,* even if one lead has a shorter distance to travel than the other. If the total distance from your signal source (turntable, CD player, tuner, tape deck) to your speakers is long, place the amp close to the speakers so the amp-to-speaker cables can be short, and extend the interconnect between amp and preamp as necessary. Speaker cables seem more critical than interconnects, especially with tube amps.

The backs of your components can start to look as if you threw a bowl of spaghetti at them. This makes it hard to untangle matters when you want to disconnect or replace a component, and, more important, wires crossing and tangling together can cause hum and noise problems. Keep them neat.

The power cords should not run parallel either to each other or to any interconnects or cables. When the magnetic field created by the AC cord cuts across an interconnect conductor, a 60-Hz voltage is induced in the interconnect because the AC magnetic field is constantly switching direction. This is particularly important to protect against when the signal is very small, as from the turntable and preamp, because any distortion introduced here interferes with a fragile signal and will be the most amplified. The AC power cord may cross other wires at right angles without causing harm.

Interconnects can run parallel and close together but not crossing. This not only keeps them neat but also, according to Dave Salz, helps to reduce RFI. You can buy tie-wraps and clamps to neatly bundle wires together at Radio Shack or from Monster Cable.

Support Surfaces

The function of good setup is to protect the system from its acoustic environment (speaker/room interaction), electrical environment (wall current plus hum fields and the like), and mechanical environment (resonances and vibrations). The surface a component is supported on provides the primary protection from this last. The surface's stability and resonance resistance are therefore critical. This applies to the preamp and amp as well as the table and speakers. Tubes, in particular, are microphonic and should be protected from vibrations, but even solid-state amps will benefit from protection from their environment. CD players, despite their hyped invincibility of "perfect sound forever," also greatly benefit from isolation from the environment, among other tweaks. (This isolation is covered in greater detail in "Turntable Setup," p. 230).

Components should be fully supported and carefully leveled so they cannot tip or wiggle, however slightly. A three-point system offers the most stable and level support, whereas four points can be very hard to get all exactly level. Three points describe one plane, whereas four points describe two planes—it is hard to get two planes exactly aligned.

Component supporters like the Sound Organization table, the Lead Balloon, and the Torlyte table, as excellent as they are, must themselves be supported on a firm and stable surface. Just as important as what surface your component sits on is what surface that surface rests on. (We also cover this in the section on "Turntable Setup," where it is particularly critical.) If the component support rests on a wobbly surface, such as a wood floor, then even the best coupling or decoupling at the component/support interface cannot overcome a bad coupling at the support/ground interface. So if your floor moves easily, you may be best off securing your component supports to a bearing wall, meaning a wall that is part of the structure of the building and not just a relatively flimsy partitioning wall.

There are two basic approaches to protecting against vibrations: high mass and low mass. As you may remember from the discussion in the chapter on tables this same duality crops up in many areas that involve controlling vibration. You can mass-couple the component to its support surface by means of spikes, or else you can damp the resonances and vibrations to prevent them from ever reaching the component in the first place.

These two basic approaches are realized in Mod Squad's Tiptoes and other spikes and in Audioquest's Sorbothane damping feet. Both these approaches help to control vibrations while preventing the addition of more vibrations. Either method will help ensure that the component cannot shake on its support—the spikes because a point is inherently a more stable support device than a larger surface, and the Sorbothane because it squashes beneath the component's weight and so fills in any gaps that could otherwise allow wobbling.

Spikes mass-couple the component to the surface beneath it. Providing the spikes are level so the component cannot rock on them, the component when so supported becomes linked to the supporting surface as solidly as if it had far higher mass—the number of pounds per square inch on those tiny points is enormous. In order to ensure the greatest effect of mass coupling per point, you should use the minimum number possible, preferably no more than three unless the component is very large.

There are three things to know about using Tiptoes: They should be placed point down on the supporting surface (with the surface protected by a coin from being impaled if you desire), the minimum number that will support the component should be used, and using the tall ones wherever possible will provide a greater improvement than using the smaller ones. The smaller ones are for use where height is restricted, as on a shallow shelf or a rack, and also for lighter components that may be a little unstable on the tall Tiptoes. However, simply using

Tiptoes—either type, either way up—brings about the greatest part of the improvement.

A Sorbothane foot, which looks essentially like a hockey puck with a depression in one side, decouples the component from its mechanical environment. Sorbothane has an extraordinary ability to absorb mechanical energy, a process known as damping. It is a soft, sticky compound that bonds tightly under compression and so absorbs externally induced resonances. It then dissipates this energy by converting it to heat within the material.

There is a general rule of thumb about when to use which approach, mass loading or damping. If a component suffers from a goodly amount of mechanical vibration, such as a table that is not well protected against a lot of acoustic feedback, then *decouple* the component from its environment by using Sorbothane feet. If the component is already on a pretty rigid, stable support and very little vibration is involved, *mass-couple* it with Tiptoes or spikes. An additional suggestion is that if a component is heavy, use a coupling foot like Tiptoes, but if light use a decoupling foot like Sorbothane. The feeling seems pretty universal that in the case of speakers, spikes, not decouplers, work best. Incidentally, hardware stores offer much cruder and less expensive alternatives to Tiptoes, including the all-metal furniture glides that used to be called Domes of Silence (appropriately enough, for audio).

Just to add the joker to the deck: Sal Demicco of Discrete Technology and Larry Smith of Perfectionist Audio both prefer acrylic plastic feet to anything else around and use them as supports for all components.

Again, both these approaches are quite system and room dependent. Both spikes and decoupling feet are excellent when they work, but they are not surefire solutions. You must experiment to determine for yourself what works best in your system. This is one of the greatest frustrations of being involved in high-end audio—not so much the need to experiment as the absence, or at least the rarity, of a "leading library" approach where one could borrow briefly before buying. We strongly sympathize with the dealers' side also, and understand full well that such privileges not only invite but often receive abuse. It is a conundrum that the audio societies sometimes are able to help out with.

CONNECTING THE COMPONENTS

Faced with all the input/output choices and lots of wire, you may think this area is complex, but in fact everything goes together in a very logical way, one connection at a time. Be sure you are using good interconnects—this makes a significant difference in sound quality (see p. 187).

Each connection represents an opportunity for distortion to be introduced, so the quality of the connection itself is also important. The electrical signal is often likened to water in its behavior. Imagine it flowing through a series of pipes—if the joints between the pipes are dirty or loose, the water will not be able to flow as easily. Be sure all connectors are clean and tight.

Follow the direction of the audio signal when connecting your components—first the music source(s), then the amplification stage, whether preamp and amp or integrated amp or receiver, and finally the speakers.

Front-End-to-Preamp Connection

Turntable to Preamp

The cartridge signal is conveyed to the preamp for RIAA correction and the first stages of amplification via the tonearm cable. In the case of all less expensive arms and about a third of better arms, this lead is permanently attached to the arm. The other end with the RCA phono plugs goes into the back of your amplifying component (preamp, integrated amp, or receiver) where it says PHONO or PHONO INPUT. The red plug for the right channel goes into the right jack, the white plug for the left channel into the left jack. Be sure not to reverse these or you will have reversed the phase. This does no harm to the equipment, but it can cause bass cancellation, muck up the imaging, and altogether make the music sound less good.

The ground wire, which grounds the cartridge, may be part of the tonearm interconnect or it may be a separate thin black, green, or gray wire terminating in a U-shaped prong. Either way, ground it to the preamp chassis. Some preamps provide a screw or other connector marked GROUND; otherwise just loosen a screw on the chassis and secure the ground wire under this. If your table has only a grounding terminal and no wire, use a length of bell wire stripped bare of insulation; connect one end to the table's grounding terminal, the other to the preamp chassis.

The turntable should be plugged directly into a wall outlet, not into an extension cord, or even worse, into the back of the preamp.

Turntable to Head Amp to Preamp

If you are using a head amp—needed in the case of a low-output moving coil cartridge and a preamp without an MC signal boost stage—the tonearm cable should first be connected to the input jacks of the head amp, then the head amp to the preamp. Run an interconnect from the head amp's output to the preamp's phono input.

Tape Deck to Preamp

Tape decks are line-level components, putting out a signal strong enough to go directly into the line stage of the preamp, bypassing the first signal boost and the RIAA correction of the phono stage.

You will need two pairs of interconnects, one for recording and the other for playback. On the back of the tape deck, one of the two jack pairs is labeled PLAY, TAPE OUT, or LINE OUT. Run one interconnect from here to the corresponding pair of jacks on the preamp, labeled TAPE IN or LINE IN.

The second interconnect should run from the other pair of jacks on the tape deck, labeled RECORD, TAPE IN, or LINE IN, to the corresponding jacks on your preamp, labeled REC OUT or LINE OUT. Follow the correct color coding: red is for the right "hot" channel (associations may help you remember—red = right = hot = fire engines = the devil), black or gray or white is for the left.

Now plug the tape deck into the wall socket and you're all set. Though the backs of many receivers and integrated amps include AC outlets, it's better to plug straight into a wall outlet to keep potential RFI and other interference away from the preamp and amp.

Tuner to Preamp

The tuner also puts out a signal strong enough to bypass the phono stage and go directly into the line stage of the preamp.

One pair of interconnects goes from the back of the tuner (labeled simply RIGHT and LEFT; red goes to right, the other goes to left) to the input jacks labeled TUNER RIGHT and LEFT on the back of the preamp. Plug the tuner into the wall socket. Set up your antenna (see p. 91).

CD Player to Preamp

Set up the CD player the same way as the tuner. If the back of your preamp is not labeled with a specific CD input, use any high-level input, such as TUNER, TAPE, AUX, VIDEO, DIGITAL—these all bypass the phono/RIAA stage in the circuit. Keep the player well away from the phono stage (usually on the left side of the circuit board) of integrated amps and preamps and also away from the tuner's front end, or you run the risk of increased noise.

Take care with CD player placement—vibration, both acoustic and environmental, is known to increase the error rate and therefore the need for error correction.

PREAMP TO AMP

(Skip this step if you are using a receiver or an integrated amp.) Place the amp well away from the sensitive front end of the tuner and preamp, as it can be a great noise producer.

On the back of the preamp, locate the jacks labeled OUTPUT or PRE–OUT. On the back of the power amp are two jacks labeled INPUT or PRE–IN. Run interconnects between these pairs of jacks. Remember—red goes to right, the other color, black or gray usually, to left. Plug the preamp into the wall. It is especially important to avoid using an extension cord with the preamp if at all possible, as this can introduce substantial hum into the system.

Amp to Speakers

("Right" and "left" refer to the speakers *as you face them.*) On the back of the amp are two pairs of terminals, one pair for the right speaker and one for the left. On the back of each speaker, a comparable pair of terminals (ranging from the cheapest screws to quality five-way binding posts) are marked plus (+) or red for hot, and (−) or black for ground. Some amps have terminals for two pairs of speakers—these may be labeled A and B or MAIN and REMOTE. If you're connecting only one pair of speakers, it doesn't matter which pair you use. The connection at the back of the speaker should be tightly secured—this is an electrical connection and you want no chance of "arcing." While not dangerous, an insufficiently tight connection will add a slight distortion to the sound. As a rule, spade lugs provide the most positive contact as they can be tightened down most thoroughly. Monster Cable's X-terminators are banana plugs that also make a very positive connection—the shaft expands when tightened down to provide a tight fit and high contact area. These can be used in conjunction with spade lugs.

In the case of tube amps, match the amp's impedance (see p. 126) to your speakers. The tap on the back of the amp that is marked with its impedance value is the hot tap; the terminal marked MAIN is the ground or "common" terminal. No solid-state amps and not even all tube amps offer this option.

On tube amps that do offer the choice, you can experiment with which tap sounds better—it is not always the one you would expect. You cannot damage the speaker regardless of which tap you connect it to; you can only improve or degrade the sound. Connecting to a lower-ohm tap may improve sound, as the signal will be going through fewer windings of the transformer and therefore may be slightly less degraded.

With transistor equipment, the difference in the power an amp puts into a 4-ohm speaker and an 8-ohm speaker is significant. As the speaker impedance halves, the amp's power delivery doubles—so an amp that can deliver 100 watts into an 8-ohm speaker will deliver 200 watts into a 4-ohm speaker.

The speakers must be hooked up in phase, or low bass will be diminished and imaging will be ethereal rather than solid. This is a simple matter of correctly hooking up the cables to the speakers, so plus goes to plus and minus to minus. (This must also be done correctly at the cartridge and tonearm.) All speaker cables, whether pennies-per-foot 16-gauge zip cord or many-dollars-per-foot speaker cable, have a positive and a negative side and all provide some clue to distinguish the one from the other. The two sides may use different-colored insulation; one side may have a raised rib or some similar mark while the other is smooth. In the case of zip cord, for example, the rough part of the wire goes to hot, the smooth part to ground. If you buy terminated speaker cable, then the terminations will likely be marked with red and black.

First lay the wires in place without connecting them. Then connect one of one pair—it doesn't matter which—and note which side of the cable went to which terminal. Hook up the other end so the same side goes to the same corresponding terminal. For example, say you hook up the right speaker first, using cable with one side ribbed for identification, and the ribbed side goes to the hot/positive/red terminal of the right speaker. Then go to the left speaker and hook it up the same way, ribbed to red, which is hot. Then at the amp, connect the ribbed side of the right speaker cable to the hot or positive terminal for the right speaker. Repeat for the left speaker.

You've now wired up your speakers *in phase* (relative). What this means is that the radiating surfaces of both speakers are moving in the same direction at the same time. If the speakers move in opposite directions—one pushing outward while the other is moving inward—then low bass will be canceled and the stereo image lessened.

To confirm that your speakers are in phase, disconnect one speaker as the system is playing. If the sound seems louder with only one speaker, they are out of phase. If it seems softer, they are in phase. Repeat this experiment several times, then hook them up correctly.

If you still sense you may have a phase problem even though your connections are correct, then perhaps the drivers themselves were incorrectly hooked up (wrong polarity). However, it is sometimes an intentional part of the design to have the midrange drives out of phase. If you reverse its phase, you will change (not correct) the overall design. Check with the manufacturer.

To test that the drivers have correct polarity, connect a 1.5-volt battery and two short wires to the speaker's terminals. Connect the positive battery terminal to the red speaker terminal, and the negative battery terminal to the black speaker terminal. Closely observe the woofer's direction of movement—it should move forward for correct polarity. If it moves inward, its polarity is reversed. This is easily changed just by removing the driver, desoldering and reversing the leads to its terminals, and then resoldering and reinstalling. Double-check with the manufacturer first.

Absolute phase is the equivalent of the "relative phase" just discussed, but as applied to the whole recording/playback chain. It is unimportant how many times the signal goes out of phase in the system, *providing* that it finally emerges from the speakers in the same overall phase condition as it began. (A preamp that inverts phase is not because of this bad, providing it inverts phase twice, restoring the output to correct phase.)

Sound consists of pressure waves that have peaks and valleys. If absolute phase is reversed, then a signal in the recording that represents a positive pressure in the air at the original mike will create a negative pressure in your listening room. A bass drum, for example, first pulls air in as the mallet contacts it, and then pushes air back out. The drumbeat being played back should also start with a pull followed by a push or it is out of phase.

What difference could all this really make to the sound? Peter Moncrieff offers a neat analogy: Say the word "puff" but *inhale* as you say it instead of exhaling. The word is the same but the sound quite different.

Correct absolute phase producers better stereo imaging and more forceful transient reproduction. Minimalist recordings will show this the best. Multimike recordings may have no absolute phase (perhaps a contributing factor in how bad some of them sound) since the mikes may all be out of phase with each other. Recording engineers rarely consider they question of absolute phase and so it is not consistent from record to record—in fact it may be inconsistent from cut to cut and even from track to track!

Some people are very sensitive to absolute phase, others not at all. Since you can experiment for free, it's worth finding out if you can hear a difference on your system. If you can't, don't fret. Just keep in mind to try the experiment after your next upgrade (whether of component or set-up quality), at which point you may be able to hear the difference.

Ken Kessler offers several quick tests to determine whether or not your system inverts. Sit to the left or right of your sweet spot (what Kessler calls the hot spot). If the phase is preserved from recording mike to you, you should be able to hear the far speaker. If it is phase-inverted, you won't. Inverting (correcting) the phase by switching the leads at the speaker terminal not only lets you hear the far speaker but, when you return to your hot spot, reveals improvements in sharp transients and greater depth.

Another test demonstrates the effect inverted phase can have. Take a good live minimalist recording and listen to the applause. If it sounds like real people clapping flesh-and-bone hands together, phase is correct. If phase is inverted, the clapping will sound like the snap, crackle, pop of Rice Krispies.

A third test is just to reverse the connections to both speakers, so they remain in phase relative to each other but the system's absolute phase has been inverted. A signal impulse that previously produced a compression—the driver pushing out—now yields a rarefaction or inward movement.

If you can hear differences with any of these tests, you may want to consider a preamp that provides phase-inversion switching. A flick of a switch, while it adds a small sonic degredation, beats constant reversing of speaker terminals. *Hi-Fi News & Record Review* has offered a switching device called the Phase Shunter that performs the same job.

Plug Polarity

This is another important fine point that some will consider belongs in Ripley's *Believe It or Not*. Which way a component's AC power cord plug is inserted into the wall socket can affect the sound of your system. In truth, it *will* affect it, the only question being whether or not your system is sufficiently revealing to allow you to hear the difference. Incorrect polarity results in incorrect grounding, and incorrect grounding results in hash and other nasty distortions.

Enid Lumley was probably the first to point out its effects in her baptismal column in *The Absolute Sound*.* Ms. Lumley has often been dismissed as a "fringe lunatic" but has usually been proven right eventually. What she has to say is very much worth following and she doesn't get coy when she has something new to say. She has written in both *IAR* and *The Absolute Sound*.

Anyhow, the importance of plug polarity has subsequently become sufficiently acknowledged that Namiki sells a special plug-polarity tester called the Direction Finder. A volt-ohmmeter works equally well and many people even use their ears perfectly successfully. Incidentally, you can get very inexpensive VOMs at Radio Shack that will perform the basic functions. Beckman meters are excellent—the Circuitmate DM25L does a great deal at a very good price.

By volt-ohmmeter: Disconnect all interconnects to the component you are testing but leave it plugged in. Set the voltage meter to DC 5 volts. Hold or clip one lead to a true ground (see below). Hold or clip the other lead to the chassis. Make a note of the voltage reading, then reverse the plug and take another reading (if it's a three-pronged plug, put on an adapter, also called a grounding cheater, which converts a three-pronged to a two-pronged plug, so you can reverse it). Most people say that the correct plug orientation is the one that gives the lowest reading on the chassis. Sal Demicco says his experimentations have shown

*No. 20, December 1980.

that the orientation is correct when all the readings for the entire system are closest together. He doesn't know why, but the difference can be clearly heard.

Mark the proper orientation on both plug and socket with red nail polish or another permanent mark, so when the component gets unplugged, you will know the right way to plug it in again.

Also, while you are doing all this, make sure the fit of plug in socket is snug. A loose fit can add to distortion—either slightly spread the prongs apart or squeeze them together to snug up the fit.

Grounding

A system needs to be grounded because of the slight AC leakage voltages that develop on equipment chassis. It should be grounded to a true ground *at one point only,* or you run the risk of setting up grounding loops with 60-Hz hum and all the harmonics of 60 Hz extending up into the midrange.

The components are all automatically grounded to each other by the interconnects' RCA jacks, which ground the chassis. Now you want to ground *one* component only to a true ground. (True ground is the ground screw on your wall outlet, the third hole in a three-way wall socket, or a cold-water pipe—a cold-water pipe comes up from the ground, while a hot-water pipe runs only to the furnace or water heater, neither of which represents a true ground). Conventionally, the preamp chassis is grounded, but Lumley reports much better results with grounding the amp.

If any component (except the one you are grounding) has a three-pronged plug on the AC power cord, this will set up a ground loop, and therefore a hum, because the unit is now grounded in two places—the wall and the interconnect. Add a grounding cheater to the plug to convert it from the three-pronged to the ungrounded two-pronged type.

Ground the tonearm grounding wire to the preamp chassis.

System Tests

Many test records are virtually useless without test equipment. Telarc's *Omnidisc* is one of the better ones and also has good instructions. Among CD test discs, the Opus 3 discs actually help teach you how to listen to music and recording techniques. They are also, like everything else from Opus 3, excellently recorded. The *RCA Test Compact Disc* does not have great recordings, but it has some useful tests that do not require special equipment, as well as a good instruction manual.

Playing interstation noise from your tuner gives you a very basic test. The signal should seem to be coming from a point right in the middle, between your speakers. If it is not, then you have a problem somewhere in your system.

TURNTABLE SETUP

As said before, the turntable is literally a *phonograph,* and the *phono* it is trying to trace is the microscopic writing on the record. Vibrations and resonances that you are likely to dismiss as meaningless, or don't even recognize the existence of, will very seriously interfere with the accurate retrieval of music from the record. However wonderful the rest of the system may theoretically be at giving you *all* the music becomes a moot point if all the music never makes it off the recording. Simply put, if you don't get the music off the record, it matters little what you spend on, or do to, the rest of the system—the music cannot be retrieved somewhere downstream.

Of course, good setup starts with a good table—a poor one is so distorting that it matters less where you put it. However, even in the case of a mass-fi table, improved setup can make a surprising difference. It cannot turn mediocre into good, but it can prevent mediocre from being worse.

The acoustic signal the table has to extract from the recording is minuscule and very fragile, as is the electrical signal that passes from the cartridge to the preamp stage. The slightest spurious resonance is enough to add distortion that will ride right along with the music signal throughout the system and come out greatly amplified—some 30,000 times—through the speakers.

Borrow a stethoscope from a friendly local medical practitioner (whether treating humans or animals) and amaze yourself and your friends with what you can hear happening to your table. Listen to the plinth, the platter, the table support, even the tonearm. Listen both with the motor on (obviously you cannot listen to the platter itself while it is turning) and with it turned off. Listen during the day and at night—you may be surprised at how much quieter the microenvironment can be at night. A stethoscope is almost certainly cruder than a stylus, but it will give you some idea of what the stylus has to contend with. Add to this that the friction of the stylus riding in the groove itself introduces a whole new generation of vibrations, including vinyl ring and needle chatter.

If your hands are very steady, you can also very delicately hold one end of a jeweler's screwdriver to the tonearm while a record is playing, hold your ear up to the other end, and listen to the vibrations. However, do this *only* if you have an unshakable hand, are playing an old and expendable record, and are prepared to risk losing the cartridge if your hand shakes.

A very crude but also revealing test is to place a dish of water on your table and watch to see if the surface vibrates as you walk around. A shallow glass dish is the best choice—the water's surface is unobscured by the clear glass, and because it is shallow, minimal weight is added to the table.

To protect the turntable from acoustic (airborne) energy, do NOT set it up in front of the speakers or near the speakers, and certainly not on the same shelf—acoustic feedback will muddy the sound, even if you don't consciously hear this. Also, don't push the turntable up against a wall as the sound waves from the speakers, reflecting off the wall, may cause acoustic breakup.

The table's plinth and to a lesser extent the dustcover offer some *limited* protection against acoustic feedback, but certainly few turntable covers are genuinely acoustic-protective. Most careful listeners remove the cover while listening. The drawback is that all the time you are listening, dust is falling on both table and record.

Table Support

Along the lines of the mass/no-mass conundrum, there has been debate on whether it is best to place the table on a massive support to protect against vibrations or to use a very light support.

It used to be believed that a massive support was the right solution, because sheer weight would prevent it from moving and so no vibrations would be transmitted up into the turntable. Unfortunately, though this type of support may not move much it will still move a little, and the movement occurs at a very low resonant frequency. The table suspension cannot provide protection against this low resonant frequency, and so it is passed through the table system and travels into the amp and speakers, where it intermodules with the musical signal, causing serious sonic deterioration.

A lightweight, stable support effectively filters out this low resonant frequency. It passes the higher frequencies, but the turntable suspension is designed to handle these. Put your ear to the ground outside your house and you'll probably hear the noise, even from blocks away, of machinery, air conditioner compressors, heavy traffic. Put your ear to the floor of your house and this noise will be reduced. The light structure of the building (relative to the earth) filters out much of the low-frequency energy. Adding another even lighter structure like a shelf further filters and isolates this noise.

So a light support of minimum size that is still compatible with rigidity is the consensus. You want quick transmission (rather than storage) of energy, and a light material that filters out low-frequency energy and minimizes low-frequency resonances.

Therefore, to help isolate the table from mechanical energy such as footfalls or even distant traffic, the best solution is a light but stable support placed on a *nonflexing* section of your floor. If you have severe vibration problems and/or a springy floor, mounting a light shelf on a wall will help isolate the table from vibrations and will certainly protect it from floor movement—just be sure that no part of the shelf support touches the floor. Make the shelf deep enough from back to front so that you can move the table out a little from the wall—the one disadvantage of wall mounting is that you can get strong reflections bouncing off the wall, causing problems of acoustic breakup.

A bearing wall is preferred to a partition wall—the former is more solid and so less likely to transmit vibrations into the table. A building's outside walls are always bearing ones and some internal walls may be as well. Apartment walls, particularly those through which you can hear your neighbors, are seldom bearing walls. Choose the one that seems most solid when you pound on it. Mount brackets firmly to the wall and then just rest, do not bolt, the shelf on the brackets. A lightweight shelf material like plywood is generally preferable to heavier materials such as particleboard. By the way, before trusting your expensive turntable to it, first make sure that the shelf won't come tearing out of the wall by loading it down with both volumes of the compact edition of the *Oxford English Dictionary*.

The table support, if it sits on the floor rather than being a shelf, is best coupled to the floor by spikes, whether these are screws that the table legs sit on (see below), or Tiptoes, or the three-pronged metal furniture glides that are an inexpensive though not ideal hardware-store substitute for Tiptoes. Spikes not only provide a solid connection to the floor but also act as a high-pass filter. This means that only the short-wavelength higher frequencies can pass through them and not the long lower frequencies. These higher frequencies are fairly easily dealt with at the component/support interface by whatever coupling or decoupling device is doing its job there. If the table support sits not on bare floor but on carpeting, spikes are especially important since otherwise the carpeting precludes a really solid, stable connection and allows the legs to rock.

Where you have the option, always use a three-point support system rather than a four-point one. Three, because they describe a single plane, are much easier to level and make rock-solid than are four, which describe two planes. This is one particular advantage of the excellent table support called the Lead Balloon. When supporting your table on a shelf, use three points instead of the table's four feet to ensure greater stability. In fact, it is always a good move to replace the four rubber feet with cones or Sorbothane pucks (see p. 219). A really cheap and dirty method is to use the screws that held the rubber feet in place, and add a hex nut to lock each screw down. If you don't mind adding another small hole to the underside of your table plinth, use two of the existing screw holes but put the third screw in the center of the opposite side so you have a stable three-point setup.

It really is critical that the table be level—*use a level to check this*. Otherwise, the platter will not spin evenly, the stylus will not sit in the groove properly, and the music will not be well retrieved from the groove.

Setting Up the Table System

If you are setting up a suspended subchassis table from scratch for the first time, do not be daunted. It is time consuming, aggravating, might even try the patience of a saint, but the reward is worthwhile in terms of music. You also enjoy a pleasing sense of accomplishment once you are done. If you always break anything you touch, then by all means pay someone else to do it for you.

Here is the basic procedure. First, buy yourself a nice bottle of wine or some other reward to partake of once you've completed the job. Then set aside several *uninterrupted* hours. Do not let yourself be rushed, whether through enthusiasm, impatience, or allotment of too little time. Your tonearm is probably already mounted on the table. If not, order a predrilled tonearm board for your particular arm from the table manufacturer and follow both the table and the tonearm manufacturer's instructions for installation.

These are the basic steps for table setup: (1) Carefully read the manufacturer's instructions; (2) set up the table on a level surface that allows you any needed access to the underside of the table to set the springs; (3) fill the bearing well with oil and insert the platter shaft; (4) set the springs; (5) move the table to its permanent position, making sure the surface it sits on is *level*; (6) set the belt onto the pulley and around the periphery of the platter; (7) dress the tonearm cable; (8) set up the cartridge; (9) connect to wall current and to preamp, being sure to keep the channels correct.

Here are some notes on the steps:

1. Read the manufacturer's instructions all the way through at least twice before you begin.

2. If you need to gain access to the underside of the table to adjust the springs, support the table on a surface high enough off the floor so that you can get underneath it easily. (If your table's suspension can be adjusted from the top, blow a kiss to the designer for saving you from having to crawl around the floor on your hands and knees.) An expandable dining room table is excellent—without inserting the extra leaf, spread the table halves apart just wide enough to support the table. If you don't have such a table and have to make do with supporting the turntable between two stools or on high piles of books, just be sure that the table cannot be inadvertently knocked off or over. Also be sure the support is absolutely level or, more accurately, that the turntable plinth is absolutely flat. Use a 6-inch level to check this.

3. Preparatory to installing the inner platter, be careful not to overfill the well or the shaft will not seat. Wipe up spills—a Q-Tip dipped in a little alcohol works well here. It's well worthwhile using the thick, dark Merrill and Linn bearing oils, as these can make an important sonic improvement over the standard thin, light-colored oils. These high-viscosity oils prevent the bearing from swimming in the shaft and cut down on friction.

4. Before starting to tune the springs, be sure that everything you will be using is on the table so you have an accurate weight to tune the springs to. This includes the platter, platter mat, record clamp, and the record (use one you don't care about). With a two-part platter, place the platter's outer ring upside down over the shaft and lay every-

thing else on top of it. Keep a clear view of the tonearm mounting board so you can tell as you tune whether or not it is level.

You can tune the springs by rotating either the spring itself or just the nut at one end. This will raise or lower the suspension. You want to tune the springs so the platter is *exactly* the same distance off the plinth *all around.* It should "float" about a quarter of an inch above the plinth. Also look at the tonearm board to be certain it remains parallel to the plinth surface. When you push directly down on the platter near the spindle, it should bounce straight up and down, not oscillate in a circle. If it moves circularly, go back and readjust the springs.

5. Set up the table in its final resting place and again test for perfect levelness of support surface, table plinth, and, most important, platter. A *bubble level* will do, but you can get a more accurate reading by using a *bullet level,* which is short enough to fit comfortably on the platter and plinth but long enough to provide an accurate reading. It is even more important than with pivoting arms that turntables mounted with straight-line tracking (SLT) tonearms be absolutely level.

6. Wash your hands before installing the belt as oil on your fingers will reduce the necessary traction between belt and platter. Handle the belt as little as possible. Dusting it with talcum powder or even cornstarch will help improve its traction. Be sure that everything—platter, platter mat, record, clamp—is in place upside down before installing the belt. Installation can be slightly tricky, so just work slowly and patiently. If speed is changed by the belt's position on the pulley, make sure you have it on the right part of the pulley for 33⅓ or 45 r.p.m.

Confirm that you have it positioned correctly by turning on the motor—the belt should ride right in the center of the pulley and of the platter rim. If it keeps slipping off, either it is greasy and should be dusted with talc, or else the springs have been adjusted so the platter rides at the wrong height, either too high or too low. If the belt slips up off the edge, the platter is too low and should be raised. If the belt slips off at the bottom, lower the platter.

7. Secure the tonearm cable with a P-clip to the inside of the plinth so that it cannot pull in any way at all on the suspension. Adding a second P-clip to the subchassis makes it possible to adjust the arm cable and clamp it in place so as to impose no tension on the suspension. This is called "dressing" the cable and is very important. Otherwise, the cable's pull can negate much of the benefit of the suspension, with bad sonic results.

8. To set up the cartridge, see below.

9. Be sure not to invert phase when connecting the tonearm cable (and therefore the cartridge signal) to the preamp.

FINAL TABLE, ARM, AND CARTRIDGE SETUP

How carefully you set up the cartridge goes a long way toward determining how good the music will sound. The amount of information the cartridge can extract from the groove is the *maximum* the system will ever see—it only goes downhill from here. If your arm and cartridge are set up poorly (or are poorly designed even though well set up), you will lose a lot of information and your cartridge will mistrack. This sounds like the attack of the killer bees—*zizzzzzz*. Very unpleasant, but even worse than unpleasant is that any mistracking increases the friction between stylus and groove walls and therefore increases wear. Serious mistracking can actually chip and gouge groove walls. The more careful you are about cartridge alignment, the more you will gain in improved tracking, lower distortion, greater clarity, increased focus, better stereo imaging.

Even though stylus alignment from the manufacturer is not always perfect, tonearm tangency is rarely ideal, records more commonly than not are poorly pressed, warped, perhaps even miscut, and despite all the other imperfections of playback, *nonetheless* you must be meticulous about optimizing arm/cartridge/record groove geometry. Any errors here either cost you details of the music or add distortion, which is then magnified along with the music signal. You must be as precise as possible in all those aspects over which you have control in order to compensate somewhat for errors in parts of reproduction and playback where you have no control.

There are three different planes in which the cartridge—more accurately the stylus—must be correctly aligned with the groove. The first is *lateral tracking angle*. Visualize the cartridge from a bird's eye view: It must be oriented so its arcing movement across the record maintains the stylus in the same relation to the groove as the cutting stylus's straight-line tracking across the record. The second plane is *azimuth*. If you're viewing the cartridge head on, the stylus must be absolutely perpendicular to the groove so it does not favor one groove wall and therefore one channel over the other wall and channel. The third plane is *vertical*

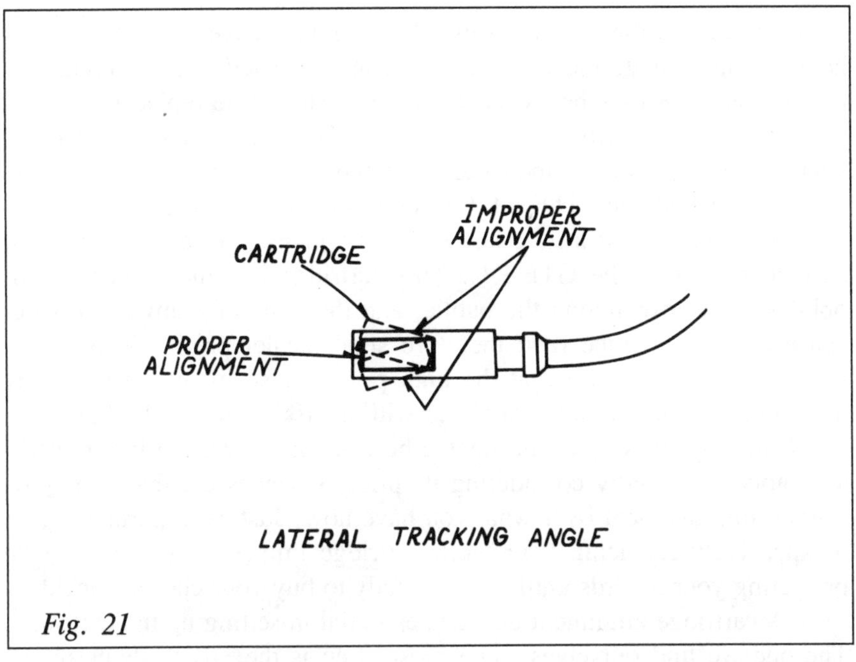

Fig. 21

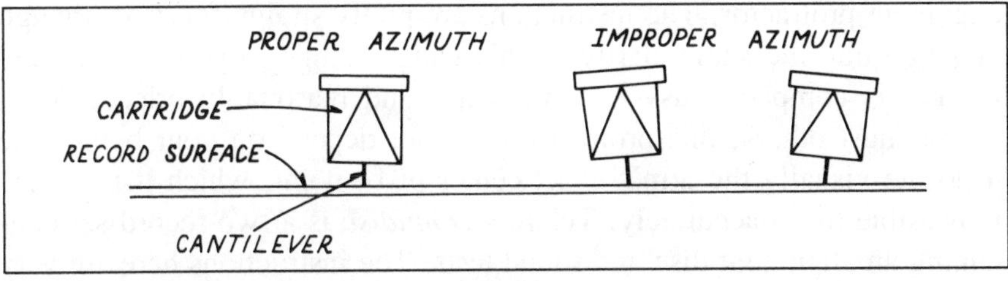

Fig. 22

tracking angle/stylus rake angle. Viewed from the side of the cartridge, the stylus must sit vertically in the groove, at right angles to the record's surface (see Fig. 23).

Regardless of whether the dealer has just set up the cartridge for you, or whether you have been listening to it this way for years and you think it sounds just fine, check the cartridge geometry. The dealer is unlikely to have fine-tuned it as well as you can, unless you have found an unusually careful and caring dealer.

As for the fact that you may have been listening to a poorly set-up cartridge for years, that doesn't prove a thing. Do it correctly now. In any case, if it's years old, you should be replacing the cartridge. A worn stylus not only can but definitely does damage your records. Worn enough, or worse yet chipped, it becomes literally a "record eraser," tearing away at the groove walls. Even if you have not put a lot of hours of use on it, the cartridge does have a shelf life, estimated as being around 18 months. After this time, it should be replaced.

If you can't afford to replace your cartridge, or haven't decided what to buy, go out immediately and buy the *least expensive* Grado cartridge, called the MTE + 1 (or some similar name—Joe Grado periodically upgrades it a little and each time gives it a new first letter; it used to be called the GTE + 1). This cartridge is famed among audiophiles, a sleeper among the public, and the bane of many dealers because of its low price (and therefore small dealer profit). This is Joe Grado thumbing his nose at the high prices of so many cartridges by designing and producing a cartridge with a $100 sound and a $20 price tag. Naturally, it is by no means the best of cartridges, but it is remarkably good, especially considering its price. Chances are that it may be a sonic improvement over what you have now. Just as important, by so inexpensively replacing your worn cartridge immediately, you will be protecting your records until you are ready to buy your chosen cartridge.

A cartridge alignment gauge is essential in setting up the cartridge. The one we find ourselves using most often is the DB Systems phono alignment protractor. The instructions are pretty straightforward (though lacking quite the same clarity as this gauge brings to your music) and the gig is compact, easy to work with, and reasonably priced. Also, unlike most others, this protractor does not depend on your being able to locate visually the arm's exact center pivot point, which it is almost impossible to do accurately. Telarc's *Omnidisc* is a two-record set containing an alignment disc and sound tests. The instructions here are very clear. Another good one is Mobile Fidelity's *Geo-Disc,* a thick plastic "record" that you can buy separately or get included in Mobile Fidelity record sets. Whatever alignment gauge you choose, do get one and use it.

Be sure the hole in the alignment gauge that goes over the turntable spindle fits snugly. If it does not, it might be off-center or could shift, making it impossible to get accurate results. If it is too large for your particular spindle, wrap tape around the spindle until the fit is snug. Just be sure that the point at which the tape begins is the same point (several thicknesses apart) at which the tape ends—if you overlap by only a partial turn around the spindle, then the built-up thickness of the tape on one side of the spindle will be greater than on the other, resulting in setup inaccuracies.

The series of cartridge setup steps must be followed in a particular sequence because each has a specific effect on the subsequent step. Change the order and the setup results will be wrong. This procedure is the same for both pivoting and SLT arms, with one exception: SLT arms do not incur skating force and so do not need an antiskate mechanism.

Tonearm and cartridge setup should be performed with the turntable in its permanent location. Use a level to determine that the platter is perfectly level. If it is not, you can either adjust the support the turntable sits on or else shim the feet of the turntable as needed.

(If you want to buy only one level, there are places where a bubble level is essential, so buy a bubble—it must also be lightweight so a plastic casing is an advantage. However, if you are prepared to spring for two levels, a bullet level, which is about 6 inches long, will give you a more accurate reading in places because you will be able to determine levelness over a broader area. For leveling turntable plinth and platter, therefore, a bullet level is more accurate. It should be lightweight and so is best encased in plastic.)

Next make certain that the tonearm mounting board is also level and parallel with the turntable. If it is not, then the tonearm will not swing across the record in a single plane and tracing forces will vary across the record. Place a small bubble level on the mounting board. If it is level, proceed.

If it is not, then you have several choices. If the arm came mounted to the turntable from the manufacturer, return it, because you probably cannot repair it and would be better off getting it replaced. If your dealer mounted a separate tonearm on your table for you, you can either return it to the dealer for repair or attempt to fix it yourself. The dealer should have checked for levelness; that this was not done may suggest the dealer won't correct the problem when you take it back. (On the other hand, everyone makes mistakes and perhaps this is one of them—only you can judge that of your dealer.) If you want to try fixing it yourself, loosen the screws that hold the mounting board in position and insert shims between the underside of the board and its support until the board is level when fastened down again. This is generally quite simple to do, but if you have qualms, do not attempt it. Of course, if you mounted the tonearm yourself, then you goofed and you can probably remedy the problem easily.

Also confirm that the distance from the center of the arm pillar (the upright post) to the spindle is correct. This *L dimension* varies with every pivoted tonearm. Your turntable instruction manual should list the L dimension, or else check with the manufacturer. However, if you cannot adjust the tonearm on the mounting board, or if the arm came premounted on the table, then whether this dimension is correct or not is a moot point, as you cannot adjust it.

Now comes the really fiddly part of setting up the cartridge geometry. This is not hard, but it is painstaking and can tax your patience.

You must have an alignment gauge in order to set up your cartridge, even if it is only the flimsy paper template that usually comes with a turntable or tonearm. You will also need a stylus pressure gauge, or tracking force gauge, for accurately setting tracking weight. A magnifying glass or one of those plastic magnifying cards will be very helpful, though not essential. You absolutely will need a very good, strong light that you can focus exactly where you need it. A set of jeweler's screwdrivers, small needle-nose pliers, and pointy tweezers to hold the nuts will ease cartridge setup.

Before we proceed, here are some fine points on cartridge-mounting hardware. While it is supplied with the cartridge, in many cases it appears to be more of an afterthought than a careful part of the design. The hardware should be considered in terms of its mass, strength to withstand torquing, the amount of space it requires in what is already a very constricted area, and ease of manipulation.

Sumiko sells a mounting kit with allen-head bolts. An allen wrench snugged into a closed slot is often easier to manipulate than a long screwdriver in an open-sided slot. The wrench also permits greater torquing. Shure hardware is lightweight aluminum, adding minimal mass. Monster Alpha II hardware uses round, knurled nuts that take up very little space and provide a good grip. Linn's hardware is very strong but also very heavy and will, in many situations, add too much mass. But you could crack the headshell and distort the cartridge body before these bolts would give under torque.

Obviously, ferromagnetic metals should be kept well away from the cartridge, because the possibility exists for a subtle electromagnetic interaction to occur between metal and cartridge generator.

Mount the cartridge in the headshell and, if the headshell is a removable one, mount the headshell on the tonearm. The headshell screws should be finger-tightened just enough that the cartridge cannot fall off, but still sufficiently loose that the cartridge can be easily moved around.

Where possible, work with the stylus's little safety cap in place, even though most of the time it has to be removed.

Disable the antiskate mechanism to prevent the arm from pulling to the outside. Make sure the counterweight is in position on the back of the arm and set roughly to counterbalance the weight of the cartridge. Immobilize the platter so it cannot rotate during setup. Otherwise, if the platter keeps shifting slightly your alignment measurements will not be accurate, and you run the very grave risk of having the stylus slip off either the protractor or the platter, with usually disastrous results! Stick the platter down firmly with masking tape and/or insert wedges underneath. Wedges are not always secure with a suspended subchassis design, as they may not brake it but just push it up a little so it can still shift. Be sure that you secure the platter without in any way altering its height or its levelness.

Wherever you need to use a record to set up the cartridge, use one that is disposable—accidents happen and you should not have to worry about the record being hurt in addition to the stylus.

Lateral Tracking Angle

With these preparations completed, the first step is to set the lateral tracking angle. This is the angle at which the stylus tracks across the record and should replicate as much as possible the angle at which the cutting stylus originally tracked the master disc. It can be adjusted through a combination of altering the length of the arm tube (by adjusting the *cartridge overhang*) and adjusting the *tangency* by angling the cartridge in relation to the groove. Cartridge overhang is the distance that the stylus tip protrudes beyond, or overhangs, the middle of the spindle. Overhang and tangency are both established in setting the *null points* (see Fig. 24).

These adjustments require a headshell with slots, not round holes, for cartridge mounting; replace yours if necessary. The Audioquest and Sumiko headshells are well regarded. If necessary, try filing out the headshell's mounting holes to extend them into longer slots that will allow greater travel. If the cartridge needs to be twisted in the horizontal plane more than the headshell allows, try filing the holes wider to allow more play for adjustment.

For SLT arms, which replicate the passage of the SLT cutting head by traveling straight across the record, the cartridge body simply needs to be squared up and aligned with the tangency lines of the setup gauge.

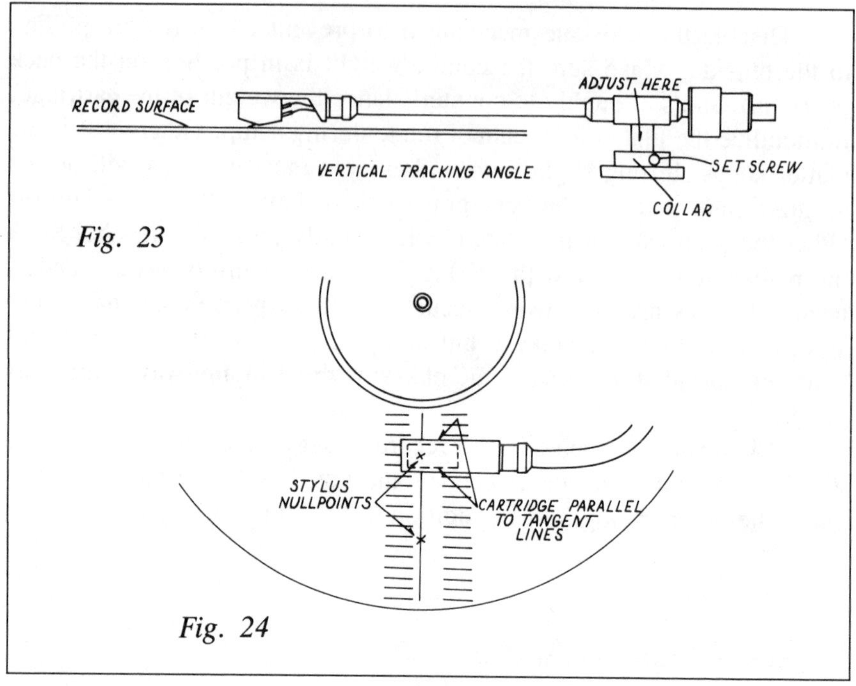

Fig. 23

Fig. 24

Null Points

These are the two points at which the lateral tracking error is zero degrees, meaning that the tracking angle will exactly match the original cutting angle. If the cartridge is perfectly parallel to the record grooves at these two points, tracking distortion will be optimally low across the entire record. Unless your tonearm manual specifies otherwise, assume you should use the common null points at the radii of 66.04 millimeters (2.60 inches) and 120.90 millimeters (4.76 inches) measured from the center spindle.

Follow the instructions provided with your alignment gauge—different gauges use slightly different methods. If your gauge uses both null points, keep adjusting between the two points, angling the cartridge body in the headshell, until overhang and tangency are good at both points. If your arm is one that cannot be adjusted for both points, optimize it at 66.04 millimeters as this is the area of most difficult tracking. Be sure, as you square up the cartridge body with the alignment gauge's markings in order to align the cartridge with the grooves, that the sides of the cartridge itself are square, or your alignment will be wrong.

When all adjustments are correct, tighten the cartridge-mounting screws. Be careful, as it is quite easy to throw the cartridge out of alignment again. The best way to prevent this is to keep a firm grip on cartridge and headshell together and to tighten down one screw delicately a turn or so, then the other screw a turn or so, and so on back and forth. If you torque down one screw all the way, the torquing action is almost certain to twist the cartridge out of alignment. Once the screws are tight, you then want to tighten them just a little more to really lock the cartridge to the headshell and so minimize the risk of resonances. A word of caution: Do this with the headshell removed from the arm, or you can torque the bearings too and damage them. If the headshell is not a removable one, be positive that you are not twisting the tonearm tube as you torque down the screws, because this can hurt the bearings.

Before doing your final tightening, go back (first replacing headshell on tonearm if necessary) and recheck that the overhang measurement hasn't been altered. Then torque down the screws well, and if necessary reposition the headshell on the tonearm.

Azimuth

Before torquing down the headshell for a final tightening, set the correct azimuth. Azimuth alignment establishes the stylus at right angles to both groove walls to ensure proper right- and left-channel separation. It is adjusted by rotating the headshell on the tonearm. Either set the stylus down on a clear, blank portion of a disc so it serves as a mirror, or else remove the record and gently lower the cartridge onto a small, thin mirror such as a pocket mirror—it must be no thicker than a record.

Look at the cartridge head on. If it is correctly aligned, the stylus and cantilever and their reflection will together be a continuous, unbroken, single straight line. If the alignment is off, then the line will break in two at the stylus/mirror interface. Adjust accordingly. This is a very important alignment. To make it easier to see the stylus and cantilever, use a magnifying glass or one of those flat plastic magnifying sheets. These are also very useful for establishing SRA (see below) and for seeing more clearly just how grungy your stylus really is.

Another way of checking azimuth, recommended by Dave Salz, is to cue up the arm over the record surface and place a small bubble level on the headshell. Adjust accordingly. Of course, it is essential that the top of the headshell be absolutely flat in order for this to work. If you do not cue up the arm, you may crush the cantilever with the added weight of the bubble level.

If the headshell is not removable, and the tonearm does not have a special azimuth adjustment device, then you will have to shim the cartridge to correct azimuth. A shim of thin paper or a business card between cartridge top and headshell will correct allignment. Naturally, you will have to loosen the screws in order to insert the shims and so you will have to double-check all the above alignments before fully torquing down the screws again.

Vertical Tracking Force

Vertical tracking force (VTF) must be set now, before moving on to anything else. This would more accurately be called vertical tracking mass—averaging about 1.0 to 1.5 grams, it counterbalances the weight of the tonearm and cartridge. Refer to your cartridge instructions for optimum tracking force. Like all others, these recommendations are not infallible, so it's best to make the final adjustment by your own ear. For example, the Grado Signature 8 lists as tracking at 1.5, but is recognized as sounding best at 1.8.

First defeat the antiskate mechanism or set it to zero, and then balance the arm. This is done by shifting the counterweight back and forth along the arm until the arm is level and balanced. As this has to be done with the arm removed from the arm rest, and the cuing device in the down position and out of operation, the stylus is at high risk of getting bounced and damaged. Be very careful. You cannot protect the stylus with the stylus guard (unless it is a permanent part of the cartridge body, in which case use it to provide protection) as this will change the arm balance.

Secure the arm in the arm rest, move the counterweight to where you think it ought to be, take the arm out of the rest, and move it over the platter to check its balance, then return it to its rest before shifting the counterweight again. By ensuring the arm is secured before adjusting the counterweight, you reduce the risk of having to go out and buy yourself another cartridge tomorrow.

To help the arm handle warps, you want the counterweight as close to the pivot point as possible while still balancing it.

Now, once the arm is beautifully balanced, return it to its cradle, lock it in, and set the tracking force according to your cartridge instructions. You will need a tracking force gauge, also called a stylus pressure gauge, for this. A very good one is made by Acoustic Research, and though it looks like something sold in Woolworth, it functions fine. Technics also puts out a good one.

Vertical Tracking Angle

Vertical tracking angle (VTA) is the angle between the cantilever (when sitting in the groove, with VTF already set, and therefore somewhat retracted under load) and the record's horizontal surface. Setting the VTA adjusts the stylus vertically along the length of the groove so that it is aligned with the axis of the cutting stylus that made the original master disc. (All previous adjustments—except VTF—deal with the *lateral* geometry of the stylus.) Some years back, cartridge designers and the disc-recording industry agreed on (but don't always follow) a standard of a 15-degree angle for VTA, though there seems to be a consensus, in the high end at least, that in fact playback is optimized when VTA is at a 20-degree angle.

There is another stylus/groove setting called SRA (see below) and it is impossible to optimize *both.* Which takes priority is a matter of some debate, though the majority opinion favors VTA. SRA only became a factor with ellipticals and then the later, even more setup-critical designs like the Shibata and line contact—it does not apply to conicals. In any case, VTA and SRA must be set to sound best in a given system in a given room. The dealer's setting may not sound good when you get it home.

The easiest way to rough in VTA is to align the tonearm tube parallel to the record surface by raising or lowering the tonearm at the back. Then make any further minor adjustments needed to align the cartridge body. Though your purpose is to align the cartridge itself rather than the arm, in most arm/cartridge combinations the two are parallel—and it is much easier to read the tilt of a long arm than a short cartridge. Set the stylus down on a record, eyeball the tonearm tube as being either parallel to the record or not, make a note as to whether the back of the arm therefore needs to be raised or lowered to bring it into adjustment, then before doing anything else restore the arm to the arm rest and lock it into place. Before proceeding, be sure you have set VTF and set it correctly, as changing the tracking force alters the deflection of the cantilever and therefore VTA. Now adjust the arm pillar height.

You can make yourself a very useful gig for VTA, using a piece of light cardboard or stiff acetate. Make it about 2 inches high and 4 inches long. If you feel in the mood, paste a little support on the back, like that on a photo frame, so you can balance it on the record just behind the tonearm. Meticulously draw a series of precisely parallel lines along the length of the cardboard, spaced one sixteenth or, at most, one eighth of an inch apart. With this gauge, it is very easy to see the tonearm profiled against the cardboard. The top or bottom edge of the arm will either run parallel with one of the lines or else cut across several of them. If it is parallel, you are in business. If it intersects several lines, you need to make an adjustment. Of course, if your tonearm tube is tapered, this gauge is useless and you will have to adjust according to whether or not the top of the cartridge body parallels the record.

Another method for gauging parallelism is to use a small bubble level. The headshell, of course, *must* have a flat top in order for this to work. Match the plane of the tonearm to that of the record and you're all set.

Adjusting arm height on most tonearms is a real nuisance. Usually it is a matter of releasing a set screw on the arm pillar and then sliding the pillar up and down in its collar (see your tonearm manual for exact directions). Unless it has a special VTA adjustment feature, there is a likelihood that the arm pillar will drop precipitously as soon as the holding screw is released. Instead of the fractional adjustment you were aiming for, you are suddenly faced with a gross alteration and have to backtrack from there. So the method is distinctly crude for an adjustment where differences of only a minute or so of arc can be clearly heard. The eye can distinguish differences of 1 minute but the ear is capable of hearing 60 times more precisely than that.

This is the tremendous advantage of arms with a special VTA adjustment feature that allows you to tune in VTA and SRA for each record as you are playing it—then the sound is truly the best every time. Sumiko sells a VTA adjuster that can be used on any tonearm with a 16-millimeter mounting post. Even if you do not reset it every time for each record, it will at least facilitate setting up the arm optimally in the first place.

One way to prevent the arm's precipitous drop when the set screw is released is using business cards as shims, jamming in a bunch to support the pillar before releasing the holding nut and then either building up a few layers and subtracting a few as needed to adjust the height.

IAR, however, offered us a far more intelligent approach—employing the precision feeler gauges that car mechanics use to set the points on distributors.

This is not only a lot easier than fiddling with business cards but is also repeatable. If you use a selection of cartridges, for example, you can just make a note of the right feeler gauge or combination of gauges to get proper VTA for that cartridge. Of if you are experimenting with optimizing VTA, which *must* be done by ear and not by the relatively crude method of paralleling the body to the record, then you can keep a running record of the gauge numbers you have experimented with and which you prefer. Incidentally, you can get these at any auto parts store or places like Sears or, if you have a friendly mechanic and you dare explain your application of the gauges (you may be laughed right out of the garage), perhaps you can get one there.

You can get a good picture by listening to music of whether or not you have optimized the VTA setting and, if not, what needs to be done to correct it. When the arm is too high and needs to be lowered at the arm pillar, the sound will lack deep bass or the bass will be thin, highs will be edgy, the midrange harsh—overall the sound is hard and bright, definitely a formula for listener fatigue. Dynamic range is reduced as low-level details between the musical notes are obscured by distortion. Transient attacks may be too sharp. When the arm is too low and needs raising, you will find the sound dull and damped, with the highs rolled off and the lows muddy and lacking definition. Transient attacks are dull.

The best approach is to tune in VTA gradually. Start with it set too low, with the sound dull and damped, and very gradually raise it little by little, first to the point where it is parallel to the record, and then so the back of the cartridge is tilting up. Keep a record of your feeler gauge settings and your opinion of each and then, having tried a wide range of options, return to the one you like best. Proceed slowly with each change; it may take several minutes to notice the differences between one setting and the next. Women are often quicker than men at picking up the differences and choosing the more correct setting. Where VTA should be set alters with the cartridge, the arm, and even with the record.

The farther away from "correct" the alignment is, the more difficult it will be to notice small changes, but as you tune in VTA each physically very small, incremental change will be sonically substantial. Finally, everything will snap into focus.

Stylus Rake Angle

SRA, compared to VTA, occurs on a level of microgeometry. It is becoming recognized as even more critical than VTA. SRA is the relative position of the stylus contact area to the groove. In the years when the only stylus profile was conical, SRA was not a factor, indeed really did not exist. You cannot orient a point in any particular direction—a point is the same all around.

Then when the conical stylus was stretched out into the elliptical, Shibata, and line contact styli, and the contact area became no longer a point but an oblong, then the orientation of the stylus contact area to the groove became critical.

If the SRA of the playback stylus does not match the SRA of the cutting stylus, then obviously the playback stylus will not properly match the groove modulations and so will not be able to trace the path of the cutting stylus accurately. But at the same time that the SRA is correct, the VTA must also match that of the cutting stylus.

Most styli are mounted at right angles to the cantilever tip. If, to maximize rigidity, the cantilever is not bent at the tip, then any stylus that is not conical will not have a proper orientation to the groove. The VTA will have to be adjusted to compensate.

It is commonly impossible to match both exactly, so there must be a compromise. This is why the final setting of VTA and SRA must be tuned in by ear to ensure the best compromise.

Antiskate Force

The tonearm has a tendency to move in toward the center of the record while playing to such a degree that, left uncontrolled, the stylus would always be pushed against the inner groove wall. This would cause mistracking, in extreme cases a total loss of the right-channel information contained on the outer groove wall, and certainly excessive wear on the inner channel. The other problem is that the cantilever would be skewed in relation to the cartridge generator and so the signal would be further distorted.

To prevent all these terrible things from occurring, one can quite simply set the antiskate mechanism, which applies an opposing force and balances everything out. Bill Seneca, designer of the well-regarded Promethean Green cartridge, believes the best way to set antiskate is to use a record with a good wide run-out—2 inches or so—or easiest of all, if you have it, is to use a blank disc. Blank discs have less resistance than grooved ones. You want the arm to drift outward, away from the label, so when centrifugal force and friction are dragging the arm in, the antiskate is compensating and pulling it out. If the arm is sitting still, apply a little more antiskate until it actually starts to drift outward. Again, this is something to finalize by ear when you are listening to music. If image placement is skewed a little off center, or if things don't quite seem locked in solidly, experiment with the antiskate.

Connecting the Cartridge

The color-coded wires or connector pins on the tonearm wire tell you how to connect them to the pins on the back of the cartridge so you do not inadvertently reverse the right and left channels and thus reverse phase. The connector pins may also be color coded, in which case it is a simple matter of matching colors. More often, the cartridge pins are just marked for hot and ground. Red is the right-channel signal, white is the left-channel signal. Green is the right-channel ground, blue or black the left-channel ground. It can be a little confusing because the color coding is not consistent with the rest of the system, where red is hot and white is ground. Here red and white are both hot. *Gently* slip the wire prongs over the pins and push them home firmly. Needle nose pliers or tweezers really help here. Be very careful that you do not maul the joint between prong and wire as this can break quite easily.

FINE TUNING

The difference between a good system and a passable one is a matter of subtleties. The illusion you are aiming for is for the hardware to disappear and the music to arise without seeming to come from the speakers. The performers should almost appear, like turning up the lights on the first act of a play.

Read the section on fine tuning at the beginning of "System Setup" (p. 199). Coming up with refinements is really a matter of understanding how a system works and what it is supposed to do and then being able to "sense" what would benefit a signal. Some people have a stronger instinct for this than others. No good cook follows a recipe by rote—subtle adjustments are constantly made according to the particular ingredients available and the mood and tastes of the cook. The great thing about fine tuning is that it can be done at a cost of curiosity and time, with minimal expense.

Even the room's air quality can make a difference. If the air is very dry, the high frequencies are absorbed more and you may get a slightly "duller" sound. When the air is saturated, the sound can even become overly bright. Many musicians recognize these changes in sound and will even talk about the particular "bloom" one can get just before a thunderstorm. In a system, though, summer high temperatures and humidity can cause one to leave the system turned off much of the time because the sound is hard and bright. Air conditioning certainly does help here. Temperature and humidity also affect the operation of the cartridge.

A number of the points covered under "System Setup" would be considered by some to be "tweaks" rather than basics. In fact, it becomes very difficult to distinguish a tweak from an essential because, once you hear the results, many tweaks will no longer appear to be refinements but become fundamentals. It is the same way with food or wine or other learned appreciations—if all you know is a steady diet of cafeteria food or Wonder bread, these may taste pretty good. But once you realize the existence of something else, perceptions change. What to one person is as fundamental as using fresh, rather than canned, chicken stock may appear to another as outré as breeding your own fish for your dinner table.

Two levels of improvement come about through fine tuning—one sharpens the focus of what is already present and the other brings into focus what before was not even known to be there.

An improvement that when first made is quite obvious soon becomes a part of the everyday sound of the system, and so its distinctiveness as a change tends to be lost. However, take away the upgrade and its effect is again as clear as ever.

Most tweaks are reversible. Those that are not are probably closer to modifications than simply tweaks. Anything that is not reversible should be undertaken very carefully and only after a good deal of research.

Just about anything that has to do with isolating the components, and hence the audio signal, from the mechanical and acoustic environment is really fundamental to good sound and therefore not a tweak. Spikes, Sorbothane, Tiptoes, speaker stands, component supports, and the like are not a matter of fancy dress but the essentials of a basic wardrobe. Nor is the quality of wire used for interconnects and speaker cable a matter of mere tweakiness (by now this has been largely accepted)—wire is a component that can be upgraded like any other and that can have a surprisingly gross effect on sound quality in any system that has progressed past mid-fi.

Some tweaks can be done once and then forgotten, at least until time for the routine six-month system checkup—these include such things as damping the tonearm or using Sorbothane tube rings. Others require a more conscious and more frequent effort and their benefit may be only a subtle improvement. Removing the speaker grilles before listening (and replacing them afterward to provide some dust protection) is an example. With these, you must choose for yourself the tradeoff between convenience and the niceties of better sound. What is blatant to some ears is subtle to others.

One of the most important tweaks is to keep your system maintained. Like a garden, a system can drift back to an untweaked (unweeded) state much faster than it can be tweaked (weeded). So maintain your system and do not lose the efforts you have invested.

Your tools and equipment should also be maintained in good order. You may find yourself with an assortment of interconnects and cables, cartridges and cartridge-mounting hardware, a set of tools, miscellaneous tubes, jacks, caps, resistors, solder, damping materials like liquid latex, Mortite, and other such oddities. An excellent means of storage and organization is one of the Kennedy mechanic's roll-away chests. These come in different configurations of drawers and sizes. They are well made for long service and roll conveniently out of the way when not in use.

THE TURNTABLE SYSTEM

Replacing the standard thin oil in your turntable platter bearing with the very thick, dark Linn/Merrill-type oil makes a noticeable improvement—providing of course that your system resolves sufficiently well to reveal the difference. Subtle but valuable differences are audible even on an AR table. Even pretty junky mid-fi systems may benefit. The financial investment is minimal—under $10 to experiment.

Cartridge "Tiptoes": An idea first propounded by Joe Grado is that interposing a small metal plate with raised bumps between cartridge and headshell makes a better connection. Mod Squad now has a similar object made of plastic. Such items do not work equally effectively in all situations—best results are reported to occur with cartridges and headshells that have large mounting areas. How you mount your cartridge to the headshell takes priority over what, if anything, you choose to insert between the two (see p. 249).

Cartridge body, headshell, arm tube, and counterweight all benefit from damping—even the most effective mechanical grounding loop cannot funnel away all vibrations. Vibrational waves reflect at boundaries (as happens with speakers) so standing waves are set up between every pair of opposite parallel surfaces—the benefit of a tapered arm tube is that it offers no parallel boundaries. A number of materials can be used to damp these resonances—anything that is pliable, does not harden and is easy to apply. Plasticine or Mortite or England's famed Blue-Tac are all good. Apply only a small, thin layer to minimize added mass. On the arm tube, apply only to the underside.

The very thin cosmetic-grade latex used by actors allows greater control in the application. (Bob Kelly sells it in New York.) Brush this on in thin layers all over the tone arm tube, the top of the headshell, the sides and bottom of the cartridge body (staying well away from the cantilever). Apply also to the counterweight. Let each thin layer dry before applying the next. Use a small, disposable brush and between layerings, soak the brush in water to prevent it from drying out. If you are not happy with what you hear, the latex can be quite easily peeled and gently rubbed off the arm, somewhat like rubber cement.

Another method is to sheath the arm tube in shrink-wrap tubing. Sold at electronics supply houses, this material forms a neat covering for the joint between wire and connector when making up cables and interconnects. Applied loose, and then heated by a hairdryer, steam, or a similar heat source, it shrinks to a snug fit. Latex is, however, easier to work with and more controllable; it allows you to build up layers as thin or as thick as you want.

Do NOT apply any kind of damping material at any coupling joints, such as between headshell and arm tube, between cartridge body and headshell, between counterweight and tube. You want joints to couple solidly.

Your tonearm cable must be flexible, but many are not. A stiff cable connected to a floating subchassis can interfere with the suspension. Dressing the cable with two P-clips as described in "Turntable Setup" (p. 236) helps but may not always solve the problem. About two thirds of the better arms use a detachable tonearm cable, terminating at the arm end with phono jacks or a five-pin DIN plug, which can therefore be replaced, if need be, with a very flexible lead or with an interface box. Straightwire's replacement tonearm lead is very flexible so it does not foul the suspension. Sumiko's PIB—Phono Interface Box—mounts on the rear of the table plinth; the arm lead runs straight out of the back of the tonearm and plugs into it, then a separate interconnect runs from the box to the preamp. The arm lead never goes near the suspension.

You can also experiment with the material of your tonearm-mounting board—metal, acrylic, wood, and wood composites all have slightly different sounds.

Matching Cartridge and Preamp Impedance

The internal or output impedance of a component should match that of its load, i.e., the input impedance of the next component. This makes possible the most efficient transfer of power. Specifically, in this case, the cartridge's output impedance must be matched to the input impedance of the preamp. Most preamps are designed with a 47,000-ohm (47-K) input impedance because it has been found that this is what moving magnets typically sound best with. However, it may be worth either experimenting for yourself, checking with the manufacturer (who may not know or may not have the right answer), or asking around about your cartridge, as some MMs sound superior at much lesser loads.

The cartridge's impedance can be changed, as needed, by changing the resistor, which is usually done across the preamp's input. The standard 47-K load is very high impedance, so nearly all the signal from the cartridge is going into the preamp circuit. Altering the resistance effectively serves as a tone control for the cartridge—by increasing the load the cartridge "sees," you can electromagnetically damp the cartridge and make it less bright. This also reduces cartridge gain, as increasing impedance diverts some of the output and feeds it back to the cartridge. Too high an impedance can overly brighten the sound (in which case, load it down); too low can dull it. Start with the manufacturer's recommendation and then, if you want to, experiment from here.

COMPACT DISC PLAYERS

These "paradigms of perfection" respond surprisingly well both to the basic setup covered earlier and to a certain amount of tweaking. A second disc piggybacking on top of the one being played is perhaps the most widespread home CD tweak to date. The quality of CD discs varies, even between copies of the same title, depending on the number of minute punctures and pin holes in the reflective aluminum coating. Each of these is a defect that has to be "covered up" by the error detection/correction circuit. The density of the aluminum also appears to be a factor, with an apparent link between greater density and better sound.

Placing a second disc on top of the CD being played serves to stabilize the playing disc so it cannot flutter as it spins, thereby changing its relationship to the laser beam; this also damps resonances and improves reflectivity, like the opaque backing on a mirror. Though the laser focuses only on the embedded pits and not on the surface, it may be that blacking out the back of the disc improves the intensity of the returned light. Though this will not affect the actual signal, it may influence the operation of the focus servos and so effect the error detection/correction rate.

In addition, the CD is poorly supported in players and, though made of rigid polycarbonate plastic, its very rigidity increases vibration, caused by acoustic feedback, mechanical energy, vibrations from the spindle motor and the optical pickup motor. The servomotor and the transformer both add vibration as well. Though the information itself may be captured in numbers, the playback methods are as subject to vibration and distortion problems as any other playback medium, plus having to go through extra digital-to-analog conversion steps. In theory, any slight movement of the disc will be compensated for by the servo-mechanisms; in practice, disc vibration leads to greater error rates, more work for the digital circuitry, and the chance of error concealment rather than error correction occurring. This vibration problem is least at the beginning of playback, i.e., at the center of the disc where it is clamped and best supported, and increases with approach to the unsupported perimeter. (Thus, interestingly, both CD and analog suffer from end-of-play deterioration problems.)

Instead of a second disc, use one of the purpose-made CD damper discs such as Mod Squad's. Any stabilizer must be exactly centered on the disc, as imperfect centering will make matters much worse than no stabilizer at all.

THE AMPLIFICATION STAGE

Aside from positioning, interconnects, or internal modifications, the VPI Brick may be consistently the most important improvement you can make to preamp and amp. The improvement is not dramatic, but once you have heard it, you will be unhappy if the Bricks are taken away again—the grunge returns. Placed over the transformers, they can reduce high-end harshness, improve the soundstaging, increase bass. Weight is a factor—placing an ordinary brick over the transformers helps, but VPI Bricks help more. Exactly why is uncertain, but the Bricks may localize the magnetic flux fields that form around the transformers and so prevent them from interfering with other elements of the circuitry and power supply. One important point: The Bricks must be very close to the transformer to work. If the protective cage over amp or preamp is any distance from the transformer, you will hear less benefit. Some say an inch is the maximum.

If you use tubes, then which tubes you use can radically alter the sound of your system. Tube hunting can turn into an odyssey—people collect tubes from China, Russia, Czechoslovakia—is Ruritania next? Tubes are covered briefly in "Maintenance and Troubleshooting" (p. 283), but this is definitely an area to explore further.

Most tubes are microphonic—tap them lightly with a pencil and you can hear the clinking clearly through the speakers. As you don't want this noise added to your music, it is important to protect the tubes from being rattled or vibrated. Proper positioning and support are essential; Audioquest's tube dampers are a worthwhile investment. These are Sorbothane rings or collars that fit snugly over the glass envelope and significantly cut down on tube noise (microphonics). These are only for the "acorn" tubes—12AX7, 6DJ8, and the like. They are not for the amp's output tubes or power supply tubes. The smaller the signal, the more fragile its state, so if you don't want to collar all your tubes, do those in the preamp's phono stage.

Some of the most significant tweaks with electronics can come about through upgrading of passive components such as capacitors and internal wiring, but you really have to know your way around a circuit. The quality of the solder you use to perform these changes can also make an audible difference. Such changes, of course, work only with components in which really good passive parts have not already been used, either for reasons of marketing and price or because the component predates the advancements made in passive parts.

You want to use a solder that is eutectic—that quickly goes from liquid to solid without the pasty stage in between that increases the risk of making a cold joint. Ersin is a good standard brand. SN95 (95 percent silver, 5 percent lead) has good conductivity and ten times the strength of the common SN60 (60 percent tin, 40 percent lead) solder. However, it has a higher melting point than SN60 so, unless it is worked quickly, the heat can damage delicate circuitry. Wonder solder is for many "the solder of choice," used by a number of small high-end companies like Superphon for all their equipment. It flows very easily, hardens quickly, melts at a low temperature. In addition to these material merits, it is also considered to make equipment sound much better than other solders. A 25W soldering pencil is fine—be sure to keep wiping its tip clean with a damp sponge while soldering and keep a supply of replacement tips on hand.

A hookup wire consistently recommended is made by Randall Research: soft, 24 gauge, oxygen free, and high density.

Recommending specific modifications of the circuitry or the mechanics of components is well beyond the scope of this book. Some good modifiers are Andy Fuchs of GSI or Mod Squad for electronics; George Merrill of Underground Sound for turntable mods and upgrades. Other reputable, experienced modifiers can be found across the country as well.

However, be aware that modifying is an art (and sometimes a huckster's art). As with other matters of art, the results may not be to your satisfaction or taste. This happened to a friend with a prized Marantz 8B—a seemingly straightforward upgrade of capacitors and internal wiring by a reputable modifier resulted in an absolute butchering of the sound. Modifying components can be a little like restoring artwork—sometimes the question arises of whether you are just cleaning off the grunge, or also stripping away some of the brushwork and delicate shadings.

Mods are often irreversible. Changing the caps and resistors and wiring can improve the sound but the change can also be for the worse. The original components you remove cannot generally be replaced, unless the parts are very carefully desoldered with the express expectation of putting them back in.

SPEAKERS

Speaker setup is really all a matter of fundamentals. Pretty much everything was covered under "System Setup" in terms of speaker stands, spikes, weighting the tops of the speakers, and of course the all-important room positioning. Be sure to keep the cables away from the stands if these are metal. Be sure your stands are sand, lead shot, or sand and lead filled.

You can improve the wiring used in the crossover, upgrade the caps and other components of the crossover, get inside the cabinet and improve its rigidity and bracing, add more acoustic insulation material. But these are all fairly major alterations, not to be undertaken lightly. Read Martin Colloms's book *High Performance Loudspeakers*; read back issues of Ed Dell's *Audio Amateur* and *Speaker Builder* magazines. Proceed with great caution.

THE BREAK-IN PERIOD

Probably every piece of equipment needs a break-in period. Certainly preamps, amps, cables, and speakers do. These can totally change their characteristics as they go from brand-new to well broken in. Some components, in fact, sound horrible before they are "burned in," so much so that you may become convinced you have made a horrible mistake and that everything you've ever read and heard about the component has been a flat lie. Be patient. If you listen to it sporadically during the break-in process, you will hear it gradually improving. If you have not played your system for a couple of weeks, it will need a small amount of break-in time again to sound its best.

The best way to burn in an entire new system or any one component is not simply to turn it on but to run noise or music through it. Interstation noise from a tuner works fine and is perhaps less disturbing than actual music if you will be staying in the vicinity—however, this has no bass to it, so music is preferred. A CD player also comes in very handy as you can set it to recycle and continually replay music with a strong bass line and transients, while you spend the day out somewhere else.

Keep the volume low, both for the sake of neighborly peace and also so as not to damage the speakers. If you want to suffer less from the sound, you can drape the speakers with towels to muffle the sound. (Be sure the speaker grilles are in place so you don't accidentally dent or damage the drivers.) However, exercise caution when you do this. A friend fried a pair of tweeters once (admittedly ones known to be susceptible to frying) by muffling the speakers with layers of towels *before* turning on the tuner and setting the volume. The result was excessively high volume, a too-constant high-frequency signal that allowed the tweeters' voice coils no chance to cool off, and therefore very well cooked tweeters. Set the volume control first and to a low setting, then add the towels.

With speakers, it is the woofers in particular that need breaking in, so you should not expect full bass response from an unbroken-in speaker. Several hours of playing should be sufficient.

A new preamp or power amp, whether solid state or tube, may need 24 hours to a week of running time or longer to start sounding its best. Never run a preamp or amp without a load, meaning simply that you should not put a signal in if there isn't anywhere for it to go. Always hook up a preamp to an amp, and an amp to speakers before playing. However, don't leave a transistor amp idling but with no input if it is connected to speakers—it may pick up stray electromagnetism in the air, think it is a signal, and try driving the speakers. It can do itself damage this way. It's best, if you want to keep an amp on to help break it in but don't want to play music through it, to idle it with no load and no input.

Wire needs at least two days to break in and settle down. Wire tends to be directional, meaning that it sounds better when hooked up in one direction than in the other. Try it one way, listen, then reverse it, and listen again. One way may sound distinctly better than the other.

Many wire manufacturers now mark the preferred direction with a series of arrows on the shield or by the direction of the writing—the signal should flow in the same direction as the writing. Yes, it sounds crazy, but it really is true. And after all, it does you no harm to run it the right way, does it?

ROOM TREATMENT

It's not just an intellectual flourish to assert that a musical instrument cannot have a sound without an acoustic space for it to occur in. Instruments do not have a fixed sound; they have a sound that varies according to where they're being played. This is a crucial concept. Carnegie Hall didn't become world-famous because of its lovely red-velvet seats, nor did Avery Fisher Hall go through millions of dollars of renovations, re-renovations, and re-re-renovations because of poor decor.

What you want your system to be able to do is to give you as accurately as possible the sound of the instrument in the space in which it was originally played, because that is in fact what is really meant by "the sound of the instrument."

If you close your eyes during a live performance, you still know the position of each performer and can define the exact locations of walls, floor, and ceiling because of how the sound bounces off them. In fact, most of what you hear in a concert hall is reflected sound.

An important part of that reflected sound is the low-level detail generally described as ambience. This lets you know the violins are at the front, stage right, and the harpist is toward the rear, stage left. We take for granted the kind of extremely subtle nuances and discernments our ears are constantly making. But getting good sound and enjoying good sound are precisely about these nuances and subtle discernments. Ambience is a major factor in whether recorded music sounds live or canned.

With a good system, you can hear the sound of the room the music was recorded in. So you really don't want to add the sound of your own room on top of the music. The point of acoustically treating your room is to minimize your room's sound—you can seemingly restructure your room's architecture by treating surfaces so they absorb rather than reflect sound. Obviously, the acoustics of a 600,000-cubic-foot concert hall cannot be re-created in the typical room of 3,000 or so cubic feet, but you can minimize the sound of that room superimposing itself on the concert hall's acoustic.

Be aware that much the same tradeoff between detail and dynamics that exists with equipment exists also in room acoustics. By cleaning up the sound, you may reduce its character. If you overdamp your room to get rid of colorations, you may also lose out on hearing the performance's original environment in your room—it too will have been damped right out of existence before it can be heard. This is as much a distortion of the music (or at least of the recording, of which the recording room's acoustic was an integral part) as are the colorations an untreated room imposes on the music. While the detail of the instruments may now be unblurred by your room's reverberation, resonance, and standing wave distortions, this ''detail'' may occur in an unrealistically, even unpleasantly, sterile environment. An anechoic chamber is a completely ''clean'' environment—if you've ever walked into one of these, you know this is *not* how you want your room to sound.

Sound reaches you in two parts: (1) the sound traveling directly from the source to the ear, and (2) the indirect sound, which reaches you only after being reflected one or more times from the room surfaces. Direct sound, once its source stops, also stops. But indirect sound waves will continue to travel back and forth between room surfaces, and you'll hear them as a continuation, or echo, of the sound after the source has stopped. With each successive reflection, the sound waves lose energy by absorption and the sound gradually dies away. This prolongation of the sound after the source has ended is called reverberation or resonance.

Consider that, as a rule of thumb, sound travels about 1 foot per millisecond, or about 1 mile in 5 seconds. Meanwhile, each subsequent note from the speaker is adding reverberation—the first note is still audible when the second note is produced, and so on. Excessive overlapping of notes can lead to mushy, confused sound.

Your listening room's degree of resonance is a function of its size and relative dimensions, and also of the nature of its surfaces and furnishings. If sound dies out very slowly, the room is called live, or even excessively reverberant; if it dies out very rapidly, the room is described as dead. An extreme example of a live room having a great deal of resonance is a tiled bathroom. The hard, smooth surfaces reflect sound almost as well as mirrors reflect light.

Reflected sound will usually be less loud than the direct sound for two reasons: The reflected path is always longer than the direct path, resulting in a greater reduction of loudness due to distance; and all reflected sound loses some of its energy at each reflection. On the other hand, in a highly reverberant room, constant and repeated reflection of sound from one hard wall to another, with little absorption, builds up the sound. Music reproduction will seem louder because you are hearing both direct and reflected sounds.

In determining the sound of concert halls, early reflections have proved to be of immense significance. These are the distinct reflections that, having bounced off a few surfaces, arrive within about 0.2 second of the direct sound, prior to the welter of diffuse reflections that constitute the acoustic's reverberant field. The directions from which these reflections arrive (wall, floor, ceiling), their relative strengths, and their frequencies are all critical factors in a room's acoustic colorations. It appears that the best-sounding halls are those in which the strongest early reflections are from the side walls. The trick is to have strong early reflections but controlled reverb time, so that the sound dies away soon enough not to muddy up the following notes. Long reverb time is like holding the sustaining pedal all the way down while playing the piano.

The accepted wisdom is that the reverb time ideally should be around 0.3 to 0.4 second, with the value held constant to within a few percent right across the frequency range, from bass to treble. Some prefer a slightly longer reverb time; others prefer a rather "dry" sound with a relatively shorter reverb time.

The balance throughout the frequency range is the real problem. For one thing, between any two parallel room boundaries, standings waves are set up—between floor and ceiling, side wall and side wall, end wall and end wall. Here, the wave bounces back and forth between the two parallel surfaces with very little loss of energy. The reverberation therefore takes longer to die out than it would normally and the result is to emphasize a certain frequency and add hangover to it, impairing both smoothness and detail.

In addition, most materials that absorb sound absorb little at bass frequencies and more at midrange and treble. Few rooms, therefore, have a constant reverb time; instead, the unabsorbed bass generally lasts considerably longer than the midrange and upper frequencies.

This is where room treatment comes in. Your audio system and your room really do exist in a symbiotic relation. You can spend a great deal of money and time on your system but may still end up with "dime store" acoustics, which can negate much of the worth of your system. In a sense, your room can be compared to a loudspeaker enclosure. Just as cabinetless dipoles offer a certain clarity of sound, a treated room in which the acoustic colorations have been minimized offers a certain clarity of recording.

Even with acoustic treatment, most acoustic materials work only with the upper half of the piano keyboard; all other frequencies are left uncontrolled. Only very thick acoustic panels—3 or 4 inches—have substantial absorption down to 500 cycles. The more common thicknesses don't help until about 900 Hz, which is well up into the midrange. If your room has a lot of soft, sound-absorbing surfaces like curtains, rugs, and stuffed chairs, then the mid- to high frequencies will be largely absorbed but the bass will remain unaffected, resulting in a frequency imbalance.

There is a limited choice of acoustic materials specifically sold for home audio—these are all quite expensive unless you need only a very small amount. So first, here are some home remedies you might try. Mark Levinson uses futons on the walls of his Cello showroom—about 4 inches thick, these are quite effective. Bill Firebaugh uses polyurethane-foam hospital bedpads, either suspended between two poles or hung from the ceiling. These are very inexpensive, come in 72-by-24-inch panels, and look and act like expensive sound-deadening material. "Egg carton" foam—molded like the inside of an egg carton—is also effective. Furniture-moving pads, though very thin, can help absorb some high-frequency problems. A parachute suspended over the system acts much like seaweed in water to "break" or dam the sound waves.

Movable acoustic-panel office dividers can build a temporary small listening room within a much larger space or can create a more symmetrical room within a very irregular one. Brewster panels work very well and come in a variety of configurations and degrees of absorbency, as well as different color choices. This is not a *cheap* solution, but is a very convenient one that can work very well. Tibbet acoustic panels can be added for extra absorbency in some places.

More conventional approaches include Sonex panels, Distech panels, and Tube Traps. Tube Traps are the only commercial acoustic product that can absorb low frequencies. They have a marked effect on the sound—in some situations, they make a substantial improvement; in others, they can be a substantial drawback. Borrow before you buy.

LIVE END/DEAD END (LEDE): THE THEORY

In the LEDE approach, one end of the listening room is live and the other is absorbent—where there is debate is at which end you should place the speakers and at which end the listener. Convention places the speakers at the dead end; experience sometimes places the listener there. This approach is based on work done by Haas.

In 1972 he showed that acoustic anomalies of rooms have almost no effect on the perceived sound from speakers, provided that the direct sound from the speakers arrives at the listener's ears well before the sounds reflected off adjacent room surfaces. Under these conditions, the listener can largely ignore the reflected sounds and accept the direct ones as the only ones present. Furthermore, if the earliest reflections are eliminated altogether, these will not interfere with the speaker's output, resulting in a far smoother response. This can be done by damping all wall surfaces near the speakers—a process that can be expensive. An alternative is to surround the speakers with acoustic absorption panels placed between the speakers and any reflective surfaces. Floors should be carpeted for at least 5 to 10 feet out from the speakers, and ceilings may also need some acoustic treatment.

ELECTRICAL ENVIRONMENT

Since electricity plays such a major role in the quality of music reproduction, it is essential to have as clean and regulated a source as possible. Music is essentially sound in time. Alter either the sound—pitch, tone color, dynamics—or the time and you alter the music. Yet line current fluctuates around the ideal of a steady 120 volts, and has constant spikes and other dirt riding along on the power. These problems will interfere with accurate turntable platter rotation, causing at least time, and therefore pitch, aberrations; it will interfere with the ability of your preamp and amp to enlarge the signal accurately, or will at least place additional stress on their power supplies.

Your system should never be connected to the same electrical circuit that carries the refrigerator, air conditioner, furnace, or any other major appliance that cycles on and off. Low-voltage dropouts, such as when the fridge kicks in, are particularly damaging to sound quality.

Ideally, your system should have its own dedicated line, but that is generally impractical. Try to tap a circuit where nothing else is in use while you are playing the system.

The fact that a system generally sounds noticeably better in the small hours of the morning is not just imagination or light-headedness—the demand for power is at a minimum then, so you are getting a cleaner, steadier supply, which is adding less distortion to the music. Keep in mind that when you take power from the wall, which means power from a public supply, you're amplifying everyone's garbage right along with the musical signal. The worse your electrical environment, the more you'll notice the difference between late-night listening and other times when the electrical supply is in greater demand.

There is growing recognition of the importance of regulating and filtering the electricity coming into the stereo system. Therefore, turntable manufacturers have been increasingly adding "power conditioners" to their motors. *Regulation* is more important than noise filtering—this means ensuring that the wall current actually operates at its rated 120 volts, eliminating spikes and dropouts. *Noise filtering* means removing the noise and hash that piggybacks along on the current.

The line conditioners in use for computers and other electrical-supply-sensitive equipment have been explored for audio applications as well. Experimenting with a wide variety of designs, while the sound definitely benefits in important ways from being cleaned up, it also tends to get "strip-cleaned"—some of the low-level detail, the high frequencies, the texture and subtleties of the music are stripped away along with the grunge. If you are listening for the effects on grunge, you may be initially very pleased because in some cases the improvements are substantial. However, over time, you may find that you have lost more than you have gained.

More and more research is being done in this area and there will probably be some important developments over the next few years.

OPERATION

CORRECT TURN-ON, TURN-OFF, AND DISCONNECT PROCEDURES

Each time you flip a switch to turn a component on or off, a transient surge and switching pop or spark are generated. These can fry resistors, punch a hole through capacitors, or send a sudden strong signal through your speakers, blowing the woofers or tweeters.

To protect against possible damage to the system, you want to minimize these thumps traveling through the system. Your system should be turned on and off in a very specific sequence of steps. Also turn the volume all the way down or engage the mute switch before you turn the system on or off. That way, if there are any surges, at least they will not be amplified and so damage to the speakers may be minimized.

Always turn the system on by following the flow of the signal from the source to the speakers—turn the preamp on first, then the amp, then, if you're using active speakers or subwoofers, the servos. Always wait a moment after turning on the preamp for any surge to subside before turning on the amp. This way, any preamp surge will be able to go no further in the system.

When turning the system off, reverse this sequence, letting the signal flow out again—servos first, then amp, then preamp. If you turn off your preamp first, any surge caused by the turn-off can travel forward through the entire system. But if the amp has already been turned off, it will neither be damaged itself nor amplify the surge to damage the speakers. It may help you to remember the proper sequence if you think of the signal as a tide flowing in when you turn the system on, and flowing out when you turn it off.

So, as a general rule, never turn a preamp on or off when it is connected to an amp that is on. Never turn the preamp and an amp connected to it on or off at the same time. Always be sure that an amp connected to a preamp is turned off long enough for the power to drain out of the capacitors before turning the preamp on or off—a minute is pretty safe. Never leave an amp not connected to a pair of speakers on for more than a few minutes. You might fry your amp. The risk is even greater if a signal is going through the amp. Some amps use relays to protect the careless or ignorant, but don't count on this. Generally, a preamp can be left turned on and not hooked up to anything.

It is good practice to *turn the volume all the way down* before placing the stylus on the record, removing the stylus, using the selector switch, or doing anything else other than listening to music. This is especially important with a powerful system.

It is best that the entire system be turned off before you plug in or unplug any interconnects. Failing this, at least be sure the particular component you plan to disconnect is first turned off. Before turning the amp back on, wait five minutes. Then when you turn everything on again, wait at least ten minutes or so for all the circuitry to stabilize. It won't harm the system to play it immediately but it just will not sound quite as good.

However, there are times—for example, if you want to make A/B tests of components or cables—when waiting the necessary ten minutes plus will spoil the comparison. If you are prepared to take some risk, you can minimize the chance of damaging the equipment by observing the same signal flow as you would when turning the system off. Specifically, if you are disconnecting amp and preamp with both components still on, disconnect *first* from the amp and *then* from the preamp. If you are disconnecting speakers and amp, disconnect first from the speakers and then from the amp; if disconnecting preamp and signal source, first from the preamp and then from the signal source. When reconnecting, reverse the sequence: first reconnect at table end, then at preamp; at preamp end, then at amp; at amp end, then at speakers.

If you have more than one signal source—table, CD player, tuner, deck—always turn off whatever is not being used at that moment. For example, do not leave your tuner or tape deck turned on when listening to records (unless you're recording). Some *cross-talk* will almost certainly occur if more than one input source is on. Cross-talk is simply the distortion that occurs when some signal from the source that you are not listening to leaks into the circuit of the source that you are listening to.

Preferably, any signal source you are not actually listening to should be disconnected from the preamp. If left connected, the input of any ancillary signal source is in the signal path of the source you are listening to, with inevitable negative effects. Experiment with this, and if you can hear a difference, balance the sonic improvement against the slight inconvenience.

Warm-up Time

All amps and preamps benefit from some warm-up time, ranging from a minimum of 20 minutes up to a couple of hours, depending on the component and when it was last played. If it was not played within the past 48 hours, longer warm-up time will be needed to restore the component to sounding its best.

Tube equipment generally needs a warm-up period of about an hour to sound as good as it can. Few people realize this of solid-state equipment, but the capacitors need to be charged up, the transistors and resistors must be at operating temperature, and whole circuits have to be burned in. Usually about 20 minutes will do it, but sometimes an hour or more is needed.

Leaving Electronics on Permanently Versus Turning Them Off

One benefit of leaving electronic components on is instantly good sound whenever you want to listen without having to wait through a warm-up period. Leaving solid-state gear on all the time may also extend its lifespan, since solid state ages from the shock of turn-on and warm-up more than anything else. Tubes are also most stressed by turn-on and turn-off, like a light bulb, but unlike solid-state equipment they can be replaced. However, if when left on they run hot enough to stress other passive parts in the amp, then turn them off between listening times.

As a general rule, solid-state preamps should be left on all the time, and solid-state power amps turned off between listening sessions if they get much above "warm" when left on. Another consideration is that solid-state amps consuming more than about 100 watts per channel on idle will certainly raise your electric bill if always left on. Opinions on tube equipment vary more, but probably it should be turned off. You might consult the designer—Lazarus, for example, recommends its preamp never be turned off. In fact, it doesn't even have an on/off switch; you have to unplug the unit from the wall if you want to turn it off.

If you will not be listening to your system for a while, unplug all the components. Also unplug them during thunderstorms to protect against lightning strikes.

AT THE CONTROLS

The Volume Control

The volume at which you listen to a recording has a critical effect on how it sounds—it is itself a "tone control." This is largely because of a psychoacoustic factor called the Fletcher-Munson curve, which was established by H. Fletcher and W. A. Munson in 1933. Sounds of different frequencies, when played at the exact same volume intensity, will not be heard as all having the same volume. The ear's sensitivity to a given sound varies according to the frequency of that sound.

As the volume is increased, low tones and the midrange produce equal sensations of loudness but the ear becomes more sensitive to the highs, so these sound "boosted." As the volume is reduced, there is a considerable loss in the bass and only a small loss in the treble. The purpose of the "loudness compensation" on mid-fi preamps is to boost the bass when you are listening at low levels. (You will not find this on high-end preamps because the extra circuitry adds distortion, and because the bass boost is inevitably nonlinear and distorts the music. Loudness compensation is fine for purposes of background music.)

Because of this psychoacoustic curve, when you listen to a recording at the "wrong" playback volume, you are hearing an out-of-balance rendition that is very distorting to the music. Volume has a significant effect on the balance of the musical ingredients—it actually alters the proportions and relationships of the elements of sound. It is important, where practical, to play at volume levels close to live. This is why small ensembles can sound better on many systems than large ones—you generally cannot convincingly reproduce the sound of a large orchestra in your living room.

The volume setting is best "tweaked in" for each recording—a tiny shift can lock the sound right into focus. The volume control actually acts to focus the sound and tends to push it back or bring it forward. Listen at the wrong levels and you will get a distortion in perspective. Each recording has its own "right" volume setting—depending on such factors as the size of the ensemble, the size of the room performed in, the intensity of the music ranging from *pp* to *ff*, the placement of the mikes.

A higher volume also tends to sound better because then the volume control itself is not restricting the sound. The signal as it goes to the preamp's volume control is always operating at its loudest—the control must actually restrict the sound in order to reduce the volume.

How loudly you can safely play your system is usually limited more by your neighbors and your eardrums than by your system. You are more likely to damage tweeters with a low-powered than a high-powered amp—each time the amp clips through being overdriven, it puts out a square wave, which is very damaging to tweeters. Tweeters will self-destruct with input of as little as 3 or 4 watts if it is *continuous*, but music is not made up of a continuous signal. A high-powered amp is more likely to damage the woofers, but you should get fair warning before this occurs. As soon as you hear a kind of crackle or click, immediately turn the volume down. This is the sound of the woofer cone "bottoming out" as it is driven to the full extent of its physical range.

Balance Controls

These are essential (unless you use dual volume controls instead). The recording, the cartridge, or some other element of the system, including speakers and room, almost invariably has a minor channel imbalance. Room imbalances can be corrected with judicious use of acoustic materials; speaker imbalances can usually be corrected through a compensating setup. But component imbalances, where one channel puts out a stronger signal than the other, need some way of being corrected. Otherwise imaging, soundstage, the whole experience of the music is subtly or grossly disturbed. Unfortunately, even ordinary balance controls are expensive and all, even the best, degrade the sound to some extent.

One choice some designers have made is to use dual volume controls instead of balance controls. The volume of one channel can be increased slightly to compensate for the weaker signal of that channel; a shift of just a hairsbreadth can suddenly lock the image and the music into focus. The drawback is that having to adjust two knobs instead of just one is somewhat inconvenient; some people find them extremely annoying to use, while to others it quickly becomes a habit. A mute switch, in this case, becomes even more valued.

Another approach, used on the Lazarus preamp, is a single volume control plus separate right- and left-channel attenuators, which are switched into the circuit only if you need to adjust the balance. When you switch on one attenuator, the volume for that channel is off and you use the attenuator as a volume control for that channel.

Tone Controls

These degrade sound, unquestionably and significantly. On the other hand, some musically wonderful, sonically horrible recordings are rendered listenable through the judicious application of bass or treble adjustment via tone controls. The ideal solution may be to have two preamps, a no-control one for listening to decent recordings and a tone-control one for listening to wretched recordings. (Though this is a legitimate suggestion, and would be a solution, it is not offered as *advice*.)

Tone controls are not intended to, nor capable of, correcting problems with your *system* or your *room*; they are intended to correct problems with poor recordings (leaving aside their role as marketing devices). If you have as many controls as the cockpit of whatever the latest fighter plane is, then you have more than you could possibly need in order to correct mediocre recordings, and in fact have so many that their sheer presence in the circuitry will instantly render *any* recording mediocre.

An old Scott 340-B tube amp (acquired by being there just at the moment it was being tossed into someone's garbage) was really an extremely nice amp. It was a lot nicer when stripped to its essentials—eliminating tone controls, scratch and rumble filters, even removing the front panel's on/off light. This last made a sonic improvement that was slight but startling, considering it had been done with some cynicism. (Sadly, the amp's cans eventually leaked irremediably and have not yet been replaced. It sits, decently wrapped in an old sheet, awaiting its next resurrection.)

PLAYING YOUR LPS

How you play your records is going to affect how long you will enjoy listening to them before they become damaged and noisy. The procedure outlined below will extend their life. It may seem quite laborious but, after the first few times, is quickly done. With LPs becoming increasingly scarce, treat yours well—you won't easily replace them.

One of the most essential points is to *keep everything meticulously clean.* Some people go so far as to handle their records wearing the low-lint white gloves that film editors use. This is highly recommendable if you can bring yourself to it.

Before *every* play, take a few seconds to clean the record and clean the stylus. The reward is cleaner sound. The next time you think to yourself, "I don't want to be bothered with all this fussy business, I just want to listen to the music," shrink yourself down in scale to the microscopic level of dirt and groove. That dust in those grooves is the relative size of boulders; you've got a high-speed (*high*-speed!—it's traveling at 20 centimeters per second, with accelerations higher than 1G), very sharp object, with an effective weight of tons per square inch, barreling around the curves until it suddenly hits up against a dust boulder and *whammo!*—you've got another microcrack in the groove wall that will forever more accompany the music, as a tick or a pip or a pop or other variation of noise. Get enough of these and it's like listening to bacon fry.

Be sure the turntable's platter or platter mat is also clean. To hear for yourself how important this is, pick out a record that you play on a favorite side but never or rarely on the reverse side. Play the reverse side—that side is "virgin" but you'll hear ticks and pops anyhow. Why? Because even though the vinyl is never touched by a stylus, the dirt from the mat is ground into the LP just from the enormous stylus downforce on the side you play. To help keep dust to a minimum, always keep the dustcover over the table when not playing a record. If you can't hear any difference one way or the other, keep it on even when playing; sometimes the cover degrades the sound, in which case you'll have to battle dust some other way.

Having placed a clean record on a clean mat, you then must clean the record of its layer of fine lint. Use a carbon fiber brush (unless you have just vacumm-cleaned it—see below). The superfine fibers lift the microscopic particles of dust out of the groove and hold on to them long enough to actually remove them from the surface of the record. Each time the record is played, more dust gets into the grooves, so this must be done every time. Even when a record is stored in its jacket, fine dust in the air can still penetrate. To neutralize the static electricity that "bonds" the lint to the vinyl, you may want to first use a destaticizer (such as a Zerostat), which generates charged particle ions. Some people destaticize, delint, and then again destaticize because the drag of the carbon fiber against the vinyl can rebuild static electricity. Be sure your carbon fiber brush does not shed, leaving its superfine hairs on the record.

A Discwasher velvet pad is good, but not *as* good. The fibers are coarser and don't penetrate the groove as effectively; also the velvet pile does not hold on to the dust as well, so some of it is released back onto the record surface. The pad must also be kept meticulously clean. Discwasher look-alikes are no better, and some are even worse because they release their own debris from the padding.

To use a carbon fiber brush, it's easiest if the platter is turning. Hold the brush *lightly* and so the bristles are slightly angled down to sweep against the direction of groove travel. This way, the dust more easily gets wedged into and stays between the bristles, rather than dropping back onto the record. After the record has made at least one complete revolution, and it appears that you've picked up all the dust, then, without lifting the bristles off the surface, slowly slide the brush sideways toward the outer edge of the disc and off the record. This way, the bristles are off the record before they spring back to their normal position, dumping their load of dust.

Never touch the brush with your fingers: The oil present on even the most pristine, just-washed-in-carbolic-soap hands will wick right up the fibers and in turn be spread all over your records. To knock the dust off, shake the specially designed handle back and forth across the bristles a few times. To clean the brush, periodically dip it in a shallow dish of 99 percent pure isopropyl alcohol, shake off the excess, and leave to air-dry. Just be sure the bristles are positioned exactly as you want them to dry.

The dirtiest thing likely to come in contact with your LPs—probably the dirtiest object in your entire house—is the cartridge stylus. When did you clean it last? Yet it has been faithfully plowing its way through a mile-long groove that is filled with record mold-release (a waxy substance that prevents the vinyl from adhering to the record stamper mold), dirt, dust, grease, and other forms of caked-on sludge, and it's been getting coated with this filth while scraping it up. Under the heat of friction, this becomes actually baked onto the stylus tip, which reaches over 350 degrees Fahrenheit. Left in this condition, the stylus will perform as a record destroyer. A dirty stylus increases friction, record wear, and groove damage, and significantly reduces a record's lifespan. It is also a major cause of distortion, mistracking, and even groove skipping. *Clean your poor beleaguered stylus each time* before putting it down on a record. This preserves your records, protects the music from being turned into noise, and lengthens stylus life.

A stiff brush may be needed to scrape off the accumulation of caked-on gunk. There are a number of very stiff stylus-cleaning brushes on the market. These *can* be dangerous to use if incautiously handled. Always stroke from the back to the front of the stylus and stroke *downward* toward you to protect against bending or loosening the cantilever or even ripping it right out of the cartridge body.

Never use your finger to try to clean the stylus as this will only dirty it more. Any finger leaves a slightly oily deposit, which the stylus spreads all over the record and which will also attract more dirt to the stylus. Electronic stylus cleaners, which vibrate the dirt off the stylus, would seem to be a perfect solution. But they can also vibrate the stylus right off its shank. And if you don't happen to notice this in time, you'll rip your record to shreds playing it with a raw metal tip.

If you are meticulous about cleaning your records well and cleaning the stylus *each time you play a side,* then a small soft brush, especially in combination with a stylus cleaner and preserver like Stylast, will work just fine. This is a great deal safer for your expensive cartridge than either a stiff brush or an electronic cleaner.

Stylast treatment is also supposed to reduce friction, thus lengthening both stylus and record life. The only caution is to apply any cleaner sparingly—it can wick its way up the cantilever and into the suspension, where it may over the long term cause harmful effects. Joe Grado, for one, advises against using any stylus cleaners on his cartridges.

While you are cleaning the stylus, turn the volume up to almost normal playing level. The amplified noise of brush scraping stylus is pretty nasty, but you will be able to hear whether you are being too rough much more easily than you can see this. Stroke smoothly and evenly, toward you only. With the sound turned all the way down or the mute engaged, it is a lot easier to have an accident.

As you become familiar with the sound of your stylus being cleaned, and therefore the sound of your system, then as you clean you can tell a lot about the condition of the system. If something is drifting a little out of tune, you may catch it more quickly when you hear it through a single noise rather than with complex music. This is a little like listening to your car engine if you work on it yourself—you can quickly tell by its sound when all is well and when it needs a little tuning.

Periodically check the condition of your stylus with a magnifying glass. Those flat plastic magnifying sheets are handy; a linen tester or thread counter also works well. You will need plenty of strong light focused on the subject. Propping up a white business card, folded in half the short way, behind the stylus helps to silhouette it more clearly.

You will clearly be able to see any accumulations of gunk. You won't be able to see wear or damage, unless really gross.

Plan to replace your cartridge regularly, anywhere from every 6 to 18 months, depending on use—a worn stylus damages the grooves. In addition, the cantilever suspension material has a limited lifespan of about 18 months, after which the sound of the cartridge will start to change. While it is possible with some cartridges to replace just the stylus/cantilever assembly, you really are better of replacing the entire cartridge (see p. 373).

So—now you have a clean record on a clean mat ready to be played by a clean stylus. There are some playing conditions to observe. Don't play the same cut twice in an hour—a record goes through a very tough time when it's played (see p. 42) and the heat built up by friction between stylus and vinyl actually liquefies the surface of the record. Unless the record is allowed a sufficient period to recuperate fully from playing, it may become permanently (though not visibly) deformed, with the result of worse background noise. Playing when the room temperature is over 90 degrees Fahrenheit should also be avoided as this places too much stress on the record.

Proper storage is covered under ''Recording Care and Preservation (p. 291).

Cleaning the Record

Before you play a new record for the first time, clean it. The grooves are filled with a combination of pernicious mold-release and the accumulated grime picked up during shipping and storage. It is essential to deep-clean all of this out of the grooves. LAST's Formula I is intended specifically for this purpose; or if you have a vacuum record cleaner, using that is sufficient.

After the first deep cleaning, a regular maintenance cleaning with an aqueous-base formula is fine to remove loose dust, airborne soot, and oily film from cooking, oil heating, and smokers. Think how quickly mirrors and windows become dirty. Even if a record has been properly stored and unused for six months, it should be cleaned of this thin film of grime. Wherever air can penetrate, dirt follows.

There appears to be no limit to how many times a record can safely be cleaned. Records involved in LAST's long-term testing over a period of years have been cleaned and played and cleaned again and again hundreds of times, with no evidence of any kind of degradation.

It is essential, of course, to use the correct cleaning fluid (see p. 277) and to make certain that everything that comes in contact with the record during cleaning is itself kept clean.

Using a Discwasher brush wet, you run the risk that the velvet pile may not be able to penetrate down far enough into the groove. Thus all the dirt is not picked up from the wet record surface but just collects as mud in the bottom of the groove, awaiting the stylus. You must be very careful to get up as much dirt as possible.

This is the major drawback to cleaning a record without a vacuum cleaner—how to remove the water, and all the dirt along with it, from the record surface. The little applicators LAST provides are quite effective but nothing is as good as a vacuum record cleaner. Some high-end dealers and record stores that own such a cleaner for their own use will rent them out.

Vacuum Record Cleaners

If you have a sizable record collection, one of the very first things to do is to buy a vacuum-type record cleaner, such as the VPI or Nitty Gritty. The improvement to the sound of *any* record, including a brand-new one, is remarkable and very well worth the investment. A clean record reveals more of the music in the groove because the stylus is tracking the actual groove walls instead of a buildup of dirt, sludge, and mud that will subtly alter the groove's shape. By cleaning a record before you ever play it, you remove the grunge left in there from the pressing process, plus dusty handling and storage conditions, *before* it does any permanent damage. Surface noise is reduced. The one drawback to these cleaners is that they are all very noisy.

If you are cleaning a particularly dirty record, first let the fluid sit on it for several minutes, then vacuum it clean. Then repeat for a thorough cleaning and rinse.

The best way to apply the fluid is to go buy yourself a good artist's brush. The ideal—but it will cost you—is a French sable brush, 3 inches wide, with a blunt chisel end. Find something that is as close to this as possible, but affordable. It must be natural bristle and it must have a blunt chisel end. The hairs should have a good taper to them so they are fine enough to penetrate to the bottom of the groove. The brush should be soft but stiff enough to resist being easily bent as you are working the fluid into the grooves. Check with the store owner (if knowledgeable) or with the manufacturer to be sure the glue used to hold the bristles is not alcohol or water soluble. Shake the brush thoroughly to be sure it won't shed its bristles in your record grooves.

Place the record on the platter and turn it on. If you store your fluid in a narrow-necked or squeeze bottle, pour out a thin ribbon of fluid onto the turning record surface, being sure to keep it well away from the label. While this doesn't hurt the record, a wet label when suctioned is likely to get torn. This butchers its appearance and damages resale value. Work the fluid into all the grooves, avoiding both label and outer edge—you don't want fluid spilling over the edge. Then turn on the vacuum suction and let the record complete two full revolutions. Repeat for the other side. Your record is now pristine and ready to play.

These fluids should be used in a well-ventilated area. The cleaning fluid and all the dirt mixed with it gets atomized as it is sucked off the record. If you are working in a broom closet, you might just as well be drinking the stuff—something any competent doctor would advise against.

Be sure to keep the cleaning equipment clean itself. A dirty brush will only spread dirt from one record onto the next. Brush the velvetlike lips of the vacuum intake tube often with a stiff, clean brush to remove dirt or lint accumulations. Wipe off the inside of the cleaner periodically too. The brush should be left hanging out to dry in the open air.

RECORD-CLEANING FLUID

This safe formula is the same as archival commercial preparations, except that you are mixing it yourself and therefore it costs you a fraction of the price of ready mixed. It can be used for both hand and vacuum cleaning. It is a 25 percent solution of isopropyl alcohol in water, with a drop of surfactant. Ethyl alcohol, sometimes applied to records in the form of vodka, is more damaging to vinyl than is isopropyl. Use it only in an absolute pinch.

Drugstore isopropyl contains too many impurities to qualify it for record cleaning. Use technical or lab-grade isopropyl, which is extremely pure. Reagent grade is unnecessary and far more expensive. Water should be steam distilled, triple de-ionized. Both of these are readily available at a chemical supply house, which should sell them to you in pint and gallon sizes.

You also need to add a drop of surfactant, or wetting agent, to reduce the surface tension of the water so the formula can penetrate down into the grooves. Very high frequency grooves, in the range of 15 kHz, can be as small as four millionths of an inch, according to Walt Davies of LAST. Though alcohol itself helps somewhat, you still need a wetting agent. Two excellent and safe choices are Triton X-114 from Rohm-Haas and Monolan 2000 from Diamond Shamrock. Both of these are nontoxic—but don't take them internally—and biodegradable. Very importantly, they leave behind no residue on the record. They are harmless in these small amounts to record vinyl and, as far as is known, to any of the conceivable by-products and impurities likely to be found in record vinyl.

Kodak's Kodaflow is sometimes recommended as a wetting agent. Do *not* use this, as it contains chemicals in addition to surfactants that would leave behind residues bad for both record and stylus. Kodak recommends against this application.

MAINTENANCE AND TROUBLESHOOTING

MAINTENANCE

Like everything else, a stereo system is subject to the laws of entropy and will in time drift out of tune. Maintaining a system properly not only ensures a high level of performance but also mitigates wear and tear. Ignoring good maintenance ensures slow degradation of sound quality—occurring so gradually that you may never be aware of why you find yourself less and less drawn to listening to music and less and less satisfied when listening.

It is at this point that many systems are scrapped as being ''outdated'' and replaced *in toto,* at sizable expense. This is a great mistake—what was once a good component remains always a good component. Better ones may be developed, and the ''best'' may be surpassed, but nonetheless once good remains always good.

The mind can psychoacoustically compensate for a bad-sounding stereo, as is demonstrated by the dominance of mid- and mass-fi and the awful sound of most TVs and of telephones. Accomplished musicians are notorious for owning disgraceful sound systems. Musicians find stereo so unbridgeably distant from live music that they see no point in even trying to narrow the gap. Few, as a result, have ever heard a good system.

The point is that just because you think your system sounds OK doesn't mean it couldn't benefit from proper maintenance. The time, labor, and money involved are minimal and you may be pleasantly surprised, even astonished, by the results.

Connections and Switches

Maintenance is, as much as anything, a matter of keeping the system clean in a dirty environment. It is an excellent idea to keep *all* your equipment covered when not in use, as this is likely to prolong its sonic life significantly. All chassis have vent holes through which heat is released, but these are also entry points for dust. When the component is turned off and cool, cover the vents.

Connections oxidize and become coated with smoke, cooking oils, furnace soot, and other airborne films. This very fine layer interferes with good surface contact, resulting in a degraded connection and in distortion. Connections can loosen over time, producing a connection that is constantly, invisibly, broken electrically, causing arcing, sonic degradation, and eventually probable damage. Disconnect and reconnect all cables and interconnects (all nonsoldered, noncrimped connectors) at least once every six months or so. Start with your cartridge pins, which must be *very gently* removed and reconnected, using a pair of small needle-nose pliers or tweezers, then proceed all through the system to the speakers. The friction of disconnecting and reinserting alone will somewhat clean the connecting surfaces and improve contact. Do not overlook the wall plugs. Plug and unplug several times to clean the prongs and be sure they provide a snug fit in the outlet. (Be sure to maintain plug polarity.)

Cramolin from Monster Cable will clean off this film. It should be used only in places where you can rub it off again vigorously, leaving behind an extremely thin protective layer. Cramolin Red is a cleaner and protector, the Blue a preserver; Red is the important one. When you're using it on internal connections such as jacks, Monster recommends diluting it heavily with alcohol. Cramolin is generally a respected product. However, some feel that a Cramolin-treated connection sounds better than a dirty contact but less good than a clean one. Do not, in your enthusiasm, clean your tube pins with it—when the pins heat up, the Cramolin burns on. While the tube itself is easy enough to replace, the socket holes will also be caramelized with Cramolin and almost impossible to get clean again.

Tweek, sold by Sumiko, when applied to contacts, protects the metal surface. It also actually improves the "sound of the contact." Apply it to metal only and keep it away from plastic.

In the case of jack connectors, you should rotate the jacks in their socket to abrade off any oxidation—this is so easy you should do it monthly. Be gentle—you do not want to stress the connection between wire and jack or break the wire.

All *switches and knobs* on your components should be rotated or flipped *every few days* to maintain friction-cleaned connections.

Periodically treat control knobs with a contact cleaner such as Chemtronics Kontact Restorer. Do NOT use WD-40, as much as this seems a logical choice—it has been known to destroy the mechanism. If the component is still under warranty, it may be wise not to clean the switches yourself, as removing the cover voids the warranty. Turn off and unplug the component at least half an hour before cleaning—capacitors store a charge that drains off only slowly after the unit has been turned off. Touch one that's still charged when you're also touching the chassis and it'll drain off into you *very quickly*. While not lethal, this is definitely startling and to be avoided.

To clean the switches, be sure the component is unplugged, then remove the cover. The backside of the control panel should now be visible—if not, remove whatever is covering it. Spray all the controls with contact cleaner. Rotate and flip them back and forth rapidly to dislodge dirt and grease, then spray again. This spray is nonconductive and noncorrosive. It will cause no damage if not wiped off. Replace the cover before plugging the component back in.

Turntables

The belt should be periodically checked and cleaned, and replaced every couple of years. Old belts tend to become stretched and can pick up airborne oils, altering the grip on the drive pulley and platter. First clean with alcohol, then dust with talc, cornstarch, or arrowroot (very effective) to give the belt a good grip.

Periodically recheck the table setup for levelness, spring adjustment, and the like. Use your level on table support and platter. Check that the tonearm board is still horizontal and parallel to the table's surface. Give the platter a sharp push straight down in the center and watch for oscillations—if it bounces vertically, it's fine; but if it oscillates sideways, the springs need to be set up again.

Check the cartridge setup. The stylus or the entire cartridge should be replaced about every 6 to 18 months. Under constant use, a cartridge—or at least the stylus assembly—should be replaced about every 1,000 hours, some say as often as every 500 hours. So if you play your records for a couple of hours every day, that's over 700 hours by the end of a year. Listen for any sonic changes.

To try to determine wear by examining the stylus tip under a magnifying glass will reveal only gross problems, such as chips, which will already have caused damage to your records. A special high-magnification microscope is needed to see the early stages of wear before it causes damage. Therefore, it is wisest to schedule regular cartridge replacement.

In addition to stylus wear, it should be noted that cartridge compliance stiffens with age. Compliance is largely determined by the cantilever's damping materials, which age through magnetic effects, mechanical wear, and chemistry. This process continues even when the cartridge is not being used, so cartridges do have a shelf life. This lifespan is harder to determine. Jim Boyk, a well-respected pianist, guiding light of Performance Recordings, avid audiophile, and audio consultant, recommends replacement every 18 months, regardless of actual use.

Tape Decks

Each minute a cassette is playing, many millions of magnetized particles pass by the tape head. Some of these particles flake off on the head; the magnetic field on the tape also magnetizes the head. The pinch roller gets dirty and flaked with minute pieces of tape or dirt, with the result that the effective diameter of the pinch roller *increases* which throws off the speed. The same applies to a dirty capstan. It is essential that these be kept clean and that the heads be demagnetized.

Head-cleaning cassettes are very convenient and effective to use, providing you clean the heads and transport frequently. If you haven't cleaned them for a while, the oxides will be so built up that you'll need to deep-clean the heads with special head-cleaning fluid or alcohol on cotton swabs. Also clean the pinch roller with alcohol, being sure not to drip any down into the machinery. Demagnetize the heads with a cassette degausser (demagnetizer). Always use clean, high-quality tapes unless you have absolutely no alternative. When you do have to use old or cheap tapes, the heads should be cleaned immediately after.

Even brand-new decks may have misaligned heads, perhaps knocked slightly askew during shipping. As the heads wear, alignment changes. It is a good idea to check head alignment every year, then either correct the azimuth yourself or get the machine serviced. A fairly crude but simple test for checking correct head alignment is to play a tape that was made on a properly set-up machine. (If you are uncertain about this last factor, use several different tapes that you at least believe were recorded on an aligned machine.) As you listen, periodically switch to mono. If the treble drops off in mono, or you hear a *whoosh* from frequency cancellation, chances are your heads need checking.

The other method is to play a special azimuth test tape and adjust the head tilt until you obtain maximum output as indicated by an audio voltmeter. If your deck has VU meters that are mechanical rather than electronic and can therefore register fine differences in signal level, and if the meters read playback level, these can be used instead of a voltmeter. If the azimuth alignment that gives maximum output to the left channel differs from that to the right channel, you will have to compromise between the two.

It is best to use a test tape that includes both a low-frequency tone around 5 kHz and a high-frequency tone around 12 to 15 kHz. First adjust azimuth using the 5-kHz tone and then fine-tune it with the higher tone. If you adjust on the basis of a high-frequency tone alone, it is possible to get false azimuth peaks that are lower than the true azimuth peak output, in which event your heads will be misaligned.

In the case of separate recording and playback heads, align the playback head first. Then, to align the recording head, simultaneously record and play back a high-frequency tone and adjust the recording head for maximum output in playback.

Tuners

There is effectively no maintenance you can perform on a tuner, other than keeping it clean. Keep it covered to protect against dust. Periodically clean the connections and treat the switches and knobs.

CD Players

There is little maintenance you can perform yourself on CD players, aside from keeping them covered when not in use. You may not even be able to get access to the push-button switches to clean them periodically.

If you find you are suffering from more faulty discs than you used to, it may be worthwhile to have the machine checked for a dirty laser—especially if your player is a year old or more. This can be cleaned much the same way you clean a tape head—except, unfortunately, you cannot do it yourself as it is not placed where you have access to it.

The average life of a laser head is about 5,000 hours, according to Steve Harris of Marantz Audio. However, there have been a number of reports in the audio press about premature laser-beam failures, some after only weeks, others after a year or so, far less than the statistical lifespan of 5,000 hours. Replacement is not inexpensive.

The Amplification Stage

The amp fuse should be replaced regularly as it oxidizes and degrades sound, though subtly.

Tube amps will need periodical retubing and rebiasing. Roger Modjeski of Ram Tubes estimates average tube life at about 1,000 hours, at which point you get degradation of sound. So if you listen a couple of hours every evening, the tubes should be replaced every year and a half or so, to maintain optimum sound. Check also with the designer regarding tube life—some amps run their tubes closer to the limits of the tubes' tolerances, which tends to shorten their lifespan. This can also make the unit's sound particularly sensitive to what tubes are used. Keep a fresh set on hand. As you approach the estimated end of the first set's sonic life, substitute the new set and listen for a difference. If you hear no improvement, return to the first set and get a little more work out of them.

You can check for tube aging by looking at the *getter,* the silver dome at the top of the tube. If you see a very faint whitish ring, this indicates that the getter has receded from its original position, which means it has been around for a while.

Tube quality varies substantially and tube sound will differ from one company to the next, and from one tube to the next. Experiment and/or follow the amp manufacturer's recommendations. Many feel that Ram's tubes are perhaps the most consistently good. Others report positive experiences with Gold Aero. Some good tubes have been coming out of China. Mesa Boogie, considered the Rolls-Royce of music amps, carries a 12AX7 that sounds very good and is consistent in quality. It is manufactured to the company's specs by Sylvania.

Every time you replace a tube in an amp (not a preamp) you must rebias the component. Set the bias and check it again after a few hours, then after a day, then again after a few days—bias can change as the tubes burn in. In between tube changes, bias should be checked periodically. Bias drift can cause the image to wander and overall sound to become degraded. Some tube equipment does not allow "user biasing," requiring the unit to be returned to the manufacturer for both rebiasing and retubing. This is a real drawback, as you will be without your equipment for probably a minimum of ten days (also incurring the risk of shipping damage and the expense of shipping) while this very simple procedure is being carried out by others.

Speakers

Speakers are fused as protection against being blown by excessive amp power, clipping, or other sudden surges in amp power or distortion. These fuses should be periodically replaced, as old ones may corrode and certainly oxidize. Use the same amperage. Do not use slow-blow fuses (unless this is specified by the manufacturer) as they may not react quickly enough to prevent all damage to the speakers.

Since the music signal must pass through the fuse, obviously this has some effect on the sound. The correct fuse will cause a subtle but not unimportant improvement in the clarity, detail, and imaging qualities of the sound. Some listeners replace the fuse altogether with a same-sized rod of solid silver from a jewelers' supply house, hearing less signal degradation from the silver than a fuse. However, while the speakers may sound great, they are also now unprotected. Proceed at your own very real risk.

With dynamic speakers, it is also a good idea to retighten periodically the screws securing the drivers to the cabinet, as the constant vibration tends to loosen them.

TROUBLESHOOTING

If NOTHING works, relax. This is often the easiest situation to correct. Check to make sure everything is plugged in, that the outlets you have plugged into are live (test this by plugging in a lamp to see if it works), that no fuses or circuit breakers are blown. If a fuse keeps blowing, you have too much plugged into that line. Don't try to get around the problem by replacing the fuse with a larger one; instead correct the problem by lessening the line's load.

If just one component doesn't work, check its fuse. This is usually at the back of the component, beside its AC power cord. Remove the fuse and see whether it has blown. Inside the glass tube capped with metal ends is a thin wire or bar of metal. If the wire is broken or the glass looks smoky, the fuse has blown. Replace it with an identical match for value (amperage) and type (slow-blow, fast-blow, or neither)—take the fuse with you to the electronics store. If the replacement fuse blows too, take the component in for repair.

If the components light up but you have no sound, check the controls to be sure they're not switched to "tuner" when you're trying to play a record, or to "tape monitor" or "speakers off." Be sure the volume control is not turned all the way down and that the balance control isn't turned all the way to one side. Be sure the speaker connections are tight—if they're not, turn the system off before securing them.

If you are getting strange noises, the first step is to determine the origin of the problem and then see whether you can fix it yourself or will have to take the component in for repair. First, try all the sources—turntable, tape deck, tuner, CD player. If the problem is common to all signal sources, then it must be in the speakers, preamp, or amp, the only components common to all sources. To find the specific component causing the problem, follow the same methods as for tracking down hum (p. 289).

If you have no sound or distorted sound in both channels, the problem is probably in the amplification stage—the odds against both your speakers' blowing at the same time are very high, unless you've been abusing them.

If the problem is in only one channel, say the right channel, then start downstream and work back toward the source. First check whether the problem is in the speakers by reversing the leads at the speaker. Take the right-channel lead and connect it to the left speaker, the left-channel lead to the right speaker. If the problem remains in the right speaker, then that speaker is the problem. If the distortion is now in the left, instead of the right, speaker, then the speaker cannot be the problem and the source is further upstream. Assuming the speakers are fine, restore the cables to their original positions.

Next find out if the problem is in the speaker cable by reversing the cables at the amp (turn the equipment off first). If the problem changes channels again, then restore the cables to their correct positions and move on to the next point upstream, the amp stage.

If you have a separate preamp and power amp, you can determine which has the problem by reversing the interconnect between them. If the problem changes channels, it's in the preamp. If it doesn't, it's in the power amp.

The Turntable System

The turntable system is a very delicate instrument that must be carefully set up and maintained. Most problems are simply a matter of the table's having drifted out of tune. (See pp. 230 and 280 for full details.) If the sound seems worse than it used to be, or if it is generally distorted and breaks up and "shatters" during high-level passages, check for the following problems. First be sure the stylus is clean. Then check tracking force: Be sure it isn't set so high that the stylus has receded up into the cartridge body. Too light a tracking weight also causes distortion. Use a stylus pressure gauge to reset the tracking weight according to the manufacturer's specs—set it toward the maximum end if the cartridge was tracking too lightly. Check that the tonearm is properly balanced so that it "floats" when the tracking force is set to zero. Check the antiskate, especially if one channel sounds fuzzier than the other; try setting it a little lower than recommended. If your stylus is a year old, *replace it.* Worn styli are record erasers and the damage they do is irreversible. If you happen to be broke at the moment, get the Joe Grado $20 MTE + 1 cartridge.

A sensitivity to groove skipping or jumping may indicate that the table is not level. Place a small level on the platter and adjust the table until it is truly horizontal. You can usually raise or lower one or more of the four corners of the table as needed by screwing in or slightly unscrewing the rubber feet.

Speed inconsistencies where there used to be none may indicate the need for a new belt on a belt-drive table. On direct-drive tables (of which the only audiophile-approved models start at over a grand), alter the speed/pitch control, or you may want to consider replacing the table if it is a mass-fi one.

Hum is often caused by a grounding wire that has come loose—check at the back of the table and the back of the preamp. Also check the cartridge leads for tightness and correct placement. Reverse the table's line cord. Plug the power cord into the wall instead of the back of the preamp. Experiment with reversing the plug to determine correct plug polarity (see p. 228). Move your preamp a little farther away and to the right side of the table.

Rumble or a boomy sound suggests the table is suffering from acoustic feedback and should be moved farther from the speakers, and/or should be placed on a more solid support.

Cassette Decks

The tape heads and transport must be kept clean or the sound of your tapes will deteriorate. The heads must also be regularly demagnetized. If sound quality has been worsening, the first step is to clean and demagnetize the deck (see p. 281).

Tape squeal, flutter, or wavering speed is suggestive of a problem in the mechanism of the cassette tape itself. However, if this problem comes up consistently on a number of tapes, the problem may be in the deck, which should be serviced. Test for this problem using new commercially recorded tapes, since, if you use your home-recorded tapes, you cannot know if the problem is in the turntable you used to make the recording. Buy new tapes because the problem may be that all your tapes have just become old. Wow or flutter, providing you're sure it's not on your tapes, is a sign that the deck needs a belt replaced—this requires expert service.

Distortion and hissiness on home-recorded tapes suggests you may be using the wrong recording levels or tape bias. Check the instruction manual to set your deck properly for the kind of tape you're using (or see pp. 78 and 332).

Dull high frequencies can mean several things: The heads may need demagnetization and the heads and transport cleaning; you may be incorrectly matching playback equalization to your tape; or if you make your own recordings, you may be using too high a bias setting.

Tuners

The major problem with FM reception is multipath distortion, which is characterized by a nasty, variable noise. Tuners differ in their susceptibility to this problem but it can be largely alleviated by the antenna. Check that the antenna connections on the back of the tuner (or receiver) are correct and tight. Be sure no stray strands of wire are crossing the two terminals. Move the antenna around the room to try to find the best location. You should consider replacing an indoor dipole antenna (a twin-lead wire that forks in two), which is probably what came with your tuner, especially if old. There may be breaks in the wire. (For more on antennas, see p. 91).

If your component has a muting circuit—this treats a signal below a certain point as noise and cuts it off—it may also be cutting off the signal you want to hear. Switch out the muting circuit, though this may leave you with a noisy signal; or, if you can, adjust its level. Sometimes switching to a mono setting will help minimize distortion.

The Amplification Stage

The electronics are the least likely to go wrong and, if they do go wrong, the most likely to need professional repair. The control switches may need cleaning—dirty ones will produce static and sometimes an intermittent signal that you can hear over the speakers. Also, the connections may be faulty—check that all are clean and tight (see p. 278 for switch and connection cleaning). With tube amps, when a tube begins to go, you will hear a rushing, hissing sound through the speakers. Always keep spare tubes on hand; replace one tube at a time until the problem clears up. An overall degradation of sound may indicate that it's time for a complete tube change and rebiasing. With the exception of a few components, you can easily do this yourself. Read the instruction manual or contact the manufacturer.

Speakers

Speakers can blow a fuse (in which case they won't work), can blow a driver (you'll lose all treble if the tweeter blows, all bass if the woofer goes), and can distort a signal. But they can't generate a signal—if you hear a noise when there's no music signal going through, the speaker is not the problem. Problems occurring in both speakers are probably caused further upstream—each speaker carries only one channel and for both speakers to become defective simultaneously is very unlikely. If both speakers are damaged, the origin of the problem is probably up the line. Track it down or it will recur and again damage the speakers you just got repaired. For example, blown tweeters probably mean your amp is overdosing them with high-frequency signals.

Defects that are specific to the speakers are generally mechanical sounding and intermittent. Uneven response, buzzing on low notes, and squealing on high ones are typical symptoms. Electrical-sounding and continuous problems such as humming or hissing are probably not speaker problems. (To track down their source, see above in this chapter.) Incorrect speaker phase can degrade the sound (see p. 225).

Room acoustics may be the problem. To check, physically exchange the speakers along with their cables: If the problem that seemed to be in the right speaker remains on the right side when the speakers are exchanged, then the problem is with the room (see p. 203). However, if the problem moves with the speaker, then it is either in the speaker itself or in that channel.

Hum

Hum and system noise can be one of the most frustrating and annoying gremlins to track down in your system. Otherwise placid souls have torn their systems apart to find its source. Hum has all the irritation of a mosquito's buzz but worse, as it never stops. Hum, like a mosquito, should be vanquishable, the listener feels, and therefore sets out determined to vanquish rather than endure. Unfortunately, it can be maddeningly elusive.

There are innumerable sources from which stray electromagnetic fields can creep into the sound: Every connection point and every chassis has the ability to pick up the electromagnetic radiation that surrounds us. We hear it as 60-cycle hum (the same sound you hear from just about any motor, or a fluorescent light fixture's ballast, or a defective streetlight).

A very loud hum or buzz is most likely from a loose ground wire. Be sure your system is correctly grounded (see p. 229). Milder hums may be the result of faulty interconnects or cables—heavy inflexible wiring can cause broken connections at plugs and jacks, as well as broken strands of wire inside the jacketing.

Here's how to track down hum methodically, according to Roger Modjeski of Ram Tubes. When listening for hum, adjust the system's volume to your "normal" listening level. The importance of listening at normal levels is that this replicates "real-world" circumstances. If you can hear hum at maximum volume, but never listen that loud, how much does it really matter that the hum is there? Though it's nicer to be without it, it could take forever to track down such a small hum.

Checking the Turntable

Turn on the table motor, as this is often a source of hum. Cue up the arm over the platter to check if the motor's magnetic field can induce hum in the cartridge—a phenomenon you can depend on in the combination of an AR table and a Grado cartridge. Do a preliminary check to discover if the table is the source: Listen on other inputs—to a quiet section of an FM broadcast, to the pauses on a CD disc. If you listen to a cassette tape, don't use a homemade one—you may have recorded hum onto it.

Better yet, disconnect the table and insert shorting plugs into the phono inputs at the preamp (where the tonearm cable would connect). What shorting plugs (available at Radio Shack) do is in effect to replace all the wire in the cartridge and arm with a very short length of wire. Able to take the table out of the system this way, you can tell if the hum is also out of the system, in which case the table is the source. If the hum remains unchanged, then the table is in the clear and the hum is further down the line.

If the table is the source, do the following: First check that the cartridge isn't picking up hum from a nearby power cord or transformer. You can usually tell by moving the tone arm—if the hum changes, then you know the cartridge is picking it up. Move either the hum source or the table. If the hum doesn't change as you move the arm, then check the connections: (1) Check that the ground wire is connected between table and amp. If it isn't, connect it; if it is, disconnect it. (2) Reverse the power cord plug. Be sure it is plugged into a wall outlet, not the back of the amp. (3) If you use a moving coil cartridge, move the leads from the table to transformers or preamp as far away from any power cords as possible. If the hum doesn't drop when you short out the input jacks, then you know the hum is not in the table but in the preamp or amp.

Checking the Amplification Stage

Turn the volume all the way down on the preamp. If the hum also goes down, then the preamp is the hum source. If the hum remains the same, proceed on to the power amp.

If you have established that the hum is in the preamp, check for loose wires—experiment with running a grounding wire from the chassis to a true ground (a cold water pipe, the grounding screw on a wall outlet). The preamp may need servicing.

Assuming the hum is not in the preamp, next short the inputs of the power amp with the amp hooked up to the speakers. You should be able to put your ear up to each speaker and hear almost total silence—and, from a foot away, true silence.

Though none of these steps may themselves cure the hum, they will help to track it down to a specific component.

RECORDING CARE AND PRESERVATION

Considering that retrieving the music from the recording is the entire purpose of this whole complicated business of high-end audio, one of the most important aspects of setup and operation is the recording itself. How well this is maintained establishes the maximum level of quality the entire system can attain. If the recording is worn, scratched, warped, or suffering any other damage, the system will inevitably register this.

Recordings are the universal storage medium for the human musical experience. Yet we tend to treat these parts of our history as just so much plastic. This is like regarding paintings as so many square feet of canvas daubed with pigment, photographs as pieces of paper coated with a microscopic layer of silver. If we accept that recordings are the museum of our musical heritage, then all of us are the keepers of the archives. (Americans, incidentally, buy nearly half the world's recordings.)

Unfortunately, you cannot expect to be able to replace your recordings when they become worn out from poor care. Not everything is kept in print. But even beyond this, the master tapes are slowly but inexorably aging, fading, sometimes even getting lost. The recording companies appear to have little more than a perfunctory interest in preserving them (the companies can always produce a "remake" of the Beatles' songs, another interpretation of Reiner's Beethoven's Fifth). But once the originals are gone, they're gone forever. Before too long, a pristine version of a very good pressing will be better than the faded master and will become the reference for future generations. Remastering to CD is not the answer—the transfer from analog to digital results in sonic degradation; digital master tapes store even worse than analog tapes; CDs themselves, regardless of all claims, are far from impervious to misuse.

Recordings, including CDs, are fragile and must be handled with care. Caring for your recordings is like performing your daily ablutions. The problems that eventually develop from, say, failing to brush your teeth are far greater than the momentary inconvenience of keeping them clean. So the best way to preserve recordings is not to abuse them in the first place—once they've been dirtied, you've created a problem that need never have been. Even when the damage can't be seen, it can be easily heard. But a modicum of care will preserve a collection worth handing on to your children and grandchildren.

LPs, CDs, and cassettes are each in their own way equally fragile. The most basic care demands that the recording, regardless of format, should go directly from jacket to player and then back to the jacket with minimum exposure to dust and other forms of abuse. Always keep recordings in their protective wrappers when not actually being played. When handling, *keep your fingers off!* This includes CDs, however much they're advertised as also making great Frisbees. Store all recordings away from heat, out of the sun, and protected from dust. Keep the player clean, whether turntable and stylus, tape heads, or CD drawer, and your music will play for years.

LPs

LPs are no more delicate, finicky, or harder to maintain than other recording formats. And there's a lot you can do to preserve them—LPs have been around long enough for a lot of information to have been collected on their long-term care. Cassettes, on the other hand, are much more limited in how much they can be protected against tape fading or mechanical problems like the reel mechanism inside the case wearing out. CDs are only recently being recognized as needing care at all, so there is little information on maximizing their lifespan.

Store albums vertically. Do NOT stack records one on top of the other. Unless you keep them *precisely* lined up, one record will be sitting slightly off-center from the next and *they will warp.* Warps are not easily flattened. The weight of the records alone will grind the ubiquitous dust particles into the vinyl, causing pops and ticks.

Store them upright, close together so they support each other but not tightly squashed like canned sardines. Preferably store them in a closed shelf to cut down on dust. Or keep them in covered record boxes. The tops lift off and you can see the full jackets as you flip through them, as in a record store, rather than having to peer crablike at the spines. If they are stored on shelving, dividers should be spaced about every 6 inches or so to prevent the records from all leaning to one side and ending up warped.

Store them well away from sun and other sources of heat, in a dry place, away from dust, and away from the kitchen. Cooking oils, furnace fumes, cigarette smoke, pollution, and dust will harm any recording.

Inner sleeves are essential. The paper sleeves that most albums come in are very handy for writing up laundry and shopping lists but NOT for LPs. They release as much paper dust as they protect against external sources of dust. Use the "rice paper" sleeve, as sold by Unique Vinyl or Discwasher, or else buy high-clarity polyethylene sleeves—these are inert.

First slip the record into the inner sleeve, then the inner sleeve

LAST

Playing a record has the unfortunate side effect of also wearing it out. After even just a few plays, some of the high-frequency information is lost and surface noise starts to increase. In addition, wear defects appear not as a linear function of the number of plays but as an exponential function. With a vertical tracking force of 1 gram, the pressure of the stylus tip on the vinyl is anywhere from around 30,000 to 70,000 pounds p.s.i., depending on the stylus shape. As the stylus traces the groove, several hundred degrees of thermal heat are generated and the surface of the groove walls actually becomes semiliquid. The passage of the stylus over the groove walls produces a shock wave. When a shock wave hits slight imperfections in the vinyl (which are all too common), vinyl fragments will be literally blown off the groove, leaving behind a "pothole" often of craterlike proportions to the stylus. The flying vinyl fragments will gouge the groove walls, or become heat and pressure welded to the walls, setting up the potential for further damage.

Every pit, pothole, microcrack, or piece of pressure-welded debris becomes the site of a whole new set of wear on the stylus's next round. So what started out as a minimal imperfection before playing has now been aggravated into a pop, click, or other auditory assault. Each successive play worsens the potholes and so increases surface noise.

While keeping both record and stylus clean is essential in minimizing the damage, this alone cannot elimate it because defects in the vinyl itself are as much a cause as dirt and dust. Enter LAST (Liquid Archival Sound Treatment), brainchild of Dr. Ed Catalano and Walter E. Davies, which is claimed to be a record preserver and distortion reducer. A number of people have come to agree with its claims and it is used by museums, radio stations, archivists, and anyone else who cares about preserving records.

LAST is not a coating or film that lies on the surface of the record (these can attract dust and dirt and also interfere with the stylus's accurate tracing of the groove wall). Nor is it a lubricant—self lubricating like Teflon, it is very slippery, yet nothing comes between the record and the stylus. The slipperiness reduces wear on both groove and stylus, extending the life of both. LAST does not alter the character of the vinyl itself, but modifies the molecular bonding structure—it increases cohesiveness so that shock waves cannot as easily shatter the integrity of the vinyl. It also stabilizes the vinyl and retards breakdown by ultraviolet light. LAST is supposed to last for 200 plays or ten years (whichever comes first). Much more detailed discussions of LAST are found in *IAR Journal,* no. 5, and in literature from the company.

One hesitates a lot before applying any substance to a record—museums are filled with horror stories of misapplications made in all good faith to preserve an object, until 20 years later the damage finally shows up. However, many serious record collectors and preservers now use LAST on our most-played and most-precious LPs. Some will use it only on old records that have become worn—LAST can help to rejuvenate them. It actually can improve the sound of even a new record, but its greatest attraction is its claim to reduce wear. The LAST company has LPs that were treated over 8 years ago and have been played over 400 times with no increase in noise. Usually the first dozen plays alone of an untreated record cause an audible increase in noise and loss of the high frequencies.

As Walt Davies puts it, "The entire acoustical heritage of all of the world's cultures is stored on a medium which is subject to wear and environmental degradation. It is possible to protect and extract the information without measurable wear." Hooray!

inside the jacket. Slip it in slowly, don't jam it in by force—you will add microscratches to the record surface. Slip it in so the open edge of the inner sleeve is to either the spine or top edge of the jacket, leaving a closed edge facing the opening of the jacket. Again, every little bit helps to keep the dust out. Do NOT place the open side of the inner sleeve so that it faces down to the bottom of the jacket—when you come to pull it out again, the record will end up on the floor!

Discard the album's shrink-wrapped outer sleeve and replace it with a loose plastic sleeve. There are two problems with shrink wrap: If stretched on tight enough, it may actually warp the record (a problem to watch for when buying); and it generates static electricity, attracting dust like a magnet. The outer sleeve provides one more dust barrier if you put it on so it closes the open edge and also protects the often-beautiful artwork. A number of jackets have become valued collector's items.

If you collect duplicates of your records or have a backlog of ones you have not yet listened to, do NOT leave them sealed. At least slit open the shrink wrap and preferably discard it, replacing it with an outer sleeve. Sealed records have a strong likelihood of warping.

CASSETTE TAPES

Cassette tapes self-destruct far more quickly than LPs or CDs. A half-dozen or so passes across the tape heads and the highs begin to drop off as the oxides flake away. The oxide dust building up on the tape heads and on the guides and pulleys contains a lot of the music. The tape heads also demagnetize the tape a little more each time it's played and so the noise builds up and the highs go away. As the magnetization builds up on the heads, this too partially erases the higher frequencies, taking away still more of the music. Your tapes soon sound dull and lifeless. It is essential to demagnetize the heads *each time the deck is turned on* to ensure even mid-fi results over the long term. The turn-on and turn-off transients of most recorders immediately magnetize the heads enough to take the machine out of spec. The entire tape path, not just the tape heads, should also be regularly demagnetized.

Just as with LPs, dust is a major enemy of cassette sound quality and longevity. Dust collects on the cassette tape, on the tape heads, capstan, and pinch roller, and on the edges of the tape guides. Dust deposits can scratch the highly polished surface of the tape heads, foul the transport mechanism, and in relatively short order destroy your tapes.

Unfortunately, cassettes deteriorate not only when played but even when stored and stored properly (unlike LPs, whose shelf life, properly stored, is indefinite). High frequencies become duller, the overall sound warmer and more veiled. Audible pre-echo can develop—the music on one section of tape prints through to the adjacent section of tape and so one hears both the current music and the upcoming section.

Cassettes must be stored away from heat, dust, dirt, and moisture. These can deform the tape transport mechanism inside the cassette shell and cause the tape edges to curl. The result is garbled sound and tape jamming.

Tapes stored after a fast wind tend to have uneven stresses and sometimes uneven edges that protrude and can become damaged. Normal speed tends to be much smoother, resulting in more even tension and edge alignment on the tape. This is why many pros store their open-reel tapes "tails out" rather than rewinding before putting them away. It is a good practice for cassette tapes also. Certainly try to avoid fast winding.

Tapes should also be stored at least several feet away from magnetic fields, including your speakers and any equipment with power transformers or motors. Like LPs, they are best stored vertically.

Tape itself cannot be cleaned. So keep the deck clean and demagnetized to prevent adding to dirt on the tape.

Prerecorded tapes are usually less good than what you can make for yourself at home. The tape of a disc won't be as good as the disc itself but still is likely to be better than the prerecorded version.

COMPACT DISCS

Compacts discs are "open sandwiches," as Walt Davies describes them. On the label side, which is where all the information is recorded, they are protected by only a thin acrylic shield. A scratch on this side and information has been wiped out that no error correction circuit can recreate, however much it may compensate. This is another of the strengths of LPs: Even a worn record, its grooves as smoothed away as the Appalachian Mountains, can, when properly cleaned and played with a deep-groove stylus like a microlinear, still provide a deep emotional experience. A damaged compact disc, on the other hand, loses the information outright and irretrievably. NOTHING can restore it. CDs, sold as impervious to damage in contrast to vinyl and tape, are in fact vulnerable.

Before loading the CD in the player, always inspect its underside, which is part of the optical system. If it has any microscratches, these can refract the light—like fine sandpaper scraped over a mirror. Error correction may "cover them up" but at the cost of nasty distortion. In addition, if there are any specks of dust, and these become transferred to the hub on which the CD is supported, then any CD will load slightly crooked until the dust specks are removed. Access to the hub for cleaning is very difficult unless you have one of the discontinued top-loading machines.

Regardless of anything you have heard, CDs cannot be used as Frisbees or coasters, nor can they survive anything other than delicate handling. Dirty CDs may be rejected from loading, will definitely sound worse as error correction attempts to compensate for fingerprints, and may sound really bad as error correction gets overloaded. If your player's sound quality has deteriorated, it may simply be because the cleanliness of your discs has deteriorated.

Immediately after playing, return the CD to its ''jewel case'' hard plastic box. If it only has a cardboard sleeve and no box, it is quite vulnerable to dust and should be treated especially carefully. Handle it only by its edges.

Clean CDs regularly and often. Cleaning should be performed not in the LP's rotational direction but radially, like the spokes of a wheel extending from the center out to the edges. Nitty Gritty has a machine that will do this for you. Believe it or not, it has been reported that, like LPs, even brand-new CDs sound better if you clean them before playing.

Microscratches can be polished out with LAST CD cleaner, which also leaves the surface so slippery that fingers inadvertently applied won't leave prints (don't therefore think you can get away with fingering the CDs). Never use alcohol as a cleaner, as this causes fogging and hazing on any polycarbonate material. Walt Davies also recommends Brillianize as an alternative to LAST CD cleaner.

PART III.

RECORDINGS

RECORDING APPROACHES

The main hindrances to good sound are not poor recordings but poor equipment and, just as important, improper use of equipment.

A good, natural recording played back well on even a modest system will provide enough sonic information to re-create much of the visual information of a live performance. Built up from subtle sonic detail, an almost holographic image identifies where each player is positioned, whether seated or standing, the kind of acoustic space the performance occurs in, the details of a page being turned, a creaky chair, a tapping foot.

There's a tactile quality to good recordings—violins sound like violins, not steel strings; the saxophone has the breathy, sometimes gurgly sound of a live sax; you can hear the snap of the drum skin, distinguish between a ridged or smooth surface on the cymbals, or when a pillow has been used to muffle the bass. You can hear the breath in a singer's throat, and almost "see" lips and tongue shaping a sound.

Ideally, you would just hold the recording to your ear to hear the music and dispense with the complications of audio components. It is a central and fundamental verity of audio that *the recording is the heart and soul of the HFS system.* For even though you must contend with putting together and maintaining a good system, it must not get in the way of the recording—the equipment is meant to be seen but not heard. What you want to hear is the music, not the system's interpretation of that music. Far too often stereo systems instead block the sound!

Your playback system is only as valuable to you as your recordings, for its function is to reveal them. Boasting about great equipment is like praising a pianist's instrument—it tells you nothing about the piano player. The piano and your system are equally useless without the input of musical information.

Largely unaware of the experience recordings can bring, we tend to mistreat them as disposable items, readily replaced when damaged. It is only recently that the recording, long viewed as an inferior substitute for the live performance, is coming to be acknowledged for what it is—not a toy or novelty item or even a mass medium, but an art form.

Recordings are a living museum of our musical heritage, the universal storage medium for the human musical experience. And while many of us have great museums—anyone with even a small record collection almost certainly owns a few special moments in recorded history—few of us realize it because we have never heard the full depth of detail locked within the records in our collections.

A performance, normally fleeting, is by recording frozen in space and time. The recording provides an extraordinary link between the two worlds of past performance and present audience, with the playback equipment serving as a kind of time machine. Like a window onto the once-live moment of the music, a recording lets you hear and see into reality. (Like a window too, the recording can never be as transparent as an unobstructed view, but it can come remarkably close.)

What printing did for the written word, recordings have done for music. Even if you could devote your entire life to traveling the world to hear live performances, it would be impossible to hear as many performers, conductors, nationalities, and varieties of music as you can hear on recordings at home, whenever and as often as desired. Just as printing brought about a proliferation of books, since hi-fi was developed there have been far more orchestras and more performances of live music. Recordings created a large enough audience with the desire to experience the original that many more towns are now able to support an orchestra and other musical events.

RECORDING AND TECHNOLOGY

While the recording industry during the past 100 years has been continually seeking to develop equipment that would more faithfully capture the live event, somewhere along the way the emphasis came increasingly to be put on the process and technique of recording rather than on the results. Recording is above all an artistic pursuit, but it is being stifled by an overemphasis on and overconfidence in technology. Science provides the tools and materials for a painter or sculptor, just as it also provides the materials and means of recording and playback. An artist who confuses material and technique with talent and communication achieves work of only a short-lived reputation at best.

Whereas poor playback equipment for many years obscured the subtle sonic detail captured on many recordings, their musical detail is today readily revealed by good equipment. But poor *recording* techniques permanently obscure subtle musical details that no playback equipment will ever be able to reveal because they were lost to the recording.

It's a pervasive misperception that technology continuously advances, making all preceding developments obsolete. It leads us to the bankrupt conclusion that stereo is inherently superior to mono, transistors to tubes, digital to analog, none of which is necessarily true. "Newer," in recording and playback alike, is not automatically synonymous with "improved." The recording of music is fundamentally an artistic matter, so the most advanced technology is not *ipso facto* the best choice for reproducing music, just as advanced technologies for processing and preserving food don't always assure your eating pleasure.

Some of the most highly regarded recordings date from the 1950s and early 1960s, not a period usually thought of as the golden age of high fidelity. These magnificent recordings may have noisy surfaces, tape hiss, some cutting-lathe noise, and occasional frequency-range compression, but they are indisputably real, dynamic, startlingly natural, *musical,* despite minor blemishes. It's a complete myth that one has to listen to "audiophile" pressings and the latest state-of-the-art equipment in order to enjoy good sound. *Music* is precisely what one is trying to capture on a disc—black velvet backgrounds, earth-rumbling lows, and Day-Glo highs may impress but aren't music.

Regardless of the millions spent on advertisements proclaiming great leaps of advancement in recording techniques, the major labels' current releases are not significantly better than those in the early 1960s, and a great number of them are significantly inferior.

These major companies have dominated the public perception of recording, along with their counterparts among the audio equipment manufacturers. (In the earlier days of audio, companies made both recordings and equipment.) Between poor recordings and poor playback equipment, it is easy to understand why so many people have become inured to bad sound.

One of the problems is that few recording companies have any awareness of what constitutes good playback equipment; they cannot even hear what is on a recording because they play it back on poor equipment. An anecdote from Raymond Cooke, head of the KEF speaker company, illustrates the widespread use of inferior monitor equipment.*

---

*As reported in *Stereophile,* vol. 8, no. 3.

EMI executives put on a public demonstration of some of their recordings, borrowing a pair of KEF's audiophile home speakers for the event. One disc played was Pink Floyd's *Dark Side of the Moon,* famous among audio connoisseurs as one of the technically finest of rock recordings. But never having heard *Dark Side* on anything better than typical studio monitors or mass-market junk, the EMI suits were unaware that there was some pretty raunchy language on the recording, a fact readily revealed by any good playback system. Much to EMI's embarrassment, some of the audience got up and walked out.

Studio monitor equipment is selected for durability and ease of use—period. The question of sonic excellence is not at issue. Recording companies all over the country were baffled by being asked about what kind of reference equipment they were listening on. It seems most recording engineers and producers listen to mass-fi equipment, undoubtedly poorly set up, and decide the final EQ according to how the mix sounds on the lowest common denominator of such equipment. This approach seems to be based on the mistaken notion that a recording has to be specifically made to sound good on poor equipment, which is what they believe most of their audience listens on. Many say they feel (as far as they think about it at all) that by listening on better equipment themselves, they would lose touch with their market.

What they don't seem to recognize is that a good recording played on *any* equipment will sound better than a poor recording on any equipment. Nonetheless, with the exception of the premier audiophile labels (such as Opus 3, Reference Recordings, Jim Boyk's Performance Recordings, Sheffield Lab), it's a rare company that knows that (or probably cares) anything about audiophile playback equipment. So the overwhelming likelihood is that most companies are in the same position as EMI in the anecdote above—they have no idea how their recordings actually sound.

Now this would be fine if they left well enough alone instead of doctoring the sound. The Mercury Living Presence, Decca/London, and DG recordings so highly prized today were at the time of their release not fully recognized for their excellence because the quality of playback equipment was generally less good than it is now. Just how much subtle detail was actually captured on those recordings finally came to be revealed as playback equipment improved. Nowadays, though, with the "advances" in technology, those same recordings would have been EQed to make them sound "more alive" on poor playback equipment and so, when listened to on a good system, they would have their subtle musical detail buried beneath EQ's electronic smog.

You can clearly hear the negative effects of misapplied technology by following a performer's recording career. The best recordings of a performer are frequently the earlier ones, before he or she became famous—because the recording company wants to minimize its risk on an unknown artist, the simplest recording techniques are used. With less electronic gadgetry and geewhizardry involved, there is also less electronic smog and distortion. As the artist becomes more successful, recording company and studio engineers alike want to impress and so pull out all the stops on the latest techno-wonders. And the sound quality goes down the drain. This is not a case of misapplied artistry; it's a case of the almighty buck and perhaps mistaken artistry. Many times we have to accept mediocrity, but must we really believe in it as well?

A number of famous rock recording artists and producers boast about using a portable radio or car stereo to test the final mix-down. The Rolling Stones in particular have always taken a perverse pride in bragging about how little attention they give to good sound—an attitude we've always interpreted as being inverse snobbery.

Good sound is not a form of elitism. The intent behind achieving sonic excellence is simply to permit better access to the music—imagine having to view a great work of art through a dirty window. The transparency of medium and equipment is what allows the music to come through and really grab the listener's heart. Bad sound short-changes not only the music and the listener but also the musicians, who may play their hearts out during a performance only to get considerably less than the best recorded sound possible.

Nonetheless, a poor recording of great music is always better than the reverse. In painting, Magritte's technique was very sloppy—this doesn't show when looking at reproductions of his work, but just take a look at the originals. Vermeer, in contrast, was excellent at both content and technique. But few would be prepared to miss out on Magritte just because he wasn't painterly.

THE TWO BASIC SCHOOLS

Recording and playback are mirror images, with the recording itself representing the plane of the mirror. Many of the principles of good playback hold true also for good recording. The importance of minimalism, for example, is just as critical in recording as in playback. Circuitry—any circuitry—unavoidably adds distortion. The smaller the amount of electronics, including wire and cable, between the live performance and the final recording, the more musical and natural the sound will be.

Just as in playback, the problems that develop during a recording's production tend to be cumulative. Problems, once existing, can never be entirely eradicated except by doing the recording over again. Attempts made to correct the initial recording error may only compound the problem. You can't just pull a bottle of sonic bleach or audio spot remover off the shelf and try to remove the stain. The best you can hope for is to doctor the recording electronically in an attempt to camouflage the mistake. But this very process, even assuming it works, will degrade the recording's overall sound, somewhat the way cleaning fluid leaches out a little of the fabric color along with the stain, leaving a larger, slightly faded area. The frightening part is that a large number of recording engineers would flatly disagree with this. They rely on the availablity of audio spot removers and believe negligible degradation results.

As a general rule, the minimum number of mikes, used in the most straightforward manner possible, with the least manipulation of the recording both during and after the performance, will yield the most natural sound and the most transparent recording. Of course, when the final musical experience is fashioned in the studio by the engineers, as in much rock and pop music, this maxim of minimalism may seem not to apply. However, with only slight rephrasing, it remains pertinent: *Use the least equipment and least processing necessary to get the desired results.*

As we said at the opening of this section, the purpose of a recording is to transport the musical performance faithfully from one location to another, through time and space. If, in the course of transportation (either in the studio or your living room), you also scour off subtle sonic detail through excessive use of circuitry and effects—then you've scoured off some of the aesthetic content of the music. You are left with a mere documentation of the experience rather than with its resurrection.

From the earliest recordings in the 1920s until the early 1960s, when multitrack was introduced, the recording technique was very simple, employing a minimum of microphones and electronic circuitry. Simple recordings made by skilled engineers are sonically among the best.

However, with the advent of multitracking, engineers started miking each individual instrument and vocal to take full advantage of the separate control made possible by the many tracks. This made an entirely new form of "studio-created" music possible, started by Les Paul, brought to a high art by the Beatles in *Sergeant Pepper's Lonely Hearts Club Band,* and burnished on Pink Floyd's *Dark Side of the Moon.* But at the same time it also allowed sloppy recording habits to develop, because now so much "correction" could be accomplished after the fact in the mix.

This new method and the older one have fundamentally different philosophies. Adopting terms from painting, call them the *representational approach* (representing reality) and the *interpretive approach* (an interpretation of reality). The interpretive approach has a further subdivision we have labeled the *expressive approach,* because it expresses a new reality.

Representational Recording

This produces a recorded document of the live acoustic event. While taking full advantage of improved equipment, this approach essentially carries on the recording tradition of minimalism. Its adherents maintain that *any* electronic processing must degrade sound quality to some degree and so should be kept to a minimum. Representational producers and engineers therefore take great pains *before* recording to ensure that mike placement and room acoustics are just right so that little or no additional studio work is required—just as a carefully selected and properly set-up playback system requires no equalization or balance controls.

The amount of cable and circuitry the signal must travel through, both during recording and throughout processing, is kept to an absolute minimum. The performance is captured precisely as it happens live, and then transferred with minimal alteration direct to disc or master tape. The LPs, cassettes, or CDs are then duplicated from this disc or master tape. Records that epitomize this purist approach include many of the excellent Opus 3, Reference Recordings, Sheffield Lab, and now out-of-print Mercury Living Presence recordings.

Generally, two mikes are used, representatives of the listener's not yet present ears and also providing the two channels of a stereo recording. A third mike is sometimes added to prevent any risk of "hole-in-the-middle" effects, with the output of this third mike being fed equally into the other two channels. (Bob Fine of Mercury first used this three-mike array back in the 1950s in the [never-fulfilled] anticipation of three-channel sound.) Occasionally, additional spot mikes reinforce weak instruments or correct for serious acoustic problems.

Mikes are positioned to capture the sound as it would be heard by a live audience. Because of the variation in the relative amounts of direct and reflected sound, this is quite different from the sound heard by the performers—while closely miked performances can be exciting, natural they are not. The objective is not to inflate the players into ten-foot giants or to project them out of the soundstage into your living room, as if swinging on a trapeze. Rather, one wants to be sonically transported to the place where the music was originally performed, so as to experience the performer and performance in the original acoustic space.

Recording an entire performance all at the same time using minimal-mike/minimal-tape-track techniques captures much of the immediacy and impact of the musical event, that all-important sense of aliveness. You can "feel" the presence of players behind their instruments, their human warmth and connectedness. One can hear the "voice" in the playing—the energy, the spirit, the mistakes. This is what makes one want to go up and shake Louis Armstrong's hand after his rendition of "St. James Infirmary."*

Really the essence of representational recording lies in *absence,* the absence of excess electronics, the engineer's imprint, and anything else not part of the original performance that would obscure the music. This art of absence requires self-confidence, musical scholarship, and a real mastery of the medium in order to be carried off successfully. Representational recording demands a *Tonmeister* (as they are called in Europe)—a person with expertise, vision, and heightened perceptions of the music and the goal of recording. In this sense, it is far more demanding than the interpretive approach, which, in its worst cases, can be reduced to a simple formula, which is often executed by equally simple souls.

Interpretive Recording

Representational recording requires that most of the music and sound decisions be made *before* the performance. Once it is recorded, these

*On *The Best of Louis Armstrong,* Audio Fidelity AFSD 6132.

decisions are usually irreversible. In contrast, the whole idea behind the interpretive method is to manipulate the musical signal in any manner desired AFTER the performance is recorded, by employing multimike and multitrack techniques.

With each instrument and vocalist miked separately and fed through a multichannel console onto a separate tape track, individual performers can be individually manipulated on tape to create the desired effect for the final master. The control is taken out of the hands of the performers creating the performance and put squarely into the hands of the engineers, who can and do manipulate and "re-create" the music in any way they deem "appropriate." The audio mixing console can be the equivalent of Frankenstein's laboratory, with the original performance lying on the table.

The major labels largely use "interpretive" recording, and since these conglomerates control 90 percent of the American record market, interpretive recording is what you most often hear.

In *multimiking,* instead of using a simple stereo mike with possibly a few spot mikes to capture the entire performance, just about every performer or group of instruments is miked separately and recorded on an independent tape track. The individual instruments are all miked, but not the sound of the acoustic space they're performing in. So this is really a multichannel mono recording more than a true stereo recording. True stereophonic recording aims not just to capture the sounds of the instruments, but to capture those sounds in their original performing space.

Multimiking and overmiking tend to make the instruments and players sound like the "cameo" inserts added for the hearing impaired on certain TV shows—not really a part of the overall performance. In some cases, really close spot miking will make it seem as if the player steps right up to the mike, tootles a little tune in your lap, and then goes away again.

Multitrack recording, instead of using a tape that has just 2 tracks for stereo (a.k.a. half track, because each track uses half the tape width), uses one with 12, 24, even 46 tracks. Because each track accepts one mike's feed, each can be individually manipulated. Every instrument is separated within its own sonic envelope. The more tracks are crowded side by side onto the tape, the more compressed the signal has to be. Signal-to-noise ratio is poorer and there is far more likelihood of crosstalk with the tracks jammed together. There is much less dynamic range and contrast possible, compared to simpler recording techniques.

In addition to convenience, the original intention of multimike and multitrack techniques was to ''improve'' sound quality as heard on mediocre playback systems. By spotlighting the quieter instruments and making them louder, they could be heard even on opaque playback equipment. This made the recording more vivid for the majority but at the same time spoiled the natural dynamic range and contrast, hall perspectives, and tonal balance for playback on accurate systems. So this technique started as an attempt to ''popularize'' the sound for mid-fi equipment.

One prime reason now for the widespread use of multimike and multitrack techniques is simply economics. The cost of paying performers and renting a hall or studio is substantial. So in most of the recording industry, the prevailing attitude is to have the performance taped and ''in the can'' as quickly as possible so the expensive musicians and the expensive recording location can be released.

Often the players don't even perform together, instead playing alone to a previously taped recording of other performers. This means the musicians engage in a one-way reaction, rather than a two-way or multiple interaction. With its players isolated in this way, whether in space by separate acoustic boxes within the studio, or in time by performing solo to a tape recording heard through earphones, a performance is no longer that of an ensemble and loses the character and creative vigor derived from the group's communication as they play. With each performer individually miked and taped, each is recorded in a separate sonic envelope; these multiple envelopes cannot be perfectly matched into a whole and so leave noticeable and distracting ''seams.''

On top of this loss of spiritual aliveness, the extensive electronic processing and reprocessing inevitably adds electronic smog and sonic congestion. The thousands of feet of mike cable needed to run all the mikes back to the console in the control booth literally acts as a filter. The more that's used, the worse the sound. Especially when recording large groups like orchestras, the engineers often locate the sound control booth 500 feet away from the stage. They don't listen to the live music. Instead, they sit tucked away in their control bunkers, listening on a set of monitors or headphones. Then they try to improve this degraded sound with signal processing, rather than directly capturing the live sound as exactly as possible. This adds to the punishment of studio reworking, as the signal is fed over and over through the console to be corrected, mixed, and remixed. The end product is Gerber's strained music.

When amplified instruments, which already have built-in haze and distortion from their own electronic circuitry, are multimiked and multitracked, the sonic problems are compounded. This is one reason why so much rock sounds as if it were recorded in a radioactive phone booth. Amplified music has two layers of electronic glaze—one from the instrument itself and one from the recording/playback process. Acoustic music has only one layer, imposed by recording/playback electronics.

Some speculate that the heavy electonic glaze of rock music is harmonic distortion. Listening to live loud amplified music, you can clearly hear the spurious overtone (harmonic distortion) over the music because it is LOUD and separate from the music—it's like a steady shriek, or whistle, or warble. Club musicians (who sometimes deserve to be called club heads) commonly seem to turn up their equipment until it reaches this shriek and then, satisfied, leave it there.

A multimike, multitrack recording means one can patch everything together at leisure, often over weeks, even months—set all the levels to obtain the right balance with all the mikes, use pan pots to distribute the instruments across the stage. Equalize to change the timbre of the instruments "to suit"—adding a little zap to a violin here, punching up the poor mike placement there. Then "sweeten" with artificial reverberation to "restore" some of the acoustic so intentionally multimiked out in the first place. The fact that what's added by the engineer to replace the original in terms of fake acoustic, reverb, and other sound effects is neither realistic nor musical, at least in terms of acoustic music, does not seem to be of much concern.

The recording is finally "assembled" by dubbing and overdubbing snippets of one tape track onto another tape track, and then mixed down to a two-track master. Each dubbing takes the tape a generation further away from the original master; with each generation the sound quality is irrevocably degraded. Distortions build at each stage.

The final tape ready for producing the recording is easily a fourth or fifth generation, already sonically degraded just from being a copy of a copy of a copy and so on, even though it's still called the master. All this adds up to electronic erosion, where the tracks have been so worked over so many times that the sound is really just plain messed up.

By the way, the term "original master tape" should not be confused with "first-generation tape"; an original master may be the seventh or eighth generation and therefore sonically quite degraded. A good first-generation original master tape is better than any pressing you can make from it. But if you ruin the master by putting it through umpteen mix-downs, then you end up with terrible-sounding recordings.

Electronics pervade a recording. It's like flavoring food—if you use too much oregano in a dish, you've destroyed it. However many tricks you try to camouflage it, the flavor of oregano pervades the dish—all you'll achieve is an overlay of the mush of additional flavors you're adding in an attempt to correct the initial flaw.

Listen for example to the Mobile Fidelity reissue of Cream's *Wheels of Fire,* a two-record set* (or try to get an English pressing). The first record is all studio work; the second is live at the Fillmore. Admittedly, the sound quality on both is not as good as it could be, but this is standard for pop recordings. And the second album, on a high-resolution system, has a realism and sonic vitality that's completely absent from the studio recording. The first record is certainly great music, but there's a sterility to it. You can hear that the engineers ran the music back and forth excessively through an lot of electronics and scoured some of the life right out of it.

Some engineers feel they need to give a recording that "little something extra," to make it "better than real." Ken Kesey describes the kind of atmosphere this occurs in: ". . . a huge recording studio . . . that looked like Disney had designed it for Captain Nemo and hired Hugh Hefner to decorate it."†

However, interpretive recording, used as a tool of art rather than a substitute for craft, and in its proper milieu of pop music or avant-garde classical and jazz, can allow tremendous artistic and engineering freedom. This variation on interpretive recording is what we call the expressive approach. The original recording is seen simply as pliable material to be used to create an entirely new work. Done expertly and with the appropriate music, this represents an art form of a high order.

Expressive Recording

Expressive recording has no pretensions to recall a live experience exactly, but instead creates an entirely new auditory experience that would be impossible or exceedingly difficult to produce in real life. Perfectly suited to rock recordings, which are largely synthesized out of the musicians' performances with the help of engineers, it makes possible a conceptual result where the recording itself becomes an integral part of

---

*MFSL 2-066.

†Ken Kesey, *Demon Box* (New York: Viking, 1986), p. 305.

the musical expression. This use of the live performance as only one ingredient in a recorded work was brought into artistic flower by the Beatles, who stopped performing live as they became more interested in the music they could create in the studio. The undisputed musical classic *Sergeant Pepper's Lonely Hearts Club Band* is, as a recording, the technical equivalent of D. W. Griffith's *Birth of a Nation*.

The expressive recording is a very tricky technique to get really right. Any studio cowboy can throw a bit of everything in the pot and come up with a sonic Mulligan stew. In the hands of a recording artist/engineer, like the synth pop composer Vangelis, this recording process itself becomes a musical instrument, making possible the creation of music that otherwise would never exist. The recording becomes a stage to be filled in with invented sound.

The problem is that this technique is often applied as a matter of expediency or, worse yet, as a substitute for artistic skill. It is often used with inappropriate music, such as acoustic folk, which it can rob of its intrinsic character and aesthetic. Expressive recording can blur the distinctions between an *expression* of personal reality by an engineer's genuine artistry and mere sloppy technique.

Each recording approach has its arguable advantages. The minimalist or representational approach, done well, *benefits the listener* because it results in the most musical, natural, "alive" recordings. But it cannot create music that couldn't be performed live. The interpretive and expressive approaches are more economical, flexible, and convenient *for the manufacturer* and perhaps the performers. When the interpretive/expressive method is used to create new forms of expression, then it's an art in its own right. But when the method is superimposed on natural, acoustic music, the results for discerning listeners are disappointing—less musical, natural, and alive.

Interpretive recording techniques, unfortunately, readily lend themselves to a lowest-common-denominator approach. A purist record producer recently reported that the mastering lab to which he sent his master tape to have a record made decided first to reequalize and otherwise "improve" his tape before making the mother. They just assumed that was what he'd want. Unfortunately, it was a favor he was devastated to receive. It is real technological arrogance for engineers to believe they "know best."

With the sole exception of expressive recordings, the art of the recording engineer is NOT to enhance the art of the musicians. On the contrary, good recording engineers are marked by their apparent *ab-*

sence—they should perhaps be seen but definitely not be heard. (True also about playback—a good system should be seen but not heard.)

This is like a story about *Stravinsky in Rehearsal* on the French Columbia pressing. There he is, conducting away perfectly happily, when the producer cuts in over the mike and asks him to speed it up a little. Stravinsky says that he likes it just the way he's doing it. The engineer replies that it'll match better with the other sections already recorded if he picks it up a bit. Because it's technologically possible to do things piecemeal, the engineer, not the artist, is often given license (or takes it) to direct artistic matters as well.

The purpose of a recording is to reveal what the artist is doing, whether that artistry is in acoustic music or in "studio-created" music. The sound of a recording should therefore be consistent with the character of the sound of the music performed live. This is the same purpose as that of the home playback system, the mirror image of the recording process—to reveal what the recording has to offer without superimposing its own sound on the music.

Clearly, how well the playback system succeeds is as much the responsibility of the listener as of the equipment producer, because it must be set up correctly. Equally, the quality of the recording is really as much the responsibility of the artist as of the engineer and producer. Though artists are obviously not directly responsible for *creating* the recorded sound quality, nonetheless they can demand a certain minimum quality standard. Unfortunately, many, if not most, are themselves unaware of good recorded sound, having never heard, let alone owned, a good playback system. They also seem to believe the engineers' line that everything can be "fixed" in the remix. Taking this attitude, they relinquish not only their responsibility, but also their control, and even their artistry to a "techie." It's all very well to say, "I'm not an engineer, what do I know about all this?"—but the fact is that if you take that attitude, you are forced to accept the record producer's artistic judgment. Does the producer know more about the artist's work than the artist?

Recording quality is permanent. Once done, nothing can alter it—neither home equalizers nor digital remastering nor any other trick. Recordings should be recognized for what they are—a living museum of our musical heritage—and not dismissed by producers or listeners as mere fleeting entertainment.

HOW RECORDINGS ARE MADE

A BRIEF HISTORY OF RECORDING

For the first 50 years of recorded sound, starting with Thomas Alva Edison's playback of "Mary Had a Little Lamb," all recordings were acoustic. Absolutely no electronic equipment was involved at any stage—unless you want to count in the light bulbs used to see what was going on. Recording relied entirely on the acoustic energy of a performer's voice or musical instrument going directly into the microphone. One lone microphone, responding to this very close voice or instrument, caused a stylus to etch the physical track of the sound waves directly onto a hard wax record *as the performance was actually occurring*. Back then, all recordings occurred only in real time. Performers had to play vigorously or sing directly into the microphone to be loud enough to make the recording—hence the numerous operatic recordings from that time.

Because there was no electronic amplification, much instrumental music could not be recorded and symphonic music was out of the question, as the instruments could not all be crowded close enough around the lone mike. Unique instruments that have never been heard from since were specially created during this brief era just to provide accompaniment to voices. Playback volume depended on the power of the performer's voice or instrument, as well as on the type of playback needle used (cactus provided less volume than steel), and on whether the doors of the Gramophone cabinet were left open or closed.

This was truly direct-to-disc recording (tape did not exist) because the discs or wax cylinders being engraved with the performance could not be duplicated—each record was unique, like an original handwritten manuscript. Duplication of a very limited sort was achieved by setting up a battery of recording machines, as many as 20 at a time, each with its immense horn pointing at the performer. Of course, the nearer horns produced the better records. Recording artists often had to repeat the same performance 60 times a day to meet demand.

If a performer made a mistake, that mistake (if not too gross) remained recorded for posterity. Nowadays musicians, having grown up with tape recording, assume a recorded performance must be "perfect''—unlike a live performance. A flaw on a recording that one anticipates and waits for each time the recording is played can be potentially annoying, but on the other hand, the degradation in sound quality as bits of tape are dubbed and spliced and remixed is also irritating, as are the sometimes rather sterile or mechanical performances that can also result.

From the time of Edison's first experimental talking machine in 1877 to the turn of the century, the ''recording industry'' flourished. But competition and rivalry also flourished, with Emile Berliner's disc and Edison's cylinder presenting alternative methods of recording and playback, each with advantages and each produced by a company holding patents that left the other without some element necessary to improve its product. In 1901, the rivalry reached a head—the entire industry was shut down by the courts and all recording ceased. In 1902, the major interests arranged an agreement pooling the patents. The advantages of the disc were combined with the advantages of the cylinder's engraving process and literally millions of records were sold over the next 20-odd years—until the arrival of radio, which nearly killed off the phonograph but which also provided its means of survival.

In 1925, electronically amplified recordings were introduced, with characteristic hoopla and overblown claims. In acoustic recording, the microphone mechanically controlled a cutting stylus. But in electronic recording, the mike converted the energy of the airwaves into a minute electric current. This tiny electrical signal was then electronically amplified many thousands of times to control a cutting head, which, just as in the earlier acoustic method, etched a physical representation of the sound waves directly into a hard wax platter. Here again, the recording process had to take place while the performance was actually occurring—direct to disc. There was no convenient way to make a test recording first, listen to it, and make revisions before doing the ''real take.''

These electronic recordings were made possible through the development of a unique amplification devise: the vacuum tube, or valve as the English call it, developed earlier in the century for radio amplification. A tiny electric current fed into the tube could be made to control a much larger current that would take on the pattern of the smaller. Now, instead of requiring performers to stand close to the mike and sing loudly or play directly into it, recordings could be made from a distance and capture quieter sounds. Fidelity was greatly improved. In addition, by removing major sections of the recording and playback process from mechanical form into the electrical form of vibration, electronic techniques avoided many of the distortions of forced mechanical vibration. With no mass or weight or substance, electricity could respond extremely accurately to the mechanical signals of the mike and record groove. Electronic recording and playback unfortunately also introduced four new sources of distortion in the form of transducers—the mike, cutting head, playback cartridge, and speakers. All recordings still remained direct to disc until after World War II.

During the 1930s, a heated controversy developed over which was preferable, the single-mike technique, which some considered gave the most natural results, or the use of several mikes set up around the orchestra and singer, their electrical output then mixed together before being fed to the cutting head. This controversy has never been effectively settled and is still being actively debated today. Curiously, the advent of digital recording may settle this debate—it is being found that simpler miking techniques produce better results.

The next revolution came with the ability to record onto tape and then transfer the taped performance onto a disc. Developed by the Germans during World War II to facilitate propaganda, tape recorders had advantages that were quickly recognized and seized upon by recording studios. Tape recorders rapidly replaced direct-to-disc cutting equipment after the war. The great advantage of tape was that it was a semipermanent storage medium that could be replayed immediately without damage and could be readily cut and edited. This opened up enormous versatility. Instead of having to be satisfied with choosing from among at most a few takes of a performance, which were all that were normally commercially feasible on direct to disc, now engineers found that *many* experimental takes could be run on tape, listened to, altered slightly, and done again. The engineer could even take parts from one tape and splice them together with the good parts from another tape, creating a composite of the best of several versions of the performance.

Two-track recording equipment was introduced in the 1950s, and so stereo recording, which had already been partly worked out back in the 1930s, now became commercially feasible. Multitrack arrived in the early 1960s with the introduction of three- and four-track machines capable of ''sync'' recording, meaning that as the tape was played back, a new track of music could be recorded alongside it. Eight-, 16-, and 24-track recorders followed. Forty-six tracks can be created by bridging two 24-track machines together, using 1 track from each for the bridging. And so today we have the Cuisinart approach to recording.

Digital recording and playback methods were pushed to center stage with the introduction of the compact disc in 1982–1983. Digital sound has been steadily improving since then, but some would say it's only improved from the unbearable to the tolerable; others feel it's a distinct improvement over what they're used to hearing. That may sum it up best, for now at least—digital is an improvement over much run-of-the-mill mid-fi equipment but not as yet an overall improvement over really good analog, though some CD players are beginning to be able to compete with some high-end systems.

All recording is inherently imperfect—in that none perfectly captures reality—and each form of recording, from 78s to CDs, has had its different imperfections. It is a question of which imperfections are preferred and what other tradeoffs and compromises are required.

Digital Recording

A breakthrough occurred in digital techniques in 1986, one just as important as the development of digital itself—it was shown that digital could sound good, good enough even to compare with analog.

This advance came not from the research labs of Sony or Philips but, in the tradition of most significant audio developments, from the small labs of audio designers whose pursuit of technology is guided by their passion for music.

However, and this must be stressed, the work done by Theta, Distech, Mod Squad, CAL, and a few others has as yet been incorporated into very few CD players. For the moment, unless you buy one of the few high-end players, analog remains the preferred recording/playback medium for music.

The introduction of digital is comparable to other historic changes in recording techniques: the switchover from acoustic to electric recording in the late 1920s, the postwar change from 78s to 33⅓ microgroove, the conversion from mono to stereo in the 1950s. At all these points (as well as the introduction of the tape recorder, solid state, and multitrack,), the reception has been divided—one group recognizing the very real losses incurred by the new technology, another group hailing its benefits and overlooking the drawbacks. Each new format is proclaimed by some to be "indistinguishable" from the live performance. This began with Edison's recording of "Mary Had a Little Lamb" and continues to this day with digital. For all the advantages of each new format, there have also been definite tradeoffs.

A new technology is not *ipso facto* better than the now "old-fashioned" technology. Digital is a major change but it is not, or certainly not as yet, necessarily a change for the better in terms of music. It is natural that listeners admire all the things the new medium does better than the old. And, initially at least, they pay little attention to those areas where the new technology is less good than the old because they take for granted from long experience with the old that these aspects are OK. It takes some listening time to adjust the ears and recognize that while the new does offer advantages, there are also disadvantages compared to what came before. Digital, whether better or worse than analog, is just another way to make a recording.

Digital sound, as currently available, presents a different mix of strengths and weaknesses than analog. The important issue is to compare and balance these strengths and weaknesses. Instead, the common attitude has been to proclaim digital obviously superior to analog simply because it is superior in *certain areas* where analog is relatively weak, while minimizing or ignoring those areas in which digital is inferior to analog's many strengths. It is important to identify what you want and should expect from recorded sound—if you've never heard a good analog recording played back on a good system, you may be easily impressed by digital sound, just as you can be impressed by a "frozen gourmet entrée" if you've never enjoyed the taste of a well-prepared meal.

It would have been informative, when first digital came out, if LPs had been released in both the digital and analog formats to demonstrate the clear superiority of digital—a method of demonstration used effectively during the switchover from mono. Audiophiles urged this, but unfortunately it was not done.

The trouble is that digital is being sold to the public not for what it actually is but for its highly promoted name. Sooner or later, people catch on that all is not as it's being represented, and there may be a backlash against a fashion that claims more than it delivers.

Take the proclamation "Perfect sound forever." Now consider that in the four years following the CD's introduction in late 1982, the players have gone through a number of different generations (is perfection perfectible?) and that all players sound different. There's a mismatch there somewhere between promise and reality.

However, the work of Mike Moffat (Theta) and others has demonstrated that digital has a sonic as well as a commercial future. If Sony and Philips had had more interest in *quality* sound, then instead of costing the CD its credibility among high-end listeners, they could have done a lot better than the mass-fi results that they labeled "perfection" in a classic rerun of the emperor's new clothes.

Digital recording is based on a theorem developed by Harry Nyquist in the 1920s, which states that if two points on a wave form are identified, then the wave's entire shape can be defined. This theorem in turn is based on theories developed by an 18th-century French physicist and politician, Jean Baptiste Fourier. Digital was first commercially used in 1978 to produce digitally recorded LPs. In 1982–1983, the compact disc was released by Sony and Philips, giving digital its own unique format.

For the past 100 years of recorded sound, sound waves have been stored in their "natural" analog form. In digital recording, by means of an analog-to-digital converter inserted between the live sound source and the recording tape recorder, the music is converted from its normal analog wave form into a series of digital numbers. This circuit takes a series of "sonic snapshots" of the audio signal—about 44,000 times per second—which are then translated into a binary code of *1*'s and *0*'s. Sampling of the wave form occurs at a frequency—44.1 kHz—roughly twice that of the highest audio frequency recorded, to ensure each wave form is sampled at two points. It is this code of binary numbers and not the original wave form that is preserved on tape and then encoded as microscopic pits and smooth places on a compact disc.

In order to be made audible again, the code numbers must be converted back into analog during playback. The numbers instruct the CD player's digital-to-analog decoder how to "reconstruct" the encoded sound. Unlike analog, the sound one hears is not what is on the tape itself (if this were so, all one heard would be electronic gibberish) but is the synthetic result of the D-to-A circuitry carrying out the encoded instructions.

The chain from live analog music to digital encoding and back again to analog is immensely complex. Nearly all of it involves new or recent technology and there are numerous opportunities for things to go wrong.

As it stands, no evidence has yet come to light either that digital is inherently unsuited for music recording or that it will be superior to analog. It is simply another approach that, while the technology is so new, offers at least as many problems as advantages. The technology is still not fully understood even by those whose job it is to use it.

Digital is promoted as an excellent storage medium because it's so stable. Once whatever's being recorded has been converted into numbers, those numbers remain unchanged until they need to be converted back into their original form. At least in theory, a number recorded onto tape is not subject to the same degradation as an analog signal recorded onto tape. In practice, this does not appear to be the case. Engineers and designers have heard degradation from one generation to the next. In addition, the digital master tapes store far less well than analog master tapes and, for safety, need to be copied over every year. If sonic degradation occurs between generations, as has been heard, this is not an encouraging prospect.

Digital in theory also benefits by eliminating two of the transduction points required with analog—the playback cartridge and the cutting lathe's cutting head. Wherever energy is converted from one form to another (for example, the cartridge transduces the mechanical energy of the LP groove into electrical energy) there is a major source of distortion, so reducing the number of transduction points is a clear advantage. On the other hand, as there are no digital recording microphones or digital speakers, the conversion of the live analog waveform into digital at the recording session, and then back again to analog during playback, introduces an entirely new realm of sonic problems.

It becomes irrelevant that the numbers can't be distorted during recording and reproduction, or that extraneous noise is greatly reduced (the CD's vaunted silent background), if the digital recording process captures only an approximation of the music signal and then plays back another ''approximation'' of the analog music signal. One of the more disturbing aspects of digital sound is that quiet musical passages in digital are the most distorted, while the loud ones are very clean. This is the direct opposite of analog and has made a large contribution to the CD's reputation. Analog is quiet in the soft passages, where distortion is actually most disturbing, but more distorted in loud passages, where the distortion is less harmful to the music.

Analog is an open-ended format—its limitations are basically those of the recording and playback equipment and of the artistry of the recording engineers. Those old recordings from the 1950s, so well regarded then, still challenge most recordings made today.

Digital, on the other hand, is a closed format, limited not just by the equipment and recording artistry but also by the format itself. A standard of limited resolution was designed into the digital medium and internationally agreed upon. (Such industry-wide agreement is in itself remarkable. The last time that occurred was when the LP's RIAA standard was finally established back in 1953 after years when each recording company used its own individual standard. The previous industry-wide agreement was back in 1902, when the flat LP was chosen over the cylinder.) The limits set by digital are permanent, whereas better playback of an analog recording will reveal more of the information contained in the recording. While it is true that digital playback systems are improving, there is a limit to how much "more" is available to be revealed on a digital recording—as the old saying goes, the numbers tell it all.

The present digital format could be improved by raising the sampling standard. In fact, this has already been done since digital's introduction—it's been raised from a 14- to a 16-bit sampling rate and oversampling has been introduced. Unfortunately, those recordings made under the old standard cannot be improved or upgraded to the new one. So those who sang their hearts out on 14 bits are going to stay entombed there. What's criminal is that great art is being recorded for history using a medium that is still incompletely developed, when an excellent recording medium exists in analog. Nonetheless, digital recording has taken over much of audio, at least among the big labels. No major orchestra now has a long-term analog recording contract. No major label is now releasing new recordings in anything other than digital.

Digital has also been steadily improving since its commercial release, in terms of both the recordings and the compact disc players. We hope this improvement will continue until digital is truly as good as or (could it be?) even better than analog. We hope digital will not rest on its commercial success and accept the popular response of "good" to mean "good enough."

THE RECORDING CHAIN

Recording and playback are mirror images, with the recording itself representing the plane of the mirror. The scale of the music signal ranges from full-size at the live performance to not quite life-size coming out of the speakers. In between, it is microsonic. The goal is to "unrecord" the recording so as to gain the illusion that the original live performance is occurring in your living room.

The acoustic energy produced by the performer's voice and/or instrument is converted by the microphone into electrical energy that can be used by the engineer in the control room. The mike's diaphragm, as it vibrates in response to the sound waves, produces a variable voltage. This is the reverse of the playback speakers, in which the speaker diaphragms vibrate in response to a variable current from the amp, and produce in turn acoustic energy analogous to the sound waves of the original live performance.

The mixing console usually comes between the mike and tape recorder so the engineer can fiddle with the sound before it's laid down on the master tape. The signal may pass through the mixing console more than once. Here the sound is equalized or "EQed," which achieves the engineer's desired balance in the frequency spectrum, increases or decreases the presence of certain bands, and alters the output or gain. The signal also travels through mixers, faders, compressors, limiters, reverb, overdubbing, remixing; is sliced, diced, and otherwise reconstituted—all with the goal of "improving" the sound.

In minimalist recordings, the mixing console may be totally eliminated, the sound being recorded straight onto the tape, or at least the mixing console is put to minimal use. Often, the studio's "monster" is replaced by a portable "mike mixer," which is a simple mike preamp with minimal EQ. In direct-to-disc recording, the sound goes directly to the master disc, eliminating even the tape stage.

The tape mix (except in the case of direct-to-disc) that is finally approved by the engineers, producers, and anyone else involved is called the master tape. From this master tape is made the reproduction master; and from this, copies are made by the thousands. This sequence of steps is essentially the same for LPs, CDs, and cassette tapes.

Long-Playing Records

Since the ascendance of digital and the compact disc, many people have mistakenly come to believe the LP is the equivalent of the dodo. Unwittingly, they are blaming the faults of their playback equipment on the record. Ignorant of how to select and correctly set up a good "record player," most people never hear the extraordinary amount of detail waiting to be revealed on an LP.

Ironically, despite its mass-market decline the LP is steadily gaining new status beyond connoisseur circles as more thoughtful listeners begin to compare carefully the sonic qualities of CD and LP. Many are opting for the musical strengths of the LP over the strengths of the CD. (Digital LPs seem to combine the disadvantages of both worlds with the benefits of neither.)

In the earlier years of CDs, audio enthusiasts generally consigned it to the mid-fi regions, giving the analog LP unmistakable sonic top place. But as CDs improve their sonic quality in response to the complaints of the audiophile community and as LPs improve their pressing quality in response to the CD "cleanness" challenge, the two *may* come to represent simply alternative media of comparable sonic worth. The main argument against this occurrence is a practical one: Neither retailer nor manufacturer will be eager to stock *two* inventories. One medium will almost assuredly have to eradicate the other, just as LPs wiped out 78s in a short time and stereo instantly antiquated mono.

A note of caution: In your first frenzy of excitement over CDs, do NOT dump your LPs. (Or if you must, please dump them into welcoming arms.) Even as the vinyl disc is superseded, the enormous and irreplaceable repertoire of artists and performances on LP will continue to be in high demand. Even if the analog recording is rereleased in digital, the sound of the digitally remastered recording can never be as good as in its original analog form.

The LP is also one of the more durable of storage media, contrary to its reputation. A CD even slightly damaged (which is far easier to do than has been advertised) loses large amounts of information, which, while covered over by the error correction circuit, results in very nasty distortions. Cassette tape fades, bleeds through, and generally deteriorates much faster than LPs. If the tape jams or breaks, as can happen quite easily, then the whole tape is unusable. LPs, in contrast, if scratched will make a nasty tick, but this lasts only a moment. If one side is seriously damaged in an accident, you still have the other side.

In order to reveal better all of the music on an LP—to be a better "unrecorder"—it helps to understand a little about how an LP is made. Recording techniques for the analog LP are essentially the same as for any other format. Whether an LP is manufactured from an analog or a digital tape, the production process is essentially identical. The only difference is that the digital tape must be retranslated by computer back into analog form before going to the cutting head.

The four steps of manufacturing that critically affect quality are (1) the *disc cutting* or *lacquer mastering,* (2) *plating,* also called *matrixing,* (3) *pressing,* and (4) *packaging.* Pressing and packaging are completed in the same facility; mastering and plating are often each performed by a separate company.

The master tape represents the best the record can be—whether it sounds as if it were recorded on an answering machine or transports you to the original performance. Then each additional processing step adds its own layer of distortion.

The master disc, or master lacquer, is like the original engraving of the live music from which all the copies will be made. A separate master is made for each record side from the two-track stereo master tape (analog or digital). How many minutes of music to fit on each side is an important question. (Of course, in symphonic works, length of side is largely determined by where the music permits of a natural break.) In general, the wider the music's dynamic range, the greater its bass, and the faster the tape-mastering speed, the more room the music will take up—and, in both cases, the less music will fit on a side.

Trying to squeeze in more music results in a clear degradation of sound quality—cramming the grooves closer together requires compressing the dynamic range so the grooves can be narrower; and distortion increases the closer the grooves come to the spindle, called end of side, because cartridge/groove alignment becomes progressively worse toward the center. If the music stops some distance away from the spindle, i.e., if there's a wide run-out of blank grooves, then the music will be subjected to less distortion. When buying a record, look for a total playing time for each side of about 20 minutes or less—this at least suggests some attention to good sound.

Incidentally, the numbers and letters you see engraved in the run-out next to the label are the *matrix numbers* assigned to the master tape for each side and used for identification throughout the manufacturing process.

To make the master lacquer, an aluminum disc prepared with a thick coating of lacquer is engraved by a cutting lathe with a physical analog of the original sound waves. The cutting lathe is like a big, extremely heavy-duty turntable. In fact, it's the direct counterpart of your turntable at home, with the cutting head being the mirror image of the playback phono cartridge. Instead of following a groove and producing an electrical signal, as does the playback cartridge, the cutting head follows an electrical signal (from the master tape) and produces a physical groove. To more easily cut the continuous spiral groove into the disc in as exact an analog of the live sound waves as attainable, the cutting stylus is heated.

Every motion of the cutting lathe head is guided by a special disc-mastering console through which the master tape is played. The RIAA equalization (see below) and any special treatments such as noise reduction, equalization, speed alterations, and the amount of "land" or space between the grooves can all be specified at the console immediately before the cutting of the master lacquer. Wow, flutter, and rumble, if any of these problems are present in the cutting lathe, may be cut into the record right along with the music. Rumble from the lathe certainly can often be heard on a good playback system.

Quality recordings are mastered in ''real time,'' meaning the same length of time taken by the original musical performance is required to make the master. Speeding up the tape in order to hasten the mastering process makes production cheaper, but at a high cost in fidelity.

Some engineers can ''read'' the lacquers and tell the kind of music by the grooves' width, depth, and pitch. You too can ''read'' the LP grooves at home and tell something about the quality of the mastering job before you ever hear the record. Large grooves indicate that the music was not unduly compressed in order to squeeze more onto each side—you can expect the dynamic range to be good. If the inner grooves, which are always more distorted, stop well away from the label leaving at the very least an inch of run-out, this also indicates mastering care. With a little observation and experimentation of your own, you can also pick up a feel for sound quality by the particular sheen on the record—some have a rainbowlike gloss suggestive of careful cutting and clean pressing quality.

Mastering, when done properly, is at once art, craft, and labor of love. Though learning the basics of how to operate the cutting equipment takes only a couple of weeks, disc masterers are generally apprenticed for several years. Some never really learn the art, despite calling themselves professional disc masterers. Also, no matter how accomplished a masterer, adjustments in the mastering room cannot improve a poorly engineered tape or mediocre music, despite the forlorn efforts of cutting room impressarios.

Before the final master lacquer is cut, acetates, or reference lacquers, are made, which can be played only a few times. These are used for final approval by musicians, producer, and others involved. Because these acetates have a tendency to sound somewhat duller than the final vinyl version, they can sometimes lead inexperienced or indifferent listeners astray—requesting the disc masterer to ''brighten up'' the sound on the acetate may result in a finished record that sounds overly bright.

The master lacquer obviously can't be used to press records directly, so a copy is made. Plating is the first step in converting the master lacquer into the molds or *stampers* used for mass-pressing the vinyl records. Lacquers should be plated within 24 to 48 hours of being made and must be kept under refrigeration until they are plated.

The lacquer is coated with a thin film of silver and electroplated in a nickel bath. The nickel plating now bears an exact negative impression of the lacquer, which is peeled away and discarded. A positive "mother" is formed from this negative metal mold, by again electroplating the mold to provide a positive impression identical to the original lacquer. This is the mother or pressing master from which all the stampers that actually mold the records are made. Mothers can be stored safely for 20 years. From the mothers, the final negative molds are made, producing stampers strong enough to sustain the force of pressing the records. Each generation of negative-to-positive-to-negative transfer increases the presence of imperfections and adds further distortions, causing a slight loss of sonic transparency.

A stamper can make only a few thousand pressings before becoming worn. The earlier in the pressing run, the better the LP's pressing quality. The producers of excellent-quality recordings may allow far fewer pressings to be made before the stamper is discarded. Obviously, unless a special edition of only 1,000 or so LPs is being made, numerous stampers have to be used for each recording and each one will come out a little different. One pressing may therefore sound better than another of seemingly the same recording; even though the master tape through to the mother were identical, the stampers were different and also undoubtedly reached different stages of wear.

To press the records, the stamper for each side of the record is placed in a molding machine (distantly related to a waffle iron). A hot biscuit of vinyl, sandwiched between two labels like an Oreo cookie or ice cream sandwich, is placed between the stampers and then hydraulically compressed. Bingo!—a record. This is repeated every 30 seconds, producing 120 records an hour. The method is called *compression molding*. Vinyl temperature, room temperature, and humidity all affect the quality of the pressing. Improper cooling, or *curing,* results in warped records.

The polyvinyl chloride used may be *virgin vinyl* (unused and the best grade) or a mix of virgin and *regrind,* which is made of ground-up and melted-down defective records and *flash,* the raw edges trimmed off after pressing. In some records, you may even find actual *chunks* of old record label—you can imagine what this would do to your stylus, let alone your ears. The better the quality of the vinyl, the less the surface noise—pops, ticks, clicks, and the notorious "record fart." This burping noise is caused by *no-fill,* a tiny pinhole in the groove caused by a bubble or speck of dust in the vinyl or a defect in the stamper.

Premium virgin vinyls, such as Teldec, can be half again to double the price of the standard mixed grade. One way of identifying virgin vinyls is that they are commonly translucent (hold them up to the light), being colored with ink rather than the carbon black used for nonvirgins. Carbon black, unfortunately, is granular and adds to surface noise. Radio stations often receive special pressings of virgin vinyl to keep surface noise off the airwaves.

Forty-fives are often made by a cheaper pressing method, called *injection molding.* This uses polystyrene, a harder and more brittle plastic than vinyl. Hot liquid styrene is poured into the mold, then quickly baked and cooled, much the same way that cheap plastic toys are made. This method is twice as fast as the compression method and the styrene is cheaper than vinyl. However, the records wear out faster and tend to register greater background noise.

The RIAA Curve

Record manufacturers are forced by purely mechanical difficulties to distort the recording deliberately. The ideal record would store in its grooves a precise analog of the sound from the live performance. However, this would mean the grooves would have a large amplitude at bass frequencies, restricting playing time, and a low amplitude at high frequencies, causing signal-to-noise problems. So in practice, the music signal is first passed through an equalization network that cuts the bass and boosts the treble. This equalization, standardized in 1953 as the RIAA (Recording Industry Association of America) curve, is reversed during playback, in the preamp's phono stage. (Tape deck, tuner, and CD, which don't require the RIAA curve, are connected to the preamp after this phono stage.) How precisely the preamp corrects the RIAA curve is, of course, critical to how your music sounds.

The treble is boosted because of record surface noise, most of which is in the upper midrange and up. By increasing the strength of the higher musical tones in a recording before the disc is made, you can reduce background noise during playback. When the preamp's phono stage equalizes the signal and cuts back on the treble, it also cuts back on the surface noise. The treble is brought to its correct original level while the surface noise, which started at "normal," is reduced to below normal, improving signal-to-noise ratio.

TAPE

The controversy over reel-to-reel versus cassette is all but dead now, with cassettes the clear victors in the consumer marketplace. In fact reel-to-reel has been so thoroughly vanquished that the last source of prerecorded reel music tapes, Barclay Crocker, closed down in mid-1986.

However, shortly thereafter, Teac brought out an "economy" model of a reel-to-reel deck, comparable in price to a good cassette deck. Open reel's superior sound may still keep it alive.

When the cassette deck was first introduced by Philips in 1964, it was never intended to be a high-fidelity medium. Then tape formulations were improved and, most importantly, noise reduction was introduced. These factors significantly improved cassette's sound, but many still disputed its candidacy as a hi-fi medium. Many still do. Nonetheless, 1984 was the first year that prerecorded cassettes outsold LPs—largely thanks to portable cassette players. Both tape and tape deck quality have continued improving to the point that cassette is becoming a worthwhile medium for quality listening.

While cassette recordings are still sonically inferior to open reel or LP, their convenience and economy ensured rapid success. Cassette players can be taken just about anywhere for recording or listening, and they are about half the cost of open reel to operate.

All tape, whether for reel-to-reel or cassette, is a ribbon of thin, flexible plastic coated with a film of magnetic particles suspended in a binder or glue. Signals are recorded by varying the patterns in which those particles are magnetized. In playback, the process is reversed and the varying magnetic field on the tape is translated back into an electric signal.

Fidelity in tape recording is determined by the speed at which the tape is recorded and played back, the width and thickness of the film backing, and the thickness and quality of the coating, which is the actual recording material. On all of these counts, cassette tape is substantially inferior to open reel. In addition, commercially recorded cassettes are generally less good than a recording you carefully make yourself on a good machine. In one area only does cassette tape currently exceed the quality of open reel and that is in the quality of the coating material itself. Exotic oxide formulas that would be exceedingly expensive on open reel are practical when applied thinly on the narrower, shorter cassette tape.

Reel-to-reel is the oldest magnetic tape format and of course is still used commercially for recording. It is simply a spool or reel wound with tape that, during playback, simultaneously unwinds from the one reel and winds up onto an empty reel—whence its name. It is not only sonically the best but also provides the best reliability, durability, and, for editing, flexibility. Because higher speeds are used than with cassette tape, more tape passes under the recording head in a given time, and a given "quantity" of music signal has more tape over which to spread itself. The signal is in effect stretched, with more room for details to register, which is another way of saying that because there is more room on the tape, the signal is less compressed and so the fidelity is better. This is similar in principle to LPs, where the less music per side, the more room the grooves have to spread out, and so the less compressed the music signal.

The cassette format, in contrast, while cheaper, more compact, and more convenient, does sacrifice some fidelity. Because there is less tape in a cassette, it must be run more slowly to cover a reasonable amount of time—generally 1⅞ i.p.s. compared to open reel's 7½ to 15 i.p.s. on domestic equipment, or 15 to 30 on commercial equipment—and so all the problems of wow, flutter, and splice audibility that are alleviated by higher speeds are now clearly exposed.

A small tape imperfection will at slow speeds loom comparatively larger than the tiny width of a moment's worth of signal. Also, as a signal varies from low to high, the corresponding change magnetically impressed on the tape from millimeter to millimeter is more drastic or rises more steeply than when stretched out over 5 or 10 millimeters. Thus, with any slight jerk or lag in the movement of the tape (more commonly known as wow or flutter), the tape head will "see" a much sharper change in the signal than if it had been laid down with a more gradual increase per millimeter on fast-moving reel-to-reel tape.

Since the area of tape that the recording head influences is not infinitely thin, but has a certain width, the more slowly it moves by the varying signal source, the more the pattern of each instant will overlap with its neighbors and be less distinctly "itself." Sharp distinctions of each moment's detail are the essence of high fidelity. But as the moments are piled one on top of each other by slow-moving tape, their individuality is forever lost. This is known as compression.

A cassette is similar to open reel except that the two reel hubs and tape are miniaturized and enclosed in a polystyrene shell. The tape is about half the width of open reel tape, and also thinner in order to fit enough into the small housing. Because of the thinner plastic film, the tape can stretch or break more easily. There is also a higher incidence of *print-through* than with open reel's more durable, thicker coating on a thicker tape base. Print-through occurs when the signal on one section of tape bleeds-through onto the adjacent piece of tape, resulting in "pre-echo." You hear the music that *will* be coming up before it actually *does* come up, sort of like a preview of coming attractions.

A disadvantage of commercially prerecorded cassettes is their manner of production. Cassette tapes are gang-produced at a superfast speed, as much as 64 times normal listening speed, on special mass-production high-speed duplicators that add noise and distortion. In general, the higher the reproduction speed (as opposed to recording speed), the greater the loss of high frequencies and the greater the tape hiss. Cassette producers seeking better fidelity will reproduce either in real time (the most expensive method since a tape with 36 minutes of music will take 36 minutes to duplicate), in half time, or at a still relatively low ratio of 8 or 10 times playback speed.

This same attitude represented by gang production can be found in other areas of quality control. As many as half of the prerecorded cassettes you buy are likely to have one defect or another. Because the cassette is such a convenient medium, and most people listen on low-grade decks, they expect neither good sound nor good QC. Poor quality is accepted almost without notice or comment. Manufacturers, receiving only this feedback of indifference, continue happily to produce low-grade cassettes.

A serious drawback—and there is some suspicion that this happens more with commercial recordings than with home recordings—is that the recorded signal tends to deteriorate quickly. After some months, the high frequencies become duller and rolled off, the overall sound more veiled, and pre-echo more pronounced. Print-through is more likely to occur when a tape is recorded at a high speed. Most of it occurs during the first few days of storage and is more severe when stored under conditions of high temperatures and if subjected to a slight magnetic field.

When buying a prerecorded tape, you don't have any choice as to which grade of tape you buy—if you want the recording, you have to accept whatever tape it comes on. But if you make your own recordings, blank tapes are offered in a potentially confusing array of choices. The least expensive tapes often end up being actually very expensive because the housings jam and malfunction easily. The most expensive, on the other hand, may offer more than you need. For example, taping off AM radio seldom requires the best tapes as the fidelity of the AM signal leaves a lot to be desired anyway. On the other hand, if you want a good recording of a live performance off FM, a high-fidelity tape is worthwhile. Match the fidelity to the end use. Don't buy cheap cassettes—if you've put in the effort to record something, presumably you want to preserve it, at least for the short term. You don't want your tape to turn out defective.

By the way, you can protect against accidental erasure by breaking out the plastic tabs in the cutaway holes in the top (thin edge) of the cassette. These engage a safety interlock in the recorder that governs the recording and erasing circuits. With the tabs removed, the deck will neither record nor erase. If you later change your mind and decide to erase or record over the existing recording, just tape over the tab holes. If you want to protect (or unprotect) just one side of the tape, here's how to tell which tab goes to which side: When you hold the cassette so that side A faces you, the side A tab is the one on the top of the cassette near the left end. The other one is for side B.

Unlike LPs, cassettes have no single, standardized tape format. There are four different tape types, requiring four different bias and equalization settings. In addition, precise bias-setting requirements for recording vary slightly from brand to brand, even within the same tape type. The instructions for your tape deck will generally specify which tape type will produce the best-quality recordings on that particular machine. But the manufacturer may not have experimented with everything available, so it's probably worth your while to experiment with a variety until you're satisfied. You can use up all the less successful tapes for recording radio shows or some other lower-fidelity use.

Tape Formulations

The three basic formulations of cassette tape are ferric, chrome, and metal. Tape formulations are also broken down into four "types" assigned by the International Electrotechnical Commission. Each basic tape formulation, whether ferric, chrome, or metal, has a different ability to receive and retain an audio signal and each requires a different magnetic strength, or bias setting, to record the signal properly. These characteristics in turn determine each tape type's frequency response, dynamic range, signal-to-noise ratio (how much hiss will be present), and saturation levels (how much audio information the tape will hold before distortion or signal loss occurs).

Bias setting adjusts the magnetic field strength applied to the cassette tape during recording. Normally, magnetic particles don't respond linearly in a magnetic field. Adding the correct amount of an inaudible, very high frequency signal ensures that the particles all respond linearly, and thus prevents distortion.

Because bias needs can vary from brand to brand even within the same tape type, it's a good idea either to stick with the deck manufacturer's recommended brand for which the deck has been specifically calibrated, or else to do some serious experimentation and come up with a brand that sounds the best. Or if you already have a brand you prefer, the deck can be recalibrated to match.

EQ or equalization corrects for different tapes' varying responses to different areas in the frequency range. Equalization "equalizes" the frequency response across the audio band. Most tapes are marked to show which EQ to use; those that aren't almost always are Type I and require a 120-microsecond setting.

Noise reduction capabilities, such as the various Dolby methods, will reduce hiss and improve the signal-to-noise ratio. Signal-to-noise characteristics vary from tape to tape. All cassette tapes have a certain amount of noise or high-frequency hiss, which can be heard during quiet passages, blank spots, or when the volume is low.

Dolby HX Pro, developed jointly by Dolby and Bang & Olufsen of Denmark, is a recording process that requires no special decoding for playback. This is not a noise reduction system but a headroom extension circuit that increases the high-frequency storage capacity of a tape.

The four IEC tape types are as follows:

Type I: commonly referred to as "standard-bias" or "normal-bias" ferric or ferrichrome tape. Requires the normal 100 percent bias current and 120-microsecond EQ. This is the oldest and most economical formulation and can be used successfully on any cassette deck, from the cheapest boom box to the best professional machine. Top of frequency response falls within the range of 10,000 to 15,000 cycles.

Type III: seldom-used ferrichrome. Low fidelity. Requires 70-microsecond EQ and a low to medium bias—use low-bias setting.

Types II and IV are considered to give better fidelity and are also more expensive. They are "high-bias" tapes, requiring bias starting at 150 percent and 70-microsecond EQ. They have better tape saturation, lower hiss, greater ability to reproduce high-frequency sound, and greater ability to reproduce music of wide dynamic range. In general, the higher the bias required, the better these characteristics. The main drawback to these chrome and metal tapes, aside from their greater expense, is that the backings are highly abrasive and tend to wear out the heads faster. They can also be successfully played back only on machines that offer the capability of playing them.

Type II: chrome and pseudochrome or chrome-equivalent formulations, requiring high bias (roughly 150 percent) and 70-microsecond EQ. Originally formulated with chromium dioxide, this was developed and patented by Du Pont, but competing companies quickly came out with chrome substitutes. Type II represents a compromise between cost and fidelity.

Type IV: In these tapes, the magnetic materials are made of particles of pure metal alloy rather than of metal oxides and so can be magnetized more intensely than ferric or chromium tapes. Metal tape is also more expensive. It requires 70-microsecond EQ and high bias settings. Can be played on any deck but, in order to record with these, the deck must have the metal tape position.

COMPACT DISCS

Digital technology is in its infancy, even though it has been under development for about 15 years. Commercial release of the CD was premature—perhaps out of need to recoup the enormous sums put into development, or from eagerness to revive a flagging recording industry—and the cost was to the CD's credibility. The mid-fi press embraced the medium without reservation, and Herbert von Karajan became so enthused as to proclaim that "all else is gaslight." But high-end listeners and press, used to enjoying far better fidelity from their analog systems, gagged on the sound and said so vociferously. We have these people to thank for the subsequent advances in CD sound.

Those digital proponents who acknowledge that digital recordings are flawed—now a steadily growing group—generally try to place the blame anywhere but on the digital method itself. First the miking techniques were blamed as being unsuited to digital (interestingly enough, the simple miking techniques favored for "purist" analog recordings are now increasingly employed for digital, a trend started by Jack Renner of Telarc). Then the playback electronics were faulted—most players contain an analog playback section in their circuit that would put even the cheapest boom box to shame. Players in which this section has been upgraded do indeed sound better. In the haste to ship vast quantities of a product whose technology was barely understood even by those whose job it was to use it, many mistakes were made. Unfortunately, nearly all digital recording equipment still has an awful analog section.

The CD is forcing a reassessment of sound quality, even though it is not setting the pace. It has renewed the public's interest in audio. Compact discs' virtues are undeniable. And for the many people who have been listening on shoddy turntables and/or poorly set-up tables, CDs can represent a great sonic step forward.

Curiously, people who come into a store to buy a CD player often find, on comparing CD and LP, that they prefer the analog recording, and so are instead walking out with a top-quality turntable. Many of the early buyers of CD players who had moderately good tables (like an AR or Thorens) were disappointed with the CDs and realized that a good table can still provide the maximum return for money invested. It is also more expensive to gain entry-level high-end sound from digital than from analog, though prices even out somewhat above entry level. An important factor is that the cost of compact discs is double that of LPs and is unlikely to come down soon (though there are indications that the price of LPs is being *increased* to reduce the gap).

While the high-end players are improving in their ability to play a CD, where improvement is desperately needed is in the digital *recorders.* All the understanding the high-end designers have put into the players has yet to be applied to the recording equipment—it is the weakest link in the digital chain. This is a worse offense than poor players, because the "software" is the heart and soul of the music system. With LPs, the software was better than the hardware for a long time. But then as the hardware slowly improved, it was able to reveal more and more of what was captured on the recordings. If CDs are poor, the better the players become, the more they will reveal the *failures* of the recordings. If the recording itself is bad, no amount of improvement in the playback can do a whit of good. Unrepeatable works of art—whether performances, compositions, or artists recorded only once or only on digital—are being stored by a medium that does not do them justice.

The Advantages of Compact Discs

The three strongest features used to sell CDs are their convenience (unquestioned), virtual indestructibility (alleged), and fidelity (occasional).

CDs are certainly convenient—as easy to use as cassette tapes and requiring none of the fuss and bother associated with LPs. Pop a small disc into its receptable, push a few buttons, and sit back and listen for 40 minutes or more.

The claim of CD indestructibility appeals greatly both to those who take a certain decadent joy in not bothering to care for their recordings but also, more positively, to those who do in fact care deeply about preserving music for future generations. It would be wonderful if music could be stored on a medium less subject than most things to the frailties of life and the second law of thermodynamics (which, roughly translated, states that all things left alone will gradually drift into chaos). Even if CD is a more enduring storage medium, the question still has to be considered whether it stores the MUSIC as well as does analog, or whether it simply stores the bad sound well.

One of the most exciting claims for digital is that there is no loss of information or sound quality between generations because the music is recorded in numbers, which cannot alter. This theory may be impeccable, but recording engineers and listeners have regrettably reported audible degradation between generations, just as with analog. In fact, digital, in both tape and compact disc form, is a more fragile medium than generally recognized. Compact discs are impervious to "stylus wear" since the laser beam makes no physical contact with the disc. But this single fact has been exploited to imply that CDs are impervious to *any* wear or damage.

Just because the laser makes no contact with the disc, and therefore neither causes wear not "reads" scratches as pops and ticks, doesn't mean you can use your CDs as bar coasters. Despite their plastic coating, they are as subject as anything else to damage. On the label side, which is the side all the information is encoded on, there is no hard plastic covering—only a very thin lacquer barrier protects an aluminum reflective layer less than seventy millionths of a millimeter thick. Scratch this and you're wiping out information that no "error correction" system can successfully compensate for.

Listening to a damaged CD with missing information is like trying to read a damaged book from which some of the pages have been torn. You can still get the gist of the story and can even fill in the gaps for yourself (as does error correction) but if there are a lot of pages missing, you'll lose the author's structure, even misapprehend the meaning through incorrect interpretation of missing information. A worn LP, on the other hand, is more like a used, rather than a damaged, book. LPs can become scratched, the groove walls worn, and the surface noisy. But the music remains in the record. A different stylus, riding below the worn area of the groove walls, can capture much of the music. Properly cleaned and played, the LP preserves the music in its entirety and so can still provide a deep emotional experience. Finial Technology of California has developed a laser turntable that plays records without any stylus contact. This would eliminate one of the main disadvantages of LPs.

This basic difference—that on CD information is lost totally, while on LP it fades or is covered over by a fine layer of noise—applies also to the digital master tapes, which are much *less* durable than their analog counterparts. Tape, like everything else, is an imperfect medium. Analog master tapes gradually fade over time, like a print exposed to sunlight that slowly bleaches away. While the music, if the tape is very faded, may become a little ghostly, and the highs will be gone, nonetheless the music is preserved. Digital master tapes, on the other hand, are encoded in a sequence of numerical bits. Because this is not the infinite sampling rate of analog, but only a discrete sampling rate, there are gaps between the bits, which during playback are essentially "reconstructed." But, when a piece of the metal oxide flakes off with aging, a bunch of numerical bits are taken along with it and there's now in effect a gaping hole in the music.

Apparently earlier tape formulations, which had larger particles, are storing well. The modern ones, especially American tapes, with very small particles scrunched together for low noise, are fading more. And the digital master tapes are not storing well at all. The tape designer for 3M says 6 dB of erasure and it's gone. Some smart engineers are copying their digital tapes over each year—but how many people know about this, and how many major companies are likely to take such trouble? So music being recorded digitally may turn out to be far more transitory than analog. Digital may turn out to be actually offering "imperfect sound for only a little while."

CD "silence"— "The music wells forth from a black velvet background"—is a major selling feature. If digitally recorded—and many CD releases are analog reissues, not digital—then CDs are indeed quiet, with no tape hiss or surface noise. But who hears a black velvet background at a live performance? The real importance of this in terms of the music is questionable. Out of that silent background can come some impressive sonic effects, but analog places real players with real instruments in a real room, something digital has yet to be able to do.

On more recent digital recordings, a form of audible background noise called *dithering,* which sounds very much like tape hiss, is intentionally added to improve digital fidelity. In our view, surface noise and tape hiss on LPs is a very minor issue—this noise is clearly separate from the music and easy to ignore, at least on any good system. Mediocre turntable systems exaggerate noise, but a good table system minimizes it so much that one wonders what people can hear in CD's great claim of silence.

The very first novelty of digital has worn off and its mere *differences* from LP and tape are no longer absorbing all attention. Perspective and balance restored, listeners are now focusing attention on the sound of the *music*, on what digital can do and what it has lost that analog does so well.

The cost of the discs themselves is a major drawback. Though this may eventually come down, the manufacturing process is an exacting and expensive one, unforgiving of shortcuts. To put together a library of CDs costs at least twice as much as LPs, and you are starting from scratch. With the price this high, CDs may discourage people from having several versions of a classical work and so exposure to differing interpretations will be limited. Also, what music you can listen to is likely to be restricted to selections chosen for being "safe" for larger sales.

Compact Disc Manufacture

A compact disc is only 4¾ inches (12 centimeters) across, made of thin plastic substrate coated with a reflective layer of aluminum (or, rarely, silver) and then wrapped in a thin layer of acrylic sealant. The information is encoded as binary numbers—strings of 1's and 0's—represented by microscopic pits and smooth places in a spiral about 3 miles long.

As the disc spins, the laser beam reads the digital code and translates it into electric signals that are fed into an amp. CDs have only one playing side, which can hold up to 75 minutes of music. Legend claims that the CD 75-minute format was chosen in order to accommodate Beethoven's Ninth Symphony, a Sony top executive's favorite music. If true, this represents one of the rare occasions when technology tips its hat to art.

In manufacture, accurately reproducing the billions of bits of information (each disc has a capacity of more than 8 billion bits) by which the music is encoded on a CD requires extremely low levels of contamination in both the raw material and in the processing plant. The tolerance is as small as for the manufacture of microchips. In theory, it is possible to make discs with very few defects, at least under laboratory conditions. But in practice, the majority have quite high levels of errors, caused by such problems as pinholes and dust. The disc players' tolerance for faults is limited. Error correction is regularly required to compensate for poor production techniques, resulting in musical degradation even if one is not consciously aware of it.

CD mastering, occurring under clean room conditions, begins with an optically polished glass disc. Coated with a layer of photoresist, it is then "etched" by a laser with the required pattern of pits. The photoresist is then developed and silver-coated. From this glass master is taken a metal master, from the metal master the mother, and from the mother the stampers. CDs to this extent follow the same pattern as LPs.

Pressing involves three principal stages. First, using a combination of compression and injection molding, the pattern of the pits is impressed by a stamper on the transparent base material of polycarbonate plastic, similar to Lexan or Plexiglas. This process is similar to LP pressing except that it must occur in a "clean air" environment to prevent dust contamination. The pressed surface is then coated with an aluminum reflective layer less than seventy millionths of a millimeter thick. Finally a very thin acrylic resin barrier is applied to protect the reflective surface.

This is the basic procedure. There are two variations, each one having its effect on sound quality—injection molding and injection/compression molding. Injection molding, usually identifiable by the see-through center of clear plastic, results in sharper definition of the pits. This is important because the detection of digital data on a CD depends not on the presence or absence of a bump but on the transition between the two. The drawback of this method is that the center hole is pressed into the disc from the stamper at the beginning, so correct centering requires very exacting accuracy from the pressing molds. While the pits may be easier for the laser to read accurately, eccentricity in the disc will cause problems.

A combination of injection and compression molding results in a disc with slightly less sharp definition of pit edges but more accurate center-hole punching, as this can be done at the end of the production with great accuracy. These discs can usually be identified by being metallized all over and having a less squared-off edge.

A new pressing technique is in the works from Teldec, as a variation of its dmm (direct metal mastering) technique. This would allow a CD master to be embossed by a stylus. Clean room conditions would be unnecessary. Done this way, CD masters could be cheaper, allowing the production of small quantities of ''noncommercial'' CDs, and the artistry and skills developed over years of cutting LPs could be applied to producing CDs.

The transparent sealant is intended to shield the disc against dust, dirt, scratches, and other damage. Though in certain ways less fragile than LPs, CDs must still be handled with great care. They should be held by their edges only and returned to their jewel boxes or jackets immediately after playing. All ad copy to the contrary, scratches and dust and fingerprints definitely interfere with the laser beam's ability to track the pits correctly. Because scratches, for example, aren't heard as pops or ticks as on LP, there is a tendency to believe mistakenly that no damage has occurred. But any alteration of the surface will cause loss of information, which can at best be disguised by the error correction circuitry but which nonetheless results in sonic degradation of the music.

There are currently no industry forces promoting *better* CDs. The prevailing attitude, at least publicly, is that CDs are exquisite just as they are and represent the millennium. The few CD-processing plants, overwhelmed with business, have reneged on promised production for the small recording companies that might have been able to show what could be done with CDs. As more plants are being built in the United States, this may turn around again. The major recording companies have no more interest in good-quality CD recordings than they have had in good-quality analog recordings over the past ten years and more. CD reviewers on the whole are doing nothing to help—*all* CDs, without discrimination, sound excellent to them. ''Perfect sound forever'' lives on in the minds of the many. If only we could all enjoy it.

Few record stores have the space and the capital to stock LPs, CDs, and cassettes in any depth. As the range of CD titles has broadened, so has the space allotted to them in the stores. This means that one of the other formats must yield room and that has primarily been the LP.

Meanwhile, CD production remains limited, with few plants worldwide able to perform the highly sophisticated processing procedures. Though plants are being built, production is expected to remain limited for some time. Limited production for a product in strong demand does not bode well for quality manufacture.

Large recording companies can afford the sizable initial investment of setting up plants or at least of booking up large production runs. By selecting "big-name" recording artists and "proven-successful" music, they recoup their investment quickly through turning out lots of CDs. This is not a promising approach for experimentation and creativity.

Small companies cannot set up their own CD-processing plants as might be possible with vinyl discs. Vinyl LPs are very low tech and production can be fairly easily set up—at one time, LPs were even hand-pressed in small workshops. With CD, control of the recorded art form is being taken out of the hands of the small companies, which often have a stronger interest in quality and in recording obscure artists who would otherwise remain undocumented. Small companies must go to one of the few CD plants, and wait on the sidelines until all the major labels' needs have been fulfilled.

PART IV.

BUYING

THE FUNDAMENTALS

Ideally, one would listen to a recording directly, without the complication, interference, and distortion of components. Unfortunately, a recording remains unfinished until played back through an audio system. It is complete only when the original performance has been made audible again.

The question is—audible in what way? Muzak can be played on any functioning system and not suffer from the mediocre sound, because it is only intended as soothing background sound, not to communicate. No message, no subtleties are missed when Muzak is poorly "unrecorded." But real music, to retain its full detail and texture, must be unrecorded so that nothing is either added to or subtracted from the original recording.

Poorly reproduced sound is like poor pronunciation—as long as what is said remains fairly simple, it can be followed well enough, second-guessing those words that are unclear. But as soon as it develops complexity, texture, detail, then guesses will as often be wrong as right and the message can come through very garbled. And it is a strain to follow someone's mumblings or odd pronunciations. One goes away tired and even annoyed. While all equipment to some extent interferes with the music communicating with you, some components interfere much more than others.

The mainstream audio magazines and even *Consumer Reports* offer guidance on whether a given component functions reliably as an appliance or "consumer good." The Health Department tells you if the restaurant is clean but not whether the food tastes good. An appliance that simply fulfills its implicit warranty of functioning for a reasonable period of time does not necessarily *satisfy*. Canned string beans may be edible and unspoiled but cannot be compared to fresh ones. Once again, it's a matter of your expectations—if you require or desire the taste of real string beans, canned ones will not do. If canned beans are acceptable, you need not invest the time and trouble needed to obtain and prepare fresh ones.

We can all compensate and compromise when we're willing to, but sometimes we accept too easily the image or "concept" of a thing in place of the reality. Equipment that sounds good as opposed to just looking impressive can be readily found once you have the necessary information, and are also prepared to use your own ears and brain to listen to the equipment for yourself instead of letting the "experts" tell you what you're hearing.

Recorded music is really too important to leave to the experts. Their wisdom may not be right for you. Unwilling to spend the time to become experts ourselves (or unable to find the needed information), many of us instead rely on salespeople, specs, and cocktail party experts as we would on a doctor, broker, lawyer, accountant, car mechanic, plumber. Instead, put faith in your ears and listen to the music, rather than trying to second-guess how the equipment will sound in the abstract.

Musicians, the very people one would expect to be reliable choosers of better equipment, in fact rather commonly settle for the mediocre. Finding such a distance between the live and recorded, they seldom attempt to bridge a gap that appears to them unbridgeable. At the same time, being so intimate with the sound of the real thing, musicians can easily take the necessary leap of imagination and fill in the gaps in the music that poor equipment leaves. But you need not be always disappointed with the sound of your system on returning from a concert. A carefully selected, set-up, and maintained system, while never the same as live music, can provide much of the emotional satisfaction and fulfillment of the live.

Trying simply to *ignore* the equipment is no solution. When you attend a live performance, you are there (aside from any social considerations) for the pleasure of just listening to the music. Yet for the performance to occur in such a way that the audience can enjoy it, there is a tremendous amount of effort put into the "show," as it is called by the producers and engineers responsible for the hall acoustics, lighting, seating, amplification, temperature control, audience control, and so forth. Any aspect of the "show," if badly executed, will interfere with the audience's ability to enjoy and appreciate the musician's performance.

Just as the "show" enables you to enjoy the performance but is not itself the reason for attending the performance, so the audio equipment enables you to enjoy the music but is not itself the reason for listening to the recording. The equipment has no value other than to enable the music to be heard to its fullest.

But poor equipment can seriously interfere with one's ability to enjoy and appreciate the music. While most people would probably recognize at a live performance that a poor "show" was spoiling their enjoyment of the music, few people ever realize to what extent mediocre equipment (and/or setup) is interfering with their enjoyment of the recording.

Since the very early 1970s, when the integrated circuit revolutionized audio by opening "high fidelity" to a mass market, recorded music has come to be ubiquitous. It is piped into supermarkets, laundries, elevators, cars, dentists' and doctors' offices, and other waiting rooms of all kinds, listened to—or, more accurately, passively heard—while eating, reading, sleeping, waking, working. It is used to soothe kine and hen in dairy and hennery; it has become as surrounding as the air we breathe and as little considered. If the air, or if sonic reproduction, is neither unusually noxious nor unusually excellent, then it is given little heed.

People tend to assume that technology by itself will provide them with music. (Technology provides the *equipment* but not the music, and the equipment restores the music to life with widely differing success.) The more advanced the equipment (commonly meaning the more gadget ridden), the better the sound, or so the thinking goes. If it is expensive as well, then its excellence must be assured. It is not at all uncommon for people to spend several thousand dollars and up for a system they have no idea how to use. The importance of stereo system as status symbol shouldn't be minimized, but then neither should the primal power of the music, which is ultimately the source of stereo's multimillion-dollar attraction.

Buying equipment should be based not on the features or price or advertising or convenience or specs, but simply on SOUND. The confusion about the respective and relative importance of music and machine arises easily enough because access to the music is possible solely through the machine. Until that access becomes effortless, attention will tend to be focused on what is preventing easy access—the equipment—rather than on what we are trying to gain access to—the music.

It is also a matter of expectations. If you never or seldom hear live music, then you have no reference point, and it may not be easy to make distinctions between "mediocre" and "better" components where "better" just means "closer to live." If you can't get fresh beans and nothing but canned ones are available to you, then your options are either to accept the canned or do without. Music, for many, is too important to do without, so they accept whatever is at hand.

THE CONSTANTS OF GOOD SOUND

Charlie the Tuna's "Good Taste" Versus Good Sound

Audio in many ways has taken a strange path in developing beyond the crude novelty of the Gramophone. In the search for better sound, it has relied on advancing technology in the belief that what makes better *equipment* must *ipso facto* also produce better *sound*. What we've ended up with today is a glamorized Gramophone, fancied up with multiple switches and flashing lights. With our faith in technology, we tend to lose sight of the goal of audio, which is to re-create the experience of music. Art, delivered via machine, is passed over to its more accessible partner, technology.

The result is equipment designed more for selling than for listening. Systems like this can be compared to a musician who has only technical prowess. Such an ability has hurt as many musicians as it has helped, because technique alone comes to be relied on until it becomes the end rather than just a means—resulting in the neglect of musical substance. Performances like this are generally cold, uninvolving, and uninviting. The analogy, without anthropomorphizing, holds true for audio systems. Presumably, you don't want to be admiring the system, you want to listen to the music.

Many mass-market and mid-fi equipment manufacturers know that gizmos (like technical prowess) sell equipment. Most of the yearly model changes consist of a redesigned face plate, perhaps a minor circuit change, and some new gizmo. To maintain a competitive price, generally something has to give and this is usually the quality—less easily seen and recognized, it does not directly help to sell the unit. But without the quality, all the gizmos in the world will bring you little pleasure—they're the audio equivalent of "go-faster" stripes on a car.

Generally, features fall into three categories: the essential; the true convenience features, such as a table's cuing device or preamp's mute button; and then the gimmicks and "fiddle controls," which at best accommodate preferences but little else. Most gadgets like this should be avoided—they're commonly a sign of a mediocre component.

Products brought to market normally have to meet a price that is in line with their competition. The market for the higher-end components is perhaps less sensitive to this, but certainly mass-fi components are stringently regulated by price considerations. Gadgets add cost. And all they do is distinguish components that distinguish themselves in no other way. If the consumer is thereby persuaded to buy that table, then for the manufacturer it's worth investing money in the gadget. But they still have to meet a price, so that gadget money has to come out of something else—generally out of the overall quality. The trade off is music for whizbangs.

So in effect, the consumer pays doubly for gizmos: once in the selling price, and a second time in the compromise and sacrifice of music quality as gadgetry is substituted for sound design. Go for the true convenience features if you want, but avoid the gimmicks and fiddle controls. Equipment that is designed for listening is generally as simple as possible.

Most specs are the equivalent of go-faster stripes as well. With no common standard, comparing specs of components is an exercise in futility—you're comparing numbers but they have no context. Since there are at least several different ways to take each measurement, the manufacturer will of course choose the way most flattering to the component. To paraphrase slightly, there are three kinds of lies—lies, damned lies, and specs. The standard specs apply only to mediocre components—and only a fool needs to go around comparing one poor component with another.

Minimal Circuitry

As Will Rogers said, anyone can make things complicated; it takes a genius to make it simple. Einstein, Thoreau, and Picasso concurred—simplify as much as possible, and then no more.

Simplicity applies as much to the basic design and circuitry as to the absence of gizmos. *Everything* has a "voice," as Ed Dell terms it. The more resistors, capacitors, wire, switches, knobs, lights, tubes or chips, in a circuit, the more distortion is introduced into the signal. Each of these so-called passive components is not only doing its intended job but also contributing unintended distortion, and thus more "veiling" between the recording and your ears. The simpler the circuit and the fewer these devices, the fewer colorations are added.

However sophisticated the design approach may be, the actual execution should be as simple as possible. The purpose of audio equipment is not to *make* the music but to *release* it from being locked up in space and time on the recording.

Incidentally, solid-state circuits may appear to be very simple, but in fact integrated circuit chips are extremely complicated. One tiny chip can contain an entire audio circuit that would otherwise take up a square foot of space or more.

Methuselahs Versus State of the Art

Most connoisseurs consider certain "vintage" components designed 25 or more years ago to compare with some of the finer equipment available today (and they are available on the used equipment market at a fraction of the cost at which anything comparable could be built today). A classic budget system of yore was an AR table with a Dynaco PAS III preamp and Stereo 70 power amp—still a very worthy budget system today, though benefiting from an easy upgrade of the capacitors in amp and preamp.

These classic Methuselahs continue being so highly prized for their musicality because the fundamental elements that go into making good sound have remained constant. These universal constants apply to all systems, regardless of vintage or origin of manufacture.

The only reason a component becomes musically obsolete is that it was never musical to begin with. "Once a good component, always a good component" is a basic audio verity. A fine musical instrument isn't transformed into a piece of junk merely by the passage of time and the "aging" of the technology used. While audio depends heavily on technology, technology is only a vehicle—engineering decisions must finally be based on musical considerations. No matter how advanced the technology, audio will only sound as good as the ear of the designer.

The Marantz 8B amp, for example, is a great tube amp from over 30 years ago, designed by Sid Smith and manufactured by Saul Marantz, and is still sought after today. It has a rosy hue, at least in its unmodified stock form, and although this is a coloration, it's a euphonic one that interferes little with the music. The original Quad English dipole speakers, with their fabled natural midrange, designed by Peter Walker in the early 1960s, continue to serve as a benchmark against which other speakers are compared. The same is also true of the Dahlquist

DQ-10 speakers, which were the first (brought out in 1973) to excel at reproducing voices.

Naturally, just because a component is old, it isn't automatically good. Early transistor equipment, and that built right through the 1970s, should be avoided. Even a classic may have been abused by the previous owner, so check out used equipment carefully before purchase.

The point is that a good system, knowledgeably assembled and well maintained, does not become *musically* obsolete. You can buy good equipment just once or you can buy cheap equipment and find you have gained little. A good basic system and a fancy mid-fi system cost about the same but what you get is quite different—fancy gives you little, good gives a lot and keeps on giving it.

Also, if you should choose to move up from your good basic system, that system still has a value and can be sold; fancy equipment has nothing going for it except that it's the ''latest''—once it is no longer the ''latest'' (which means within six months of your buying it), it has little left to offer. One of Busoni's observations on music can be applied also to equipment: ''Its ephemeral qualities give a work the stamp of 'modernity'; its unchangeable essence hinders it from becoming 'obsolete.' ''

The term ''state of the art'' is often heard about a new piece of equipment. The implication is that anything else is obsolete and must be replaced. A question is how accurately you can apply this term to art, or whether it is more legitimately suited for technology. Tube equipment never became *musically* obsolete. In fact, it has been making a slow but steady and strong comeback, not only in the highest high end but also in the budget high end.

Even if you do believe that the idea of ''state of the art'' can be applied legitimately to audio equipment, why should you be a guinea pig for testing the cutting edge of a new technology? Why not be the *last* person on your block to pay to do the manufacturer's testing?

Instead, buy equipment that has been out for a couple of years or so. This way, most of the inevitable bugs are likely to have already been worked out of it. There will probably also be a fair amount of information about it after that length of time, both in terms of reviews and of other users' experiences. This can help you decide whether the component will match well with the rest of your system, as well as providing tips on setup to enhance the performance.

Perceived Value

"All works must bear a price in proportion to the skill, time, expense, and risk attending their invention and manufacture. Those things called dear are, when justly estimated, the cheapest." —John Ruskin

"Money is a blessing that is of no advantage to us except when we part with it." —Ambrose Bierce

Buy as good a system as you can afford. Spending $500, $1,000, or more on a component if you've got the scratch is not conspicuous consumption or frivolous, gross extravagance. Music is a vital nutrient to human life—a good playback system is capable of delivering a depth and intensity of musical experience far greater than most people have yet had the chance to realize. It makes a great deal of sense to spend money on a fine music system as a lifelong investment. Remember, components age like musical instruments—once good, always good. Something better may come out, but that does not make what you have any worse than it was.

Much of the excellent audio equipment is largely handmade, assembled one at a time, each carefully burned in, tested, and listened to before being sold. Like a musical instrument, fine equipment represents a combination of art, science, and craft, all of which take time and are therefore expensive. High-end companies are commonly quite small—sometimes no more than the designer plus a helper or three—and they tend to build components with the same care and quality invested by musical instrument builders. The goal is excellence of fidelity, rather than mass-fi equipment's combined criteria of price point, ease and economy of manufacture, and marketability.

Small companies are also more expensive to operate and maintain because they cannot get the volume discounts of larger companies. Also, just because the fidelity is excellent doesn't always mean the other aspects of the company are equally polished—sloppy business practices, disorganization, variable customer service, and mixed product reliability are more common than they should be.

Buying HFS equipment should be approached with the same attitude and understanding as buying a musical instrument or a piece of art. One may look inside the Lazarus preamp—a modest but pleasingly musical piece—and exclaim, "Why, there's nothing there, what a ripoff, my clock radio has more parts than that and it costs a twentieth of the price!'' What about a dulcimer made of catgut and little thin pieces of wood probably good for little else? It's really not a question of a handful of parts. One cannot use ''cost-effective analysis'' to determine equipment value. In fact, how *does* one measure the value of a conveyor of music?

The relationship between price and performance is most often geometric rather than linear. At the beginning of the curve, the increments of sound quality are pretty directly correlated to increments in price. But as you move on, the sonic differences get smaller and smaller for each increment in price. This is known as the knee of the curve. Once you've achieved a really good system, then a perceptible improvement in its *overall* sound quality, in contrast to simply a change in tradeoffs and compromises, is likely to cost at least double.

It is not so hard to minimize, even eliminate, the grosser distortions in equipment design. As the gross ones are eliminated, lesser ones are revealed, which are a little harder to minimize. This layer of grunge stripped away then reveals still smaller distortions, like the nesting wooden dolls that each contain another smaller one inside. Each level is more difficult and more expensive to minimize; each increment in sound quality becomes smaller while the spread between prices becomes larger. Eventually, the point is reached where in minimizing one distortion you cannot minimize another, and it becomes a matter of tradeoffs among compromises rather than absolute improvements.

While music equipment should certainly be judged by its music-conveying qualities, some attention needs to be paid also to aesthetics, ergonomics, and reliability. After all, if you couldn't get into your wine bottle to drink the wine, your perception of the whole event would change. The best-sounding equipment tends to be Spartan, ugly, expensive, and/or a pain to live with and use—as Ken Kessler says, ''The mirrors in the house fog up because the product is so rude and ugly to behold.'' Some of the musically finest equipment would be rejected by *Consumer Reports* and the mainstream magazines. For information on manufacturers notorious for either good or poor component reliability, check through back issues of *The Absolute Sound,* which really brought this whole subject out of the closet back in late 1985, and the other underground magazines.

Fidelity, Equity, and the Hassle Factor

Ed Woodard of Lineage supplied the above rune for buying equipment. The first element, *fidelity,* is self-explanatory. *Equity* helps make sure you choose components of *lasting* value, not gimmick or fashion value, so you can be sure you will be able to get your money out of it again if you want to. *Hassle factor* simply means that most listeners don't want to spend their time constantly fussing and fiddling with their equipment, or waiting for it to come back from repair or the "latest" in a never-ending series of upgrades—they want to be listening to it. Keep these three words in mind as you shop and they may help keep you out of trouble.

DESIGNING A SYSTEM

Choosing the Compromises

Even the best reproduction is not perfect and so there must inevitably be compromises. Audio equipment is inherently defective. We live in a nonlinear world, meaning that what goes into a system inevitably emerges altered by its passage through that system. What comes out is not on a continuous line with what went in.

If sound could be perfectly reproduced, then all good equipment would sound the same and the only considerations in buying equipment would be its construction, its appearance, and its ergonomics. The reality is that not only do components reproduce imperfectly, but they also each reproduce differently. (And even if the components were perfect, the room would add colorations that were not part of the original recording.)

Given that all components and all systems involve compromises, both because reproduction is imperfect and because of budget considerations, it's essential to consider carefully *which* compromises are the most acceptable and least offensive to you. A key decision in the overall sound of your system is what you are prepared to give up and what you're not. Once the basics have been satisfied, some people find they value bass, others "detail," others transparency. The basics include a natural midrange, tonal accuracy, the range of dynamic contrast from loud to soft (dynamic range), and resolution of low-level detail, which helps put the performance in three-dimensional space within the air of the performing room. The absence of glare, brightness, hardness, and similar irritations is also a basic.

Which compromise you make depends on the kind of music you like to listen to most. Rock demands power and bass to sound really authoritative. One pair of mono tube amps listened to for a while was pretty unimpressive until it was used to play rock. Then, at 200 watts a channel, it made the Cream's live version of "Spoonful" on *Wheels of Fire* just spring alive. You could almost smell the Fillmore's dusty old seats, the dope- and incense-filled air, the . . . you fill in the rest. But bass and loudness, which these amps delivered, are very expensive if you also demand refinement. If you are a chamber music or jazz listener, your compromises are likely to be quite different from those of someone who listens primarily to orchestral works or to rock.

Your taste in compromises will probably guide you into choosing certain broad sonic categories of equipment: a moving magnet or moving coil cartridge, tube or transistor electronics, dipole or dynamic speakers. Budget considerations and room realities also enter in.

With electronics, for example, transistors don't begin to sound as good as tubes, for many listeners, until you get into the higher price ranges at which most tube equipment is also sold. You can buy used tube equipment for prices competitive with moderately priced transistor gear. Examples are the classic amps Marantz 8B and Dynaco Stereo 70 or mono Mark IIIs and IVs. You can also combine tubes and transistors. If you do this, go with a tube preamp and a transistor amp. The preamp signal is smaller, more delicate and fragile, so it benefits from the qualities of tubes. The amp signal is less fragile and so can more readily tolerate the disadvantages of transistors while benefiting from the better bass and oomph of transistors.

With speakers, the choice between dynamics and dipoles is not just a matter of money and music. It is very much a matter of room realities. Dipoles must be placed well away from walls and are far more sensitive to setup and room anomalies than are dynamics. Carefully read the Speaker Setup section (p. 203) before looking at specific speakers.

Component Matching

Interactions between components often affect the sound as critically as the components themselves. Just as musicians and their instruments must all work together in an ensemble, so the components, including your room, ears, and musical preferences, must also all work together as a system. How well these components—from recording to your ear—work together is one of the central elements that determine how good your system sounds. The parts of a system must be assembled holistically. All components err; you want to be sure you don't combine ones that all err in the same direction.

The same system, set up in two different rooms, can actually sound like two different systems. The same component, inserted in two different systems, can sound like two different components. The same system reproducing two different kinds of music is even likely to reproduce each with differing degrees of success.

Every component, from music source to amp stage to speakers, adds its own particular distortion or tonal coloration; any set of components combine these colorations. Some combinations work well, some absymally. Two otherwise good components mismatched will lose their virtues; two merely acceptable components can sound far better combined. When the sum is greater than the individual parts, this is known as a *complementary nonlinearity*.

This whole issue of matching components would make it appear advantageous to buy something like a rack system, where all the components have been "prematched" by the manufacturer. This is very tempting for the neophyte—it seems such an easy and neat solution to a lot of difficult and messy decisions. But the manufacturer's decisions in assembling that rack system are seldom the ones you would choose for yourself, because they were made for different reasons.

The manufacturer is trying to offer an attractive package and offer a lot of "bang for the buck." High fidelity doesn't have "bang"—it gives you music rather than fireworks. The manufacturer is very unlikely to be a great turntable designer and also great at speakers and amplifiers. So generally the components are assembled from a number of different manufacturers. As the package is being put together to meet a price, and needs a lot of features to sell itself, quality must be compromised. Generally, this whole approach is mass-fi only. There are a few exceptions—notably the English company Linn, headed by the notorious Ivor Tiefenbrun, which produces tables, amps, and speakers. The firm is still most highly regarded for its tables. Conrad Johnson, long admired for its amps, has also introduced the Sonographe turntable to some acclaim. However, this is very much the exception rather than the rule.

Therefore, you must use your judgment to select components that are innately good, that combine so that the sum is greater than the parts, that are well suited to your room, and that are successful at reproducing the kind of music you listen to the most. This extends also to accessories. A very good system can be greatly diminished by a set of cables that on another system might sound fine.

Here's an example. If you have a good but somewhat bright cartridge and comine it with a thin, bright amp and speakers that also tend to sound bright, you will end up with a system you will be very unhappy with. The components individually may qualify as high fidelity, but the overall sound falls far short. A mild problem in each component has been intensified into a serious system problem that is likely to drive you away from listening. This is especially likely with women, who tend to be more sensitive than men to such higher-frequency distortions.

If you take the same bright speaker and bright cartridge, but counterbalance them with an amp that softens or rolls off the higher frequencies, the overall sound will be euphonic and less fatiguing. Both system combinations may be equally imperfect, but one combines colorations in such a way that the results are unlistenable while the other minimizes the colorations so the music can come through. You must be very careful to avoid combining components that will exaggerate each other's colorations.

When you listen regularly to more than one signal source, you should be careful to tune the system to ensure sound good with all of them, rather than optimizing for one source. If, for example, you were to compensate for a slightly dull cartridge by choosing slightly bright speakers, the system may sound great playing records but not so good with tuner, CD player, tapes. As soon as you switch your signal source so the dull cartridge is out of the equation, the system may sound quite hard and shrill.

As a general rule, the tonearm/cartridge and amp/speaker matches are probably the most critical. If you use more than one front end, the amp/speaker match remains a constant with all signal sources, so concentrate on this and get it as neutral as possible.

The careful matching and balancing of components is equally important whether their quality is good or mediocre. Not surprisingly, the less expensive, less good components tend to have more noticeable colorations—that's what makes them less good. So it is important that the colorations work together. Better components, on the other hand, tend to be more neutral and to add less of themselves to the music, but as a result they are also more revealing. So poor matching here, while perhaps more subtle, will be cruelly exposed. Also, better components need more meticulous setup to reveal the music fully because their potential for good sound is so much greater. Colorations contributed by poor setup may be somewhat lost in the overall grunge of a lesser system, but will audibly add themselves to better equipment.

All audio systems have their own characteristic sound, just as all water has some kind of taste. The particular taste of the water will flavor your tea or coffee, just as the "sound" of your sound system will flavor your music. The goal of high-end audio is twofold: to minimize the system's "flavor," and then to make the residual flavor as euphonic and musical as possible, so as to interfere the least with the music.

Replace the System or Upgrade the Components?

It is good advice to change only one component in your system at a time. This can be a lot more interesting than replacing everything in one fell swoop. You will be able to hear exactly what improvement each change makes. Going step by step also spreads out the costs of a new system.

All things being equal, follow the system hierarchy and start upgrading the audio signal from its beginning (see p. 15 for more about hierarchy). The closer the component is to the recording, which is the heart and soul of the system, the more critical is its performance. The reason is simple enough. If the full detail of the music signal is not retrieved from the recording, it can never be recaptured down the signal chain. The components cannot improve the signal; they can only minimize the amount of distortion they add. Any error upstream tends to be compounded as it proceeds along the hierarchy.

Equally true is that a component downstream that is less good than the front end will tend to block the benefits of that front end—you need to observe some balance in the quality of all the components.

If you are planning to buy an entire system but have budget constraints—and who doesn't?—then choose your primary signal source, which is the one you listen to most, and buy it (see p. 15 for more on this). The system's secondary front ends can wait a little while until your coffers fill up again. If you splurge on geting table, tuner, deck, and CD player, you will probably have to compromise on amp and speakers and later will have to upgrade *everything*. If, more modestly, you buy a very good table (or whatever front end you choose), along with a good amp section and speakers, then you'll just need to add tuner, deck, CD player later and can buy each separately.

Of course a system can be only as good as its weakest link, so if any component is disproportionately poor, correcting this imbalance takes precedence over observing the hierarchy.

PREPARING TO BUY

Audio equipment is an expensive investment, and can also to be an emotional one, with the potential for either great happiness and solace or nagging dissatisfaction, though it may be unexpressed and perhaps even unacknowledged. Putting together a system that will bring real satisfaction over an extended period must be approached holistically and with patience.

Make haste slowly. There is no one "right way" with audio; there are just varying shades of compromise, ranging from gross to increasingly subtle. The soundcraft in this book can help you to eliminate the gross ones, and then just how far into the subtleties you want to go is up to you—this will get you started. Whatever you buy, however much you spend, there will always be something better. There are no absolutes, no one "best" component, no ultimate system. Do you want to spend your time chasing equipment or listening to music?

People tend to think of "high-end" sound in terms of money first and quality second. The difficulty is that most people don't know how to identify its quality and so cannot readily see it. You can spend just as much or more on a mass-fi system and end up with far less quality and satisfaction, yet somehow there seems to be so much more to show for your money by way of flashing lights and knobs, switches, dials, options, and "rich Corinthian leather." High-end equipment is so minimal that people may think they're being taken for a ride with the high price.

Set Up Your Present System

The first thing to do before you do anything else is to set up your present system correctly. This may seem crazy when you are going to take it all apart again to put in new equipment, but you will learn a great deal through these efforts that will help you in choosing new equipment.

The difference proper setup can make even with the most modest equipment is really surprising. All systems gradually decline and drift out of tune, and gradually your pleasure and interest in listening also decline. A new system or new component will often sound better—at least initially—not because it necessarily really *is* better, but because new connections and contacts were made and setup was improved.

You may be surprised how much better your system sounds just through correct setup. ''Better'' in audio operates on a subtle scale—music playback occurs on a literally microscopic level—so while these setup procedures may seem small and subtle, yet they can be clearly heard once you attune yourself to what to listen for and how to identify sound quality. Listen for a while over a period of days before going any further. You may even decide not to upgrade at this moment.

Of course, if your turntable is a plastic, direct-drive, suspensionless Japanese toy, or your electronics are transistor models of early 1970s vintage, then you may not hear much if any improvement, and these components will almost certainly need replacing. If, on the other hand, your electronics are 1960s tube equipment or your turntable is early Thorens or Acoustic Research, then you'll almost certainly want to keep these, if only in order to pass them on to friend or family.

Proper setup also includes using the correct accessories—these are as essential as the components proper. They are not merely esoteric refinements of a system, but as essential an ingredient as the steak in steak-and-kidney pie.

In recent years, which wire to use has been the subject of great debate. In fact, *whether* using one kind or another kind made any difference was initially the debate but, despite *Stereo Review*'s refusal to hear any differences, it is widely accepted that cables and interconnects are just as important as the other components in a good system. The problem is that how they interact with the system seems even less predictable than is the norm for the other components. Straightwire appears somewhat less system dependent than a lot of others. Straightwire's Flexconnect is very good value—it is inexpensive while maintaining many of the good qualities of the more expensive LSI. This is a good place to start if you haven't tried out interconnects before. As you bring the quality of the rest of your components up to where you want, go back and experiment further with fine-tuning your system with wire.

Learn Equipment Basics

Read the equipment chapters in this book. Understanding the fundamentals of how a system works, what a component is supposed to do as part of that system, and how to distinguish between the gingerbread and the real stuff gives you a tremendous advantage in making your choices. Though there are literally thousands of components out there, the majority are built like cheap toys, to be played until you tire of the sound and then thrown out. Weed out this plastic rubbish and then you are left with relatively few components. It becomes reasonably easy to whittle down the choice further by considering your budget, what is available in your area, and whom you want to give your business to.

The Role of Specs

The inexperienced will laboriously compare and judge components by studying the spec sheets, happily ignorant of the half-truths and limitations of this approach. What specs are supposed to measure represents only a very small part of the sonic picture, and *how* the measurements are taken varies from one company to the next, even from one model to another. In the great spec wars, whatever method of measurement will give the best *appearance* is the method used. Specsmanship has become such a marketing tool that audio circuits are actually changed just to make a spec measure better, irrespective of how this makes the equipment sound. As one reviewer expressed it, spec charts are often revealing primarily of the manufacturer's hopes, and should be accepted by the public with the admiration accorded a work of imaginative art rather than the credence granted to a mathematical axiom.

Specs are viewed as being "objective"—they promise the solid ground of cold hard facts, real data, inarguable concrete reality. Judging equipment by listening to it, which is considered a subjective approach (and therefore, according to its denigrators, unreliable, inconsistent, inaccurate—in a word, human), restores the ultimate judgment to the real world instead of the lab by evaluating the product holistically in a real-life situation. Spec measurements are not taken using music but instead using a sine wave—a far simpler wave than music. It therefore cannot really effectively test how the component will behave with *music*, which is all the consumer, as opposed to the equipment designer, need be interested in.

Even if one were to take the position that specs help to identify the musical qualities of a component on its own, specs cannot identify how two components will interact (which is the only way components are actually used, as opposed to tested). Sometimes, two components can have the same specs but will sound quite different. Sometimes, the one that sounds better actually "specs out" worse.

Specs are useful when designing equipment, not useful when assessing musical qualities. Who would make a decision to buy a particular piano, guitar, harmonica, contrabassoon, according to its specs? It's like testing food to measure "objectively" whether it tastes good.

When "acousticians" try to spec out good acoustic spaces and then apply that "hard data" to building a good-sounding concert hall, the success rate is not significant (at least not significantly good). Measurements are an attempt to gauge reality; music *is* the reality. What you want to know about a component is not how well it performs *as* a component, but how successfully it conveys the music into your listening room.

To call a component "musical" refers not only to having relatively little distortion but also to the *kind* of distortion. Given that perfect linearity—the absence of distortion—has yet to be attained, both designers and users instead strive to make the inevitable distortion *euphonic*, so that it interferes with the music minimally and blends with it in a more acceptable, even if not exactly a pleasing, manner. Irrespective of spec sheets with their THD (total harmonic distortion) and TIM (total intermodulation distortion) and other measured distortions, there are more *un*measured, *un*named, *un*identified distortions than a spec sheet recognizes. So a low listed distortion is only a negative definition of quality; it tells you only what isn't a problem while overlooking everything that is. Specs do not necessarily correlate with sound quality. In fact, THD, the most common spec, has been known for decades not to correlate to sound at all.

The dangerous thing about trusting your ears is that what they hear can fly in the face of theory and then you no longer have any experts to rely on. If your ears hear differently from what theory prescribes, then go with your ears and throw out the theory. Theories change; your ears change also in the sense that as you learn more about listening, you hear more details. But while it is easy for us to deceive ourselves, and for our ears to lead us astray, the theories have no more solid grounding than our ears do. Trust your ears.

Used Equipment

"Used" by no means necessarily means old and abused, nor second rate. Some of the best components available are still the classic Methuselahs. And there is always a goodly amount of equipment being sold off—there are many eager souls out there who have the equipment bug and buy a component when it first comes out to good reviews and then soon move on again to the next rave review. There are great benefits to staying at least a year or so "behind the times."

Buying used equipment, whether vintage or just a few years old, requires some simple precautions. Through a dealer, you should be able to get a guarantee or at least return privileges; through a private party, neither of these. A dealer will probably be a bit more expensive because of the extra service.

Prices should be about half the original retail price; if the equipment is more than several years old, perhaps dropping down to 40 percent. The higher the original price, the steeper the drop-off.

Just because the component is relatively cheap, don't be too casual about the purchase. Thoroughly check out the component's reputation for reliability. Look over the unit you are considering very carefully. Put it through all its operations. With electronic components, look inside the chassis to see how clean everything is. Switches should work smoothly and quietly. If you do not have return privileges, listen to music through it for more than just five or ten minutes.

DEALING WITH DEALERS

You wouldn't expect to be able to buy a fine musical instrument at a Woolworth's or K mart. You shouldn't expect to find fine playback equipment there either. You should go to a place that specializes in audio equipment without also selling toasters and Mickey Mouse telephones. This alone may not solve all problems—audio dealers are themselves sometimes confused about their own image as "purveyors of the fine art of recorded music playback."

Travel around to half a dozen different dealers and chances are that you will hear as many different recommendations about what to get. Each will scorn the others' advice.

From everything one hears, there are few audio dealers who can be depended on for impartial guidance. They are, naturally, preoccupied with making sales and not necessarily with educating customers. Most dealers are themselves so steeped in industry hype that their ideas are just as mistaken as their customers', except the dealers have the lingo down pat. A friend characterizes talking to audio experts as being like talking to mid-19th-century "experts" on evolution—you'll hear all kinds of crazy notions. Uninformed of the fundamentals, they nonetheless know the jargon fluently. A barrage of terminology is a potent weapon for the subjugation of gullible customers.

A retailer may try to switch you away from a new component in short supply. A retailer is likely to refer you to the manufacturer in the case of a problem rather than taking care of it directly. Some high-end manufacturers are excellent about helping out their customers, some are not—try to find out before you buy. A retailer, on hearing about a problem with a component you've just purchased from that store, is likely to conclude immediately that the problem is with one of your other components (not bought from that store) and recommend you replace that component (with one from that retailer, of course). A retailer may also recommend components that in fact do not make a good match, most likely out of ignorance but sometimes just because they are on hand.

Unfortunately, this really does seem to represent the majority of dealers (you may be able to add stories of your own). Regrettably, it also holds true with high-end dealers. Among these, you may run into another problem—the Morris the Cat routine. If you don't know the right buzzwords or have the "right" equipment, you are likely to be either cowed into submission or shown the door. Many dealers are more interested in selling you equipment than in selling you good sound.

Looking at the other side, customers can be pretty awful too. A lot of people are tire kickers. They come in knowing very little but pretending to know more than they do, and then try to wheedle an education out of the dealer, while fighting him all the way. This is most likely to occur on a Saturday at midday, when the store is at its busiest and the sales that pay the bills to keep the store open during the rest of the week need to be made! Observe basic courtesy and consideration. And don't, if you take up a dealer's time, then go off and buy the component by mail order or at a discount house or at another retailer who'll give you a slight break because he hasn't had to invest any time in you. Though you may not have stolen cash out of the till, you have just as surely robbed the dealer by taking time and attention away from another sale.

High-end stores are generally tiny businesses, often run by people who do it because they love audio. High-end dealers tend to be service oriented, unlike mid-fi dealers, who are principally order takers. They must maintain a sizable inventory in a price range from audiophile-beginning affordable to exotic, and in a design range offering tubes and transistors, straight-line arms and pivoting, dynamic speakers and dipoles, and so forth, along with a large selection of accessories. A great deal of attention may go into selling a set of Tiptoes while very little profit is made.

Audiophiles on the whole are a talkative lot and there is always plenty to talk about, what with new equipment, ideas, and controversy to keep life interesting. Customers may come in to talk even more than to buy. Listening to equipment is time consuming (and sometimes patience consuming) and requires that the dealer provide a special listening room, an unhurried atmosphere, and the willingness to suggest alternatives and to allow the customer to compare. You are dealing, as often as not, with minutiae. Even though the equipment itself is tangible, what you are actually comparing is what it does to the music, which is not tangible, and so to estimate the differences accurately may require a lot of thought.

Good dealers should be able to tell you why they carry the equipment they do, should not automatically scorn any equipment they don't carry, and in fact should be prepared and able to point out the merits of good equipment they don't carry.

Then, once the sale is made, they still have to stand behind the equipment. They should have the ability to install the components, be prepared to answer questions about it in the ensuing weeks and longer, be prepared to go to bat with the manufacturer on their customer's behalf if need be.

All around, the most satisfactory approach is to find a dealer you trust and really like, then confine your choice to one of the components that dealer handles. It is better to base your decision on the dealer than to buy a possibly slightly better table from an audio weasle and wind up with no dealer support. Who needs more misery in life? Dealer support should be a critical consideration and it's OK to base your final decision on what your dealer carries, assuming obviously that he specializes in good equipment.

Your choice of components can perhaps be broadened by buying through mail order, but this has a lot of drawbacks—namely, no dealer support, nowhere to go for advice, and nowhere to turn for help if you have a problem. There are a few exceptions, always—the Mod Squad springs to mind—but you're probably best off if you can establish a relationship with a decent local dealer.

How to Audition Equipment

Instead of floundering in an ocean of audio technology and terminology, remember that the most important factor in choosing equipment is having sufficient listening and evaluation time. (Keep in mind: "Jargon is a noise that keeps our brains from understanding what our mouths are saying," according to Russell Ackoff.) You can determine how a component sounds only if you listen to it, and only you can determine whether what you hear will be satisfying to you.

The complication, of course, is that a component will sound different depending on what other components it is matched with and the room it's being played in. Listen to the equipment in different acoustic environments so you can better distinguish between the aspects of the sound that are a matter of the particular room acoustics and associated equipment, and those that are part of the component itself. Try to keep the associated components consistent from environment to environment so you are not comparing component changes as well as environmental changes. This is very easy to say but harder actually to carry out. Best of all, try to listen to the equipment in your own acoustic space and with your own other components. If you can find a dealer who will let you borrow the equipment like this, you should be happy to do just about anything for him.

To establish some consistency in auditioning, bring your own recordings with you instead of using whatever the store offers. If you listen to the store's music, your lack of familiarity with it adds additional confusion, it is difficult to distinguish between the recording's flaws and those of the component, and the recording may have been chosen specifically to make that equipment sound good.

So before you begin the process of auditioning, select half a dozen recordings that you know very well and that typify the kind of music you listen to. Voice is an excellent test—we all are intimately familiar with voices of all kinds and can pretty readily determine when a voice is being played back convincingly and when not. Also, using acoustic (unamplified) music that has been minimally miked (see p. 307) will be more revealing than a multimiked recording of amplified music, where it is harder to tell what is the fault of the recording and what of the playback.

Listen to the recordings on your system a number of times so you really know them, and also try to identify what you like and don't like about your system. There are two reasons why it is important to be very familiar with your reference recordings: One is so you know the flaws of the recording itself, and the other is so you can distinguish between what your system does to the recording and what the various components you are auditioning are doing to it.

Van den Hul, noted cartridge designer, described his do-it-yourself "course to upgrade your listening" in *The Absolute Sound*. Use a record you like and be prepared to spend some time listening. Do it at a time when you can be *relaxed* and able to concentrate. First train your ear to listen just to the dynamics. Then, listen again, but this time listen just to the low-level detail. Next, listen to the overall sound but still not to the music; listen instead for the depth in the sound and the reverberation. A lot of systems that may have good stereo—left/right—imaging have no depth to the image; they are flat. Then listen for the definition of the sound, whether an instrument sounds like itself or like something else. For example, trumpets should sound like trumpets, not tin cans; violins like a horsehair bow touched to gut strings rather than like steel strings. Finally, concentrate on the timbre.

Then listen to the record yet again (this is why it has to be a record you really like) and listen for two of these things at a time—dynamics and low-level detail, depth and definition, and so forth. And finally, listen again, this time to the whole music. If you have allowed yourself enough time, you will notice a sharp focusing of your perceptions and you will be able to listen with more pleasure. You'll probably also notice that your perception of *all* sounds has become more acute.

Always bring the same recordings around with you from place to place and use the same cuts. (See p. 370 for good music to audition by.) Be aware that even audio salespeople don't always know (or care) how to treat records well and may put their greasy fingers all over the edges or use a dirty stylus. Constant playing will wear out any recording except a CD, so be sure to use ones that are easily replaced. Incidentally, LPs are the first choice because they are still the best commercial recording medium.

Auditioning equipment involves tedium, impatience, and frustration. It can also be fascinating because it offers an intense education in the nuances of music playback. If you run across people who can help point out what to listen for, this can be invaluable. Just be sure their tastes coincide with yours and that they are not just pointing out the obvious good points of a component and glossing over the poor ones. If you can, audition the best system you can find just so you have an idea of what is possible.

Gauge a system or component as you would music—not by intellectually pulling the sound to pieces but by listening to the whole. You're interested in the totality of the music, not in how well the component produces certain individual aspects of sound. When you listen to music, you don't really want to be conscious of the strengths of the equipment, you want not to be distracted by its flaws. The goal of good audio is to minimize the flaws rather than to maximize the strengths.

The impact of the music should be a sense of ease. Some equipment gives you all the analyzed-out bits really well—like many CD players—but the bits never all come together into an emotional experience of music. That's what you're seeking—whatever equipment will give you the most of the life and sound of the music, even if it does certain specific things less well than another component.

Keep your focus on what you're listening *to* rather than what you're listening *through*. This can be difficult when you are specifically auditioning equipment and comparing it with other components, but keep in mind that while the function of the equipment is to reproduce sound as accurately as possible, its purpose is to supply you with pleasure. Also be aware that any component you listen to will sound different from your own system, but that different does not necessarily mean better.

Don't play just a minute of music. Play through at least a cut or two per album. You need time to adjust to a new component, a new environment, to become comfortable with your surroundings so you can focus full attention on the sound. Also, you may not immediately notice that the sound is distorting. One of the most significant criteria of a system or component is whether, after listening for an extended time, you experience listener fatigue—a sense of tiredness, irritation, a desire to turn off the system, even leave the room. Music should be enticing, involving; it should draw you in so you don't want to do anything else; it should reward you for listening closely. Linn suggests the ''hum-along'' test—if you can easily hum along with the system, then it must be good. But you can also hum along with a radio very easily, so though this idea has some legitimacy, it's only the beginning.

Keep notes. As you go from place to place, or listen to the component on several different occasions, or listen to different kinds of music, you will collect different impressions. If you can keep a record of this to refer back to, it will help to clarify your thinking and reduce some of the frustration. Note most importantly your *emotional* responses to a presentation of music. Your analytical critique may lead you astray, but your emotional reactions are likely to be very accurate. Hear the same setup in the same situation again some time later and you will probably respond emotionally the same way. But you may critique it quite differently, perhaps because you have more experience and more comparisons, or just because you can verbalize your feelings another way.

The ear, it is claimed, had a notoriously fallible recollection for sound heard even just a few seconds earlier—scientific tests have been devised to prove this. Yet honest experience contradicts this proposition. Many can hold the sound of a component or system in their heads long after having heard it and can clearly and accurately describe just what they heard. We can instantly identify voices over the phone, even of people we may not have spoken to for days, weeks, months, and longer. Sometimes we can even recognize a voice heard only once some time ago. This is obviously a form of audio memory that does not conform to the ''scientific tests'' devised to disprove its existence. This does not contradict the value of keeping notes.

Do not try to compare more than two components at a time and also do not try to do A/B comparisons. This is where you listen to one component for a minute and then immediately switch to the other, and then repeat this back and forth a few times. Then you are asked to describe the differences. This can be very confusing and is really not a valid comparison. Listen to a side or more of music on one component, then listen to the same music on the other component. Assess each component immediately after listening and then compare the two of them at the end. A/B testing is the subject of a lot of controversy—how valid it is, how much the switching boxes used affect the sound, what the psychological stresses might be that would change how one hears under these conditions. What it boils down to is that this is not how you listen to music, that it does not seem to offer much in the way of real benefits and certainly seems to have some very definite negatives.

Here are a couple of other factors to consider. How the equipment is set up is critical. If proper setup at home can make a significant difference to sound quality, this is no less true at a store. Some say that having more than one speaker in the room can also alter (worsen) sound, but unfortunately it is very hard to find dealers who can afford a room with only one pair. If you are trying to compare two components at the same shop within a brief space of time, don't compare more than two at a time—two are enough of a challenge and your mind simply cannot encompass all the variables involved in any more than two. Volume levels must be meticulously matched. The component that is playing more loudly can be mistaken as sounding better.

Unfortunately—as there is little either the dealer or the customer can do about this—quality components sound significantly better after a period of breaking in. When you buy a component and start listening to it at home, you can hear the sound slowly improve over a period of hours and days. It may even initially start out sounding pretty rude. At a store, rarely will a component have had proper break-in time. Manufacturers often try to break in equipment before it leaves the factory but, at least in the case of electronics, if it has been left off for more than a few days or a week, it will need to be broken in all over again. This is also true for interconnects and cables. (Yes, you may well be saying, "Oh, come on now." But it is true and very easily audible in some cases.)

Good Music Choices

The music you bring with you should be typical of the music you listen to most. When you're getting down to a final decision, it can be revealing also to bring along some different kinds—if you listen to complex music, bring something simple and listen to how the speaker handles it. You may be missing something in the complexity that the simplicity will reveal, or vice versa.

Change the volume setting for each music selection. Different types of music need to be played at different volumes—large-scale orchestral needs the largeness of high volume whereas folk should be played more softly. Music is composed to be played by specific instruments at those instruments' characteristic volumes—the playback level should reflect the original live intention.

The voice is particularly revealing—if the speaker is good on voice, it's probably good on everything (though the voice can't reveal the quality of bass and highs). Because it is the instrument we are most familiar with, it is the most difficult to reproduce convincingly. The female voice has extensive dynamic range and power requirements, together with subtle inflections and a quality of intimacy. You should be able to hear the voice in the throat and the breathing. Speakers tend to add honkiness and screechiness to voice. Classical or complex music could hide this speaker coloration. Cyndee Peters's *Black Is the Color* and *Your Basic Dave Van Ronk* are good voice records—the music is enjoyable and the sound is wonderfully natural on both.*

Piano is probably the most difficult instrument to play back naturally—to reproduce both the transient strike of the hammer and then the resonance of the string accurately is very difficult. Time problems are particularly noticeable here.

With percussion instruments, the beginning of the strike is midrange, followed by the bass of the transient itself. The strike on the skin should be separate and distinct from the sound of the body resonating.

Strings should sound like strings, not steel instruments of torture.

The Absolute Sound, Stereophile, and *IAR* all publish lists of recommended recordings—recommended for both their music and their sound quality.

Making the Purchase

Some tips on closing the sale from your end: You should be able to have a money-back guarantee on the equipment, for something like a week or ten days, which not only covers any defects in the equipment but also allows you to listen to the equipment in your own home with your own associated equipment. With the best will and intentions in the world, equipment seemingly well chosen in the store may not sonically survive the transition home into a new acoustic environment and different system. This guarantee should be in writing and it should specify money back, not just credit or exchange—the store may have nothing else you want as a replacement.

Though we feel, given the kind of money involved in audio, that a dealer really owes this to the customer, also consider what this does to the dealer. That dealer is effectively loaning you equipment that may or may not come back to the store, and that may also come back dam-

*Opus 3 no. 7706 and Kicking Mule 177, respectively.

aged with the customer claiming this to be the dealer's fault. Equipment that was possibly damaged by the customer is a loss that has to be eaten by the dealer. Customers may also use this guarantee as a lending library—curious to hear a component at home, they may be just pretending to buy with no really serious intentions. This trick cannot be pulled too often unless they keep moving around the country, but it still puts the dealer at a great disadvantage.

Just because the equipment is in a sealed box, don't assume that it is pristine and has never been opened. Sometimes you will be sold a display sample, or one returned (and perhaps abused) by someone else. There is no problem with this if the price is dropped accordingly, but some stores will try to sell you a sample as if brand new. Have the box opened and the component checked in front of you *before* you pay for it. Operate all knobs and dials; check for the instruction manual and warranty.

THE SPECIFICS

The annual equipment directories of *Audio* magazine and *Stereo Review* may be useful as nearly complete (some high-end equipment is not included) listings of everything available, but they can also be overwhelming. These listings tell you nothing about the equipment other than the specs, which are of very limited usefulness.

Much more informative are the annual recommended listings of *The Absolute Sound, Stereophile, IAR*, and some of the other "alternative press." These will provide valuable reference points. It is always a good idea to listen to the best and then work down from there, if you can do this without driving the dealers (and yourself) bonkers.

Following are a few quick pointers on buying components. Read the full chapters on these components in this book before you buy.

BUYING A TURNTABLE SYSTEM

When you're buying a turntable system, you're in search of synergy—how well the stylus is able to release the music from the groove depends on how successfully the turntable, tonearm, and cartridge all work together. Each part directly influences the others—alter any element and you alter the sound.

Mass-market merchandisers commonly offer the turntable and tonearm as a package and may even throw in the cartridge. This is primarily a good marketing, rather than a good sound, decision. With very few exceptions, each of these components should be bought individually. A good builder of tables is not *ipso facto* an equally good designer and builder of arms or cartridges. Just to design, build, and then successfully market a good table (or arm, or cartridge) takes a great deal of dedicated concentration. Some of the "exceptions" offering very good table-plus-arm systems include the AR ES-1, Rega, Linn and Linn Axis, Well Tempered, and Sonographe.

Keep in mind, when you're selecting the table components, how the hierarchy goes: The table itself is of first importance because it supports, isolates, and drives the record, tonearm, and cartridge; the tonearm is next in importance because it controls the cartridge. Only once you have a good table and arm, with good resolving power, does it then make sense to invest substantial money in an excellent cartridge. Its ability to capture subtle detail will be largely obscured unless the table and arm can provide the right conditions for it to work in.

Only once the three elements of the table system are all very good does their importance then become equal. But until they *all* get good, observing a certain sequence of importance will yield the best sound all along the way.

Even if it means having to skimp a little on the other components, buy as good a table system as you can afford—a good front end is essential to release all the music stored on the recording. Though this may initially be more expensive, it's actually a frugal investment because you need never replace it (except the cartridge). A component that's good when you buy it will always remain good. True high-end tables don't change drastically from one season to the next—outwardly, they can remain unchanged for years. The AR, for example, is based on a design developed in about 1961; the Linn is about 15 years old. In addition, almost all of the top-quality table manufacturers design their upgrades so as to be easily retrofittable onto earlier tables. When you invest in a good table, you can be confident it will remain contemporary because you'll be able to add on future refinements for a lot less expense in time and money than it would take to sell your old table and buy a new one.

Turntables

The best tables are simple, with an emphasis on precision engineering and quality manufacture of parts. The sonic chasm between a poor table and a good one results above all from the mechanical and engineering differences. Getting the music out of the groove is a ticklish mechanical task complicated by the minuscule scale on which playback occurs. A child's toy microscope and one of laboratory quality work on the exact same basic concept. The major differences between them are in the quality of the optics, the precision of the gear mechanism, and so forth—in other words, the quality and refinement of the mechanical execution. Like a lab microscope, an adult-quality table has a much higher level of resolution, which allows it to discern details in the groove that cruder tables would blur or miss entirely.

Generally, the good tables are almost all made by small companies where pride of craftsmanship and quality of manufacture replace the mass-fi assembly mentality. The finest tables are made either by the designer's hands or at least under the designer's constant supervision.

Mass-market table manufacturers mostly attempt to substitute "high-tech" shortcuts to circumvent the need for exacting precision. Regardless of slick advertising claims, gizmos such as servo controls and strobe rings cannot be substituted for quality make and have nothing to do with providing good sound. They are marketing ploys. Yes, these may originate from an honest, if misguided, desire to improve playback. Unfortunately, though, what usually happens is the equally honest corporate imperative to make lots of money takes over, and so good-bye, good sound. Often mass-fi equipment will cleverly attempt to imitate the appearance of expensive audiophile equipment. While the outward design of a mass-fi table may visually mimic an excellent table, the quality of the engineering, which makes the real difference in sound quality, is missing. Who would trust a seismograph made of flimsy plastic, however many fancy switches it boasted?

Don't, by the way, try to base any decisions on table specs—these are about the biggest joke since Pavarotti made *Yes, Georgio*. Rumble, wow, and flutter can all be heard if you listen carefully. You don't need a bunch of numbers to tell you if you just survived an earthquake—all the numbers will tell you is how severe the quake was. Interesting if you're a geologist, or if you're house-hunting along the San Andreas fault, but otherwise not very pertinent to daily life. Also, the Richter scale is a rigorously defined and universally standardized measurement, whereas table manufacturers have a much broader latitude in how they can come up with their measurements.

You cannot bulldoze your way into good sound. The best tables are uncomplicated, with an emphasis on precision engineering and quality manufacture of parts. In good audio, form normally follows function, whereas in mass-market audio, the exact opposite is the norm. Fancy looks aren't going to charm a recording into releasing its music (although appearances may well charm people into releasing their money).

The only area where you want to get into something fancy is in the quality of the manufacture itself. Look for economy and insightfulness of design, plus precision parts and construction. When recovering information from a groove modulation a millionth of an inch in size, small, even seemingly insignificant details are critical. You're looking for a very straightforward, precision-built machine. Stay away from audio cheesecake. Uncomplicated design, minimalist circuits, and precision manufacture will allow good sound to be faithfully "unrecorded" from the record.

How to Choose the One from the Many

There are only about ten really top-end tables, and then perhaps another ten that are a step below. You can drive yourself crazy trying to decide which of these good tables to buy, or you can accept that all the high-end tables are very, very good. Don't try to figure out which is the absolute "best"—there isn't one. At most, there is a "best for you."

So it's less important which good table you buy than that you buy a good one. It's good advice to just go buy the best table you can afford and have done with it. All of the good ones are, within their various price points, very good. If you choose to at some point down the road, you can get into the minutiae of differentiating between one top-class table and the next—once your whole system has sufficient resolving power really to be able to distinguish these differences. Good equipment has good resale value, so if you do decide to change tables, you'll be able to get something for your current one. Mass-fi gear, on the other hand, is generally good only for the trash heap.

For someone just moving into the high end, buy a veteran belt-drive table made by a well-established company and sold by a well-established, knowledgeable dealer. The belt-driven Acoustic Research ES-1 is the *minimum* point of entry for good sound because it's the least expensive, established, *good* table readily available in the United States, and because anything *sonically* less takes you back down into mass-fi. (The Dual 505-2 is also a good and *cheap* table, but definitely not as good as the AR.) The ES-1 offers the additional important advantage that it can be conveniently and economically upgraded into a vastly superior table via George Merrill at Underground Sound. After some 20-odd years of existence, the AR continues to be a first-rank table in its price range. With the benefit of Merrill upgrades, its ability to remain current is assured. Merrill makes excellent upgrades for the earlier AR models as well as for all the Linns.

Between them, AR and Thorens, which also makes good tables, have been responsible for just about every major innovation that has shaped the modern turntable—with the exception of direct drive, which has proved largely a dead end.

Two other very well known and highly regarded American-made

tables are the SOTA and the VPI. Either one is excellent. Use them as a point of reference or comparison with any other table you're considering. It's probably safest to avoid an imported table, unless the company has a very secure presence here.

What to Look For, What to Avoid

As said earlier, the better tables all tend to be very simple—which doesn't mean simplistic. Great care and thought goes into working out the design concepts and precision engineering—rather than into dreaming up new ways to entice the consumer to buy *this* product rather than the competition's. Tables that play the record sideways or where the record pops out in a drawer like a CD player are definitely *nekulturni*.

NEVER buy a table that is part of another component, sometimes called a console. Likewise, if a table has a record changer, walk on by. This belongs in the same category as an electric carving knife—only worse, as it can badly damage both your sound and your records. The parts in a record changer are a wonderful breeding ground for all the resonances that will spoil your sound. Considering all that's already been said about the prime importance of the table, no more need be said here.

Automatic and even semi-automatic tables are in the same category, though slightly lesser on the severity scale. Mechanisms that return the arm to its resting position invariably add resonances without adding commensurate value. Fully automatics even put the stylus in the groove for you and then turn the table off when the side is over. Any nonessential mechanisms should be avoided because they will muddy the sound.

You're a lot better off with a fully manual table, which, by the way, is the *only* way the best tables come. It's not so tough to have to get up at the end of each side and manually return the tonearm to its resting place. You want to flip the record over anyway, or change it. Even if you're clumsy, you really can't do any damage, providing, of course, the arm has a *cuing device*—an invaluable feature, even though the cueless Well Tempered Arm has survived much use without disaster. A cuing device is a hydraulic system that, when activated, very slowly lowers the tonearm to the record or raises it up. There are certain instances where a mechanical gadget can be reliably and repeatedly more sensitive and delicate than many a human hand.

You can also buy an add-on *autolift*, which will automatically lift the arm off the record at the end of the record side. This is both convenient and minimizes any possible risk of damaging the stylus by leaving it circling in the run-out. The autolift is positioned on the chassis so that the tonearm, reaching the end of the record side, will touch its trip lever, setting off a little hydraulic arm-raiser. It's reputed to degrade sound slightly (far less than a semi-automatic table), but you won't necessarily notice this.

By the way, it is sonically preferable if the dustcover is not permanently affixed to the back of the plinth but simply rests on top of the plinth. In fact, sound quality will often improve if the table's dustcover is altogether removed while playing. If the dustcover is an option that costs extra, you can save quite a bit by building your own from foam-core or cardboard. It may not look superslick but will serve its purpose.

DON'T buy a table that doesn't allow you to change tonearms easily. If the table is designed so the arm cannot be removed and replaced, then it's almost a certainty you're dealing in poor company. Also be sure that the tonearm cable easily unplugs from the arm so you can replace it with a better one. Too low a plinth may limit your choice of arms that can be used on the table—there must be ample clearance for both arm and properly dressed arm cable.

There are a few good table companies that sell a decent table/arm package. Minimum standard for a good table/arm combo is represented by the AR ES-1. The arm is OK and can also be readily upgraded to a better one when you're ready—such as the Premier MMT. The Linn table offers two arms—the Basik Plus and the more expensive Ittok. Then you've got the Well Tempered table, which can be paired with the WTA arm, both first-rank choices and forming an all-around excellent team. Two imported table/arm combinations well worth considering, if your dealer handles them, are the Rega 3 with 300B arm (considered an excellent one) and the Systemdek.

Tonearms

Arms tend to have pretty straightforward designs without a lot of frills. You want a rigid tube, rigid bearings, and a means of tightly clamping the cartridge to the headshell and the headshell to the arm. The arm must permit fine-tuned settings for overhang, VTA/SRA, and azimuth. Be sure the weight and size of the arm will mate well with your table. The excellent Dynavector, for example, is big and heavy enough that the only readily available table it really works well on is the VPI. As far as pivoting versus SLT arms, well, the SLT choice is extremely limited and quite expensive, as well as being more finicky.

If you are a devotee of the sound of moving magnets, which as a rule are small, light cartridges with very compliant styli, then your ideal arm might be low mass and lightweight. If, on the other hand, you're a fan of moving coils—heavy cartridges with low compliance—then you'll want to move in the direction of a more massive construction.

Avoid P-mount arms—these really are all mass-market plastic junk and are unlikely ever to be developed by the good companies. Though the idea is seemingly a good one, it in fact greatly restricts your cartridge choices and limits your flexibility in correctly setting up the cartridge. Allegedly, P-mounts obviate the need for setup as it's already been done for you, but all they really accomplish is to eliminate your control.

Cartridges

There is just no point in investing in a good cartridge until you have a table and arm worthy of it. It's quite likely that a cartridge that is better than the table and arm may actually sound worse than an inexpensive cartridge with that same arm and table. A good cartridge will be more revealing and critical of flaws—it isn't designed to ameliorate poor conditions, whereas a decent inexpensive cartridge like Grado's MTE + 1 is very musical and forgiving under less than optimal conditions. Stick with this until you've got your arm/table combo worked out.

If you have a very good table and arm, but are perhaps relatively new to critical listening, don't start off buying a very expensive cartridge—less expensive ones will give you the lion's share of performance. It's the same approach used for musical instruments—you don't start off with a world-class instrument but first get your feet wet with a lesser though still good one. This way, by the time you do get to the best, you'll be able to distinguish the subtle differences that make it the best. To enjoy the full benefits of the very expensive cartridges, you really need to be experienced in divining nuances.

A moving coil cartridge can be more finicky than a moving magnet, and all but the high-output ones will require an additional gain stage. If this is already included in your preamp, then fine. If it is not, you must include the purchase price of the gain stage with the price of the cartridge and judge whether it is worthwhile. High-output MCs may not sound better than moving magnets. Again, the particular execution is more important than which design approach was employed.

The single most important thing about a cartridge is something only you can control—the physical condition of the stylus itself. Perhaps the very most significant point to make about cartridges is that they should be replaced regularly and sooner rather than later. A stylus will generally last around 1,000 hours (some say only about 500 hours), depending on how roughly it is used and also on its shape. For example, the microlinear profile is thought to have a relatively longer life.

A worn or damaged stylus can literally "regroove" the record, gouging out the grooves, shaving off some of the musical information, and chipping the groove walls. These are no longer record revealers but record erasers. A strong magnifying glass will help you see dirt, but wear can be revealed only by a very high power optical microscope. By the time you can see the wear yourself under a magnifying glass, it's far advanced and undoubtedly causing significant damage.

Cartridges, incidentally, have a shelf life, regardless of whether or not the cartridge is being used. The cantilever's damping material ages through magnetic effects, mechanical wear, and chemistry, causing the compliance to stiffen. Shelf life may be around 18 months. If you're a regular listener, the stylus needs replacement by then in any case, but if you keep several cartridges lying around, be advised that they are aging as they sit in their little boxes. Also be sure to buy from a dealer who has a regular turnover in cartridges.

The second most important thing about a cartridge is also something you control yourself—and that's how well it is set up. The best cartridge, poorly set up, can sound like fingernails on a blackboard. This may be the primary advantage of the Shure V15-VMR—it comes with its own special setup gig, which really is idiot-proof. (Regrettably it will NOT work on any other cartridge.) Sonically, though it is well liked by many, it may not be by you.

Essentially what you're looking for in any good cartridge is a strong nonresonant body, preferably one that is absolutely flat on top for maximum mechanical contact with the headshell to transmit resonances; probably a relatively low compliance stylus, so it tracks well and stays out of the groove gunk, probably with a fixed stylus assembly and a line-contact stylus profile. You also want a tip mass resonance well above the audio band and do not want the high frequencies rolled off. High frequency roll-off may be an easy way to prevent a cartridge from sounding overly bright, but you will also lose much of the subtle detail of the music, which provides the sense of ambience and air. Definitely *stay away from* P-mount and integral headshell cartridges.

Be sure to match stylus compliance with arm mass, and cartridge impedance with your preamp. Matching arm and cartridge can be a tough job. There's an equation available, but often one doesn't have enough or the right information to plug into it. That's one advantage of the Linn combination—it comes all matched. A test record may tell you, but at that point you've already invested a lot of time and money in buying the cartridge and setting it up on your arm.

Generally what it all boils down to is that it's best to rely on the experience of others with that particular combo—just be sure to solicit a number of opinions. Call both the tonearm and the cartridge manufacturers—a small company will generally share its experience with you, providing it has the experience to share and also providing that you make it clear you're not asking for an endorsement of a particular arm or cartridge, but just for advice on good matches.

Many cartridges provide a sense of detail by emphasizing one aspect of the frequency spectrum over another. Few, however, provide *definition*, which is the ability to provide all the information on the record over the entire frequency band, across the entire range from the loudest passages to the softest detail, all properly balanced in a musically natural and convincing way. This musicality is what you want to listen for.

When auditioning cartridges, be aware of two factors: They benefit from a break-in time (how long depends on the cartridge—you can hear the cartridge's sound changing as it breaks in) and, if you're listening in the summer months, the heat and humidity induce high-frequency resonances that can make a cartridge sound unpleasantly shrill and screechy.

Some cartridges are sold with replaceable styli. Instead of replacing the entire cartridge, the body of which may be perfectly fine, one can replace just the stylus and cantilever at usually half the full retail cost of the cartridge. While this is an economical design, such styli introduce more resonance because they're not permanently bonded to the body. In addition, many cartridges are discounted—at discount price, it's often not much more expensive to replace the entire cartridge rather than just the stylus alone, which is rarely discounted. On the whole, it's better to replace the whole cartridge and not buy cartridges with user-replaceable styli.

Some manufacturers will replace the stylus/cantilever assembly for you, which generally gives better results. Joe Grado, for example, will not only replace a stylus but will often at the same time upgrade the cartridge to the next level or the most recent modification (for a charge, of course). The Garrott Brothers in Australia will retip any cartridge—they are especially well known and respected for their upgrades and modifications on the English Decca cartridges.

TAPE DECKS

The two most widely well regarded manufacturers of reel-to-reel decks are Tandberg and Revox. Tandberg is historically considered to have better electronics, Revox to have a particularly good transport mechanism. The Revox is therefore often chosen for modification because, once the electronics are improved, you end up with an overall better deck.

There are really no good, inexpensive cassette decks, with the exception of the Sony Pro Walkman. The Nakamichi Dragon is very well regarded for sound quality—but beware that just because the Dragon is good, you cannot therefore infer that other Nakamichi decks are comparably good. The Tandberg 3014 is really very good, with excellent midrange and good controls.

A basic consideration is that a deck is as much mechanical as it is electronic. In this sense, it combines all the complexities and requirements of both a turntable and an amplification stage, and both elements must be equally good to result in a good deck. For recording, you will get much better results with three heads than two. It's best to avoid autoreverse unless you are using the deck only for background sound.

Avoid decks that allow you only "automatic" settings for bias, equalization, noise reduction, and so forth. Like a digital turner, what "ought to be" as determined in the lab does not always conform to "what is" out in the world. You gain slight convenience from all the settings being automatically chosen for you, but you also are likely to get less good sound. Automatic cameras may take better snapshots than nonautomatics, but they will not take better photographs—the same distinction holds for decks.

TUNERS

If you want a tuner, it is definitely worthwhile to buy a good one, even if it is not your primary source of music. It is an invaluable aid in hearing new music, but one to which you will not listen much unless it sounds good.

Tuners usually are better at some aspects of capturing the radio signal than at others. Decide which you need most in your area and then select from among the tuners that are best at this. The antenna is also a critical aspect of how well you receive signals.

A very useful and quick test for a tuner's sound quality, aside from its ability to capture the signal, is to listen to a voice talking. We are all sufficiently familiar with voices to be able to identify readily whether or not one sounds "natural." Voices talking cover a much narrower range of frequencies than music, but then the FM signal has a very narrow bandwidth anyway, so a voice does not represent much of a limitation. In any case, it falls right in the all-important midrange. You can also turn the dial all the way to one end or the other. Listen to the white noise and determine whether certain areas of sound are emphasized—you want overall balance across the frequency band.

The Marantz 1OB is probably *the* classic tuner; McIntoshes also look and sound good; Quad FM4s and even the Dynaco, Scott, and Fisher tube tuners are also very good. A lot of the Dynacos are pretty banged up so make sure the one you're looking at is in good condition—it will probably cost you around $50. Of current production tuners, the Magnum Dynalab is highly regarded and its front end is widely used by other high-end audio companies for building their own tuners. Onkyo has some good tuners—the T-22, considering its price of around $100, is remarkable.

CD PLAYERS

The good-sounding CD players come from a handful of high-end designers, most of whom modify Sony or Philips players. Unfortunately, the quality of the players they have to work with is deteriorating as competition increases and the value of the dollar decreases.

You should test the player with a wide selection of CDs of different kinds of music and from different labels—don't just use the dealer's CDs, which have already been hand-picked to sound good in that player. Also, because digital sounds different from analog, you will need extended listening time to adjust to digital's sound and so be confident that you are really distinguishing between players and not just between analog and digital.

Most specs and testing for error correction are done with a purposefully damaged disc produced by Philips. This disc is very undemanding so just about any CD player, even the cheapest, will pass the test with no problem. A better test you can easily perform is to buy a CD, scratch it up—use curved scratches as these are harder to play through than straight ones—and play it on each player you are considering.

Player weight and solidity of construction are being downgraded. Whether or not the laser system alignment is correct affects both tracking and error correction—a heavy, sturdy construction protects against vibration and physical shock and thereby reduces the risk of misalignment. Excessive heat degrades components and can cause failure of the semiconductor lasers, so good heat dissipation is important.

Despite this mechanical deterioration, the longer you wait, the better are your chances of buying a good-sounding player. CD players are continually evolving. Some recommend buying the cheapest player you can find to listen to your CDs now and waiting till things settle down a bit more before investing a lot of money. The problem with this approach is you probably won't spend much time listening to your cheap player, in which case it will actually turn out to have been an expensive investment.

THE AMPLIFICATION STAGE

The American audio establishment—despite the evidence of many ears—persists in claiming that all amps that measure the same will therefore sound the same. Don't be misled—no two amps sound alike.

The preamp must be matched with the cartridge (or other front end); the amp must be matched with the speakers. This matching will alter the sound of both components involved.

Tubes and transistors, being imperfect, each have their own sonic "thumbprint"—you will likely prefer one over the other, though you will have to make tradeoffs with each. Listen to both as much as you can before assuming tubes to be as "old-fashioned" as the "old" Coke. More and more new tube equipment is being designed at reasonable prices and there is also the used market to turn to for classic tube designs. These include the Quad tubes; the Dynaco Stereo 70 and Mark III and IV amps (all excellently modified by GSI) and PAS III preamp; the Marantz 7C and 8B.

Separates and Integrateds

There's a lot to be said for buying an integrated amp, though integrateds have long inhabited the no-man's-land between mass-fi and the high end. (Receivers are quite another story—there are probably none being made now that achieve sound beyond mass-fi, so buy your tuner separately.) Historically, integrated amps have been clearly less good than separates, though some integrateds are changing this reputation. Because both preamp and amp are contained in a single chassis and share the same power supply—both expensive items—you can get a good sonic value and convenience for a lower price than with separates. There is also a sonic benefit to eliminating the colorations of interconnects, plugs, and jacks. Compatibility is assured (at least with a well-designed unit) and you need not fuss about which interconnects sound best with your components. On the other hand, sharing a single power supply is a drawback (see p. 107), there is greater chance of hum and cross-talk, and overall quality is often lower.

Among separates, there are an increasing number in the "low end of the high end," an area that nearly went defunct some years ago, leaving a chasm between high end and mass-fi. That gap is being bridged once again, often by companies that also cover the "high end of the high end," with components from PS Audio and Superphon, as well as the Adcom 555 transistor amp and the Lazarus tube preamp.

One of the benefits of buying separates, in addition to the opportunity for better sound, is versatility. If you want to start upgrading, you can do it one piece at a time rather than replacing the entire stage. You can buy your preamp from one designer and amp from another—often a company is more inspired with one than the other. You can gain all the benefits of mixing a tube preamp with a transistor amp. The preamp can be positioned close to the turntable (where it must be because of the shortness of the tonearm cable) while the amp can be placed close to the speakers, thus taking advantage of short speaker cable runs, which generally sound better than longer ones.

The quality of the execution of the design—power supply, passive parts, circuit layout—is at least as important as the particular design approach of tubes or transistors, separates or integrated. Listen before you judge.

As for specs, it's all very well to take a lot of measurements, providing you know what you're measuring and how to interpret the data once you have it. An electronic circuit may function fine as an electronic circuit, but this doesn't ensure it is working as a musical circuit. Frankly, no one has figured out yet how to measure music or really has even a fairly good grasp of how the human mind understands music. Anyone who suggests they have a lock on the knowledge of which measurements are definitive in terms of music is a charlatan, a fool, or both.

The best "expert" you can rely on is your own ears. Rather than listening to the barbershop pundits, listen for yourself to the differences between amps. If you've tasted only frozen apple pie, perhaps you wouldn't be able to distinguish whether nutmeg or cinnamon or mace was used for flavoring, and whether in the right proportions and combinations. But as you come to taste a wider variety of apple pies, then you have enough information and experience to become more discriminating in your taste. Some people consider the tastes of apple pie to be inconsequential—apple pie is apple pie. Others can't tell the difference, however much pie they taste. If either of these cases applies to you, then go with convenience, price, reliability, and resale value.

SPEAKER BUYING

There are more different speakers on the market than any other component. Twelve hundred–plus different models, produced by more than 200 manufacturers, fill the pages of *Audio* magazine's annual equipment directory. This is a staggering quantity, but only a handful of them are musically special. Among these few, there seem to be basically two categories—the good enough and the very good.

Price does not serve reliably as a guide. For example, the economically priced Spica TC-50s have been compared by *Stereophile* and *IAR* to much more expensive and illustrious speakers like the Quads, which are almost five times the price. Until you really get into the stratosphere of high-end listening, you may do very well to settle on speakers such as the Spicas. Then invest your money further upstream where it will have a more salubrious effect on your ears.

There is an absolute basic minimum standard of quality that many speakers fail to meet and that therefore eliminates them from further consideration. Cabinet and driver configuration are easy problem areas to spot. Rap the cabinet with your knuckles—it should be solidly constructed and nonresonant, responding with a nice tight *nick-nick* sound to it, rather than the more common *boink-boink* of an undistinguished speaker. Look at the front of the speaker for baffle diffraction problems. Preferably, the grille covers are removable. Even the quality of the terminal posts used can be revealing—a simple screw should generally alert you to the existence of other problems hidden from view. The drawback to a screw is not that it isn't "fancy" enough, but that it provides a less good electrical connection with the cable.

A good electrical connection is dependent on two factors: ample contact surface area and contact area pressure. You want a "gas-tight interface," meaning a good solid connection that will keep the air out and so slow down oxidation problems. A nut and bolt with two O-rings provides good contact; a small screw on a terminal strip will strip out or buckle before you can really tighten it and also provides the minimum of contact area. Curling a length of bare wire around it does not help either—use large-size spade lugs.

Buying speakers requires that a number of broad decisions be made right from the start—to buy dynamics or dipoles; if dynamics, whether two- or three-way; with or without subwoofers; directional or dispersed. These choices should be considered in combination with your amplifier. Read "The Loudspeaker System" (p. 130) and "Speaker Setup" (p. 203) so you have a good understanding of what is involved.

The music you most often listen to will affect which is the right speaker for you (see "The Loudspeaker System"). You really have to choose between hearing the subtle differences in tone between similar instruments or the power for playing rock and full-scale orchestras at live volumes—the two are rarely combined in the same speaker, any more than in the same amp.

Here's a rough guide to the amp power needed to drive your speakers: If you listen mainly to something like chamber music in a small room, then 30 watts with medium-efficiency speakers should be fine. In a full-size room, and playing pretty much any music, 50 watts driving high-efficiency (90- to 100dB) speakers should be fine; for mid-efficiency (90- to 85-dB) speakers, use anywhere from 50 to 200 watts of amp power; inefficient speakers of 85 dB or less will probably benefit from 200 watts to get the most out of them.

Choosing any new component is time consuming, frustrating, aggravating, mind boggling, hair tearing—and speakers can be among the worst because they are so affected by their environment. Be patient and don't let it get you down—the rewards are immeasurable. Regrettably, there is no single answer, nor even a limited combination of answers. The variables involved in the specifics of equipment, room, listening habits, preferred music, volume, sensitivity to certain equipment colorations, and so on permit of no set solutions. Remember also that, providing you choose a quality speaker, if you end up not liking it after a period of time, or find that you have become more discerning, you can sell it at a fair price and look again. How often does one get something right the very first time? The search can be fascinating and will almost certainly teach you a great deal about listening.

You may want to listen to some of the classic names in speakers to orient yourself. A number of top audiophiles and designers around the country listen on the Quad electrostatics, both the originals and the ESL-63s. They are particularly known for their very natural sound and good texture—what they do, they do excellently. They don't go down very low and cannot play very loud—people have sold off their Quads for these reasons, only to go out and buy another pair again a few months later. Among dynamics, the Vandersteens and Thiels are longtime good speakers. In the less expensive world, the Spica TC-50s really stand out. The Rogers SL3/5A BBC two-way mini-monitors have spawned a plethora of variations in the last couple of decades, and have really now been superseded, though they remain very good in their own right. Celestion SL-6s are also to be checked out.

Listening at a Store

The difficulty with buying speakers is that they just plain do not sound the same in the store as they will at home. A speaker's sound is greatly determined not only by its associated equipment but also by its acoustic environment. Yours will be grossly different from that of the dealer's showroom.

There are some other points that can also substantially change the sound of a speaker. If you're comparing two speakers, the one that is playing at a higher volume, even if it's not perceptibly louder, will almost always sound better. Be sure to match volume levels meticulously—check this for yourself, don't just assume the salesperson has set it right. Loudness is also a function of distortion—the more distorted a system is, the louder it will be perceived to sound. However, it will not necessarily be perceived as sounding more distorted. Also be sure the tone controls on both amp and speakers are set to neutral. A system with a raised treble will sound livelier, at least in the store.

Check that the amps you're auditioning the speakers with are about the same power as the one you'll be using at home—again, this can significantly change the sound. If your amp at home is less powerful, it may not be able to drive the speaker properly. All the components in the dealer's setup should be of at least comparable quality to yours or you won't be able to separate speaker distortion from the other equipment colorations. (The better the equipment, the more neutral its sonic thumbprint.)

If need be, bring your own amp with you. Any store that finds that difficult to accept is not a store dedicated to good sound. On the other hand, be sure to ask first and bring it only if you have made an appointment for a listening session. The salespeople will have to take time and trouble to substitute your amp for theirs and this should be done when it is convenient for them and will not cost them other sales.

The speakers must also bear at least *some* semblance of being set up decently. Just try disturbing your own speaker setup at home and you'll hear how much worse the sound becomes. The Linn people (of turntable fame) claim that having any other speakers in the same room will destroy the sound of the ones you're trying to listen to—they were the originators of the "single-speaker demo room." A number of people who are not Linn followers—"Linnies," as some call them—agree there is something to this.

Don't compare more than two pairs at a time—this is a surefire way to become first confused and then thoroughly lost. Additionally, be aware that speakers need a break-in period before they sound their best. If you are auditioning a pair straight out of the box, this will not do them justice.

Also, don't try to do quick A/B switches. You have to give yourself a few minutes to adjust to the sound and then some more time to think about it and react to it. Play a record side. Play half of one record side and then some of a different kind of music. Don't rush. Some people are faster than others at pinpointing what they're hearing. When listening to live music, your mind may not need to adjust to the sound, but with recorded sound, it needs a chance to adjust itself to the *distor-*

tions, the "unnatural" aspects of the sound. Even if you listen only to recorded music, the distortions on a system new to you are quite different from the ones you have become used to. Even at a concert, there is a minute or two while you focus your attention and compose yourself for listening. You need to allow yourself at least this much time to make even a preliminary judgment. The more time you have, the more accurate your assessment. The more experienced your listening, perhaps the more quickly you will be able to reach an evaluation.

Bill Seneca suggests listening to a single speaker initially, rather than the pair (switch to mono and preferably use mono recordings). One speaker sounds less impressive than a pair and it's also easier to focus in on just one channel to hear the colorations. If you like the one speaker, then proceed on to listening to the pair. Dr. Floyd Toole also reports that good speakers seem to be as well liked by listeners when heard singly as when heard as a pair, whereas poor speakers are liked more when heard as a pair.

The other advantage of listening to a single speaker is that you can more easily compare two different ones using the preamp balance control, switching between the left and right channels (be sure the preamp is switched to mono). This eliminates the need to use a switching box, which degrades the sound, or alternatively to hook up and unhook the speakers, which is a nuisance.

As with all equipment buying, try to listen to the same speaker in a number of different stores so you can get an idea of how it sounds in different rooms and different systems. When you've finished a session of critical listening in a store, go home and listen to your own system and consider again what it is you like and don't like about it—this will help you tremendously in focusing your thoughts. Though obviously the goal is to listen to music, you sometimes have to listen to the equipment first to make sure it's revealing the music as well as you'd like it to. Critical equipment listening not only brings you better equipment but can also help train you to be a more musically perceptive listener as well.

What to Listen For

What you're looking for in speakers is a neutrality, or lack of coloration, so that the inherent colorations of the musical instruments and voices can be clearly heard, without the addition of such speaker colorations as boxiness, a metallic treble, or a honky midrange. Some coloration is inevitable. Rather than trying to pull the sound apart and analyze the individual sound qualities for accuracy of reproduction, listen to the overall experience of the music. A speaker that can give you the emotion of the music is more important than one that can give you all the detail, accuracy, definition, and other attributes in the world. Having all the right parts doesn't necessarily mean that, when put together, they work well. Frankenstein's monster had all the necessary parts but, when they were put together, something was still just not quite right somehow.

Overall tonal balance, also called spectral balance, is essential, with neither punched-up bass nor glaring highs—all parts of the music should be naturally balanced, with no part either exaggerated or diminished. It's far easier to design and build a speaker that emphasizes the bass or treble but, while this may sound superficially attractive when first listened to, the ear soon tires of it. Speakers with a genuinely wide frequency band are usually very expensive. So remember the heart of the music is in the midrange and focus your attention here. It is also where the speaker should be focusing its best qualities. Once the midrange is solid, you can turn your attention to the bass and treble.

Many speakers that have a *measured* wide dynamic range will, when listened to, turn out to have a narrow one. Others with a narrow measured range will sound good. This is not a measured specification but a perceived, or heard, characteristic. A perceived good dynamic range is expensive to develop; a measured spec "proving" wide range is not.

Good dynamic contrast is really more important than range. The better a speaker can render the differences between loud and soft, loud and very loud, soft and very soft, the more musically satisfying the performance will be. This has no connection with how loudly a speaker can play or how much power it can handle.

Ambience, imaging, time and phase coherence, definition, and detail all go hand in hand. The result is that the speakers can reveal all the individual instruments and performers onstage, in their precise locations, in a three-dimensional space. A excellent system will permit distinctions to be heard between a Stradivarius and a Guarneri.

THE MUSIC

Buying recordings is a little like buying food: With experience, you can tell a lot from appearances, but you won't definitely know if it's good until you've tried it—by which time it's too late to make a return. Recording companies and stores certainly don't consider such qualities as lousy sound quality, poor mastering, and wonton-wrapper-thin disc to represent a legitimate basis for return. In their eyes, these are not "defects" but simply the norm. Therefore, you have to do as much as you can for yourself to protect against getting stiffed. You can, if you know what to look for, learn a great deal about the recording—whether CD, LP, or tape—just from its wrappings before having to shell out your money.

(You can also patronize a record store where the staff is knowledgeable and the return policy is reasonable in the event of real defects. If you show the courtesy of giving your business to one store, that store is likely to return the courtesy and treat you as a valued customer. This may sound old-fashioned but it's worth a try. Just be sure to pick out a store that's worthy of your custom in the first place.)

There are four basic qualities to a recording: (1) the musical performance, (2) the record technique, (3) manufacturing, and (4) playback. Playback, of course, is in your hands, but you can probably judge quite a lot about the other aspects by culling the copy of the jacket.

Regarding the music and its performance, obviously if you already know the work of the performers, then you're in a stronger position to decide whether or not to buy. Otherwise, you have to read reviews in magazines like *Fanfare,* listen to the radio, turn to friends, borrow records from the library. *The Absolute Sound* has extensive record reviews, and *Stereophile* and occasionally *IAR* also review records. All publish short lists of recommended recordings. *Hi-Fi News & Record Review* and *Hi-Fi Answers* do the same for English releases. If you're lucky, someone in your record store will have similar taste to yours and will be able to advise you. But hearing the recording on the store system may tell you very little—most store systems are pretty awful. And not just awful but often blaring loud enough to tear off your ears—this does not engender confidence. If you're very lucky, you'll know someone like friend Deep Ears, a repository, seemingly, of ALL classical disc knowledge.

You may find information somewhere on the jacket about the recording techniques used, perhaps indicating the number of mikes, and the recording location. In an on-site rather than studio recording, representational rather than interpretive recording techniques were probably used. Even this is no warranty of sound quality—the sound quality can still be manipulated *after* it passes through the mikes.

The quality of foreign pressings is often better than American ones, because over here many of the companies cut corners wherever they can, even for a third of a cent. On the other hand, it's best to try to get a pressing from the same country the master tape is from, because rarely is the *original* master tape sent out of the country for pressings. Instead, a copy is sent that is at least two steps removed from the master tape and therefore noticeably degraded sonically from the original. Also, this copy tape is used to cut a new master disc from which the stampers are made, and the engineers, in their wisdom, will often re-EQ the tape to their own taste. Whether the tape is reequalized or not, cutting systems sound as different from one to the next as do power amps.

Japanese pressings are often admired by audiophiles as being superior to the same LP pressed elsewhere. Technically (physically), the pressings are excellent—warp free, with correctly centered spindle hole, never any no-fill, and very quiet surfaces. The tonearm, instead of performing its usual bob and weave as it travels up and down warps and sideways from the off-center spindle hole, rides true and steady. But sonically, while these pressings tend to be very "live," they are often also considerably brightened and thinned out, especially in the midrange. They tend, as a rule, to be less musical and, despite their good points, less enjoyable to listen to, we find.

There's speculation that the Japanese actually hear differently than Americans, and certainly their taste in sound must be different. Even their electronics and speakers are designed to have this same bright, somewhat antiseptic sound. However, Japanese audiophiles cannot get their hands on enough quality American tube equipment, for which they'll pay a king's ransom. Apparently you can pay for an entire trip over there just by taking over a few of the right pieces of classic American equipment.

In any case, a good rule of thumb, when you have the choice, is to buy the pressing from the country of origin of the album. For example, an English pressing of the Beatles will be better than the American pressing. *Your Basic Dave Van Ronk,* which is a wonderful album—wonderful folk music and very good sound—was recorded in England but by Americans who kept the master tape. The American release, though the actual pressing quality is inferior, sonically is far better than the English one, which sounds more compressed, darker, and strangled. Technically, an American pressing may have worse surface noise, but if the music was recorded here (or the master tape is here), the sound quality of the American pressing is likely to be better.

Regrettably, there has recently been a big stink by the U.S. record industry about the sale of foreign pressings in this country. If the industry has its way, a Stones album, for example, released in the United States could not be the original—and best—British pressing but would have to be repressed in America to be sold here. We would lose out on both counts—it would not be from the country of origin, meaning the master tape would be a copy, and it would be further degraded by poorer American pressing quality. This kind of protectionism only protects mediocrity. Music lovers prefer foreign pressings of foreign recordings because they are better. Many even prefer foreign pressings of domestic recordings because these are technically better and quieter. Improve American pressing quality, and protectionism might not be needed.

Musically, some recordings you select to buy are found to be duds—the only way to have fail-safe success is to stick only with the knowns and never experiment. When you end up with a record you don't like, put it away in a separate box. If you leave it in with the rest of your collection, you'll be depressed every time you flip past it. You'll also be misled into thinking you have more records than you actually do (at least to listen to) and this will discourage you from buying others. Keep your collection well weeded. If the ones you don't like are segregated, they're also easy to show friends for trading or presents—others may like the music even if you don't.

Recordings that are *sonically* duds are more difficult to decide what to do with. As your system gets better, the record may sound better—with less distortion being added by your equipment, more music may be revealed. If you're already familiar with the music, then the sound quality is more easily "listened around" and may be tolerable. Or you may have several versions of the same piece and value this particular one for its special performance despite poor sound. Some performances are so extraordinary that poor sound is happily allowed for.

You're likely to have to return as many as 25 percent of the new recordings you buy because of flat-out defects like warps, an off-center spindle hole resulting in wow, or dust and fingerprints. Some people are more fussy about exchanging defective recordings and others may not want to be as meticulous. But if you plan to have the records you now own still in good shape to comfort you in your old age, it figures you may as well start off with the best you can get and then take good care of them. These may be the last days of vinyl records, so take full advantage while you still can get them at all.

Some recordings sold as brand new have already been opened, used, and resealed. These may have been returns, store demos, or sent out that way from the pressing plant or distributor. Clues are dust and dirt, fingerprints, maybe faint markings around the spindle hole. Such defects will show up more clearly under strong light. Our policy is to return these—not only are you paying full price for used goods but, more important, in the case of LPs you don't know the condition of the stylus that rode in those grooves and what damage it may have done while it was there. Get another copy that's new. The recording companies, if they were interested, could readily eliminate this problem by sealing the spindle hole with foil or the like, the same as is done for aspirin to prevent tampering. One could then immediately know whether or not a recording had been played.

LP BUYING

Look for short LP sides, which suggest the music hasn't been overly compressed to squeeze the maximum time onto each LP—this squeezes sound quality too. Many album jackets will provide timing for the individual songs or else give the overall length per side—a total of about 20 minutes or less is usually a good sign. The shorter the side and the wider the run-out, the less distortion the music is subjected to.

Any record that's intended primarily to be played over the airwaves will have been *ipso facto* rigorously compressed. The stations want to play the music at maximum volume to cover a maximum geographical area—in an undoctored recording, the loud passages would be too loud and the soft ones too soft to hear, so these are electronically compressed or ''flattened out'' to a more uniform sound level, making the louds less loud and the softs less soft.

When you consider that the cost of producing most album jackets far exceeds the cost of the records they contain, and that the industry standard for record promotion is about 30 percent of revenues, then it begins to make more sense that so many records aren't made well. The money doesn't go into production, it goes into marketing.

Record jackets are often emblazoned with terms like ''Teldec vinyl'' (a good German brand of virgin vinyl), ''audiophile pressing'' (who knows what this is really supposed to mean), ''chrome stampers'' (which make cleaner pressings), and the like. But this is all so much window dressing and marketing unless the master tape itself was excellent. The purpose of all these techniques is to reduce manufacturing distortions and therefore more clearly reveal the sound captured on the master tape; if that wasn't so good, better ''revelation'' won't improve it.

Going to great lengths to reduce tape hiss, for example, doesn't mean all that much as far as the quality and enjoyment of the recording is concerned. Hiss and background noise on LPs is steady and quite separate from the music so it can be easily tuned out. As a playback system improves, the clicks and pops on recordings matter less—they're like the quiet rustlings and coughs of an audience. The music-to-noise ratio is much better on a good system and the music becomes more compelling.

Far more important in manufacturing are such things as the basic quality of the pressing technique, the vinyl, the stampers and how worn they are allowed to become before replacement. Stampers should at most be used for only a few thousand pressings. Imperfect pressing can cause the gaps or potholes in the vinyl known as no-fill. Many records are made far too thin, which means not only that they warp easily but also that distortion increases when they are played. The stylus dragging in the groove actually sets up a vibration that is picked up by the cartridge and amplified right along with the music. With heavier vinyl, such resonances are less easy to set up and more effectively damped if they are started. The mid-1970s oil crisis encouraged record companies to cut LP thickness by one third; being patriotic, they continue their conservation efforts to this day.

Proper storage immediately after pressing is essential to prevent warps and must be maintained throughout the distribution chain. A thick piece of vinyl, a substantial jacket, *loose* shrink wrap (a quarter inch or so larger than the jacket all around), and a quality rice-paper sleeve all help to protect the record. Overly tight shrink wrap is likely to warp the record. Wakefield is widely recognized as being one of the best American pressing plants. Europadisc is also highly regarded for both mastering and pressing.

At times it may require real perserverance to get finally a clean copy. CBS, for one, is notorious for its poor pressings. The Smithsonian has some marvelous recordings—including authentic renditions of Duke Ellington and Jelly Roll Morton music—but more than a dozen copies of a particular album (at that time pressed by CBS) had to be exchanged before finally finding one not smeared all over with fingerprints! The then head of Smithsonian Records down in Washington, laconically responded that fingerprints are a normal part of the manufacturing process!!! (He's not there anymore and CBS has decided to get out of the LP business altogether—it will be releasing only CDs from now on. How well it manages to press these, considering that CDs are far more demanding than LPs, will be most interesting to see.)

Pressing quality overall does seem to be improving, whether in response to the years of complaint from the underground press or in response to the challenge of CDs—either way, we're happy.

If you can't get a new copy because your defective one is the last available and the album is going out of print—an increasingly common problem—then you have to balance your desire for the music with the seriousness of the defect. A record that's just dirty on the surface can be cleaned with a VPI or similar quality vacuum cleaner.

An off-center spindle hole can be a serious problem because you will always hear the wow as the record turns out of round. No record is ever perfectly cut relative to the spindle hole—some minor error is inevitable because the hole is punched *after* the record is pressed—but there are times when the error is significant.

Warps vary in their degree of severity—some records look like potato chips. The least disturbing kind of warp is one with very shallow, long curves so the tonearm rides smoothly up and down over it without too much distortion. Small sharp warps tend to be more audible. Edge warps usually affect the music only at the beginning of the record. The easiest way to spot warps is to put the record on the turntable and squint along the edge of the rotating record. Then also look straight down onto it and look for quaverings in your face's reflection. Also put the stylus down on it and watch the movement of the tonearm, both up and down and from side to side.

The importance of scratches must be decided on a case-by-case basis. Surface noise, ticks and pops from poor vinyl, and even no-fill, are the least objectionable of the manufacturing defects. They are clearly distinct from the music, and though they certainly add noise, they don't distort the music.

Buying Used Records

You often run across used records being sold at tag sales, flea markets, in secondhand stores. As many of these are out of print, and with more LPs becoming unavailable all the time, used records can be a wonderful source of real finds. With a little skill, you can develop a sense of the overall record quality by knowing what to look for. A dead giveaway is whitish powdery dust embedded in the grooves—these records have generally been "regrooved" by a worn or damaged stylus acting as a record eraser. Or they may have just been played over and over again, so that the grooves, which were once like the Rockies, are now as worn as the Appalachians. Nothing will help records in this condition—neither a VPI cleaning, a treatment of Last, nor anything else. Buy only if the music is a must-have—it'll hold you over until you may be lucky enough to find a better copy. Unfortunately, some unscrupulous people treat the records with a light coating of oil to conceal the white haze and restore the surface to apparent newness. Watch out.

Often, the only problem with a record may be that it's dirty, in which case a good cleaning will leave you with an almost-new copy. Fingerprints are a sign that the record was carelessly handled, which suggests the grooves may also be somewhat damaged by a worn stylus. The prints can be cleaned off with a stronger cleaning solution and your record cleaner. Faint marks around the spindle hole, if extensive, also indicate sloppy handling—you should be able to match up hole and spindle without too much trouble if you're being careful.

Scratches may or may not matter, depending on their depth. Surface scratches don't penetrate down into the groove so they need not be a problem sonically, though here again their presence indicates carelessness, which may manifest itself in other groove damage. Deep scratches obviously affect the sound.

As more and more people make the changeover to CDs and foolishly throw out their LPs, there will be all the more riches for LP addicts to pick up at great prices—many of them long out of print and available no other way. Used records are definitely a resource to investigate.

PRERECORDED TAPE BUYING

Prerecorded tape is the most ephemeral medium and generally has the lowest fidelity (see p. 329). Recognize it as being primarily a convenience source. Nonetheless, it is definitely worthwhile to seek out quality tapes, because these will not only sound better but will last longer before print-through develops or the cassette mechanisms malfunction. Some record stores estimate that close to half the prerecorded cassettes sold are already defective in one way or another at the time of sale. If you get one of these, return it without hesitation for a replacement. Make sure before you buy that the cassettes aren't stored in a way that will damage them—for example, in direct sunshine or near some other source of heat.

Nakamichi, Monster Cable, and Chesky Records Realtime cassettes are all considered good.

CD BUYING

CDs are as subject to warping as LPs. Quality control has been steadily slipping as the demand has been increasing and also as acceptance has been established—it is no longer so necessary for CDs to prove themselves "perfect." Quality varies not only from label to label and title to title, but also from disc to disc. There are indications that the thickness of the silvering has an important effect on sound—or more precisely stated, a thicker backing reduces the amount of "error" that then needs "correction."

Undoubtedly, CDs, like LPs, are being sold as new when they are in fact used. This is far more difficult to identify than with LPs, as overall sound will be degraded as error correction copes with the microscratches but there may be no actual ticks and pops to hear. Return defective CDs without fail or the manufacturers may allow quality to deteriorate further.

It is tricky to predict how a CD will sound because there are so many possible combinations of analog and digital involved. Some discs are marked with the three-position SPARS (Society of Professional Audio Recording Studios) code, which identifies their lineage. The letters used are *A* and *D* for analog and digital. The first position identifies if the original recording was analog or digital; the second position specifies whether the original recording was mixed to a digital or analog recorder; and the third position specifies whether the recording was then mixed to an analog tape recorder or was directly digitally transferred into 44-K format. So an AAD code indicates that the source was analog tape, mixed to an analog tape recorder, and then transferred to a digital master.

However, how much you can do with this knowledge is questionable. Some say an analog original transferred to digital sounds better than a recording made digitally from start to finish. This was probably absolutely true with the awful early digital recorders. The present digital recorders are still pretty awful, so an analog original may give you a better first step. There are still so many variables in the playback that it is hard to establish definite judgments on the recordings. The Opus 3 CD samplers will give you an idea of what a good CD sounds like. These, incidentally, are digitalized versions of original analog master tapes.

The other problem unique to CDs is that some will load into certain players and some will not. Players are being made cheaper and cheaper and their quality control becomes poorer and poorer. Reliability is worsening. Combine this with imperfect discs and a fair number of them end up being rejected by the players.

HAPPY LISTENING!

GLOSSARY

Ambience: The acoustic characteristics of a room with regard to reverberation. A room with a lot of reverb is said to be "live"; one without much reverb is "dead."

Attenuate: To reduce the dB level of sound.

Audiophile: A lover of sound.

Cross-talk: Unwanted breakthrough of one channel into another. Also refers to the distortion that occurs when some signal from a music source that you are not listening to leaks into the circuit of the source that you are listening to.

Decibel (dB): As was discovered by Alexander Graham Bell, we do not perceive differences in volume level in a linear manner, but logarithmically—our ears become less sensitive to sound as its intensity increases. In fact, the ratio of the softest sounds we can hear to the loudest sounds is about one to a trillion (roughly 120 dB). Decibels are a logarithmic scale of relative loudness. As a general rule of thumb: A difference of 1 dB is the minimum perceptible change in volume; 3 dB is a moderate change in volume (though it represents either a doubling or halving of the electrical power involved); about 10 dB is an apparent doubling or halving of the volume, similar to turning your volume control halfway up or down (though this requires a tenfold increase in power). This gives a somewhat simplified picture, as perceived loudness also depends on frequency—our hearing is considerably more sensitive at midrange frequencies than it is at the frequency extremes.

0 dB is taken as the threshold of hearing, 130 dB as the threshold of pain.

Whisper: 15–25 dB
Quiet background: about 35 dB
Normal background, home or office: 40–60 dB
Normal speaking voice: about 65–70 dB
Orchestral climax: about 105 dB

Disco music: 120 dB
Jet plane: 140–180 dB

Distortion: Anything that alters the music signal (*see also* Nonlinearity). Distortion can be minimized but never eliminated—nonlinearity is a law of nature. There are many different forms of distortion, but all do one of two things: They either add spurious information to the signal or subtract musical information. *See* also Total harmonic distortion.

Dynamic contrast: The ability of a component to reveal the dynamic gradations between the very softest sounds and the very loudest in the music. Far more important to the music than the system's dynamic range.

Dynamic range: The range between the loudest and the softest sounds that are in a piece of music, or that can be reproduced by a piece of audio equipment without distortion (a ratio expressed in decibels). In speech, the range rarely exceeds 40 dB; in music, it is greatest in orchestral works, where the range may be as much as 75 dB.

Extension: How extended a range of frequencies the component can reproduce without distortion—i.e., how close it comes to the top end of the audible spectrum at 20,000 Hz, and close to the bottom end at 20 Hz.

Fletcher-Munson curve: Our sensitivity to sound depends on its frequency and volume, so sounds of different frequencies, when played at the exact same volume intensity, will not be heard as all having the same volume. At low volumes, one hears lower frequencies more weakly than higher ones and much more weakly than the midrange. With an increase in volume, the ear becomes increasingly sensitive to high frequencies, while low tones and midrange are perceived as equal in loudness. The curve representing this was established by H. Fletcher and W. A. Munson in 1933.

Frequency: Musical pitch. Refers to the number of complete cycles in a second. The lower the frequency—the lower the number of cycles per second—the lower the sounded note.

Frequency range: The audible band of frequencies extends from 20 to 20,000 Hz, which is a spread of ten octaves. Audio equipment rarely reproduces this full range, or at least not accurately. Where most of the music occurs is in the midrange, and you want a balanced extension out to both extremes. A component or system that reproduces an extended high end which is *not* balanced by a comparably extended low end will not be musically satisfying. Lesser extension, if balanced in highs and lows, is preferable.

Frequency response: The audio equivalent of tonal balance—the relationship of mids, highs, and lows. In audio, a system's frequency response indicates its ability to reproduce all audible frequencies supplied to it in proper balance to each other, with all the original relative strengths of the highs and lows exactly preserved. This is important because the musical mind perceives small differences in tonal *balance* as large differences in tonal *quality* and coloration. However, be aware that just because a component's frequency response *measures* flat, this does not always give you the same spectral balance as existed during the original performance.

Fundamental: The lowest frequency of a note in a complex wave form or chord.

Haas effect: If sounds arrive from several sources, the ears and brain will identify only the nearest. In other words, if our ears receive similar sounds coming from various sources, the brain will latch onto the sound that arrives first. If the time difference is up to 50 milliseconds, the early arrival sound can dominate the later arrival sound, even if the later arrival is as much as 10 dB louder. The discovery of this effect is attributed to Halmut Haas in 1949.

Harmonics: Also called overtones, these are vibrations at frequencies that are multiples of the fundamental.

Harmonic series: Harmonics extend without limit beyond the audible range. They are characterized as even-order and odd-order harmonics. A second-order harmonic is two times the frequency of the fundamental; a third order is three times the fundamental; a fourth order is four times the fundamental; and so forth. Each even-order harmonic—second, fourth, sixth, etc.—is one octave or multiples of one octave higher than the fundamental; these even-order overtones are therefore musically related to the fundamental. Odd-order harmonics, on the other hand—third, fifth, seventh, and up—create a series of notes that are *not* related to any octave overtones and therefore have a displeasing sound. Amplifying circuits that emphasize odd-order harmonics tend to have a harsh or gritty sonic signature.

Headroom: The ability of an amp to go beyond its rated power for short durations in order to reproduce musical peaks without distortion.

Hertz (Hz): A unit of measurement denoting frequency, originally measured as cycles per second: One Hz = 1 c.p.s. Kilohertz (kHz) are hertz measured in multiples of 1,000.

Nonlinearity: What goes into a system comes out changed by its passage through that system—in other words, distorted. The ideal of an audio component and an audio system is to be linear, or nondistorting, with the image on one side of the mirror identical to the image on the other side.

Overtones: See Harmonics.

Radio-frequency interference (RFI): Radio-frequency sound waves are ubiquitous. Unfortunately, they can interfere with your audio signal, causing noise and other distortions.

Resonant frequency: Any system has a resonance at some particular frequency. At that frequency, even a slight amount of energy can cause the system to vibrate. A stretched piano string, when plucked, will vibrate for a while at a certain fundamental frequency. Plucked again, it will again vibrate at that same frequency. This is its natural or resonant frequency. While this is the basis of musical instruments, it is undesirable in music-*reproducing* instruments like audio equipment.

Signal-to-noise (S/N) ratio: The range or distance between the noise floor (the noise level of the equipment itself) and the music signal.

Sound pressure level (SPL): A more accurate term for loudness. When a sound wave is propagated in the air, the pressure of the air at any point will vary above and below the normal ambient pressure; this difference from the norm is the SPL, perceived as loudness.

Spectral balance: Balance across the entire frequency spectrum of the audio range.

Stereo: From the Greek meaning solid. The purpose of stereo is not to give you separate right and left channels, but to provide the illusion of a holographic, three-dimensional image between the speakers. It is akin to the old stereopticon in which each visual channel gave a slightly different view of the subject, which, when viewed together, presented the illusion of three-dimensionality. The sound in a stereo system should not seem to be coming out of the speakers at all; instead the performance should ''appear'' quite solidly as if on a stage between the speakers. It should even be possible to point to where each player is standing or sitting in space.

Total harmonic distortion: This is a sad joke. Discredited years ago, it is still used as a spec. Its name sounds so impressive that the naïve are taken in. While some forms of distortion have been analyzed and can even be measured, new ones are constantly being identified. Rely on a pair of well-trained ears, not measurements. Even if one could measure all the forms of distortion in a given system, this would only create thousands of pages of information requiring analysis. As we still do not know much about how we hear, such analysis would be very hard to undertake successfully. Some forms of distortion are more disturbing than others—for example, those that produce odd-order harmonics (*see* Harmonic series) are unpleasant.

Transducer: A device that converts one form of energy to another. Playback transducers are the cartridge, which changes mechanical vibrations into electrical energy, and the loudspeakers, which change it back, from electrical energy coming from the amp to mechanical movement of the diaphragm, causing audible pressure changes in the air.

Transient response: The ability of a component to respond quickly and accurately to transients. Transient response affects reproduction of the attack and decay characteristics of a sound.

Transients: Instantaneous changes in dynamics, producing steep wave fronts.

Wavelength: The distance the sound wave travels to complete one cycle.

MUSICAL TERMS AND THEIR AUDIO EQUIVALENTS

Music is sound in time. Alter the sound—pitch, tone color, or dynamics—and you alter the music. Alter the time relationships and you alter the music. How much or how little sound and time are altered determines the quality of recording and playback. Here are the scientific equivalents of musical terms:

Audio frequency range/octave: The ear can respond to a frequency range of about 20 to 20,000 Hz, usually written as 20 Hz to 20 kHz. This represents ten octaves. Each octave doubles or halves hertz; for example, one octave above 60 Hz is 120 Hz; one octave below 60 Hz is 30 Hz.

Dynamics/amplitude: This depends on the magnitude of the vibration—how far or hard the string or air column vibrates. The louder you want to play a wind instrument, the greater the air pressure you must use; the louder you want a guitar to play, the harder you must pluck the string.

Note/sound wave: A note or sound wave is made up of two elements—amplitude and frequency, musically termed dynamics and pitch.

Pitch/frequency: The pitch—"highness" or "lowness" of the sound—depends on the frequency—the speed of the vibrations. The higher the pitch, the higher the frequency. The smaller the vibrating body, the faster the vibrations and so the higher the sound. Blow across the top of a bottle as you fill it up with water and the sound becomes higher, as the vibrating column of air above the water becomes smaller.

Tone color (timbre)/wave form: The quality of sound that allows you to distinguish between a flute and a violin and that ascribes a "white" tone to a flute and a "rich" tone to a violin. Tone color is determined by the number, kind, and relative amplitude of the overtones (harmonics) and fundamental. Sound-producing bodies tend to vibrate not only along their full length (fundamental) but also simultaneously in halves, quarters, etc. These fractional vibrations are called overtones or partials. The sound of the overtones is much softer than that of the fundamental note, but it also reinforces certain overtones of the fundamental. In a flute, the air column vibrates mainly along its entire length and not much in halves and quarters; violins vibrate simultaneously in many segments.

LISTENING LANGUAGE

The following definitions have been culled predominantly from *The Absolute Sound* and *Stereophile,* which have been painstakingly establishing a common language in which to talk about audio—a language that is neither that of electronics nor music, but is specific to recorded music. This is similar to the development of a common language for wine tasting.

Ambience: The ability to capture the distinctive sound of a particular space. Ambience occurs not only in the space in which the music was performed but also in the body of the instrument itself. The sound of an instrument is truly its sound *as it occurs in space.*

Decay: The way a note stops.

Dynamics: The ability to be articulate, to offer both good dynamic range and dynamic contrast; i.e., to play loudly and softly at the same time and change amplitude quickly and cleanly.

Grain: A background texture; heard in the spaces between the instruments and between the notes.

Imaging: The creation of specific images of individual players and instruments. Poor imaging creates mental confusion and fatigue, similar to your vision being slightly out of focus.

Imaging dimensionality: Identifies an image that has dimension, volume, solidity; that is not flat and maintains correct perspective. Provides the sensation of being able to walk around and behind the players. While this overlaps with soundstage, imaging focus, and specificity, dimensionality is more than providing a sense of depth or location; it provides a sense of solidity and three-dimensionality. It's the ability to make a particular sound, whether from voice or instrument, take on life.

Imaging focus or resolution: The ability to retrieve very low level detail so that it is possible to differentiate voices in a chorus or violins in a string section; to hear the space and air around individual instruments.

Imaging specificity: The ability to pinpoint a component in space, so that it occupies a specific location without wandering or shifting. This latter aspect is also called image stability.

Low-level detail: The fine detail of the music, musical nuance.

Soundstage: The correct spatial rendering of a natural acoustic environment. (Though they are often confused, this is *not* the same as imaging focus or specificity.) The soundstage should extend in all three dimensions: in width, well beyond the outside edge of the speakers; in depth, to your room's back wall; in height, enough to create a realistic illusion of the relative height of the instruments and players. This is not just a matter of actual dimensions, but of music filling that space and sound moving up from the players. It benefits from, but is not synonymous with, good ambience retrieval. With most systems, you are limited to hearing only into the first few rows of the orchestra.

Tonal balance: The balance of midrange, highs, and lows, with all harmonics present in the original remaining present in the playback. Adding or removing harmonics will change the coloration of the sound. Tonal balance is similar to frequency response, except that FR refers only to audio components, whereas tonal balance can be applied also to an orchestra or other large group of players. Measured flat frequency response also does not necessarily assure correct tonal balance.

Transparency: A good system should be seen but not heard. The aim of stereo reproduction is to create the illusion of listening in on the performance through a large window. That window should be "transparent"—there should be the absence of any barrier between you and the music. This term was first used by J. Gordon Holt of *Stereophile*. The drawback of transparency is that it also reveals all the system's flaws along with the music. Your system must have an overall balance of compromises in order to render music well, rather than pursuing any one attribute at the expense of all others.

BIBLIOGRAPHY

Books

Barzun, Jacques, ed. *Pleasures of Music: An Anthology of Writing About Music and Musicians from Cellini to Bernard Shaw*. Chicago: University of Chicago Press, 1951 (abr. ed., 1977). Try to get the original unabridged edition, which has a very good introduction by Barzun, for some strange reason dropped in the abridged edition. Both editions have the wonderful "Music with Meals" essay by G. K. Chesterton.

Burgess, Anthony. *This Man and Music*. New York: Avon, 1985. Burgess discusses music and writing, from the perspective of a musician and writer.

Colloms, Martin. *High Performance Loudspeakers,* rev. ed. New York: Wiley, 1985. "The speaker bible."

Del Mar, Norman. *Anatomy of the Orchestra*. Berkeley, Calif.: University of California Press, 1983.

Eisenberg, Evan. *The Recording Angel: Explorations in Phonography*. New York: McGraw-Hill, 1987. Defines a new art form: phonography, the art of making music on record. About the people who make the records and the people who listen to them. Filled with "ohs" and "ah-has."

Felton, Gary. *Record Collector's International Directory*. New York: Crown, 1980. Though unavoidably always somewhat out of date, this book is accurately described by Nat Hentoff as "the ultimate guide to roaming pleasure for the record collector. Indispensable!" No argument.

Martin, George, ed. *Making Music: The Guide to Writing, Performing and Recording*. New York: Quill, 1983.

Mumford, Lewis. *Art and Technics*. New York: Columbia University Press, 1952. The relationship through history between two conflicting impulses: the artistic, which is subjective, and the technical, which is objective—and Mumford's assertion that the present worship of machines and exaltation of objectivity contribute to the depersonalization of much of life today. This is a very brief, succinct book and pertinent to the debate over measurement versus listening and to the prevalent emphasis on the equipment over the music.

Rapaport, Diane. *How to Make and Sell Your Own Record.* Tiburon, CA: Headlands Press, 1984. A clear description of the record production process.

Schafer, R. Murray. *The Tuning of the World: Toward a Theory of Soundscape Design.* Philadelphia: University of Pennsylvania Press, 1980. Our sonic environment—the past explored, present described, and future predicted. Reading this will change your awareness of sound. Schafer is a full-time composer in Ontario.

Villchur, Edgar. *Reproduction of Sound in High Fidelity and Stereo Phonographs.* New York: Dover, 1965. An excellent collection of articles, first published in *Audio,* by the designer of the Acoustic Research turntable and acoustic suspension loudspeaker.

Wilder, Alec. *American Popular Song: The Great Innovators, 1900–1950.* New York: Oxford University Press, 1972. Perhaps *the* classic history in its field.

Sacks, Oliver. *The Man Who Mistook His Wife for a Hat.* New York: Summit, 1986. Includes astute observations on musical aesthetics and musical psychology.

U.S. Magazines

Absolute Sound, The
Editor and publisher: Harry Pearson
Sea Cliff, NY

Audio Amateur and *Speaker Builder* (for the builder/modifier)
Publisher: Ed Dell
Peterboro, NH

''Audio'' Annual Equipment Directory
Audio magazine, New York

Fanfare
Editor and publisher: Joel Flegler
Tenafly, NJ

International Audio Review
Publisher: J. Peter Moncrieff
Berkeley, CA

Stereophile
Publisher: Larry Archibald; editor: J. Gordon Holt
Santa Fe, NM

British Magazines

Hi-Fi Answers

Hi-Fi News & Record Review

INDEX